Detail in Contemporary Residential Architecture 2

Published in 2014 by
Laurence King Publishing Ltd
361–373 City Road
London
EC1V 1LR
e-mail: enquiries@laurenceking.com
www.laurenceking.com

A catalogue record for this book is
available from the British Library

ISBN: 978 1 78067 175 8

Consultant Editor: Virginia McLeod
Designed by Hamish Muir
Illustrations by Advanced Illustrations
Limited
Picture Research by Sophia Gibb

Printed in China

Detail in Contemporary Residential Architecture 2

David Phillips
Megumi Yamashita

Laurence King Publishing

Contents

Introduction

Residential architecture is the genesis of many things. In the past we have seen careers, movements and technologies all starting with the construction of a single house. Houses were among the first structures that man built; a simple hut to provide shelter from the elements was our first architecture. In many cases houses are the first realized projects for young architects; an opportunity to express an idea or to experiment with materials.

This book is a review of 50 contemporary houses. It focuses on the construction details, as it is in these that we can see and understand how the buildings have been constructed. A detail is a beautiful thing; it is a drawing that describes how materials should be formed and brought together. Details are ideas fixed in the form of a drawing, and the best details are elegant and simple. It is a shame that so often they are invisible once the building has been completed.

The details included tell us something about what the architects see as important in the construction of their buildings. They tell us not just how the building was built, but also why it was built in that way. The drawings provide an insight into the construction culture of the place where the building is situated. What is of the deepest concern in one place can often be of no consequence elsewhere.

Some of these homes are modest houses built on tiny sites, some are opportunistic developments of neglected parts of the city and some are remote mountain retreats. Each has been chosen because of a quality or an aspect of the design that is particular. Spread across the world, they are built from many different materials and they have vastly different budgets. They do, however, have one thing in common, and that is that they are all homes.

The way that people live in their houses is very different around the world. In the frozen north of Sweden a house is a place to shelter from the weather, in Brazil or India the barrier between inside and outside is often nothing more than a change of material. In some of the houses the space is divided into the traditional Western-style rooms for cooking, eating, sleeping, washing; in others there is just a single space that serves many functions.

Interaction with nature and natural materials is at the centre of a number of projects. Arjen Reas has used thatch in an innovative way to clad his house and likewise bamboo clads AST 77's project. Byoung Soo Cho's Earth House in Korea is buried in a pit below the ground, and Bercy Chen's Edgeland House in Texas is set into the earth, healing a scar in a damaged industrial landscape.

Building in extreme environments is always a challenge. Kjellgren Kaminsky has, with its round house in Sweden, provided a warm and stylish home in a harsh climate. SPASM in India has very different if no less harsh conditions to contend with. The architects have designed a house that works with nature to provide a pleasant environment.

Many houses in this book have been informed by the local vernacular. These houses demonstrate that traditional forms and materials such as pitched roofs, brick walls and timber windows can be modern. Indeed, the idea of what a contemporary house might be is perhaps far more divergent now than at any time in the past.

Referencing the vernacular is not the same as copying it. Bedaux de Brouwer's Villa Rotonda in the Netherlands is an example of a house that at first appears familiar. The materials and forms are ordinary, but a subtle reordering and attention to detail has given the composition new life. The same is true of H House in Hungary, by Budapesti Mühely; here a simple barn has been reinterpreted to provide a 21st century living space. In Japan Tato Architects has, in the arrangement of three simple sheds, so subtly shifted the vernacular vocabulary that the result might at first go unnoticed.

The sites available to architects in cities today are often little gaps left over from previous development; derelict land hemmed in by other buildings. Balancing the provision of space and light with issues of overlooking and planning regulations is, however, often the catalyst that produces great architecture. Architects such as Duggan Morris, Laura Dewe Mathews and Liddicoat Goldhill show us how such sites can be developed to provide beautiful places to live. These small urban sites test the ingenuity of the architect. Carl Turner's Slip House is an elegant prototype for future city living, where ecological issues are fully addressed without dominating the visual appearance of the building. Sometimes no site can be found on dry land, as increasingly land to build on in densely populated areas is hard to find. Rost Niderehe's houseboat is a prototype for a new way of mobile city living that can come with you when you need to move.

In Japan the process of building a small house is perhaps less difficult than in many parts of the world. Finding a viable site is the hard part, but the architects are designing houses that show real innovation in the development of difficult sites. Harunastsu-archi, in a rural situation on a tiny sub-tropical island, battles with a harsh climate; mA-style uses every bit of space on a tight triangular city site; Tezuka's suburban villa in the hills of Kamekura opens up to blur interior and exterior. Each house is a clever solution to local conditions.

In the hills above Locarno, Wespi de Meuron Romeo has created a small house that references the forms of medieval castles. These include an entrance door that rises up into the roof, narrow steep stairs and thick stone walls. The hut or cabin is a romantic architectural idea that has been examined many times. Jonathan Hendry's cabin by the sea is a lovely example. It is a place to retreat from the world and relax. In a similar vein, the tiny wooden house that Carlos Quintáns Eras has built in the hills of northern

Portugal is perhaps as close to the primitive hut as any of the projects in this book. It has a quality that transcends all styles and times. Although it is a basic building, it is also enthused with sophistication, charm and elegance.

Prefabrication in building does not conjure an image of originality. The Streeter House, designed by David Salmela for a father and his son, makes innovative use of prefabricated SIP panels to create a unique, finely tuned and exuberant home. Prefabrication in the form of the glass box is a modernist idea that architects have been perfecting for nearly a hundred years. In California, Swatt Miers has provided a retreat from the world that is both sophisticated and fundamental.

Houses are perfect places to demonstrate a philosophy. The house that Uwe Schröder has built in Bonn follows in a long tradition of European architecture. It is a careful essay in proportion and an examination of the relationships between the parts of the house to city.

These are not all dream houses with vast budgets. Many are realistic solutions to housing needs. H Arquitects has, on a tiny budget, made a startlingly powerful and original house with a raw materiality.

Fashions for materials come and go, and although brick has been in constant use for thousands of years, today it is a material that architects are looking at with renewed interest. A large number of the houses in this book use brick as the primary construction material. Wood is also enjoying a renaissance; this flexible carbon neutral material can be seen being used in innovative ways by many architects including Suga Atelier and Bernard Quirot.

Energy use is one of the most important considerations in contemporary architecture. Many of the houses have innovative strategies for reducing energy use. There are high levels of insulation, ground source heat pumps and solar panels all contributing to the environmental performance. A new structure is not always the most appropriate environmental solution. Dow Jones has taken an existing house and remodeled it within a metal skin into something completely new. This additional skin wraps old and new, providing substantial gains in environmental performance.

Each of these houses tells us a good deal about domestic architecture today. We hope that you will find them interesting.

David Phillips
Megumi Yamashita

Notes

Imperial and Metric Measurements
Dimensions have been provided by the architects in metric and converted to imperial, except in case of projects in the USA in which imperial dimensions have been converted to metric.

Terminology
An attempt has been made to standardize terminology to aid understanding across readerships, for example 'wood' is generally referred to as 'timber' and 'aluminum' as 'aluminium'. However materials or processes that are peculiar to a country, region or architectural practice that have no direct correspondence are presented in the original.

Floor Plans
Throughout the book, the following convention of hierarchy has been used – ground floor, first floor, second floor, and so on. In certain contexts, terms such as basement level or upper level have been used for clarity.

Scale
All floor plans, sections and elevations are presented at conventional architectural metric scales, typically 1:50, 1:100 or 1:200 as appropriate. An accurate graphic scale is included on the second page near the floor plans of every project to aid in the understanding of scale. Details are also presented at conventional architectural scales, typically 1:1, 1:5 and 1:10.

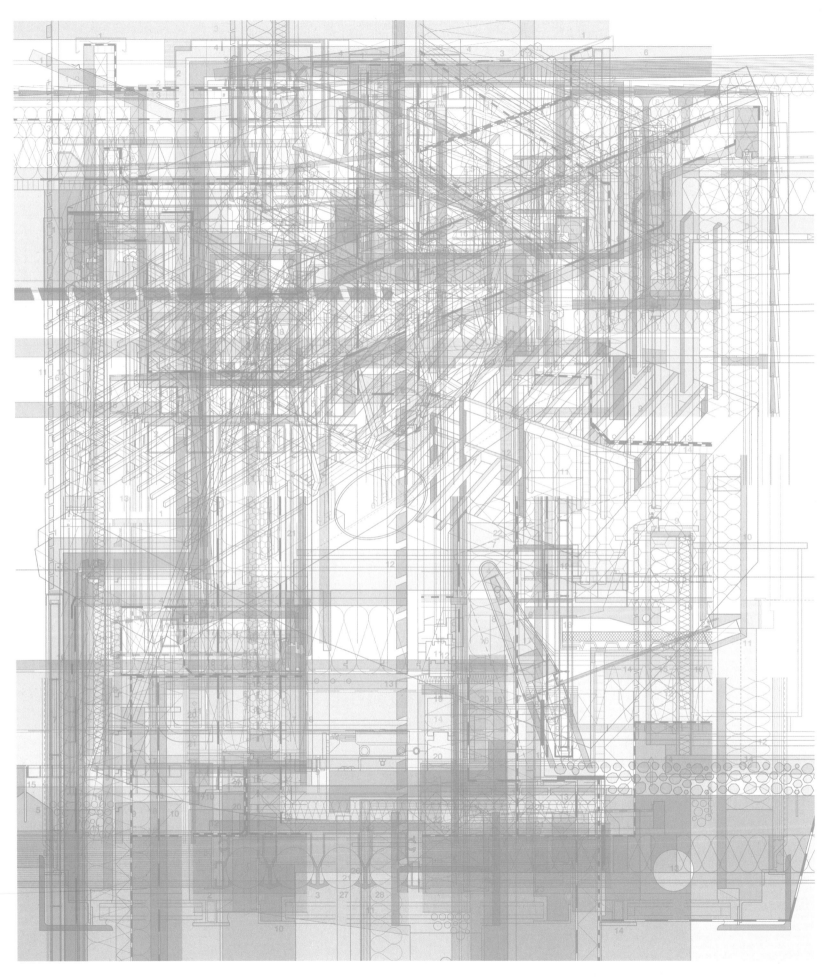

8

Wood
01–14

9

AST 77 Architecten

Rotselaar House
Rotselaar, Belgium

Client
Thijs Peeters

Project Team
Peter Van Impe

Structural Engineer
Bart Gullentops

Main Contractors
Kris Hermans, Carl Deckers,
Makke Dakwerken

This unusual bamboo-clad house is situated to the north-east of Brussels, in a forested region popular with Belgians who have holiday homes there. On a long, narrow sloping site, this family residence replaces a dilapidated bungalow. The new house makes clever use of an existing retaining wall, to improve the orientation of the building's long facades to face south and north. The unusually elongated house, at 26.3 metres (86 feet) long and only 4.5 metres (15 feet) wide, appears to emerge from the site like a sharp wedge, an effect emphasized by the roof which is pitched at the same angle as the ground.

The defining architectural feature is the exterior cladding which comprises a series of rectangular black steel frames filled with pale coloured bamboo stems to create a highly organized yet organically textured surface. Between the bamboo panels, dark glass windows reflect the surrounding forest. A punctured opening in the lower level forms a covered entrance terrace, with access on one side to the house and on the other to a small bike store. The ground floor is completely open with three main spaces stepping down from the office near the entrance, to the kitchen and finally to the living area. A series of light wells that penetrate the first floor draw daylight down into the interior. On the upper floor, four bedrooms and a bathroom are arranged along a single corridor.

The house uses a range of energy saving and resource sensitive strategies, including an exchange heat pump, underfloor heating, extensive insulation and a mechanical ventilation system. These provisions and the orientation of the house make this a sustainable and effective low energy family residence.

1 The long narrow house is partly dug into the site, with its length aligned with the contours of the forrested hillside. The north facade is divided into three strata, the vertical bamboo cladding interspersed with a variety of square and rectangular windows framing particular views of the forest.
2 The sustainably sourced, steel-framed bamboo panels that make up the facade lend a natural rhythm and texture to the otherwise precision-made structure.
3 The essentially open plan ground floor steps up in four levels across the length of the house beginning at the east end with the living and dining area, stepping up to the kitchen, then the office and terminating with the covered entrance deck to the west.

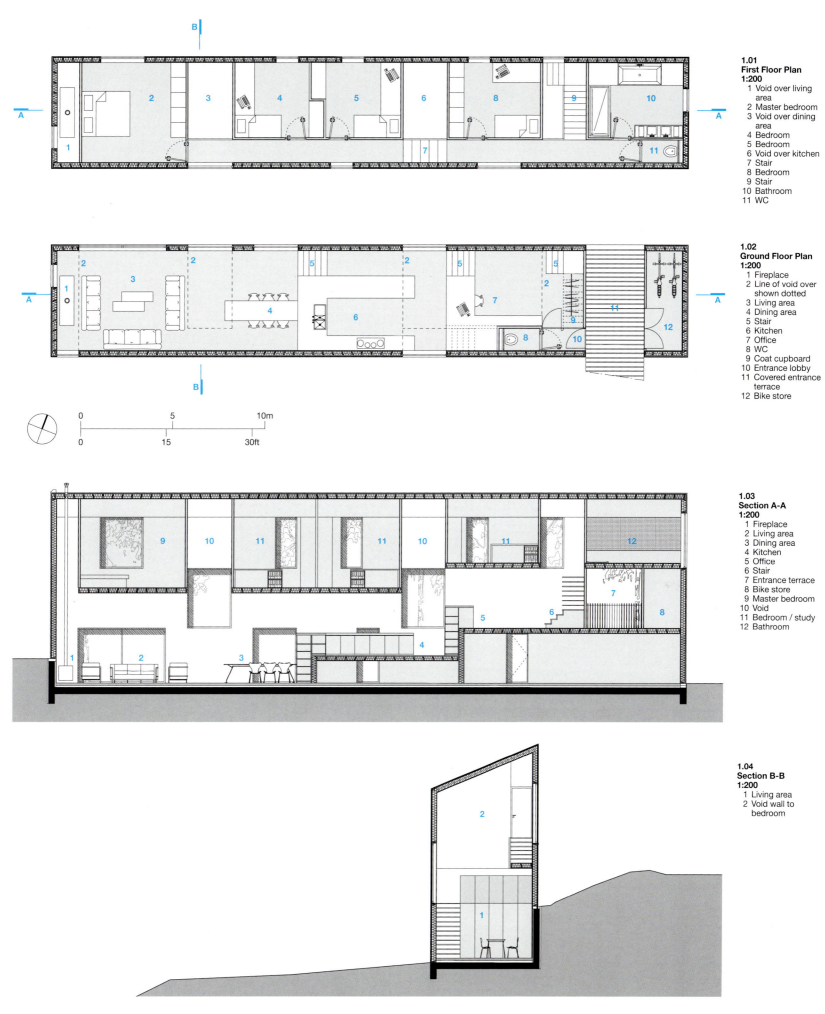

1.01
First Floor Plan
1:200
1 Void over living
  area
2 Master bedroom
3 Void over dining
  area
4 Bedroom
5 Bedroom
6 Void over kitchen
7 Stair
8 Bedroom
9 Stair
10 Bathroom
11 WC

1.02
Ground Floor Plan
1:200
1 Fireplace
2 Line of void over
  shown dotted
3 Living area
4 Dining area
5 Stair
6 Kitchen
7 Office
8 WC
9 Coat cupboard
10 Entrance lobby
11 Covered entrance
  terrace
12 Bike store

1.03
Section A-A
1:200
1 Fireplace
2 Living area
3 Dining area
4 Kitchen
5 Office
6 Stair
7 Entrance terrace
8 Bike store
9 Master bedroom
10 Void
11 Bedroom / study
12 Bathroom

1.04
Section B-B
1:200
1 Living area
2 Void wall to
  bedroom

11

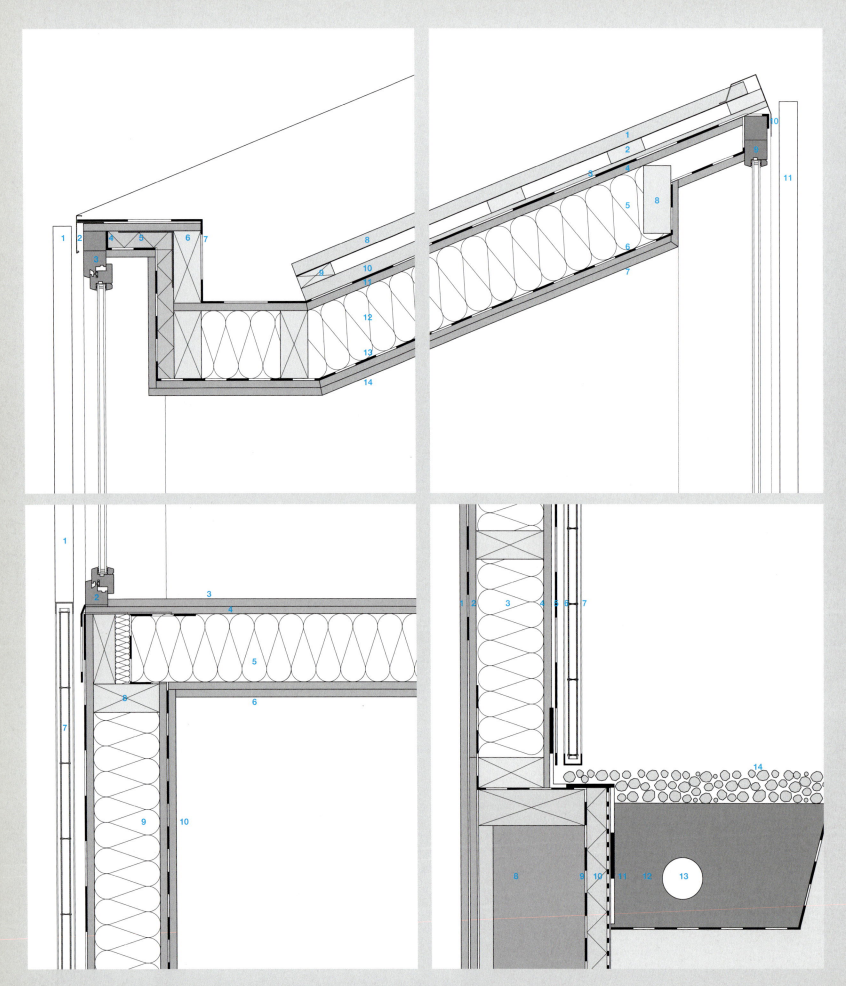

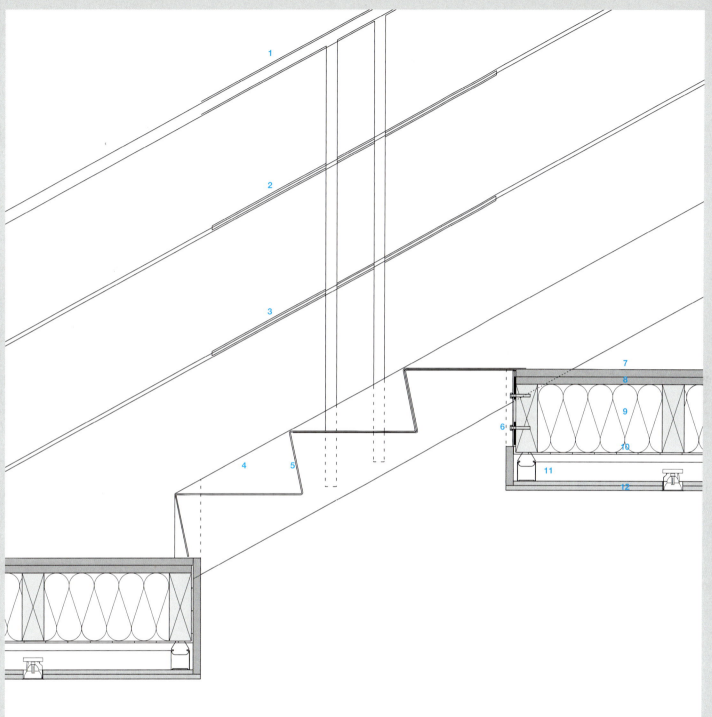

1.09
Stair Section Detail
1:10
1 3 mm (1/8 inch) welded square steel handrail
2 1 mm (1/16 inch) round steel intermediate rail
3 1 mm (1/16 inch) round steel intermediate rail
4 6 mm (1/4 inch) steel flange stair stringer
5 3 mm (1/8 inch) folded steel sheet stair riser and treads
6 3 mm (1/8 inch) steel mounting plate attached to floor structure with stainless steel bolts
7 Laminate floorboards
8 18 mm (3/4 inch) oriented strand board flooring substrate
9 180 mm (7 inch) thermal insulation
10 Vapour barrier
11 Aluminium ceiling clips and support structure
12 Double layer of plasterboard to ceiling with built-in spotlights

1.05
Roof Edge Section Detail
1:10
1 Steel frame for bamboo cladding panels seen in elevation beyond
2 Steel capping to roof edge
3 Double glazed, timber framed window
4 Vapour barrier
5 Thermal insulation
6 Timber edge beam
7 Waterproofing layer
8 Steel standing-seam roof sheet
9 16 x 22 mm (5/8 x 7/8 inch) timber roof battens
10 Waterproofing layer

11 18 mm (3/4 inch) oriented strand board
12 180 mm (7 inch) thermal insulation between timber rafters
13 Vapour barrier
14 18 mm (3/4 inch) oriented strand board ceiling

1.06
Roof Ridge Section Detail
1:10
1 Steel standing-seam roof sheet
2 16 x 22 mm (5/8 x 7/8 inch) timber roof battens
3 Waterproofing layer
4 18 mm (3/4 inch)

oriented strand board roofing substrate
5 Thermal insulation between 180 mm (7 inch) timber rafters
6 Vapour barrier
7 18 mm (3/4 inch) oriented strand board ceiling
8 16 x 22 mm (5/8 x 7/8 inch) timber roof battens
9 Double glazed, timber framed window
10 Folded steel roof edge profile
11 Steel frame for bamboo cladding panels seen in elevation beyond

1.07
First Floor Window Sill and Floor Section Detail
1:10
1 Steel frame for bamboo cladding panels seen in elevation beyond
2 Double glazed, timber framed window
3 Laminate floorboards
4 18 mm (3/4 inch) oriented strand board flooring substrate
5 180 mm (7 inch) thermal insulation between timber beams
6 18 mm (3/4 inch) oriented strand board

ceiling
7 External cladding panels from bamboo lengths in steel frame
8 Timber frame
9 180 mm (7 inch) thermal insulation
10 18 mm (3/4 inch) oriented strand board wall lining

1.08
Wall Section Detail
1:10
1 Painted plasterboard wall lining
2 Vapour barrier
3 180 mm (7 inch) thermal insulation
4 Waterproof

membrane
5 18 mm (3/4 inch) oriented strand board wall substrate
6 Wind and waterproofing layer within bamboo panels
7 External cladding panels from bamboo lengths in steel frame
8 250 mm (10 inch) reinforced concrete retaining wall
9 Waterproof membrane
10 60 mm (2 3/8 inch) rigid thermal insulation
11 Drainage foil
12 Concrete slab
13 Agricultural drain in sand bed
14 Gravel bed

Bernard Quirot Architecte & Associés

Sampans House
Sampans, Jura, France

Client
Private

Project Team
Alexandre Lenoble, Francesca Patrono, Bernard Quirot, Olivier Vichard

Structural Engineer
Le Bon Plan

Main Contractor
Maison Bois Mirbey

This compact timber-clad house is located in the foothills of the Jura mountains in eastern France. The house was designed as a vertical stack of accommodation in order to maximize the amount of land that could be dedicated to a garden. Stacked neatly over four levels, the plan and section seek to balance the relationship between the beautiful views to the north and the light from the south.

Above a storage cellar, the split level ground floor accommodates the entrance, kitchen, dining and living areas. The first floor contains two bedrooms and a bathroom and the top floor the master bedroom and bathroom, a study, and a terrace that provides a private outdoor platform with panoramic views to the north. Two smaller, similarly timber-clad structures to the north-east and south of the house – a garage and a garden pavilion annexe respectively – complete the composition.

The vertical Douglas fir cladding that wraps the entire form accentuates the height of the structure and complements the rural setting. Cut into the facades are simple rectangular windows of various sizes. A large window in the west facade brings light down into the living area through a double height void. The interior is characterized by a robust use of materials from a limited natural palette and simple details. Extensive use of wood creates a warm, domestic atmosphere in a house that appears to be completely at ease in its rural location.

1 Situated on a slightly sloping site, the ground floor negotiates the change in level through a split level built over a partly excavated cellar. The three timber-clad volumes of garden pavilion (left), house (centre) and garage (right) frame a variety of open and sheltered garden spaces.
2 The south facade is designed to protect the privacy of the occupants, with minimal openings and the use of the garden annexe to screen the terrace.
3 In the living room, which opens up to the south-facing terrace via sliding glass doors (left), a double height void provides additional light via a large west facing window.

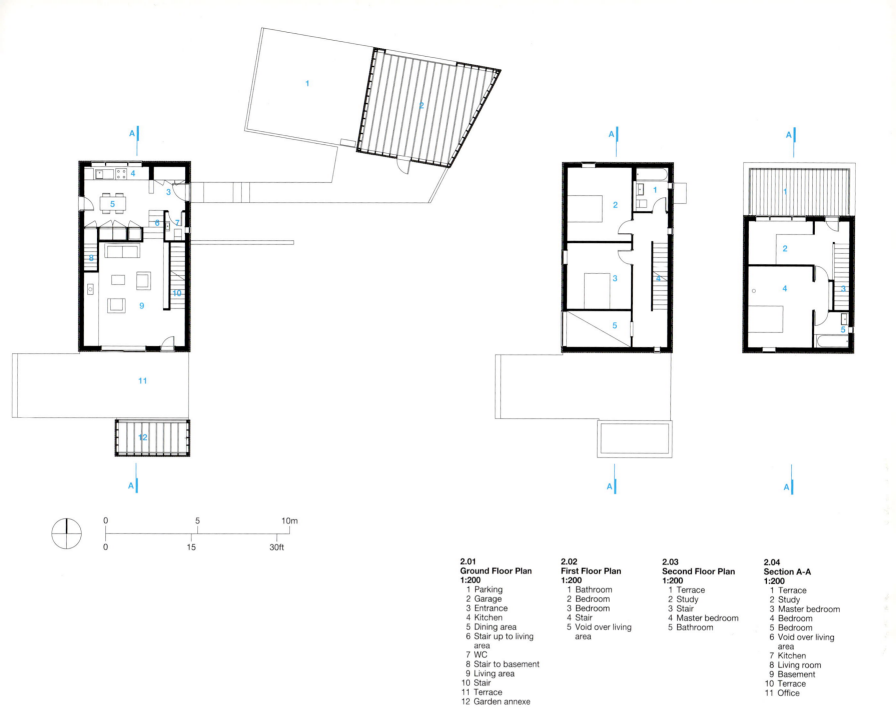

0 5 10m
0 15 30ft

2.01
Ground Floor Plan
1:200
1 Parking
2 Garage
3 Entrance
4 Kitchen
5 Dining area
6 Stair up to living area
7 WC
8 Stair to basement
9 Living area
10 Stair
11 Terrace
12 Garden annexe

2.02
First Floor Plan
1:200
1 Bathroom
2 Bedroom
3 Bedroom
4 Stair
5 Void over living area

2.03
Second Floor Plan
1:200
1 Terrace
2 Study
3 Stair
4 Master bedroom
5 Bathroom

2.04
Section A-A
1:200
1 Terrace
2 Study
3 Master bedroom
4 Bedroom
5 Bedroom
6 Void over living area
7 Kitchen
8 Living room
9 Basement
10 Terrace
11 Office

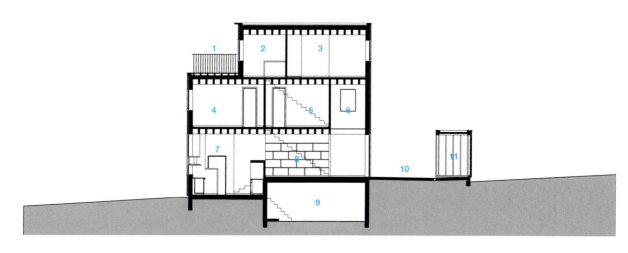

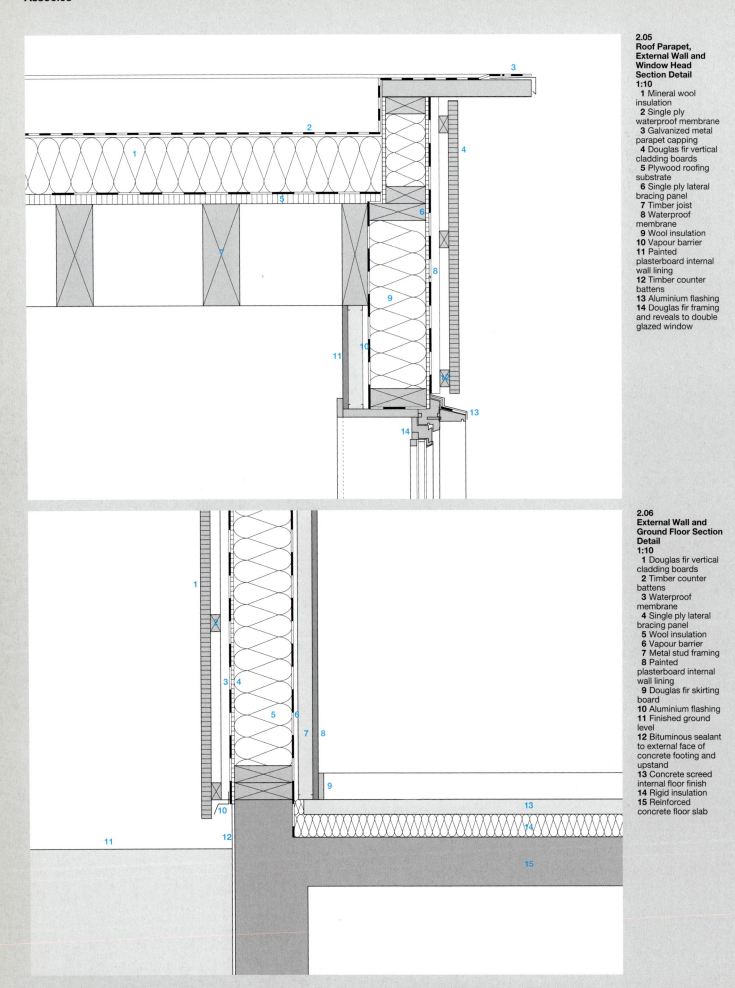

2.05
Roof Parapet, External Wall and Window Head Section Detail
1:10
1 Mineral wool insulation
2 Single ply waterproof membrane
3 Galvanized metal parapet capping
4 Douglas fir vertical cladding boards
5 Plywood roofing substrate
6 Single ply lateral bracing panel
7 Timber joist
8 Waterproof membrane
9 Wool insulation
10 Vapour barrier
11 Painted plasterboard internal wall lining
12 Timber counter battens
13 Aluminium flashing
14 Douglas fir framing and reveals to double glazed window

2.06
External Wall and Ground Floor Section Detail
1:10
1 Douglas fir vertical cladding boards
2 Timber counter battens
3 Waterproof membrane
4 Single ply lateral bracing panel
5 Wool insulation
6 Vapour barrier
7 Metal stud framing
8 Painted plasterboard internal wall lining
9 Douglas fir skirting board
10 Aluminium flashing
11 Finished ground level
12 Bituminous sealant to external face of concrete footing and upstand
13 Concrete screed internal floor finish
14 Rigid insulation
15 Reinforced concrete floor slab

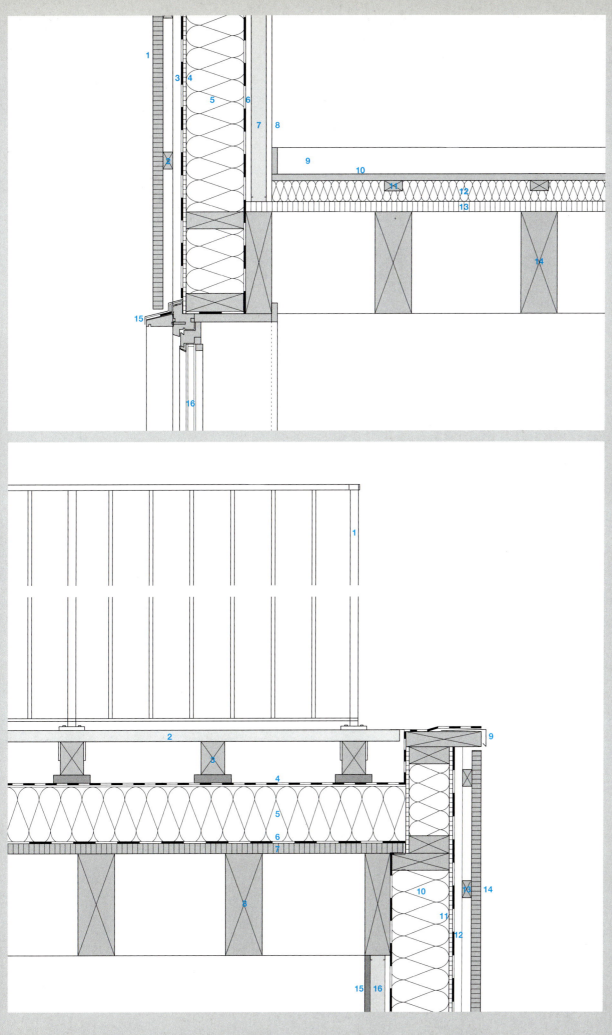

2.07
External Wall, First Floor and Window Head Section Detail
1:10
 1 Douglas fir vertical cladding boards
 2 Timber counter battens
 3 Single ply waterproof membrane
 4 Single ply lateral bracing panel
 5 Mineral wool insulation
 6 Vapour barrier
 7 Metal stud framing
 8 Painted plasterboard internal wall lining
 9 Douglas fir skirting board
 10 Douglas fir floor boards
 11 Timber joists on acoustic buffer
 12 Thermal and acoustic insulation
 13 Triple layer plywood flooring substrate
 14 Timber beam
 15 Aluminium flashing
 16 Douglas fir framing and reveals to double glazed window

2.08
Second Floor Terrace and External Wall Section Detail
1:10
 1 Steel balustrade and railings to terrace
 2 Larch decking boards
 3 Timber joists
 4 Single ply waterproof membrane
 5 Rigid insulation
 6 Vapour barrier
 7 Triple layer plywood flooring substrate
 8 Timber beam
 9 Galvanized metal parapet capping
 10 Mineral wool insulation
 11 Single ply lateral bracing panel
 12 Waterproof membrane
 13 Timber counter battens
 14 Douglas fir vertical cladding boards
 15 Painted plasterboard internal wall lining
 16 Metal stud framing

03
Budapesti Műhely

H House
Sóskút, Hungary

Client
Henriette Tompa

Project Team
Tamás Dévényi, Eszter Mihály,
Viktor Vadász

Structural Engineer
László Szőnyi

Services Engineer
József Horváth

Landscape Architect
Zsuzsa Bogner

Located to the south-west of
Budapest on the edges of a forest,
this large family house draws
inspiration from traditional central
European farm buildings. In an area
with strict building regulations, the
architects were required to work
within established guidelines including
the use of traditional materials, the 41
degree roof pitch and the distance of
the house from the road. However, the
way these constraints were
considered and applied has resulted
in a fresh and contemporary
interpretation of the peasant
longhouse typology.

The simple, single storey
rectangular plan is laid out using a 12
square metre (129 square feet) grid
which was determined by the client to
be the perfect size for bedrooms. The
interior is eight modules long and
includes along its north-west side five
bedroom modules, one for the kitchen
and two for the living spaces. A
circulation hall, deducted from the
modules on the other side of the
house, divides the house lengthwise,
and provides access to secondary
spaces such as bathrooms, the
entrance and a study. Three additional
modules are added to the south-west
end of the house to create a large
covered terrace under the great
pitched roof with its open gable end.

The strict rectangular geometry is
deliberately broken to create two
terraces, one on each of the long
facades, to create intimate outdoor
living spaces directly accessible from
the central living and dining rooms.
The timber-framed structure is clad in
traditional timber shingles which give
way to dark grey standing-seam metal
sheeting along the eaves, to the roof
of the covered terrace and to the
north-east facade.

1 The simple
pitched-roof,
gable-ended form is
brought to life through
the judicious use of
cladding materials. The
timber shingles used
for both roof and walls
are disrupted by the
introduction of
standing-seam metal
sheeting along the
entire length of the
eaves, as well as to the
gabled north-east
facade. Striped
multicoloured metal
security shutters add
additional colour and
texture.
2 The simplicity of the
roof structure is
revealed through the
open gable end to the
covered terrace.
3 The covered
north-east terrace
includes a dedicated
firewood storage area
(left) while the
generous eaves
protect the outdoor
areas adjacent to the
living and dining
spaces at the centre of
the house (right).
4 The secondary
concrete ring-beam
and column structure
is a feature of the living
space. Here, one of the
ceiling modules has
been removed to
create a double height
space (right).

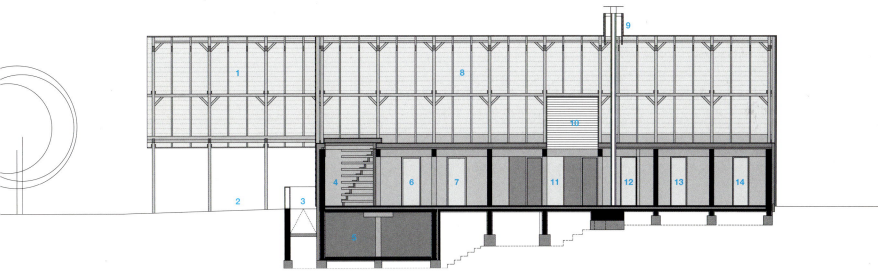

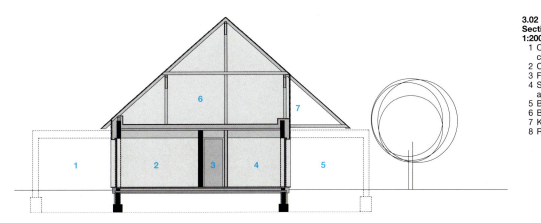

0 5 10m

0 15 30ft

3.01
Floor Plan
1:200
1 Covered terrace
2 Firewood store
3 Bedroom
4 Bedroom
5 Kitchen
6 Dining area
7 Dining terrace
8 Bedroom
9 Bedroom
10 Bedroom
11 Stair to basement
   and loft
12 Bathroom
13 Entrance hall
14 Covered entrance
15 Utility room
16 Living area
17 Outdoor living
18 Bathroom
19 Store
20 Office
21 Line of roof over
   shown dotted

3.02
Section A–A
1:200
1 Open roof to
  covered terrace
2 Covered terrace
3 Firewood store
4 Stair to basement
  and loft
5 Basement
6 Bedroom
7 Kitchen
8 Roof void
9 Chimney
10 Double height void
   over living area
11 Living area
12 Bedroom
13 Bedroom
14 Bedroom

3.03
Section B–B
1:200
1 Living terrace
2 Living area
3 Hallway
4 Dining area
5 Dining terrace
6 Roof space
7 Clerestory glazing

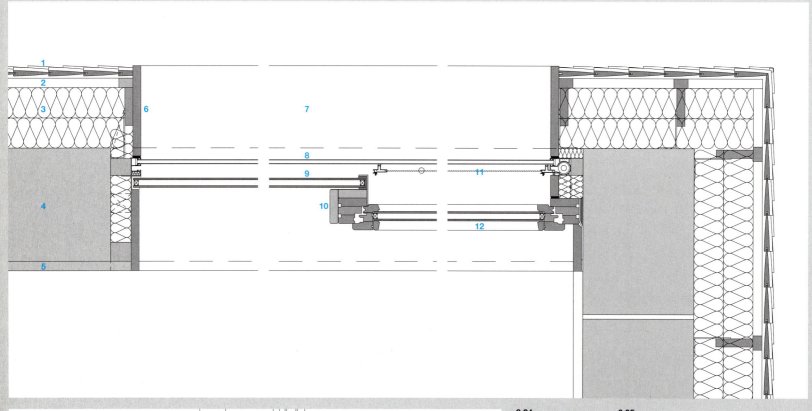

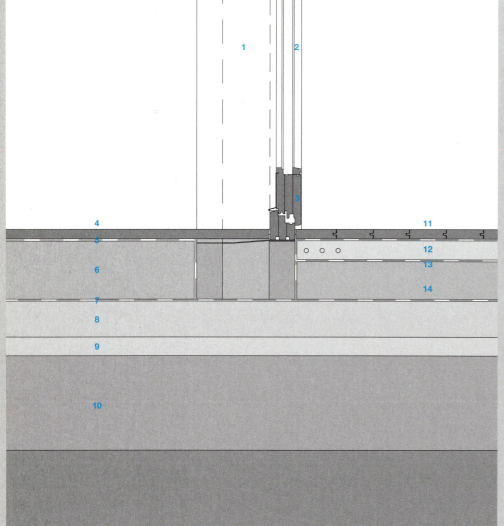

3.04
Bedroom External
Door and Facade
Plan Detail
1:10
1 90 x 400 x 15 mm
(3^{1}/$_{2}$ x 15^{3}/$_{4}$ x ^{5}/$_{8}$ inch)
Scots pine shingles
with natural finish to
external wall
2 25 x 48 mm (1 x 2
inch) battens and
counterbattens for
hanging shingles and
creating ventilated
cavity
3 80 mm (3 inch) and
100 mm (4 inch)
mineral wool insulation
4 325 mm (12^{3}/$_{4}$ inch)
thick blockwork inner
leaf of external wall
5 25 mm (1 inch)
thick cement render to
interior face of wall
6 Thermally insulated
veneered blockboard
external reveal
7 Thermally insulated
timber sill with 1.5%
fall toward exterior
8 Track for sliding
insect screen
9 Fixed double
glazing comprised of
4.8 mm (^{1}/$_{5}$ inch) solar
control laminated
safety glass, 15 mm
(^{5}/$_{8}$ inch) argon filled
cavity and 4.8 mm (^{1}/$_{5}$
inch) toughened glass
10 Timber post with
concealed fixing
11 Sliding insect
screen
12 Sliding double
glazing comprised of
4.8 mm (^{1}/$_{5}$ inch) solar
control laminated
safety glass, 15 mm
(^{5}/$_{8}$ inch) argon filled
cavity and 4.8 mm (^{1}/$_{5}$
inch) toughened glass

3.05
Entrance Door
Section Detail
1:10
1 Thermally insulated
veneered blockboard
reveal
2 Sliding double
glazed door comprised
of 4.8 mm (^{1}/$_{5}$ inch)
solar control laminated
safety glass, 15 mm
(^{5}/$_{8}$ inch) argon filled
cavity and 4.8 mm (^{1}/$_{5}$
inch) toughened glass
3 Timber frame with
concealed fixing
4 50 mm (2 inch)
wide, 25 mm (1 inch)
thick fir decking
boards
5 Foil separating layer
6 165 mm (6^{1}/$_{2}$ inch)
thick impact sound
insulation
7 Bituminous barrier
underlay
8 100 mm (4 inch)
thick reinforced
concrete foundation
slab
9 50 mm (2 inch)
thick auxiliary concrete
slab
10 200 mm (8 inch)
thick hardcore blinding
layer
11 50 mm (2 inch)
wide, 25 mm (1 inch)
thick fir floorboards
12 65 mm (2^{1}/$_{2}$ inch)
concrete screed with
underfloor heating to
bedroom
13 Foil separating
layer
14 100 mm (4 inch)
thick impact sound
insulation

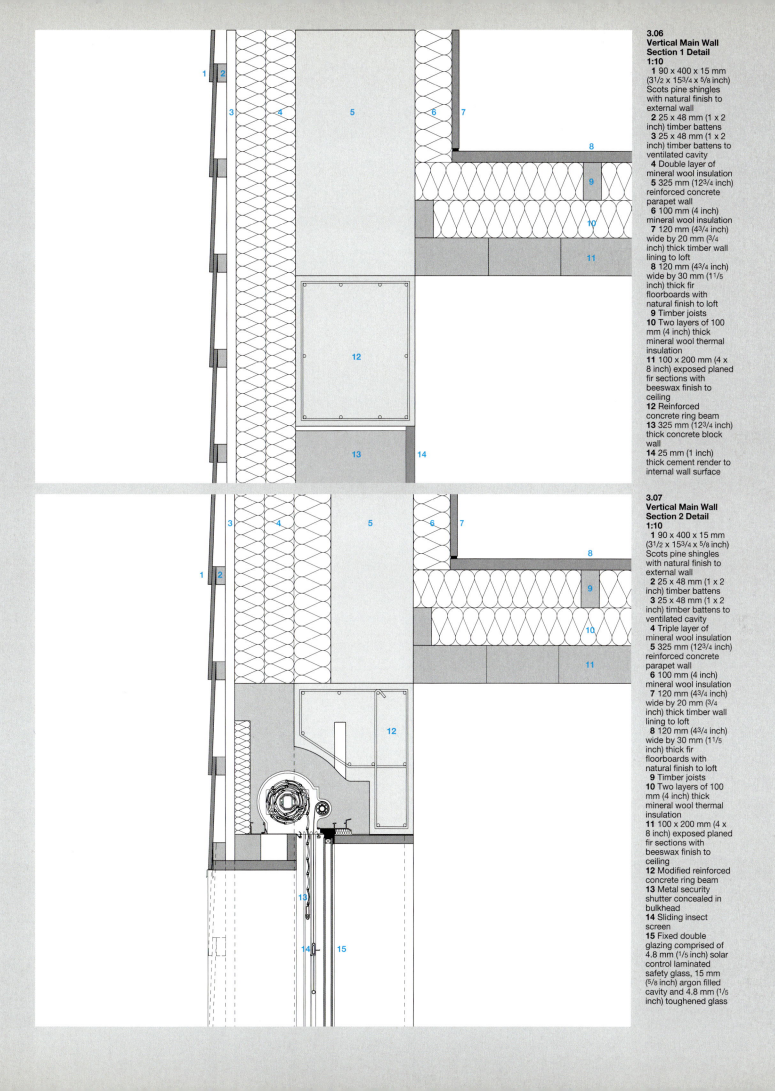

3.06
**Vertical Main Wall
Section 1 Detail**
1:10
1 90 x 400 x 15 mm
(3$^1/_2$ x 15$^3/_4$ x $^5/_8$ inch)
Scots pine shingles
with natural finish to
external wall
2 25 x 48 mm (1 x 2
inch) timber battens
3 25 x 48 mm (1 x 2
inch) timber battens to
ventilated cavity
4 Double layer of
mineral wool insulation
5 325 mm (12$^3/_4$ inch)
reinforced concrete
parapet wall
6 100 mm (4 inch)
mineral wool insulation
7 120 mm (4$^3/_4$ inch)
wide by 20 mm ($^3/_4$
inch) thick timber wall
lining to loft
8 120 mm (4$^3/_4$ inch)
wide by 30 mm (1$^1/_5$
inch) thick fir
floorboards with
natural finish to loft
9 Timber joists
10 Two layers of 100
mm (4 inch) thick
mineral wool thermal
insulation
11 100 x 200 mm (4 x
8 inch) exposed planed
fir sections with
beeswax finish to
ceiling
12 Reinforced
concrete ring beam
13 325 mm (12$^3/_4$ inch)
thick concrete block
wall
14 25 mm (1 inch)
thick cement render to
internal wall surface

3.07
**Vertical Main Wall
Section 2 Detail**
1:10
1 90 x 400 x 15 mm
(3$^1/_2$ x 15$^3/_4$ x $^5/_8$ inch)
Scots pine shingles
with natural finish to
external wall
2 25 x 48 mm (1 x 2
inch) timber battens
3 25 x 48 mm (1 x 2
inch) timber battens to
ventilated cavity
4 Triple layer of
mineral wool insulation
5 325 mm (12$^3/_4$ inch)
reinforced concrete
parapet wall
6 100 mm (4 inch)
mineral wool insulation
7 120 mm (4$^3/_4$ inch)
wide by 20 mm ($^3/_4$
inch) thick timber wall
lining to loft
8 120 mm (4$^3/_4$ inch)
wide by 30 mm (1$^1/_5$
inch) thick fir
floorboards with
natural finish to loft
9 Timber joists
10 Two layers of 100
mm (4 inch) thick
mineral wool thermal
insulation
11 100 x 200 mm (4 x
8 inch) exposed planed
fir sections with
beeswax finish to
ceiling
12 Modified reinforced
concrete ring beam
13 Metal security
shutter concealed in
bulkhead
14 Sliding insect
screen
15 Fixed double
glazing comprised of
4.8 mm ($^1/_5$ inch) solar
control laminated
safety glass, 15 mm
($^5/_8$ inch) argon filled
cavity and 4.8 mm ($^1/_5$
inch) toughened glass

House in Paderne
Paderne, Spain

Client
Private

Project Team
Borja López Cotelo, Maria Olmo Béjar

Structural Engineer
E3 Arquitectos

Main Contractor
Carlos López

This appealingly modest mountain house is located in Galicia in northwestern Spain between the provinces of Lugo and Ourense. The Lor River winds through the forested landscape, which features hectares of holm and other oaks, chestnut trees and beech forests. The area's rich architectural heritage includes a plethora of medieval stone churches and shrines, Celtic castros, or forts, as well as isolated hamlets and villages of small stone-walled, slate-roofed houses and barns.

Carlos Quintáns Eiras' house began life as one such traditional structure, which had previously been added to with an unsympathetic contemporary structure. This was demolished while retaining the original thick stone foundation walls which were used as the base for a new lightweight timber structure. The two storey house accommodates two bedrooms and a bathroom in the partly below ground lower level. Here, the timber ceiling and thick stone walls lend an appropriate degree of protection and solidity to the private sleeping and bathing places. The new timber-clad structure, built up from the old stone walls and following their non-orthogonal geometry, encloses a single, open plan, high-ceilinged living space. The kitchen is located on an elevated platform in the west corner of the plan, accessed from the dining and living space via a short flight of timber steps. Here, a tall storage cupboard divides the kitchen from the stair and the entrance behind.

The south facade is almost entirely glazed. A large fixed pane of glass in the living space and smaller glazed doors to the kitchen look out over ancient stone walls and lush grass pasture in the foreground, and across to the forested, rock strewn ridges and valleys of the mountain range beyond.

1 The north facade of the house faces a public lane and another dwelling. As a consequence, the timber cladding is uninterrupted to maintain privacy to the living spaces. The frameless entrance door, clad in the same timber, is virtually invisible.
2 The timber cladding on the east facade drops down in the centre to create a visually integrated shutter over the bedroom window.
3 On the south side the house is fully glazed, allowing far reaching views over pastureland to the spectacular mountain scenery beyond.
4 The single open plan living space is arranged over two levels. The storage units in the raised kitchen (centre) provide a screen to the entrance door and the stair that leads down to the lower level (right).

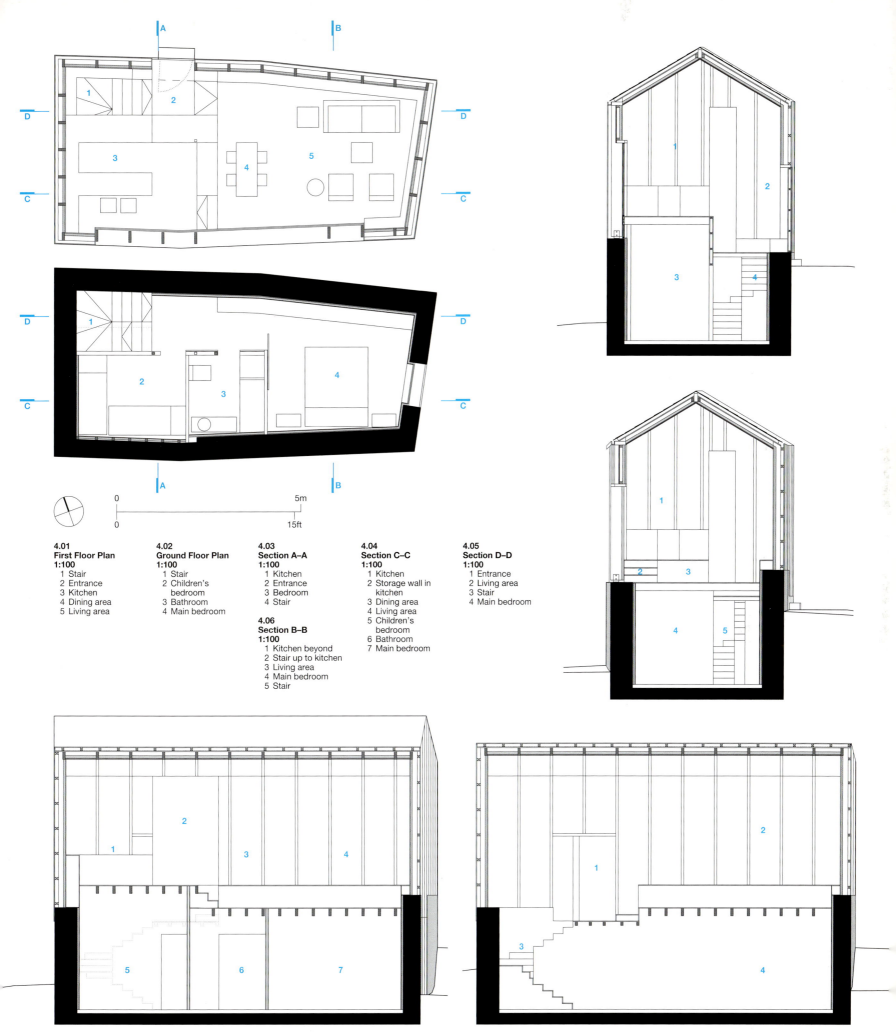

4.01
First Floor Plan
1:100
1 Stair
2 Entrance
3 Kitchen
4 Dining area
5 Living area

4.02
Ground Floor Plan
1:100
1 Stair
2 Children's bedroom
3 Bathroom
4 Main bedroom

4.03
Section A–A
1:100
1 Kitchen
2 Entrance
3 Bedroom
4 Stair

4.06
Section B–B
1:100
1 Kitchen beyond
2 Stair up to kitchen
3 Living area
4 Main bedroom
5 Stair

4.04
Section C–C
1:100
1 Kitchen
2 Storage wall in kitchen
3 Dining area
4 Living area
5 Children's bedroom
6 Bathroom
7 Main bedroom

4.05
Section D–D
1:100
1 Entrance
2 Living area
3 Stair
4 Main bedroom

0 _____ 5m
0 _____ 15ft

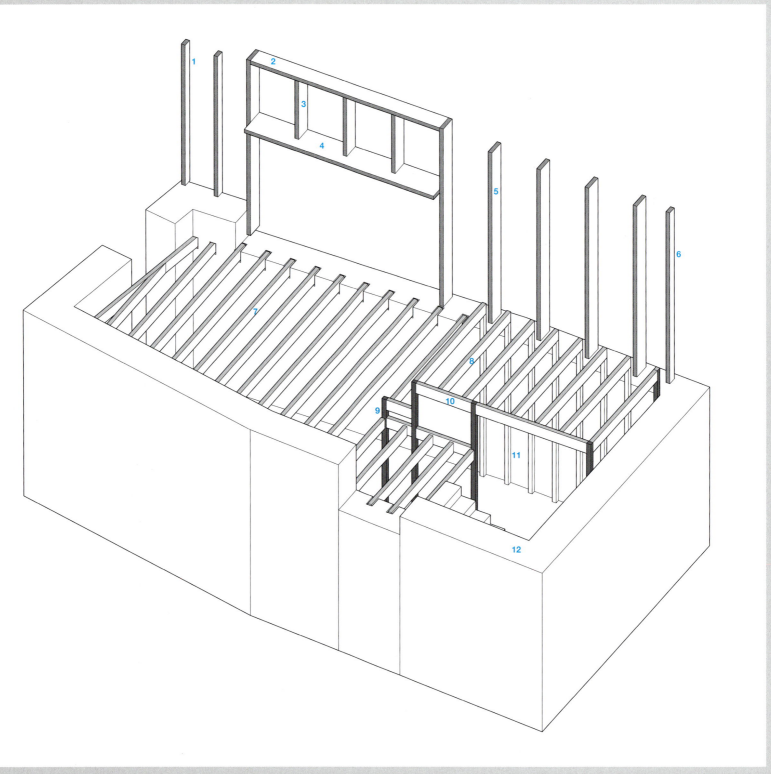

4.06
Timber Framing
Axonometric Detail
Not to scale
  1 70 x 150 mm (2³/4 x
6 inch) glazed south
wall vertical framing
  2 70 x 300 mm (2³/4 x
12 inch) south wall
horizontal framing
  3 70 x 300 mm (2³/4 x
12 inch) south wall
vertical framing
  4 70 x 500 mm (2³/4 x
19³/4 inch) glazed
south wall horizontal
framing
  5 70 x 300 mm (2³/4 x

12 inch) glazed south
wall vertical framing
  6 70 x 150 mm (2³/4 x
6 inch) corner framing
to south wall
  7 70 x 200 mm (2³/4 x
8 inch) floor joists to
living area
  8 70 x 80 mm (2³/4 x
3 inch) floor joists to
kitchen platform
  9 70 x 80 mm (2³/4 x
3 inch) column
  10 80 x 70 mm (3 x
2³/4 inch) edge beam
to kitchen platform
  11 70 x 80 mm (2³/4 x
3 inch) uprights to

base of kitchen
platform
  12 Existing stone base
wall

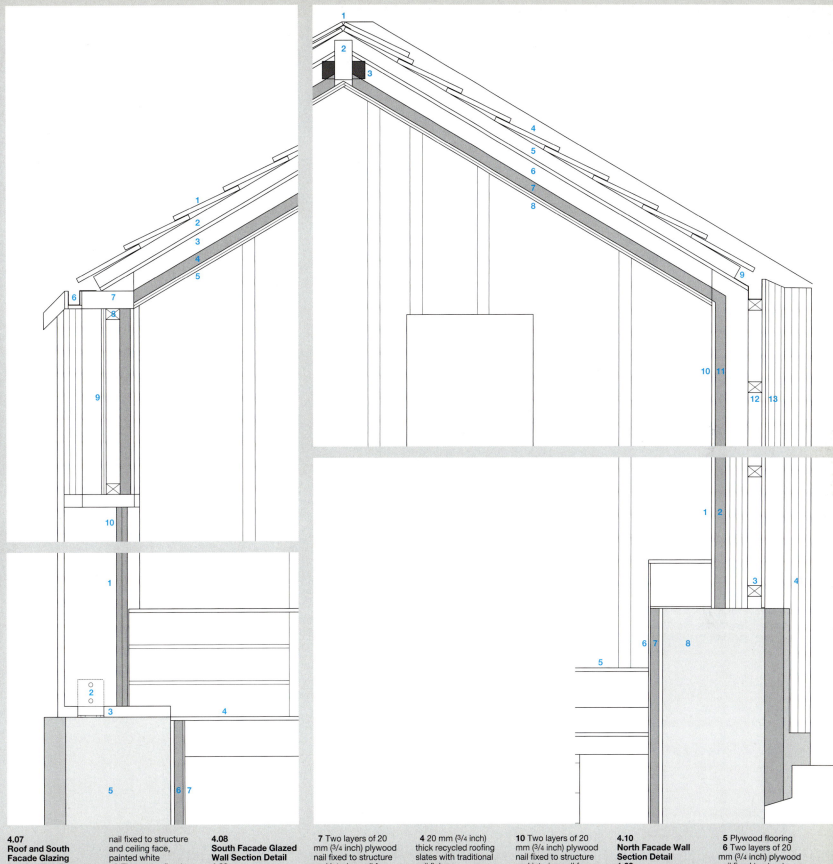

4.07
Roof and South Facade Glazing Section Detail
1:20

1 20 mm (^{3}/$_4$ inch) thick recycled roofing slates with traditional nail fixings
2 60 x 72 mm (2^3/$_8$ x 2^3/$_4$ inch) timber roofing battens
3 20 mm (^{3}/$_4$ inch) plywood
4 60 mm (2^3/$_8$ inch) thick thermal insulation
5 Two layers of 20 mm (^{3}/$_4$ inch) plywood

nail fixed to structure and ceiling face, painted white
6 Zinc gutter fixed to timber frame
7 300 x 950 mm (12 x 37^1/$_4$ inch) timber framing
8 80 x 70 mm (3 x 2^3/$_4$ inch) timber battens
9 Two layers of 20 mm (^{3}/$_4$ inch) plywood nail fixed to structure and interior wall face, painted white
10 Fixed double glazing

4.08
South Facade Glazed Wall Section Detail
1:20

1 Fixed double glazing
2 Steel plate bolted to stone base for fixing timber frame
3 Timber frame
4 20 mm (^{3}/$_4$ inch) plywood flooring
5 Existing stone wall of variable thickness, 600 mm (23^1/$_2$ inch) average
6 60 mm (2^3/$_8$ inch) thick thermal insulation

7 Two layers of 20 mm (^{3}/$_4$ inch) plywood nail fixed to structure and interior wall face, painted white

4.09
Roof and North Facade Section Detail
1:20

1 Stainless steel ridge cap
2 100 x 210 mm (4 x 8^1/$_4$ inch) timber ridge beam
3 Timber reinforcement beam

4 20 mm (^{3}/$_4$ inch) thick recycled roofing slates with traditional nail fixings
5 60 x 72 mm (2^3/$_8$ x 2^3/$_4$ inch) timber roofing battens
6 20 mm (^{3}/$_4$ inch) plywood
7 60 mm (2^3/$_8$ inch) thick thermal insulation
8 Two layers of 20 mm (^{3}/$_4$ inch) plywood nail fixed to structure and ceiling face, painted white
9 Waterproof membrane

10 Two layers of 20 mm (^{3}/$_4$ inch) plywood nail fixed to structure and interior wall face, painted white
11 60 mm (2^3/$_8$ inch) thick thermal insulation
12 60 x 72 mm (2^3/$_8$ x 2^3/$_4$ inch) timber roofing battens
13 Solid timber cladding over 20 mm (^{3}/$_4$ inch) waterproof plywood cladding

4.10
North Facade Wall Section Detail
1:20

1 Two layers of 20 mm (^{3}/$_4$ inch) plywood nail fixed to structure and interior wall face, painted white
2 60 mm (2^3/$_8$ inch) thick thermal insulation
3 60 x 72 mm (2^3/$_8$ x 2^3/$_4$ inch) timber roofing battens
4 Solid timber cladding over 20 mm (^{3}/$_4$ inch) waterproof plywood cladding

5 Plywood flooring
6 Two layers of 20 mm (^{3}/$_4$ inch) plywood nail fixed to structure and interior wall face, painted white
7 60 mm (2^3/$_8$ inch) thick thermal insulation
8 Existing stone wall of variable thickness, 600 mm (23^1/$_2$ inch) average

Wellness Villa
Sealand, The Netherlands

Client
Private

Project Team
Jack Hoogeboom

Structural Engineer
Leen Brak

Landscaping
Habo Hoveniers

This luxury villa in Sealand is located half a mile from the North Sea coast, hidden in a tree-filled area along the edge of the dunes. The owners live in Rotterdam and commissioned the architects to design a weekend house where they could relax and spend time with friends and family. In the future the house will be able to be rented out for corporate training sessions and as a holiday rental property. The house is arranged over three levels, with a spacious living and dining area on the ground floor at the centre of the design where a wall of north facing glazing overlooks a stone paved terrace and garden. On this floor, bedrooms and bathrooms arranged along the south facade, along with the double height living space create a experiential blend of loft, holiday house and hotel. On the first floor, an open gallery overlooking the living room gives access to a glass walled cinema as well as an additional guest bedroom.

The wellness area in the basement, after which the villa is named, accommodates a 12 metre (39 foot) swimming pool as well as three saunas including a regular sauna, a steam sauna and an infrared sauna. A relaxation area, an open wet room and whirlpool bath complete the suite.

Both the structure and cladding of the house are constructed from sustainably sourced timber. Other energy efficient systems include a grass roof, low-emissivity glazing, heat pump and underfloor heating. Natural materials and neutral colours – including a natural stone floor, off-white clay plaster walls and timber details – dominate the interior and contribute to a warm and comfortable atmosphere.

1 A stone paved terrace to the west of the house provides space for outdoor relaxation. An external stair leads to the wellness area in the basement.

2 The open plan living spaces include a large living and dining space to the north (left) and a circulation zone at the centre of the plan (right) defined in the living area by a wood-burning stove and firewood store.

3 The glazed north facade looks out over the garden. Clerestory glazing on the first floor bring light into the mezzanine gallery.

4 The cavern like basement 'wellness area' provides opportunities to relax in the pool, saunas or sitting area.

5.01
First Floor Plan
1:200
1 Void over living
   area
2 Technical room
3 Stair to ground
   floor
4 Home cinema
5 Storage
6 Gallery
7 WC
8 Guest room

5.02
Ground Floor Plan
1:200
1 Living area
2 Dining area
3 Kitchen
4 Stair to basement
5 Stair to first floor
6 Entrance
7 External stair to
   basement
8 Master bedroom
9 Ensuite bathroom
10 Bedroom
11 Ensuite bathroom
12 Ensuite bathroom
13 WC
14 Bedroom

5.03
Basement Plan
1:200
1 Sauna
2 Sauna
3 Sauna
4 Sitting area
5 Laundry
6 Pantry
7 WC
8 Technical room
9 External stair
10 Bath tub
11 Showers
12 Stair to ground
   floor
13 Swimming pool

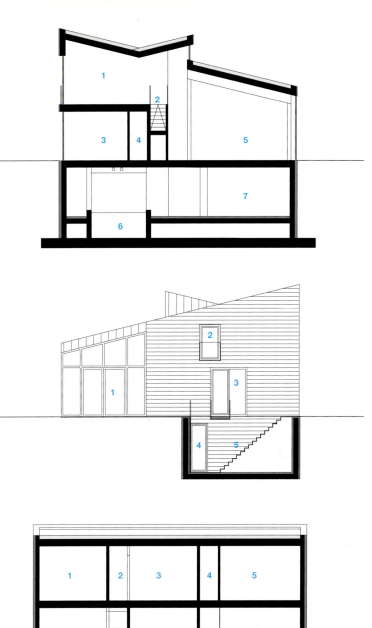

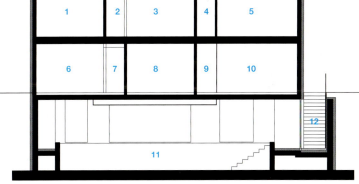

5.04
Section A–A
1:200
1 Gallery
2 Stair
3 Bedroom
4 WC
5 Dining area
6 Swimming pool
7 Sitting area

5.05
Section B–B
1:200
1 Doors to living area
2 Window to home
   cinema
3 Doors to master
   bedroom
4 Door to basement
5 External stair

5.06
Section C–C
1:200
1 Home cinema
2 Storage
3 Gallery
4 WC
5 Guest room
6 Bedroom
7 Ensuite bathroom
8 Bedroom
9 Ensuite bathroom
10 Master bedroom
11 Swimming pool
12 External stair

0   5   10m
0   15   30ft

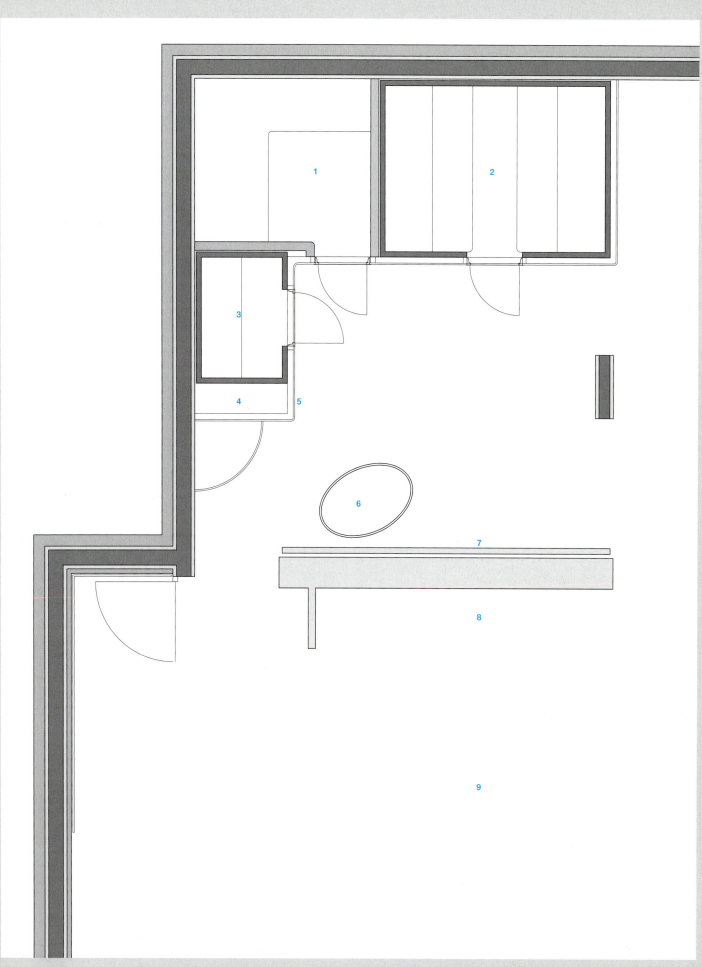

5.07
Sauna Plan Detail
1:50
1 Steam cabinet
2 Sauna
3 Infrared sauna
4 Steam generator
5 Wall finish zebrano veneer
6 Cold water tub
7 Shower wall
8 Stair from ground floor
9 Swimming pool

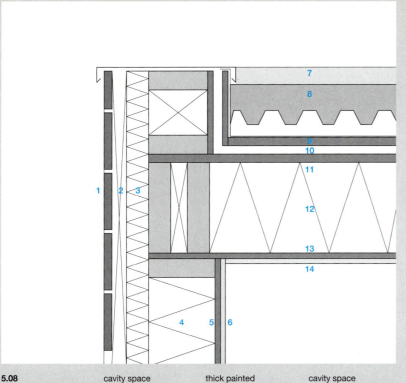

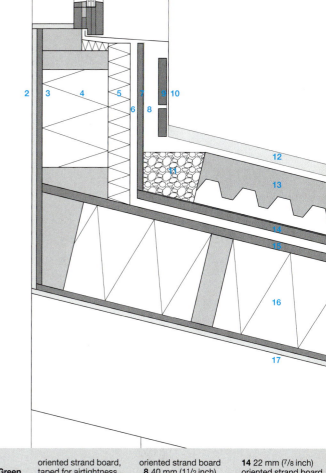

5.08
External Wall Section Detail
1:10
 1 22 mm (7/8 inch) thick untreated Western red cedar external wall cladding
 2 40 mm (1 1/2 inch)

cavity space
 3 60 mm (2 3/8 inch) wood fibre board
 4 Timber framed wall with 180 mm (7 inch) cellulose insulation
 5 15 mm (5/8 inch) oriented strand board, taped for airtightness
 6 12.5 mm (1/2 inch)

thick painted plasterboard wall lining
 7 40 mm (1 1/2 inch) thick green roof system
 8 Root-resistant roof construction
 9 22 mm (7/8 inch) oriented strand board
 10 22 mm (7/8 inch)

cavity space
 11 22 mm (7/8 inch) oriented strand board
 12 Timber beam with 240 mm (9 1/2 inch) cellulose insulation
 13 15 mm (5/8 inch) oriented strand board
 14 12.5 mm (1/2 inch) plasterboard ceiling

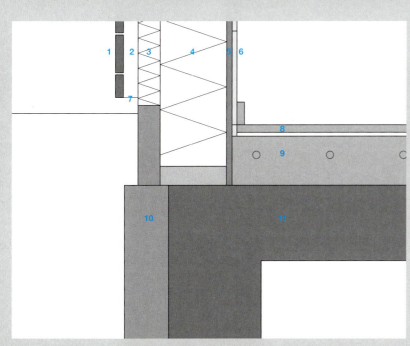

5.10
Roof Light and Green Roof Section Detail
1:10
 1 Timber framed double glazed window
 2 12.5 mm (1/2 inch) thick painted plasterboard wall lining
 3 15 mm (5/8 inch)

oriented strand board, taped for airtightness
 4 Timber framed wall with 180 mm (7 inch) cellulose insulation
 5 60 mm (2 3/8 inch) wood fibre board
 6 22 mm (7/8 inch) cavity space
 7 22 mm (7/8 inch)

oriented strand board
 8 40 mm (1 1/2 inch) cavity space
 9 22 mm (7/8 inch) timber battens
 10 Zinc cladding
 11 Gravel
 12 Green roof system
 13 Root-resistant roof construction

 14 22 mm (7/8 inch) oriented strand board
 15 22 mm (7/8 inch) oriented strand board
 16 Timber beam with 240 mm (9 1/2 inch) cellulose insulation
 17 12.5 mm (1/2 inch) plasterboard ceiling

5.09
Ground and First Floor Wall Section Detail
1:10
 1 22 mm (7/8 inch) thick untreated Western red cedar external wall cladding

 2 40 mm (1 1/2 inch) cavity space
 3 60 mm (2 3/8 inch) wood fibre board
 4 Timber framed wall with 180 mm (7 inch) cellulose insulation
 5 15 mm (5/8 inch) oriented strand board, taped for airtightness

 6 12.5 mm (1/2 inch) thick painted plasterboard wall lining
 7 Vermin barrier
 8 30 mm (1 1/5 inch) thick floor tiles
 9 130 mm (5 1/8 inch) concrete screed with underfloor heating
 10 Rigid insulation

 11 200 mm (8 inch) reinforced concrete floor slab

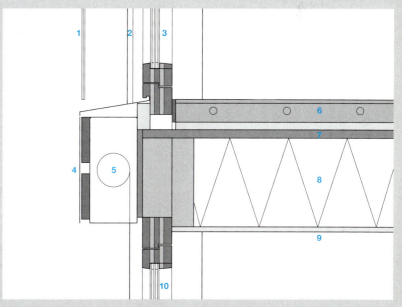

5.11
Glass Balustrade and Sunscreen in Western Red Cedar Facade
1:10
 1 Glass balustrade
 2 Rail for sunscreen
 3 Timber framed double glazed door
 4 Zinc facade on

timber battens
 5 External roller blind
 6 Concrete screen with 80 mm (3 inch) underfloor heating
 7 18 mm (3/4 inch) oriented strand board
 8 Timber beam with 240 mm (9 1/2 inch) cellulose insulation

 9 12.5 mm (1/2 inch) plasterboard ceiling
 10 Timber framed double glazed door

Summer House
Oberbergen, Austria

Client
Private

Project Team
Judith Benzer Architektur with Geiger & Walser

Structural Engineer
Merz Kley Partner

Main Contractor
Zimmerei Berchtel

Located in eastern Austria not far from the Hungarian border, Oberbergen is known for its high quality Pinot Noir production. Designed as a summer house for a soon to be retired couple – who plan to make small quantities of wine from grapes grown in their own vineyard – this rural retreat is a distillation of local architectural forms, with particular reference to the steeply pitched roofed, gable ended Kellerstöckl (wine house) typical of the region. The appealing simplicity of the form and structure gives the impression of something carved from a single material. However on closer inspection, the exterior envelope is in fact a finely textured rain screen of untreated larch battens which have been used for all external surfaces including the walls and the roof.

Despite its appearance of a single storey structure, the house has three levels. A concrete basement accommodates cellaring and wine making functions, while residential accommodation is in the timber structure – living, sleeping and bathing spaces in the main, ground floor space and an office on a mezzanine level within the pitched roof, accessed via a folded metal-plate stair.

As the house is not inhabited in the winter months, the timber skin has been designed so that it can be completely closed. Shutters of the same larch battens can shut across the openings on the east facade, or fold down on the west facade – when open they create a shade structure. Extra crispness in the detailing of the timber facade is to be found in the black painted counter battens to which the outer larch battens are fixed, and the use of folded copper to define the corners.

1 The generous timber terrace, constructed in the same larch as the cladding, has been laid down as a sort of shadow of the house. Gravel beds to the perimeter, and in line with the ribbon window, add texture to the built landscape and reinforce the idea of a built shadow.
2 The pitched roof wooden box, with its regular rhythm of openings and flat gable ends, references local agricultural buildings.
3 The larch shutters are braced by a black steel frame structure that is entirely concealed when in the closed position to retain the aesthetic integrity of the timber cladding.
4 On the north facade, a small square window to the WC forms a composition with a full height vertical ribbon window that brings natural light into the ground floor circulation zone and the mezzanine office.
5 The interior uses a simple material palette of timber walls and floor with black joinery and steelwork, including the folded steel stair.

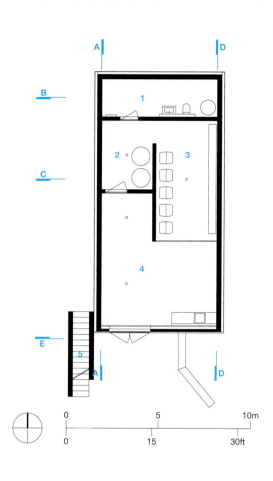

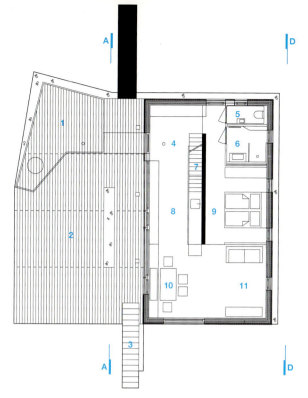

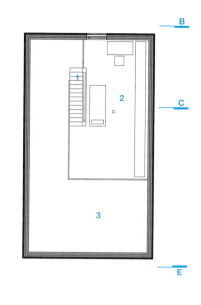

0   5   10m
0   15   30ft

6.01
Basement Plan
1:200
1 Technical room
  and WC
2 Wine making area
3 Wine cellar
4 Cellar
5 External stair

6.02
Ground Floor Plan
1:200
1 Future garden
  pavilion
2 Terrace
3 External stair
4 Entrance
5 WC

6 Bathroom
7 Stair to mezzanine
8 Kitchen
9 Bedroom
10 Dining area
11 Living area

6.03
Mezzanine Floor Plan
1:200
1 Stair
2 Office
3 Void

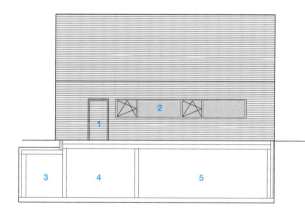

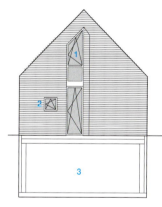

6.04
Section A–A and
West Elevation
1:200
1 Entrance
2 Window to kitchen
  and dining area
3 Technical store
  and WC
4 Wine making area
5 Cellar

6.05
Section B–B and
North Elevation
1:200
1 Window to
  mezzanine
2 Window to WC
3 Technical store
  and WC

6.06
Section C-C
1:200
1 Mezzanine office
2 Bedroom
3 Stair
4 Kitchen
5 Terrace

6 Wine cellar
7 Wine making area

6.07
Section D–D and East
Elevation
1:200
1 Windows to
  bathroom,
  bedroom and living
  area
2 Cellar
3 Wine cellar
4 Technical store
  and WC

6.08
Section E–E and
South Elevation
1:200
1 Window to dining
  and living area
2 Entrance to cellar

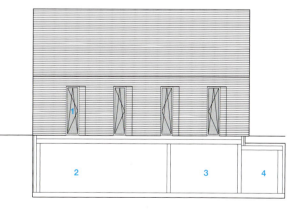

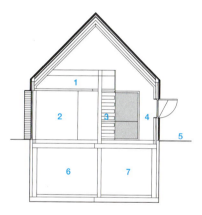

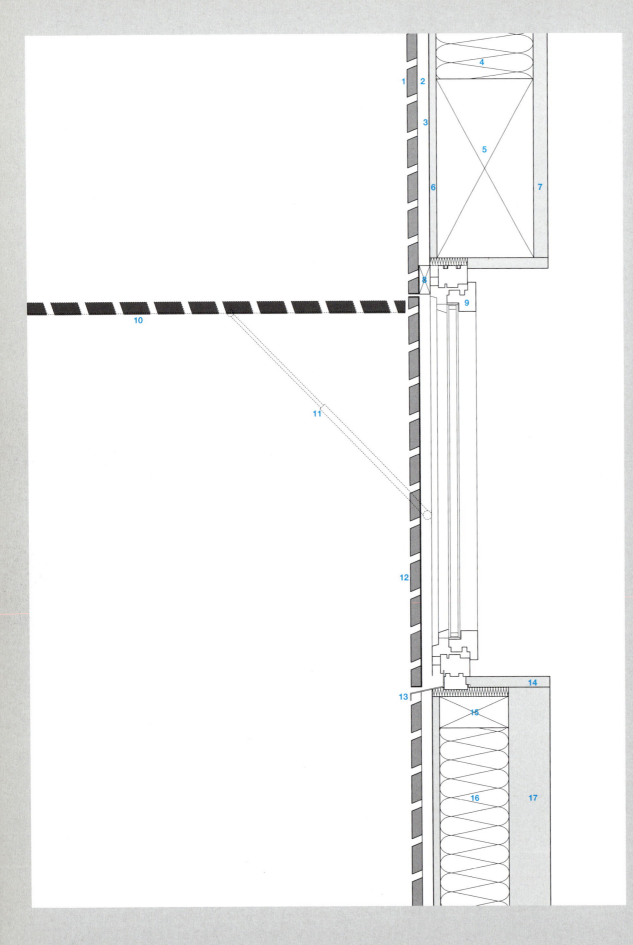

6.09
**External Wall and
Window Section
Detail**
1:5
 1 Chamfered
untreated larch batten
cladding
 2 26 x 70 mm (1 x
2³/₄ inch) black-
painted timber counter
battens
 3 Breather membrane
 4 160 mm (6¹/₄ inch)
rock wool insulation
 5 Timber wall framing
and lintel
 6 16 mm (⁵/₈ inch)
vapour permeable,
windproof, waterproof
wood fibre structural
insulating panel
 7 Cross laminated
timber internal wall
lining
 8 16 x 40 mm (⁵/₈ x 1
¹/₂ inch) timber stop
batten to window
opening
 9 Black anodized
aluminium-framed
double glazed sliding
window
10 Larch batten
shutter awning in open
position
11 Gas spring struts to
shutter awning
12 Larch batten
shutter awning in
closed position
13 Folded aluminium
flashing
14 Solid timber
window sill
15 Timber framing
16 160 mm (6¹/₄ inch)
rock wool insulation
17 95 mm (3³/₄ inch)
thick cross-laminated
timber-panel internal
wall lining

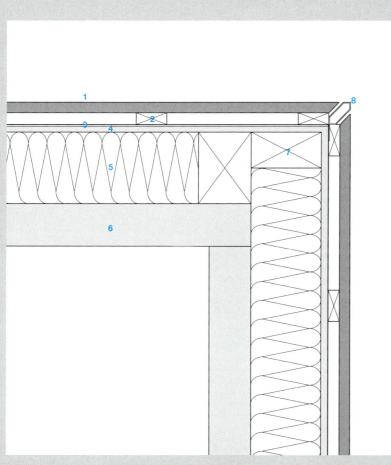

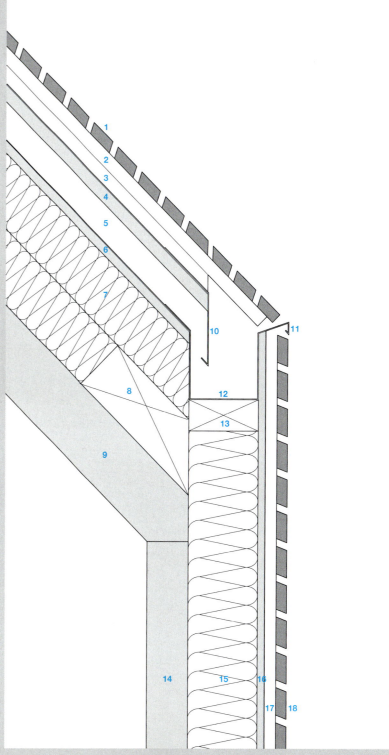

6.10
External Wall Corner Section Detail
1:10
1 Chamfered untreated larch batten cladding
2 26 x 70 mm (1 x 2³/₄ inch) black-painted timber counter battens
3 Breather membrane
4 16 mm (⁵/₈ inch) vapour permeable, windproof, waterproof

wood fibre structural insulating panel
5 160 mm (6¹/₄ inch) rock wool insulation
6 95 mm (3³/₄ inch) thick cross-laminated timber-panel internal wall lining
7 Timber stud framing
8 Folded copper corner fixed to timber counter battens

6.11
Roof and External Wall Section Detail
1:10
1 Chamfered untreated larch batten roof cladding
2 26 x 70 mm (1 x 2³/₄ inch) black-painted timber counter battens
3 Waterproof plywood roofing substrate
4 Waterproof

plywood roofing substrate
5 Ventilation void
6 16 mm (⁵/₈ inch) vapour permeable, windproof, waterproof wood fibre structural insulating panel
7 Double layer of 160 mm (6¹/₄ inch) rock wool insulation
8 Timber ceiling joist
9 95 mm (3³/₄ inch) thick cross-laminated timber-panel internal

ceiling lining
10 Aluminium flashing
11 Folded edge to external face of aluminium gutter
12 Pre-formed folded aluminium concealed gutter
13 Timber stud framing
14 95 mm (3³/₄ inch) thick cross-laminated timber-panel internal wall lining
15 160 mm (6¹/₄ inch) rock wool insulation

16 16 mm (⁵/₈ inch) vapour permeable, windproof, waterproof wood fibre structural insulating panel
17 26 x 70 mm (1 x 2³/₄ inch) black-painted timber counter battens
18 Chamfered untreated larch batten wall cladding

Villa Nyberg
Borlänge, Sweden

Client
Nyberg family, in collaboration with
Emrahus

Project Team
Joakim Kaminsky, Fredrik Kjellgren,
Oscar Arnklitt, Daniel Andersson,
Corina Bermúdez

Structural Engineer
Emrahus

Villa Nyberg is situated on the shores
of a lake in a pine forest in central
Sweden. It was originally designed as
a speculative conceptual project and
was later adapted to suit the needs of
the client. The concept makes
reference to a traditional analog clock,
seen in the circular plan with its
central atrium that captures the sun as
it moves around the house.

The open plan public spaces
including the kitchen, dining and living
areas are placed to the north-east
where they enjoy far reaching views
towards the lake. In contrast, the more
private areas including the bedrooms
and bathrooms are situated to the
south-west and feature small square
windows that protect the privacy of
the inhabitants while allowing views
into the forest. An open tread steel
stair in the gravel floored atrium leads
up to a roof terrace with panoramic
views of the lake, and to a glass
enclosed rooftop studio. A separate
building opposite the entrance
contains a garage and self-contained
studio guest accommodation.

Importantly, the house was
designed to conform to 'Passive
House' principles enabling it to
achieve very low levels of energy
consumption. The building is
extremely well-insulated and sealed
making it possible for the house to be
largely heated by secondary sources
including body heat and household
equipment. The circular form also
helps to eliminate cold-bridges and
reduces the enclosing wall area of the
house to minimize heat loss. The
building is clad in pine boards that will
weather to the same grey as the pine
trunks in the surrounding forest.

1 Seen through the
trees, the vertical
cladding references
the trunks of the pines
that surround the
house. Solar panels on
the roof are part of the
low energy strategy.
2 Simple robust
detailing seen in the
gutters, material
junctions and
functional windows
lend the house a
simplicity and
straightforwardness
that is in keeping with
a comfortable family
home.
3 The interior is
flooded with natural
light. The living spaces
have windows onto
both the exterior and
the central atrium
courtyard which leads
up to the roof terrace.
4 The simple material
palette of white walls
and ceilings with light
timber floors is used
throughout. In the
open plan kitchen
(foreground), dining
and living space, large
windows look out to
the lake.

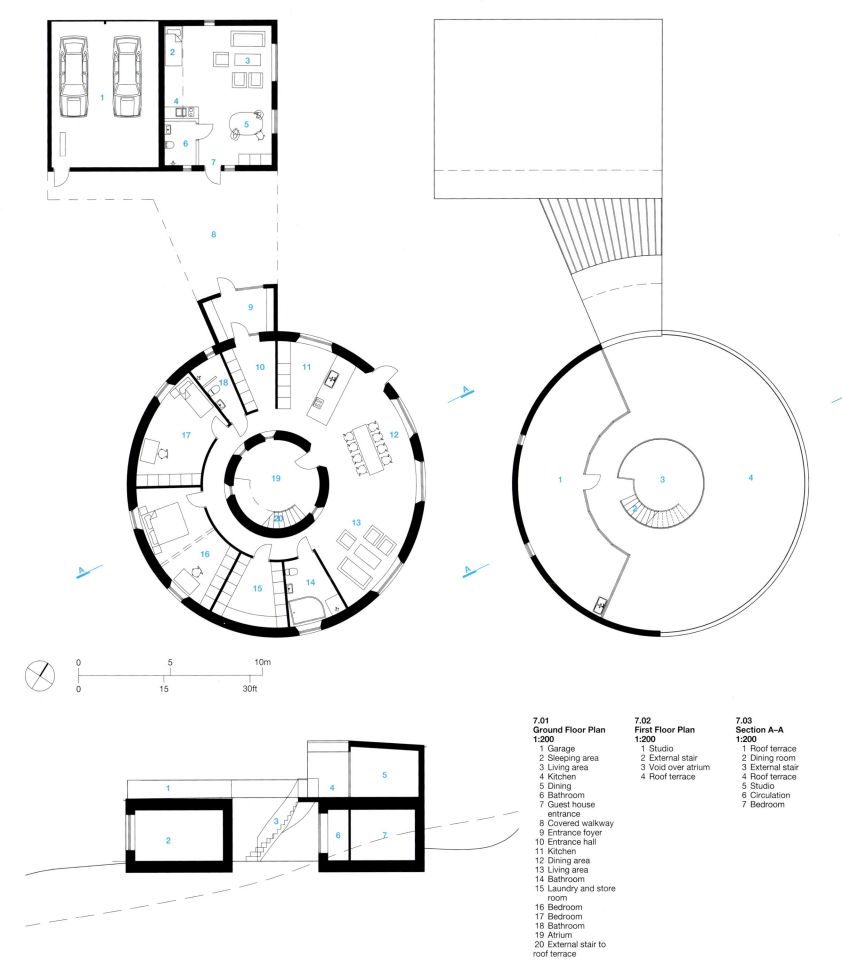

7.01
Ground Floor Plan
1:200
1 Garage
2 Sleeping area
3 Living area
4 Kitchen
5 Dining
6 Bathroom
7 Guest house entrance
8 Covered walkway
9 Entrance foyer
10 Entrance hall
11 Kitchen
12 Dining area
13 Living area
14 Bathroom
15 Laundry and store room
16 Bedroom
17 Bedroom
18 Bathroom
19 Atrium
20 External stair to roof terrace

7.02
First Floor Plan
1:200
1 Studio
2 External stair
3 Void over atrium
4 Roof terrace

7.03
Section A–A
1:200
1 Roof terrace
2 Dining room
3 External stair
4 Roof terrace
5 Studio
6 Circulation
7 Bedroom

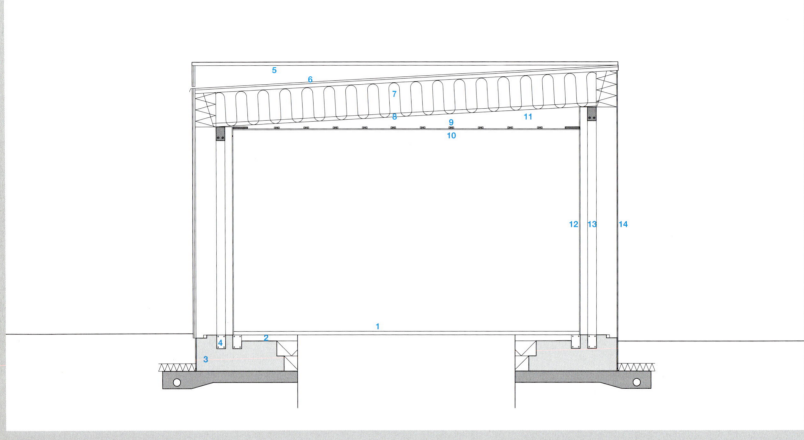

7.04
Wall Section 1
1:50
 1 45 mm (1³/4 inch)
thick timber flooring
 2 80 mm
(3 inch) concrete
topping
 3 400 mm (15³/4 inch)
reinforced concrete
edge beam
 4 Two 200 mm (8
inch) cast-in columns
 5 Steel beam
 6 Roof build up of
timber deck over
waterproof membrane,
felt underlay, 22 mm
(⁷/8 inch) tongue-and-
groove timber
boarding and variable
size 400–800 mm
(15³/4 – 31¹/2 inch)
masonite beams
 7 500 mm (19³/4 inch)
thermal insulation
 8 Inner roof layer of
reinforced plastic
sheeting and 28 x 70 x
400 mm (1 x 2³/4 x

15³/4 inch) plywood
panels
 9 22 mm (⁷/8 inch)
timber battens
10 13 mm (¹/2 inch)
painted plasterboard
ceiling
11 Steel beam
12 Polished plaster
wall finish
13 500 x 500 mm
(19³/4 x 19³/4 inch)
steel column
14 Timber tongue-and-
groove cladding

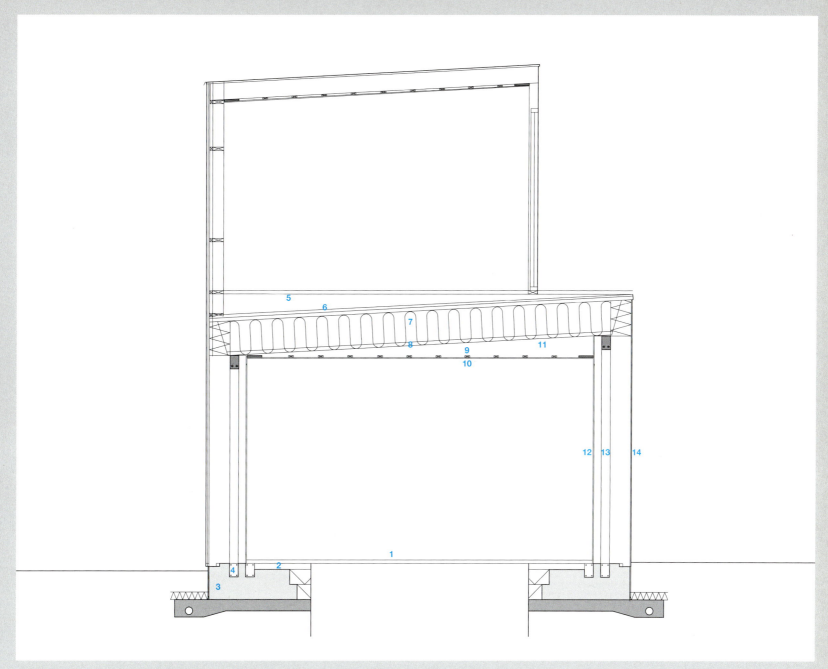

7.05
Wall Section 2
1:50
1 45 mm (1¹/₈ inch)
thick timber flooring
2 80 mm
(3¹/₈ inch) concrete
topping
3 400 mm (15³/₄ inch)
reinforced concrete
edge beam
4 Two 200 mm (8
inch) cast-in columns
5 Steel beam
6 Roof build up of
timber deck over
waterproof membrane,
felt underlay, 22 mm
(⁷/₈ inch) tongue-and-
groove timber
boarding and variable
size 400–800 mm
(15³/₄ – 31¹/₂ inch)
masonite beams
7 500 mm (19³/₄ inch)
thermal insulation
8 Inner roof layer of
reinforced plastic
sheeting and 28 x 70 x
400 mm (1 x 2³/₄ x

15³/₄ inch) plywood
panels
9 22 mm (⁷/₈ inch)
timber battens
10 13 mm (¹/₂ inch)
painted plasterboard
ceiling
11 Steel beam
12 Polished plaster
wall finish
13 500 x 500 mm
(19³/₄ x 19³/₄ inch)
steel column
14 Timber tongue-and-
groove cladding

House MJ
Novo Mesto, Slovenia

Client
Private

Project Team
Tomaž Čeligoj, Ana Grk, Blaž Kandus,
Alenka Korenjak, Tina Rugelj, Tjaša
Mavrič

Structural Engineer
PBO Osterman Miran

Mechanical Engineer
Arctur Projektiva

Electrical Engineer
Ivan Čeligoj

Located near the small city of Novo
mesto in southeastern Slovenia,
House MJ sits on the edge of a forest
at the top of a slope overlooking the
city. The timber-clad building is
arranged within a simple rectilinear
plan, however in section, the form is
divided in two with mono pitched roof
lines denoting the separation. The two
zones – living spaces to the north-
west and sleeping and bathing spaces
to the south-east – are arranged to
minimize circulation space and
maximize natural light. Light enters
through full height glazing to the
north-west wall, and through
clerestory glazing running the entire
length of the open plan kitchen, dining
and living space, introduced through
the lifted roof line. Further delineating
the plan, split levels follow the natural
slope of the site so that bedrooms are
raised up behind the living area with
two steps in the parquet floor
negotiating the change in level.

   Further down the sloping site
towards the road, a concrete garage
has been dug into the hill and covered
with a grass roof in order to eliminate
any disruption to long range views
from the house. A meandering
concrete stair and ramp cut into the
grass connects the two structures.
The highly insulated timber frame
construction, along with triple glazed
windows, sustainably sourced larch
cladding and the judicious use of
natural light makes this house a highly
energy efficient and comfortable
family home.

1 The house sits at the top of a gently sloping site looking out over the planted roof of the garage towards the city of Novo mesto.
2 A concrete stair, rising in angled sections up the sloping site, connects the street with the concrete garage (right) terminating at the entrance to the house.
3 A view of the north-east reveals the covered entrance tucked into the timber facade, as well as the two raised roofs that define the section and let south-east light into the interior.
4 Clerestory windows run the entire length of the house and bring light into the living spaces in the mornings.
5 The all white walls and ceiling are anchored by the richness and texture of the American walnut parquet flooring. In the centre of the living space there is a large wood-burning stove.

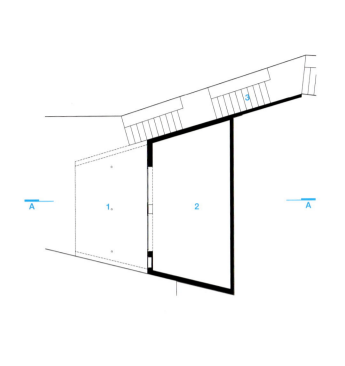

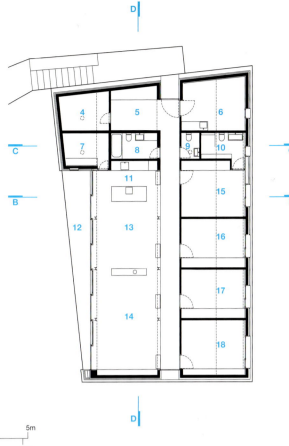

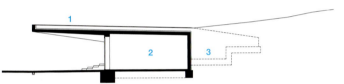

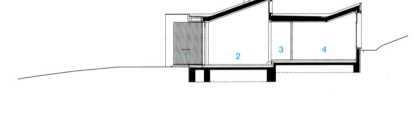

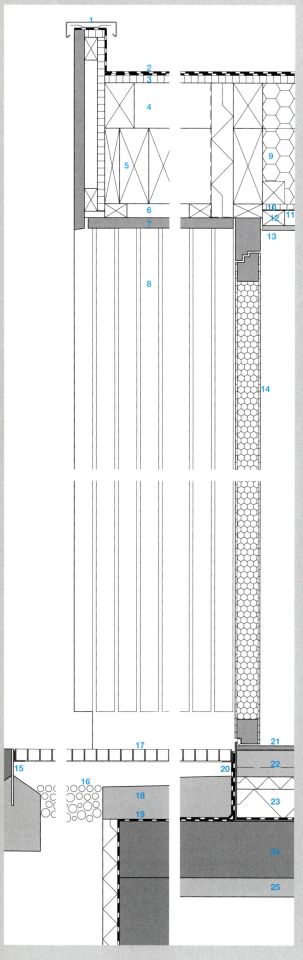

8.06
Living Area
North-West External
Wall and Door
Section Detail
1:10
1 2 mm (1/8 inch) thick painted sheet aluminium parapet cap
2 Double layer bituminous waterproof membrane
3 20 mm (3/4 inch) oriented strand board roofing substrate
4 130 x 80 mm (51/8 x 3 inch) timber battens laid to fall
5 200 mm (8 inch) structural timber framing
6 37 x 60 mm (11/2 x 23/8 inch) timber soffit battens
7 55 x 28 mm (21/8 x 1 inch) oiled larch timber soffit lining
8 Oiled larch timber wall lining to terrace
9 200 mm (8 inch) cellulose insulation laid between 200 x 60 mm (8 x 23/8 inch) glue laminated timber rafters
10 15 mm (5/8 inch) oriented strand board
11 Vapour barrier
12 40 mm (11/2 inch) timber ceiling battens
13 12.5 mm (1/2 inch) plasterboard ceiling
14 68 mm (25/8 inch) entrance door comprised of larch veneer ply outer layers with solid larch lipping and composite insulated core
15 30 x 5 mm (11/5 x 1/5 inch) steel L-angle
16 Cavity and gravel to drain
17 30 x 30 mm (11/5 x 11/5 inch) grid stainless steel bar drainage grate
18 Screed laid to fall
19 Bitumen damp-proof membrane
20 Self adhesive high-density waterproof membrane
21 60 x 60 x 12 mm (23/8 x 23/8 x 1/2 inch) ceramic floor tiles
22 70 mm (23/4 inch) thick concrete screed with underfloor heating
23 100 mm (4 inch) thick rigid insulation panels
24 120 mm (43/4 inch) thick reinforced concrete floor slab
25 50 mm (2 inch) thick lean concrete sub slab

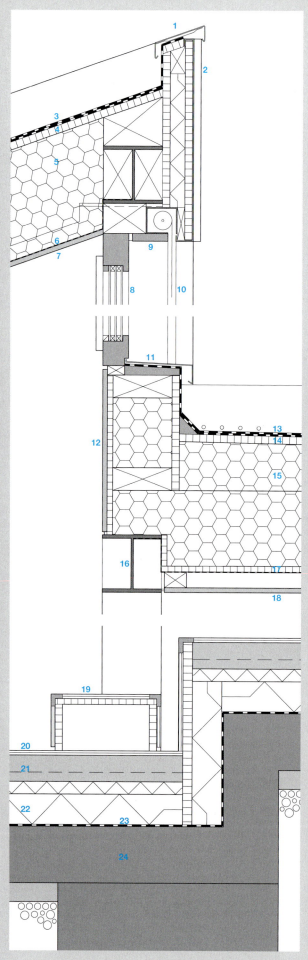

8.07
Living Area
North-East External
Wall and Clerestory
Window Section
Detail
1:10
1 2 mm (1/8 inch) thick painted sheet aluminium parapet cap
2 1.5 mm (1/8 inch) sheet aluminium cladding bonded to oriented strand board
3 Double layer bituminous waterproof membrane
4 20 mm (3/4 inch) oriented strand board roofing substrate
5 200 mm (8 inch) cellulose insulation laid between 200 x 60 mm (8 x 23/8 inch) glue laminated timber rafters
6 Vapour barrier
7 12.5 mm (1/2 inch) plasterboard ceiling
8 Larch-framed triple glazed clerestory window
9 Larch window reveal
10 Electrically operated external fabric roller blind
11 Folded aluminium sill cover
12 12.5 mm (1/2 inch) plasterboard wall lining on oriented strand board
13 Double layer bituminous waterproof membrane
14 20 mm (3/4 inch) oriented strand board roofing substrate
15 110 mm (43/8 inch) cellulose insulation laid between 200 x 60 mm (8 x 23/8 inch) glue laminated timber rafters
16 Exposed steel beam
17 15 mm (5/8 inch) oriented strand board
18 12.5 mm (1/2 inch) plasterboard ceiling
19 11 mm (1/2 inch) American walnut parquet flooring to intermediate step
20 11 mm (1/2 inch) American walnut parquet flooring
21 70 mm (23/4 inch) thick concrete screed with underfloor heating
22 100 mm (4 inch) thick rigid insulation panels
23 Bitumen damp-proof membrane
24 120 mm (43/4 inch) thick reinforced concrete floor slab

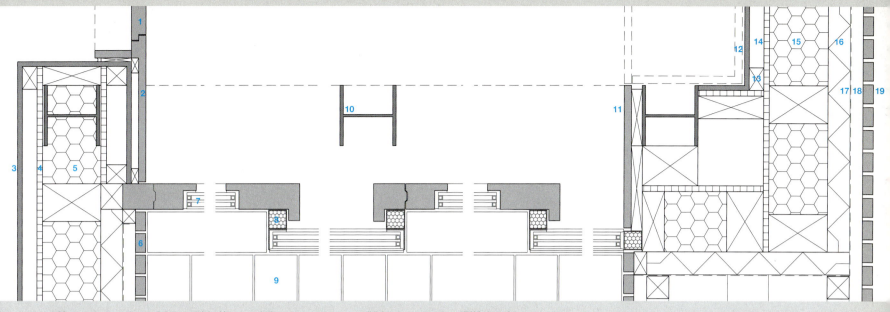

8.08
**Living Area
North-West External
Wall Plan Detail**
1:10
1 Composite
structure, flush
mounted, painted
interior door
2 19 mm (3/4 inch)
painted MDF interior
wall lining

3 2.5 mm (1/8 inch)
plasterboard wall lining
4 15 mm (5/8 inch)
oriented strand board
5 160 mm (61/4 inch)
cellulose insulation
6 55 x 28 mm (21/8 x
1 inch) oiled larch
timber batten exterior
cladding
7 Triple glazed, oiled
larch-framed sliding

window
8 50 x 50 mm (2 x 2
inch) stainless steel
square section framing
9 28 x 120 mm (1 x
43/4 inch) oiled larch
timber decking
10 Exposed steel
column to living room
wall
11 19 mm (3/4 inch)
painted MDF interior

wall lining
12 12.5 mm (1/2 inch)
fibreboard interior wall
lining
13 40 mm (11/2 inch)
timber battens
14 15 mm (5/8 inch)
oriented strand board
15 160 mm (61/4 inch)
cellulose insulation
16 60 mm (23/8 inch)
wood fibre insulation

17 Windproof
membrane
18 35 mm (13/8 inch)
timber battens
19 55 x 28 mm (21/8 x
1 inch) oiled larch
timber batten exterior
cladding

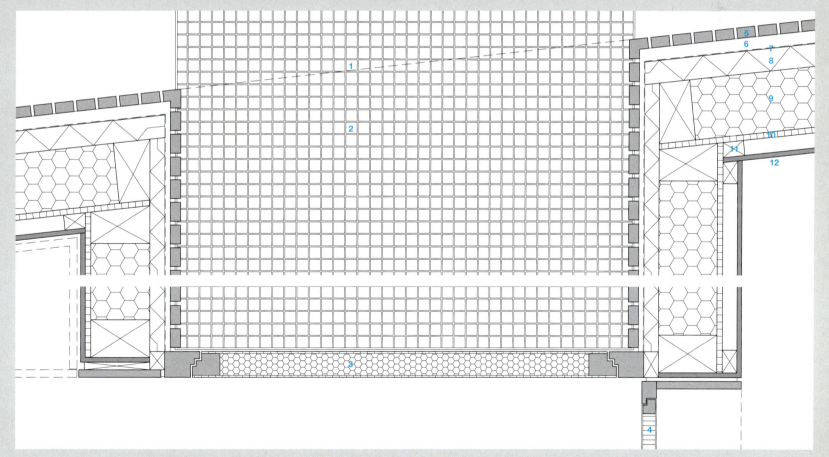

8.09
**Entrance Door Plan
Detail**
1:10
1 Line of roof over
shown dotted
2 30 x 30 mm
(11/5 x 11/5 inch) grid
stainless steel bar
drainage grate
3 68 mm (25/8 inch)
entrance door

comprised of larch
veneer ply outer layers
with solid larch lipping
and composite
insulated core
4 Flush mounted,
paint finished, solid
timber internal door
5 55 x 28 mm (21/8 x
1 inch) oiled larch
timber batten exterior
cladding

6 40 mm (11/2 inch)
timber battens
7 Windproof
membrane
8 60 mm (23/8 inch)
wood fibre insulation
9 160 mm (61/4 inch)
cellulose insulation
10 15 mm (5/8 inch)
oriented strand board
11 35 mm (13/8 inch)
timber battens

12 12.5 mm (1/2 inch)
fibreboard interior wall
lining

Toblerone House
São Paulo, Brazil

Client
Private

Project Team
Marcio Kogan, Diana Radomysler

Structural Engineer
Gilberto Pinto Rodrigues

Main Contractor
Lock Engenharia

Studio MK27's Toblerone House in São Paulo is a study in considered simplicity. Its elegant expression consists of three expansive horizontal concrete planes that sandwich the simple juxtaposition of two contrasting spaces. On the upper level, a timber box is recessed beneath the overhanging concrete roof plane. This level, containing three bedrooms, all with ensuite bathrooms, a study and a home cinema, is wrapped in retractable screens of slender timber 'toblerone-shaped' slats that lend a high degree of privacy and flexibility to the private spaces. Inside the line of the toblerone screens, which sit on the perimeter of the upper floor, blackout roller blinds and lightweight curtains together provide a multitude of ways to introduce or exclude natural light.

The lower level, containing the living and dining spaces, an office and the kitchen, are set within an entirely glazed perimeter wall set in from the concrete slab of the first floor. The floor above is supported on two rows of 14 slender steel columns running longitudinally to maximize exposure to the garden through the uninterrupted full height glass walls. A timber clad box within the ground floor contains the kitchen and a number of circulation zones, including a lift that serves all three levels, plus a stair to the basement service and staff areas. An additional, strikingly elegant open tread stair leads from the south-west end of the ground floor up to the first floor.

The relationship of the house to the garden was essential to the concept. The house has been placed along the length of the site among groves of mature Jabuticabeiras – Brazilian Grape Trees – which were retained and provide the focus for both interior and exterior living spaces, including the large terrace at the north-east end of the ground floor where a hanging fireplace creates a focus for year round outdoor living.

1 The dematerialized walls of the ground floor, enclosed by four walls of sliding glass doors, provides a striking visual foil for the timber screen-clad upper floor.
2 View of the south-west facade where a circulation zone of lift and open tread stair lead up to the private spaces on the first floor.
3 The timber screens on the first floor are constructed from triangular fillets of solid wood attached to frames that can be opened and closed to moderate light and privacy.
4 The concrete slab to the first floor extends out over a large terrace at the north-east end of the living area and into the mature garden.
5 The office on the ground floor (left) is separated from the living area (right) by a long run of double-sided joinery.

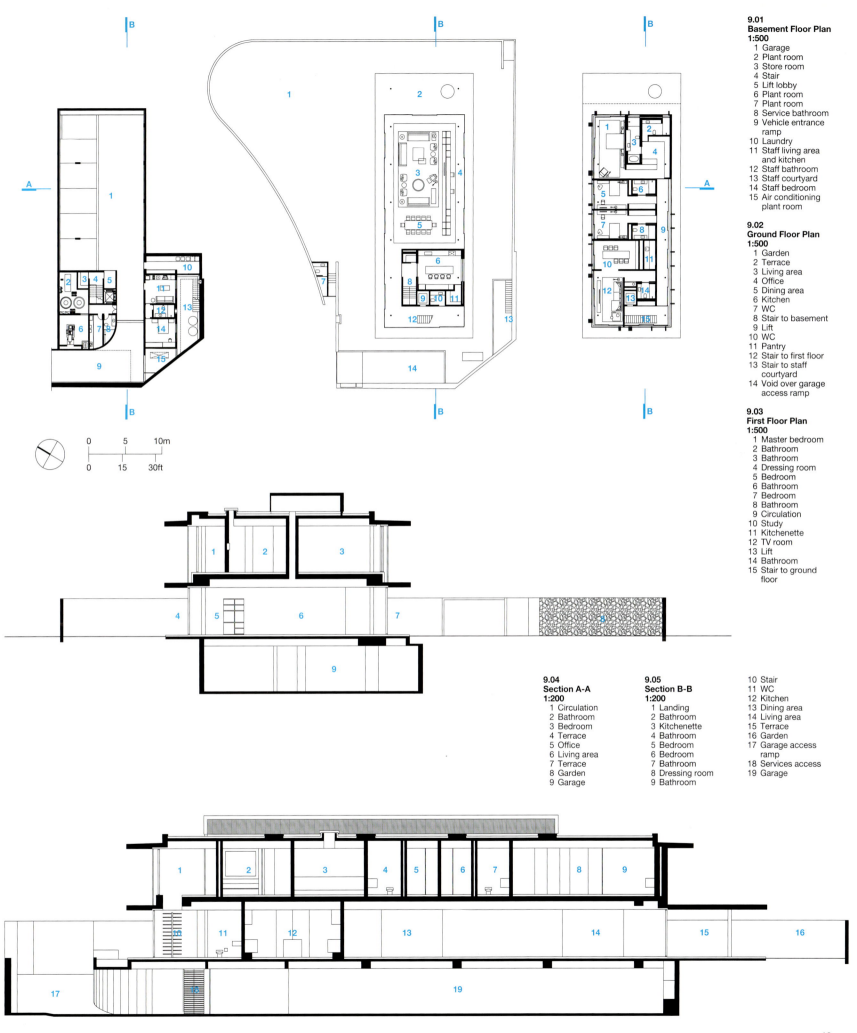

9.01
Basement Floor Plan
1:500
  1 Garage
  2 Plant room
  3 Store room
  4 Stair
  5 Lift lobby
  6 Plant room
  7 Plant room
  8 Service bathroom
  9 Vehicle entrance
    ramp
  10 Laundry
  11 Staff living area
    and kitchen
  12 Staff bathroom
  13 Staff courtyard
  14 Staff bedroom
  15 Air conditioning
    plant room

9.02
Ground Floor Plan
1:500
  1 Garden
  2 Terrace
  3 Living area
  4 Office
  5 Dining area
  6 Kitchen
  7 WC
  8 Stair to basement
  9 Lift
  10 WC
  11 Pantry
  12 Stair to first floor
  13 Stair to staff
    courtyard
  14 Void over garage
    access ramp

9.03
First Floor Plan
1:500
  1 Master bedroom
  2 Bathroom
  3 Bathroom
  4 Dressing room
  5 Bedroom
  6 Bathroom
  7 Bedroom
  8 Bathroom
  9 Circulation
  10 Study
  11 Kitchenette
  12 TV room
  13 Lift
  14 Bathroom
  15 Stair to ground
    floor

9.04
Section A-A
1:200
  1 Circulation
  2 Bathroom
  3 Bedroom
  4 Terrace
  5 Office
  6 Living area
  7 Terrace
  8 Garden
  9 Garage

9.05
Section B-B
1:200
  1 Landing
  2 Bathroom
  3 Kitchenette
  4 Bathroom
  5 Bedroom
  6 Bedroom
  7 Bathroom
  8 Dressing room
  9 Bathroom

  10 Stair
  11 WC
  12 Kitchen
  13 Dining area
  14 Living area
  15 Terrace
  16 Garden
  17 Garage access
    ramp
  18 Services access
  19 Garage

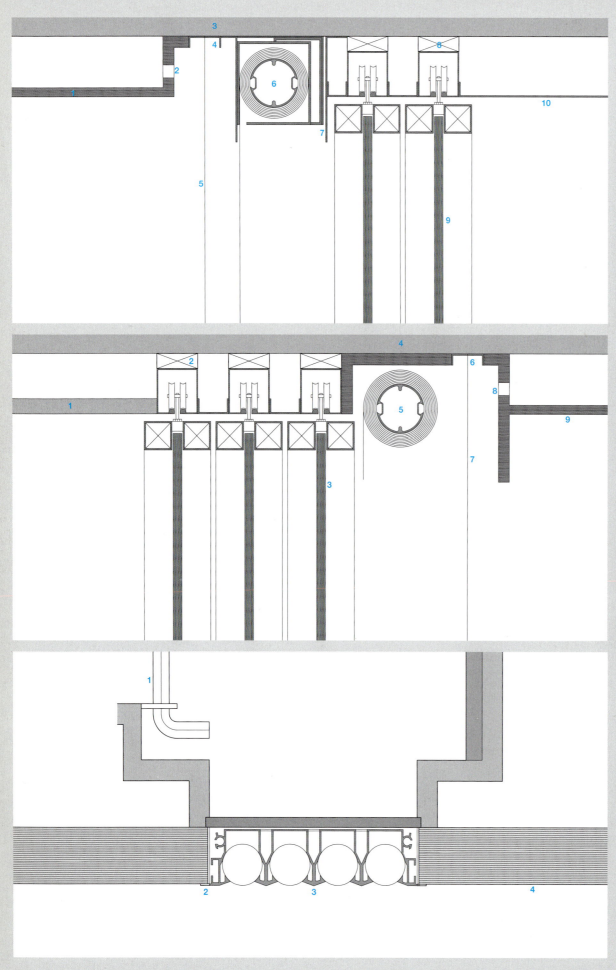

9.06
First Floor Bedroom Window Section Detail
1:5
  1 Suspended painted plasterboard ceiling
  2 Air conditioning outlet
  3 Reinforced concrete floor slab
  4 Niche for fixing curtain rail
  5 Line of curtain
  6 Aluminium profile box housing to blackout roller blind
  7 Painted profile separator plate
  8 Timber blocking for window installation
  9 Aluminium framed single glazed sliding doors
  10 Metal sheet soffit lining painted same colour as concrete slab

9.07
First Floor Master Bedroom Window Section Detail
1:5
  1 Grey limestone suspended soffit panels
  2 Timber blocking for window installation
  3 Aluminium framed single glazed sliding doors
  4 Reinforced concrete floor slab
  5 Blackout roller blind
  6 Niche for fixing curtain rail
  7 Line of curtain
  8 Air conditioning outlet
  9 Suspended painted plasterboard ceiling

9.08
Typical Bedroom Ceiling Light Diffuser Detail
1:2
  1 Hangers for suspended ceiling system
  2 Aluminium trim in same colour as ceiling
  3 Ceiling mounted linear light diffuser
  4 Suspended plasterboard ceiling with textured acrylic paint finish

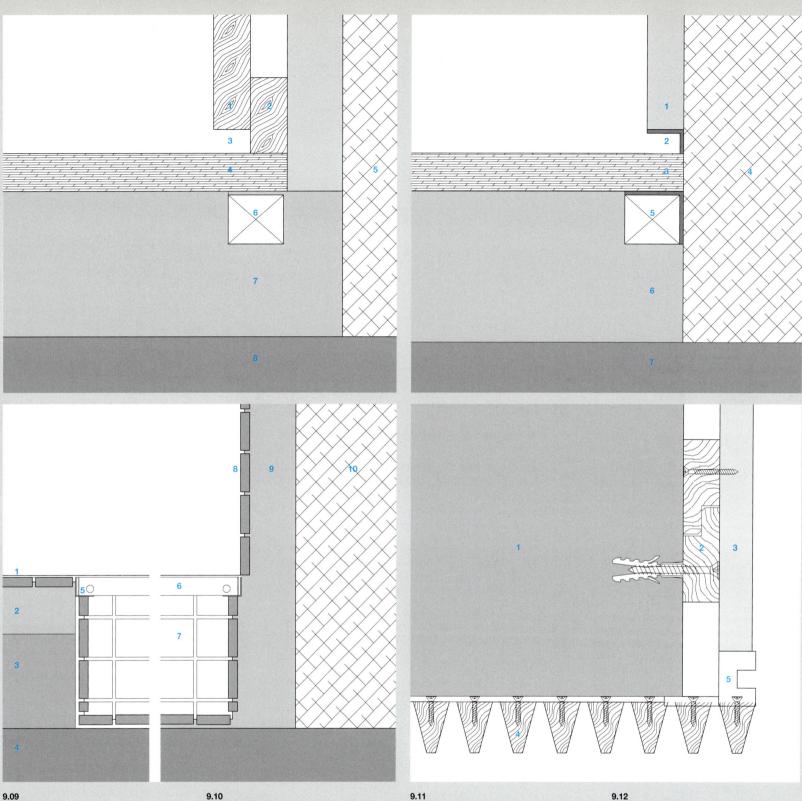

9.09
**Wall and Floor
Junction Detail to
First Floor WC**
1:2
 1 Madeira
wood-faced plywood
interior wall lining
panel
 2 Madeira
wood-faced plywood
skirting
 3 13 mm (1/2 inch)
shadow gap
 4 Solid Madeira wood
floorboards
 5 Masonry interior
wall
 6 50 x 40 mm (2 x 11/2
inch) timber battens
 7 Acoustic insulation
 8 Reinforced
concrete floor slab

9.10
**Wall and Floor
Junction Detail to
First Floor Bedrooms**
1:2
 1 Plasterboard wall
lining with textured
acrylic paint finish
 2 20 x 10 mm (3/4 x
3/8 inch) aluminium
L-angle
 3 Solid Madeira wood
floorboards
 4 Masonry interior
wall
 5 50 x 40 mm (2 x
11/2 inch) timber
battens
 6 Acoustic insulation
 7 Reinforced
concrete floor slab

9.11
**Wall and Floor
Junction Detail to
First Floor WC**
1:2
 1 Glass mosaic floor
tiles
 2 Mortar bed
 3 Concrete screed
 4 Reinforced
concrete floor slab
 5 Aluminium L-angle
 6 Aluminium grille
over floor drain
 7 Strip floor drain
 8 Glass mosaic wall
tiles
 9 Mortar bed
 10 Masonry interior
wall

9.12
**Toblerone Screen
Plan Detail**
1:2
 1 MDF substrate to
screen panel
 2 20 mm (3/4 inch)
solid timber fixing
battens
 3 Timber bottom rail
to interior face of
screen door
 4 27 mm (1 inch)
deep, 19 mm (3/4 inch)
wide solid timber
'toblerone' pieces to
exterior face of screen
panel
 5 Routed timber
finger pull handle

Flint House
London, England, UK

Client
Mr and Mrs Stafford

Project Team
Nick Willson, Amy Bodiam

Structural Engineer
Trevor Millea

Quantity Surveyor
Bonfield

Main Contractor
Modernarc

One of the primary aims in designing Flint House was to combine the latest in building technology with an element of crafted materiality. The finished house brings together a rich mixture of crafted elements including the textured flint walls, lead cladding and finely detailed timber joinery, both inside and out, which are all made by hand by specialist tradespeople.

In plan, the house is divided into four zones, two to the west and two to the east. All four areas are linked by a central, double height, glazed circulation space. Externally, each of these different elements are expressed with a subtly different palette of materials which reflect their orientation and function. The two west wings are clad in a mixture of split flint and render. The east elevation, which brings the living spaces into direct contact with the outdoor living areas and the garden, is enclosed in a ribbon of vertical oak cladding that runs from the ground floor, up through the exterior staircase to the first floor walls, extending into the terraces on both levels.

To maximize natural light and reinforce visual connections with the garden, all of the windows and roof lights frame particular views of the trees and garden, allowing different levels of light to permeate the house as the seasons change. These connections mean that although the house is situated on the outskirts of London, there is a suggestion of having escaped to the countryside. The underlying structure features a highly insulated airtight timber frame to create a highly energy efficient and sustainable building. The house also makes use of natural ventilation, a planted roof above the garage and solar thermal panels with smart meters to provide sustainable heating.

1 The garden facade illustrates the use of a mixed palette of highly crafted materials including English oak to the dining and master bedroom (left), lead to the circulation zone (centre) and flint with render to the living area and bedrooms above (right).
2 View of the entry door (left) and garage (right). The entrance hall is flooded with natural light via the south facing glazing over the door and a north facing skylight.
3 Interior finishes follow the same crafted approach as the exterior, seen here in the kitchen joinery (left), the timber stair, floor and ceiling, and the dining table designed specially for the house.

10.01
Ground Floor Plan
1:200
1 Garden
2 Terrace
3 External stair
4 Dining area
5 Kitchen
6 Living area
7 Snug / living room
8 Driveway
9 Stair
10 Entrance hall
11 WC
12 Utility room
13 Garage

10.02
First Floor Plan
1:200
1 Terrace below
2 External stair
3 Terrace
4 Bedroom
5 Bathroom
6 Study
7 Master bedroom
8 Bedroom
9 Stair
10 Library
11 Dressing area
12 Master bathroom
13 Green roof to garage

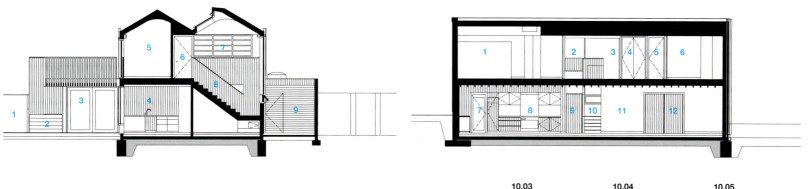

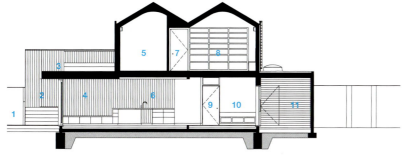

10.03
Section A–A
1:200
1 Terrace
2 External stair
3 Doors to dining area
4 Kitchen
5 Study
6 Door to master bedroom
7 Library
8 Stair
9 Garage

10.04
Section B–B
1:200
1 Master bedroom
2 Library
3 Stair
4 Cupboard
5 Door to bedroom
6 Bedroom
7 Door to utility room
8 Kitchen
9 Entrance hall
10 Stair
11 Living room
12 Door to snug/ living room

10.05
Section C–C
1:200
1 Garden
2 External stair
3 Terrace
4 Dining area
5 Study
6 Kitchen
7 Door to master bedroom
8 Library
9 Door to WC
10 Entrance hall
11 Garage

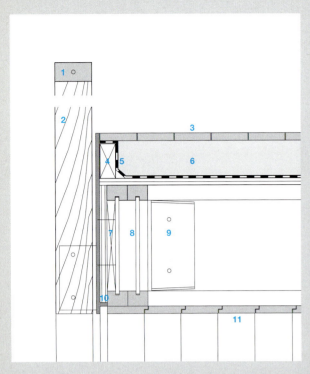

10.06
Terrace Balustrade and Roof Section Detail 1
1:10
1 45 x 100 mm (1³/₄ x 4 inch) solid English oak section with rebated connections
2 45 x 100 mm (1³/₄ x 4 inch) solid English oak balustrade fixed to galvanized flange to form flitch connection
3 22 x 100 mm (⁷/₈ x 4 inch) wide treated oak decking with 5 mm (1/5 inch) spacing
4 Tanalized timber trimmer
5 Double layer waterproof membrane lapped onto trimmer
6 Tanalized timber and galvanized framing to decking
7 Timber edge plate to I-joists
8 Timber I-joists
9 Galvanized metal bracket and fixings
10 18 mm (³/₄ inch) waterproof plywood with galvanized metal plate fixing to balustrade
11 22 x 100 mm (⁷/₈ x 4 inch) tongue-and-groove English Oak boarding fixed to timber framing

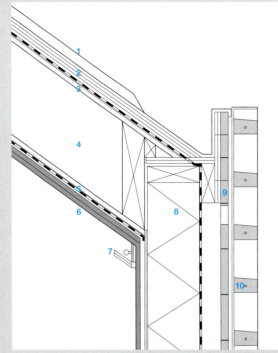

10.07
Pitched Roof and External Wall Junction Section Detail
1:10
1 Standing-seam to zinc roof
2 Zinc roofing mechanically fixed to stainless steel mesh and 18 mm (³/₄ inch) waterproof plywood
3 Breather membrane and oriented strand board
4 Roof insulation between I-joist rafters
5 Moisture barrier
6 Double layer of skimmed and painted plasterboard
7 Painted soft wood lighting slot with LED fitting
8 Timber wall framing with insulation
9 Timber boarding fixing behind louvres
10 45 x 100 mm (1³/₄ x 4 inch) English Oak louvres rebated and set into 6 mm (1/4 inch) galvanized frames

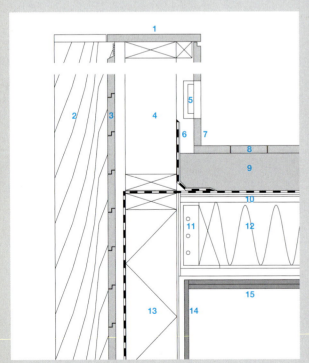

10.08
Terrace Balustrade and Roof Section Detail 2
1:10
1 Folded zinc capping bonded to waterproof plywood base
2 45 x 100 mm (1³/₄ x 4 inch) solid English oak section with rebated connections
3 22 x 100 mm (⁷/₈ x 4 inch) tongue-and-groove English oak cladding
4 Treated timber framing
5 Recessed light fitting
6 Waterproofing upstand
7 English oak cladding to terrace
8 22 x 100 mm (⁷/₈ x 4 inch) wide treated oak decking with 5 mm (1/5 inch) spacing
9 Treated timber and galvanized metal frame to decking
10 Double layer of waterproof membrane on 18 mm (³/₄ inch) waterproof plywood boarding
11 Galvanized joist bracket
12 Roof insulation
13 Wall insulation to timber frame
14 15 mm (⁵/₈ inch) fire resistant board with plaster and paint finish
15 Double layer of skimmed and painted plasterboard

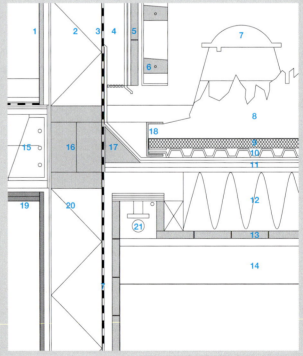

10.09
Timber Screen Wall and Garage Roof Section Detail
1:10
1 15 mm (⁵/₈ inch) fire resistant board with plaster and paint finish
2 Wall insulation in timber frame
3 Breather membrane
4 Cavity with galvanized drip
5 Treated timber boarding
6 45 x 100 mm (1³/₄ x 4 inch) English oak louvres rebated and set into 6 mm (1/4 inch) galvanized frames
7 Double glazed roof lights
8 Sedum planting
9 Sedum bedding
10 Sedum drainage layer
11 Root barrier and two layers of waterproofing membrane
12 Roof insulation
13 22 x 100 mm (⁷/₈ x 4 inch) tongue-and-groove oak cladding
14 English oak door
15 Galvanized joist hanger
16 Treated timber beams
17 Treated timber fillet
18 Metal sedum trim
19 Double layer of skimmed and painted plasterboard
20 Wall insulation in timber frame
21 Recessed low voltage external light fitting

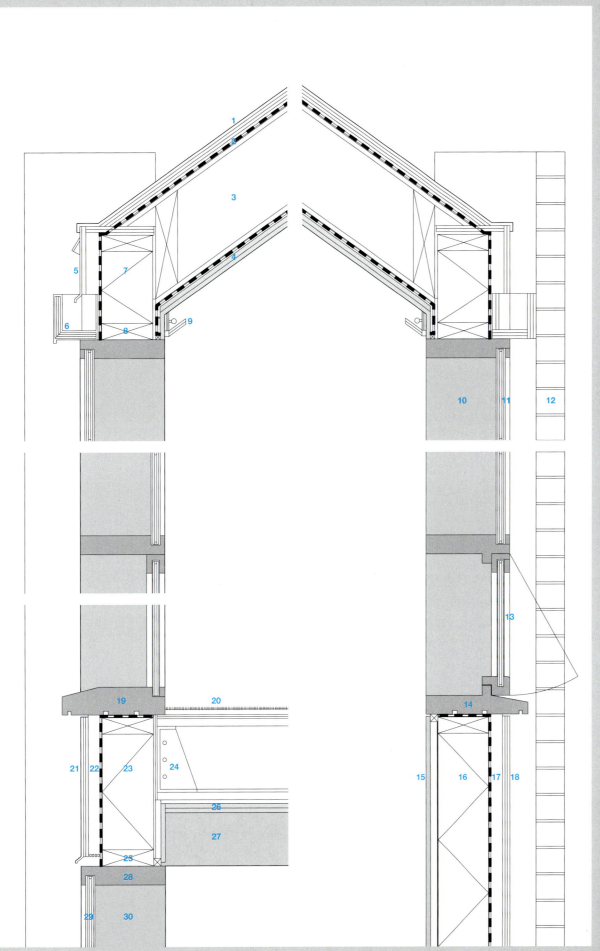

1 Standing-seam zinc roofing over ventilation mesh on 18 mm (^{3}/$_4$ inch) waterproof plywood boarding and battens
2 Breather membrane
3 200 mm (8 inch) roof insulation between timber I-joist rafters
4 Oriented strand boarding, moisture barrier and two layers of plasterboard with skim and paint finish
5 Pressed zinc vent and capping
6 Pressed zinc concealed guttering fixed to 18 mm (^{3}/$_4$ inch) waterproof plywood boxing
7 Insulation to timber framed wall
8 Timber trimmer to frame
9 Painted softwood lighting slot with LED fitting
10 Solid 50 x 200 mm (2 x 8 inch) English oak window frame
11 Fixed, double glazed low emissivity coated and sealed glazing unit with timber beads
12 22 x 100 mm (^{7}/$_8$ x 4 inch) horizontal oak cladding
13 Openable double glazed low emissivity coated and sealed glazing unit with timber beads
14 Solid English oak sill with drip
15 15 mm (^{5}/$_8$ inch) fire resistant board on battens with plaster skim and paint finish
16 Wall insulation between timber framing
17 Breather membrane and ventilation cavity
18 18 mm (^{3}/$_4$ inch) waterproof boarding with folded lead cladding
19 Solid English oak window sill
20 Carpet on 18 mm (^{3}/$_4$ inch) tongue-and-groove timber floorboards
21 Lead cladding mechanically fixed to 18 mm (^{3}/$_4$ inch) waterproof plywood
22 Ventilation cavity with breather membrane and insect mesh
23 Wall insulation in timber frame
24 Galvanized wall hanger
25 Timber header
26 15 mm (^{5}/$_8$ inch) fire resistant board ceiling with plaster and paint finish
27 Painted soft wood baffles
28 Solid English oak window head
29 24 mm (^{7}/$_8$ inch) thick double glazed low emissivity coated and sealed glazing unit with timber beads
30 250 mm (10 inch) solid English oak window frame

Eilbek Canal Houseboat
Hamburg, Germany

Client
Amelie Rost, Jörg Niderehe

Project Team
Amelie Rost, Jörg Niderehe

Structural Engineers
Buschmann und Söhne, Niderehe
Design & Engineering

Main Contractor
Rost Niderehe Architekten

Barmbek-Süd is an area of Hamburg that is undergoing rapid transformation from a former industrial area that was almost completely destroyed during the Second World War, to a popular residential neighbourhood. Part of the area, the Eilbek canal, was the subject of an ideas competition to transform it into a base for houseboats. A pilot scheme for owners and architects was initiated to explore the possibilities of a designated houseboat neighbourhood, at the conclusion of which ten winners, including the houseboat by Rost Niderehe, were announced.

The concept was to create a design that expressed the character of a boat but embraced the comfort and facilities of a family home. Public spaces, including kitchen, dining and outdoor living areas, are located on the upper deck, this being the entrance level, while more private spaces including a study, living area, bathroom and bedroom are located on the lower deck.

A number of considerable design challenges included making connections to public infrastructure, engineering logistics to comply with strict German building regulations, the minimization of energy consumption, and the need for the upper level to be dismountable to meet the required bridge clearances. Timber and steel were chosen for the structure and cladding to reflect their use in both maritime and domestic building construction. Energy use and sustainability concerns were addressed through the extensive use of environmentally friendly building products so that in the case of an accident no damaging substances would end up in the canal. The houseboat was also constructed almost entirely from recyclable materials including the steel superstructure, wood fibre insulation and timber cladding.

1 The two level houseboat is wrapped in a skin of larch battens that curve at the corners to create a seamless timber envelope designed to echo traditional boat building aesthetics.
2 The upper level accommodates a kitchen and dining area where a wall of sliding glass doors opens onto a large timber deck that wraps around the kitchen volume.
3 The boat is connected to the steep riverbank by a bridge that leads onto the upper deck and from there to the entrance.
4 The kitchen and dining area is glazed on two sides to allow expansive views over the canal and its banks. White walls, ceilings and joinery, timber floors and black painted steel are used throughout the interior.

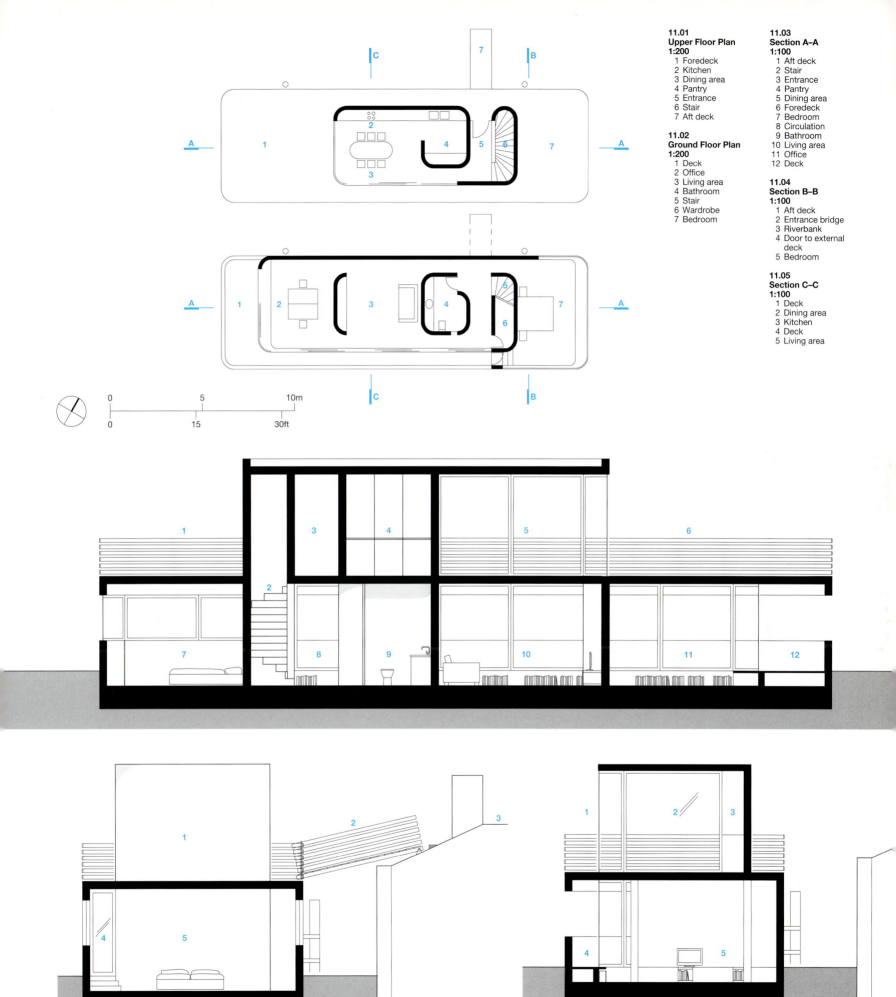

11.01
Upper Floor Plan
1:200
1 Foredeck
2 Kitchen
3 Dining area
4 Pantry
5 Entrance
6 Stair
7 Aft deck

11.02
Ground Floor Plan
1:200
1 Deck
2 Office
3 Living area
4 Bathroom
5 Stair
6 Wardrobe
7 Bedroom

11.03
Section A–A
1:100
1 Aft deck
2 Stair
3 Entrance
4 Pantry
5 Dining area
6 Foredeck
7 Bedroom
8 Circulation
9 Bathroom
10 Living area
11 Office
12 Deck

11.04
Section B–B
1:100
1 Aft deck
2 Entrance bridge
3 Riverbank
4 Door to external deck
5 Bedroom

11.05
Section C–C
1:100
1 Deck
2 Dining area
3 Kitchen
4 Deck
5 Living area

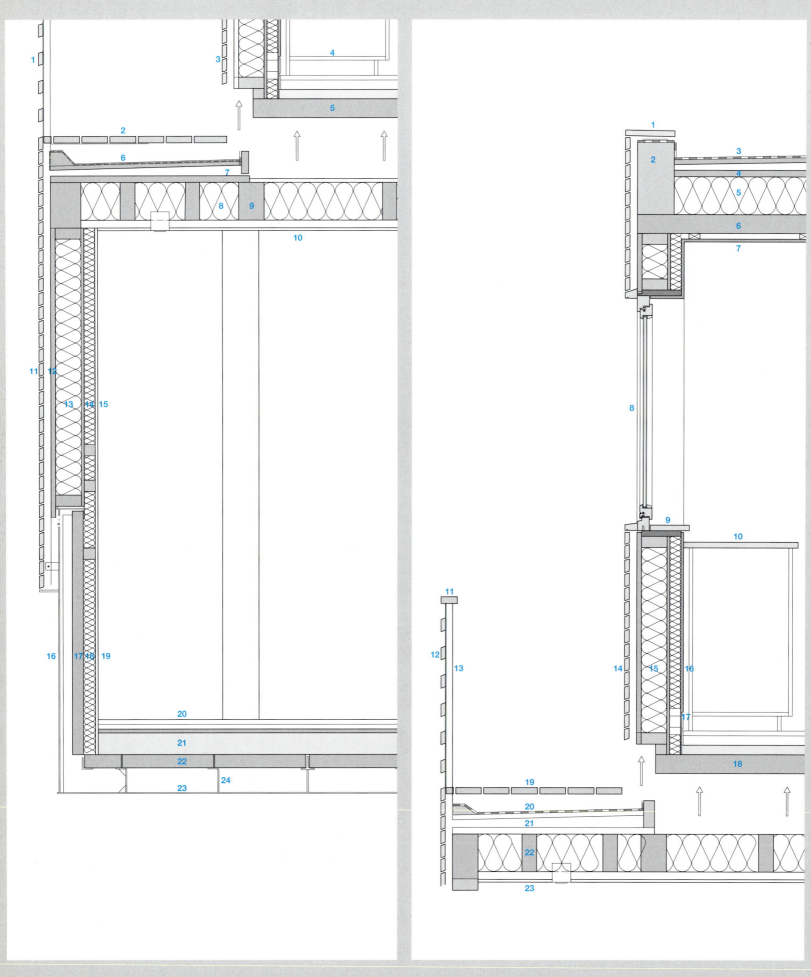

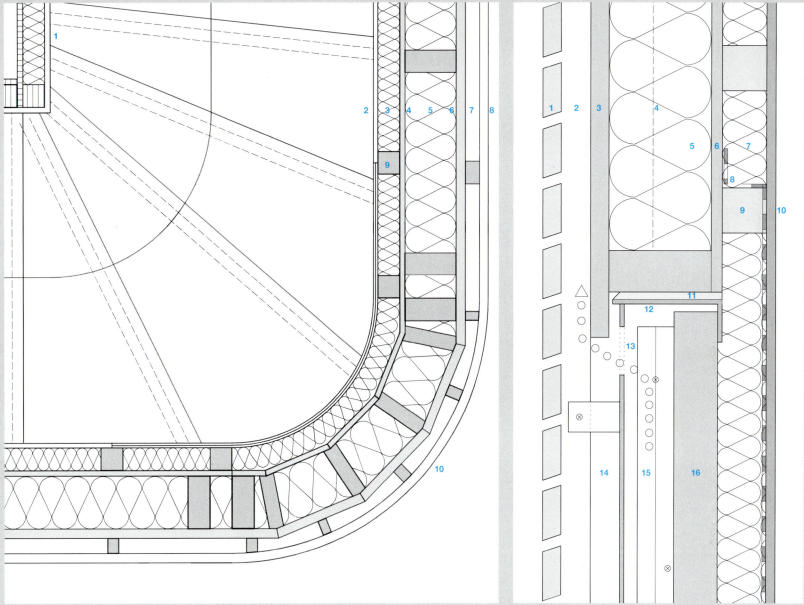

11.06
Lower Deck External Wall Section Detail
1:20
1 20 x 70 mm (³/4 x 2³/4 inch) larch batten cladding
2 40 x 140 mm (1¹/2 x 5¹/2 inch) larch boards to terrace
3 20 x 70 mm (³/4 x 2³/4 inch) chamfered larch batten cladding
4 Kitchen joinery
5 100 mm (4 inch) timber floor beam
6 Waterproof membrane
7 Sloped larch batten to floor substructure to drain to exterior vessel
8 240 mm (9¹/2 inch) wood fibre insulation
9 100 x 240 mm (4 x 9¹/2 inch) timber beam
10 12.5 mm (¹/2 inch) suspended plasterboard ceiling
11 20 x 70 mm (³/4 x 2³/4 inch) chamfered larch batten cladding
12 Waterproof membrane over 22 mm (⁷/8 inch) wood fibre board

13 140 mm (5¹/2 inch) wood fibre insulation
14 15 mm (⁵/8 inch) oriented strand board and 60 mm (2³/8 inch) wood fibre insulation
15 12.5 mm (¹/2 inch) suspended plasterboard ceiling
16 6 mm (¹/4 inch) thick ship building steel to hull
17 65 mm (2¹/2 inch) wood fibre soft board
18 60 mm (2³/8 inch) wood fibre insulation
19 12.5 mm (¹/2 inch) suspended plasterboard ceiling
20 22 mm (⁷/8 inch) pitch pine floorboards over underfloor heating
21 100 mm (4 inch) wood fibre insulation between timber beams
22 500 x 500 x 60 mm (19³/4 x 19³/4 x 2³/8 inch) cement slabs
23 6 mm (¹/4 inch) thick ship building steel to hull
24 6 mm (¹/4 inch) thick ship building steel framing

11.07
Upper Deck External Wall Section Detail
1:20
1 200 x 40 mm (8 x 1¹/2 inch) larch cover board
2 160 x 360 mm (6¹/4 x 14¹/4 inch) timber beam
3 Waterproof membrane
4 35 mm (1³/8 inch) wood fibre soft board
5 200 mm (8 inch) wood fibre insulation
6 100 mm (4 inch) timber panel
7 12.5 mm (¹/2 inch) suspended plasterboard ceiling
8 Aluminium framed double glazed window
9 40 mm (1¹/2 inch) high pressure laminated board
10 Kitchen joinery
11 30 x 100 mm (1¹/5 x 4 inch) larch handrail
12 20 x 70 mm (³/4 x 2³/4 inch) chamfered larch batten cladding
13 40 x 2 mm (1¹/2 x ¹/8 inch) galvanized steel flat upright

14 20 x 70 mm (³/4 x 2³/4 inch) chamfered larch batten to balustrade
15 140 mm (5¹/2 inch) wood fibre insulation
16 60 mm (2³/8 inch) wood fibre insulation
17 20 x 70 mm (³/4 x 2³/4 inch) high pressure laminate base board
18 100 mm (4 inch) timber panel
19 40 x 140 mm (1¹/2 x 5¹/2 inch) larch planks to terrace
20 Waterproof membrane
21 Sloped larch batten to floor substructure to drain to exterior of vessel
22 100 x 240 mm (4 x 9¹/2 inch) timber beam
23 12.5 mm (¹/2 inch) suspended plasterboard ceiling

11.08
Curved Stair Wall Plan Detail
1:10
1 12.5 mm (¹/2 inch) painted plasterboard interior wall lining
2 12.5 mm (¹/2 inch) painted plasterboard interior wall lining
3 60 mm (2³/8 inch) timber framing with insulation between
4 15 mm (⁵/8 inch) thick tongue-and-groove oriented strand board bracing panels with integral vapour barrier
5 140 mm (5¹/2 inch) thermal and acoustic insulation
6 25 mm (1 inch) wood fibre rigid insulation panels
7 40 mm (1¹/2 inch) ventilation cavity
8 25 mm (1 inch) larch batten cladding
9 60 x 60 mm (2³/8 x 2³/8 inch) timber framing
10 Laminated larch cladding to curved wall

11.09
Typical Exterior Wall Section Detail
1:5
1 25 mm (1 inch) chamfered larch batten cladding
2 40 mm (1¹/2 inch) ventilation gap
3 25 mm (1 inch) wood fibre rigid insulation panels
4 80 x 80 x 4 mm (3 x 3 x ¹/10 inch) steel structure
5 Insulation
6 15 mm (⁵/8 inch) thick tongue-and-groove oriented strand board bracing panels with integral vapour barrier
7 Insulation
8 Waterproof membrane
9 60 x 60 mm (2³/8 x 2³/8 inch) timber framing
10 12.5 mm (¹/2 inch) painted plasterboard interior wall lining
11 10 mm (³/8 inch) acoustic isolation strip
12 6 mm (¹/4 inch) steel framing with

13 mm (¹/2 inch) diameter bore holes for services
13 40 x 80 mm (1¹/2 x 3 inch) slot centered between joists
14 Steel floor joist below
15 Ventilation cavity
16 60 mm (2³/8 inch) thick wood fibre rigid insulation panels

Owhanake Bay House
Waiheke Island, New Zealand

Client
Erin and Gary Clatworthy

Project Team
Dave Strachan, Roy Tebbutt

Structural Engineer
Adam Mackenzie

Landscape Architect
Bryan McDonald for Auckland
Landscapes Limited

Located on Waiheke Island, a 40 minute ferry journey from central Auckland, the Owhanake Bay House sits below a ridge looking east over the outer islands of the Hauraki Gulf. Designed for a semi-retired couple, ease of movement and single level accessibility were requirements that set design challenges on a site with a significant natural slope. Divided into three narrow pavilions, the plan bends to follow the natural contours of the land, allowing ease of movement through the landscape with minimal excavation of the landform.

Designed for a subtropical climate, the house features banks of lifting panel windows on gas struts that open up so that the verandah posts are all that remain of the wall. Further dematerialization of wall surfaces takes the form of copper-clad fins on the west facade that frame clear-glazed apertures while protecting the interior from solar gain from the western sun. Elsewhere, the two links between the three pavilions contain bathing spaces, where the boundaries between interior and exterior are further broken down with both the east and west walls constructed of banks of glass louvres. The idea of water-based space is extended to the exterior of these link spaces where two ponds extend out, flanking the outdoor room that forms part of the central living pavilion.

Durable natural materials have been carefully chosen to reflect the context and achieve longevity in the harsh coastal environment. Oxide-coloured concrete floors cantilever over the landform, and plastered masonry retaining walls anchor the house back to the earth. The roof is expressed as a series of slender blades that lift and hover above the landscape, folding at points of water collection to form expressed valley gutters that are moored to the land by articulated downpipes.

1 The study to the south, and the guest bedroom to the north, shown here, feature double glazed extruded copper-clad boxes designed to frame specific views.
2 Overlapping monopitch roofs to the master pavilion (left), the living pavilion (centre) and the guest pavilion (right) lift up towards the north.
3 The covered outdoor dining area is directly accessed from the living pavilion (right) and features a wood-burning fire. Pools of water to the north and south, one with a bridge (centre) bookend the space.
4 Polished concrete floors are used both inside and out, seen here in the living pavilion and the outdoor room.
5 All of the windows on the eastern facade can be raised to open up the entire house to views of the Hauraki Gulf.

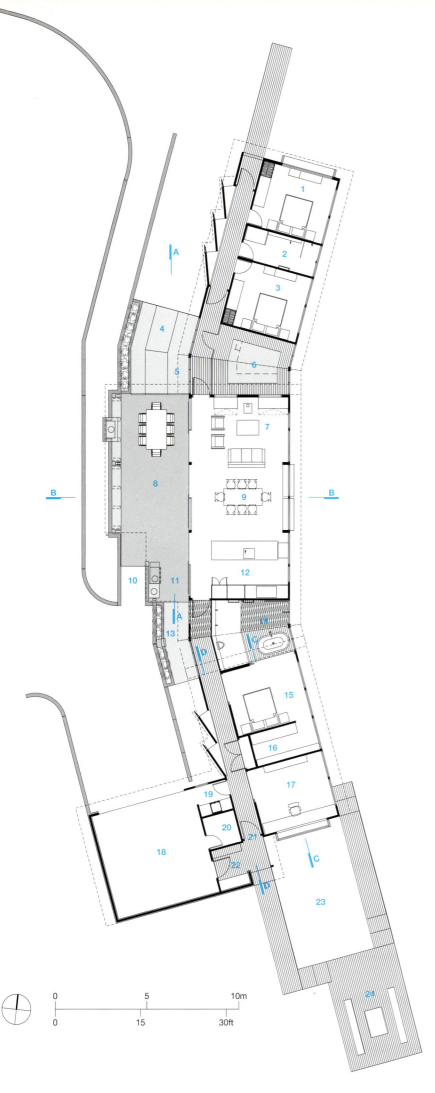

12.01
Ground Floor Plan
1:200
1 Bedroom
2 Bathroom
3 Bedroom
4 Bridge
5 Pond
6 Plunge pool
7 Living area
8 Outdoor room
9 Dining area
10 External stair
11 BBQ area
12 Kitchen
13 Pond
14 Master bathroom
15 Master bedroom
16 Dressing room
17 Study
18 Garage
19 Laundry
20 Storage
21 Entrance
22 Entrance from garage
23 Garden
24 Terrace

12.02
Section A–A
1:200
1 BBQ area
2 Outdoor room
3 Fireplace
4 Bridge over pond

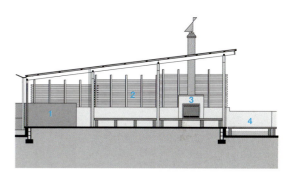

12.03
Section B–B
1:200
1 Dining area
2 Kitchen beyond
3 Outdoor room
4 External stair

12.04
Section C–C
1:200
1 Covered terrace
2 Study
3 Dressing room
4 Master bedroom
5 Master bathroom

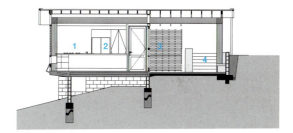

12.05
Section D–D
1:200
1 Entrance from garage
2 Entrance hall
3 Door to laundry
4 Copper panel window
5 Circulation to living pavilion

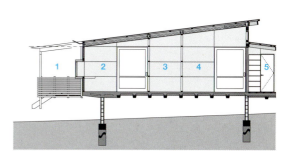

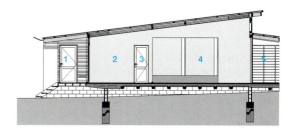

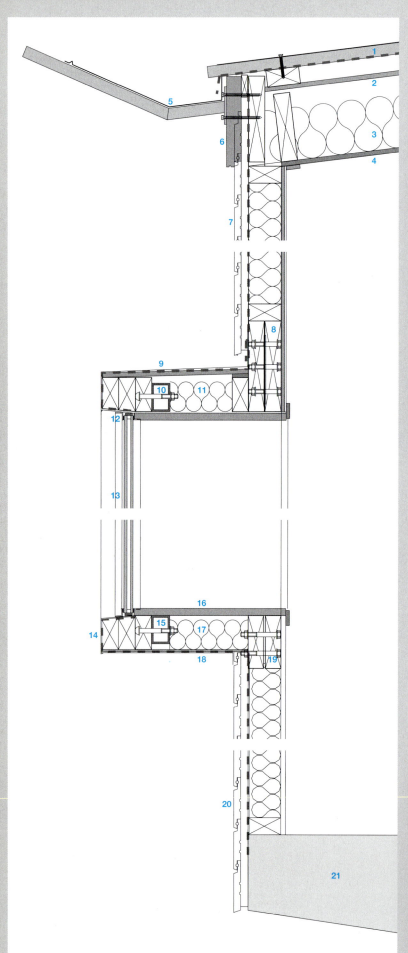

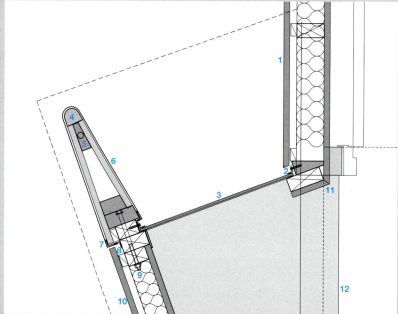

12.06
Copper Box Window Section Detail
1:10
1 Long run sheet metal roofing on underlay and galvanized mild steel mesh, screw-fixed to timber purlins
2 12 mm (1/2 inch) radiata pine plywood packer strips fixed to top of rafters beneath purlins
3 200 x 50 mm (8 x 2 inch) timber rafters at 600 mm (23 1/2 inch) centres
4 Plywood ceiling
5 Folded sheet metal gutter to match main roofing on custom brackets at 600 mm (23 1/2 inch) centres
6 250 x 50 mm (10 x 2 inch) cedar facing rebated to receive top edge of weatherboard cladding
7 Weatherboard external cladding on 20 mm (3/4 inch) cavity battens over waterproof building paper
8 Timber lintel bolted to 130 x 250 x 6 mm (5 1/8 x 10 x 1/4 inch) steel cleat welded to side of 75 x 75 x 5 mm (3 x 3 x 1/5 inch) square hollow steel section with 12 mm (1/2 inch) mild steel bolts

9 1.5 mm (1/16 inch) thick flat copper sheet cladding fixed over 15 mm (5/8 inch) thick treated radiata pine ply laid to fall
10 75 x 50 x 5 mm (3 x 2 x 1/5 inch) steel rectangular hollow section cross beam cleated and bolted between steel support arms
11 75 x 50 x 5 mm (3 x 2 x 1/5 inch) steel rectangular hollow section support arm welded at right angles to steel legs and packed locally with thermal insulation
12 20 x 20 mm (3/4 x 3/4 inch) brass angle glazing bead fixed with brass countersunk screws
13 Double glazing fixed directly into copper rebate with glazing tape to both sides
14 Copper sill flashing dressed up and into rebate in window board
15 75 x 50 x 5 mm (3 x 2 x 1/5 inch) steel rectangular hollow section cross beam cleated and bolted between steel support arms
16 18 mm (3/4 inch) cedar sill head and reveals

17 75 x 50 x 5 mm (3 x 2 x 1/5 inch) steel rectangular hollow section support arm welded at right angles to steel legs and packed locally with thermal insulation
18 1.5 mm (1/16 inch) thick flat copper sheet cladding fixed over 15 mm (5/8 inch) thick treated radiata pine ply laid to fall
19 Timber sill trimmers bolted to 130 x 100 x 6 mm (5 1/8 x 4 x 1/4 inch) steel cleat
20 Weatherboard external cladding on 20 mm (3/4 inch) cavity battens over waterproof building paper
21 Reinforced concrete floor slab

12.07
Plan Detail of Fins and Glazing
1:10
1 Timber weatherboard external cladding on 20 mm (3/4 inch) cavity battens over waterproof building paper on 75 x 50 mm (3 x 2 inch) timber framing
2 19 x 19 x 3 mm (3/4 x 3/4 x 1/8 inch) brass angle bead fixed into glazing rebate with 25 mm (1 inch) round head brass screws
3 8 mm (3/8 inch)

thick toughened clear glass fitted into copper rebate with glazing tape to both sides
4 Capped end from 50 mm (2 inch) diameter perfect half-round shaped timber with substrate for shaped copper cladding
5 19 mm (3/4 inch) diameter, 1.5 mm (1/16 inch) thick stainless steel tube support leg set into bottom of fin and cast into concrete footing
6 21 mm (7/8 inch)

thick radiata pine plywood fixed over shaped framing
7 Copper cladding to fin in 800 mm (31 1/2 inch) high panels
8 Copper back flashing at end of weatherboard cladding
9 Prefabricated fin framing connected through to wall studs with 12 mm (1/2 inch) diameter galvanized mild steel bolts
10 Timber weatherboard cladding on 20 mm (3/4 inch) cavity battens over

waterproof building paper on 75 x 50 mm (3 x 2 inch) timber framing
11 Weatherboard cladding mitred at corner over framing timbers shaped to suit
12 Edge of concrete plinth

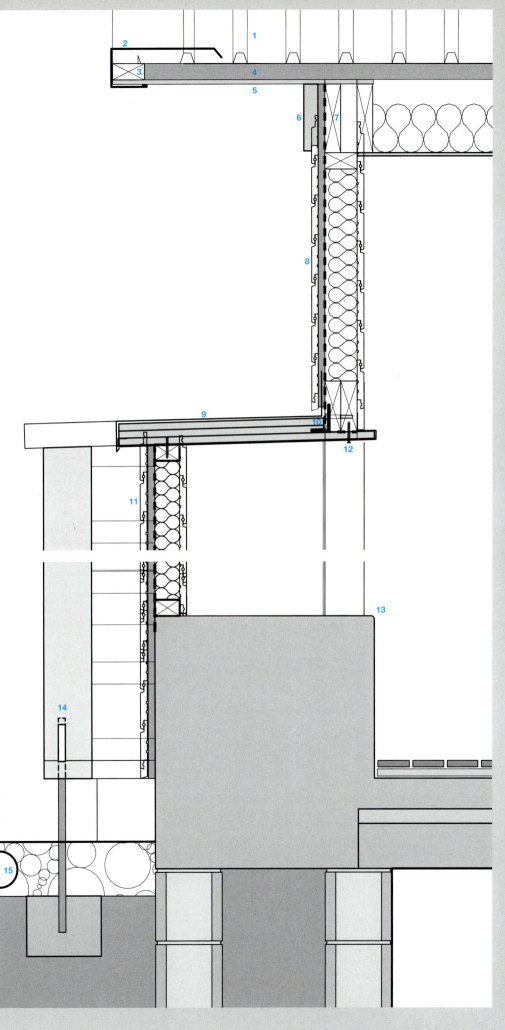

12.08
Wall Section Detail
1:10

1 Long run sheet metal roofing on underlay and galvanized mild steel mesh
2 Folded edge cap flashing to match main roofing
3 100 x 50 mm (4 x 2 inch) timber fly purlins to roof edge
4 100 x 50 mm (4 x 2 inch) timber purlins laid flat at 1200 mm (47$\frac{1}{4}$ inch) centres
5 12 mm ($\frac{1}{2}$ inch) plywood soffit lining fixed to top of rafters and beneath purlins
6 200 x 50 mm (8 x 2 inch) cedar rafter rebated to receive tapered top edge of weatherboards
7 200 x 50 mm (8 x 2 inch) radiata pine rafters at maximum 600 mm (23$\frac{1}{2}$ inch) centres
8 Weatherboard external cladding on 20 mm ($\frac{3}{4}$ inch) cavity battens over waterproof building paper to external wall with cavity closer at base of cavity
9 Three layers of 21 mm ($\frac{7}{8}$ inch) radiata pine plywood, clad top and bottom with copper flat sheet with top end turned up to form apron flashing
10 75 x 50 x 5 mm (3 x 2 x $\frac{1}{5}$ inch) steel angle bolted to lintel with 12 mm ($\frac{1}{2}$ inch) diameter coach screws to provide support to ply roofing sheets

11 Weatherboard external cladding on 20 mm ($\frac{3}{4}$ inch) cavity battens over waterproof building paper on 75 x 50 mm (3 x 2 inch) timber framing
12 Neat line of round head brass screw fixings to fix bottom of copper clad ply sheet to lintels
13 Arrissed edge to concrete plinth finished with two coats of clear concrete sealer
14 19 mm ($\frac{3}{4}$ inch) diameter, 1.5 mm ($\frac{1}{16}$ inch) thick stainless steel tube support leg, epoxy glued into bottom of fin framing and cast into concrete footing below finished ground level
15 Land drain with free draining gravel cover for rainwater collection from lower roof

57

13
Suga Atelier

House of Cedar
Osaka, Japan

Client
Private

Project Team
Shotaro Suga

Structure Engineer
Satoru Shimoyama

Main Contractor
Kimuko Corporation

This two storey house stands on a hill in an urban area of Osaka in the west of Japan. The architect wanted to design a house that celebrated the natural warmth, colour and sustainable qualities of timber. A nearby cedar forest was the source of a plentiful supply of offcuts, which although not usually used for building, were perfect for realizing this small dwelling. Smaller timber sections could be used as the structure was designed using a system of cross bracing to create the necessary structural integrity. The approach has resulted in a densely textured architecture in which the cedar is celebrated.

The most dramatic expression of this is the timber framed, aluminium trimmed glass facade in which a two storey high facade of glazing has been assembled with a variety of fixed and openable glazed panels. Inside, the primary structure is formed from multiple small timber sections bolted together in both horizontal and vertical bundles, while horizontal furring is left exposed for hanging lightweight joinery, partitions and storage units.

The house is rectangular in plan with service zones, including the laundry and kitchen at the centre with larger living, working or sleeping spaces at either end of both levels. The asphalt cladding to the two long facades is primarily solid to address privacy and orientation issues, relying on the two short elevations which face north and south, to bring natural light into the habitable spaces. In addition, a skylight over the open stair brings in additional light. Breaking the structural grid of the orthogonal layout, the bathroom on the first floor is expressed as a multi-faceted cantilevered prism attached to the west facade, cantilevering out over the entrance.

1 From the street at night the interior is revealed as a forest of cedar sections. Three small opening windows in the glazed facade allow for ventilation. The braced frame, essentially a structural tube, allows for an open, column, and load-bearing partition-free interior.
2 The timber stair is located against the west facade and maintains the concept of open framing. Treads are constructed from the same cedar offcuts as the wall and roof framing, and open risers allow uninterrupted horizontal and vertical views through the house.
3 The bedroom on the upper floor features a glass door leading out onto a small balcony and a built-in timber storage wall.
4 A view of the kitchen, dining and living areas on the upper floor reveals the forest of timber structure that characterizes the architecture.

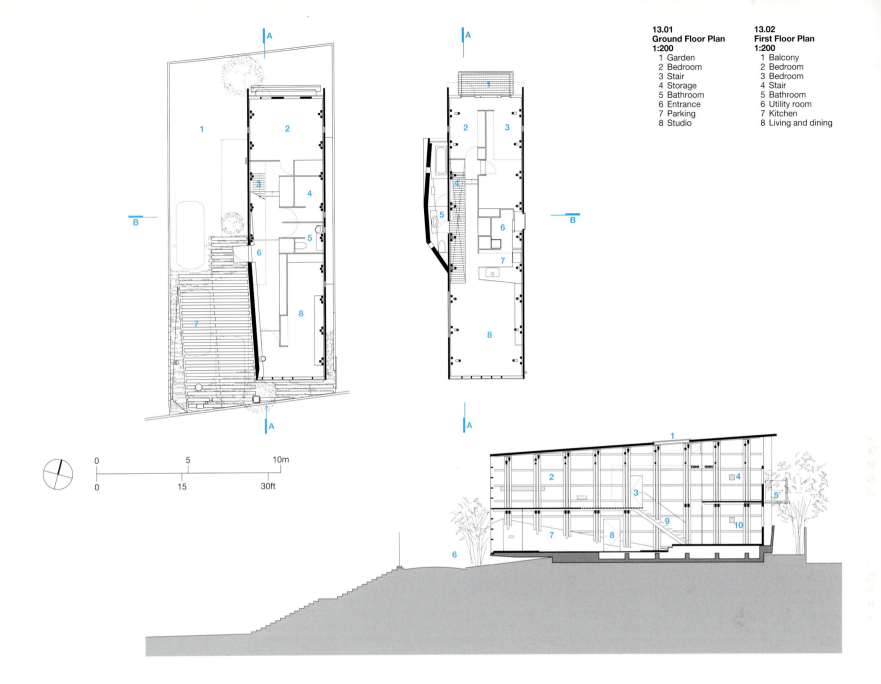

13.01
Ground Floor Plan
1:200
1 Garden
2 Bedroom
3 Stair
4 Storage
5 Bathroom
6 Entrance
7 Parking
8 Studio

13.02
First Floor Plan
1:200
1 Balcony
2 Bedroom
3 Bedroom
4 Stair
5 Bathroom
6 Utility room
7 Kitchen
8 Living and dining

13.03
Section A–A
1:200
1 Skylight
2 Living and dining
3 Bathroom
4 Bedroom
5 Balcony
6 Garden
7 Studio
8 Entrance
9 Stair
10 Bedroom

13.04
Section B–B
1:100
1 Skylight
2 Bathroom
3 Stair
4 Hallway
5 Cupboard
6 Utility room
7 Utility balcony
8 Entrance hall
9 Storage

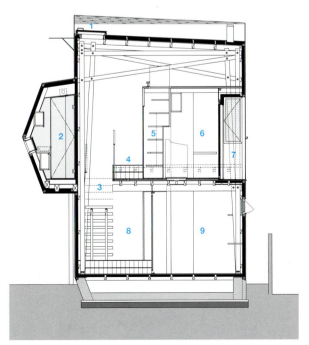

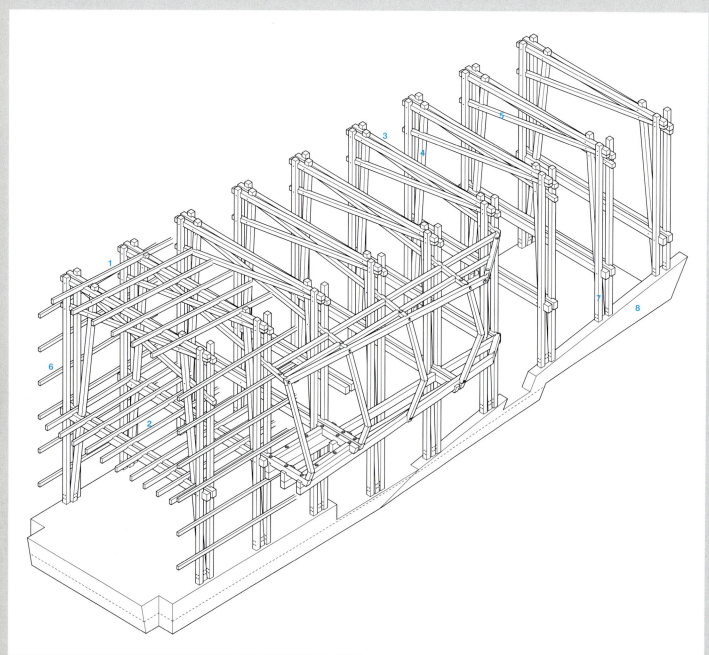

13.05
Primary Structure
Detail
Not to scale
1 90 x 120 mm (3^1/$_2$ x 4^3/$_4$ inch) timber rafter
2 60 x 120 mm (2^3/$_8$ x 4^3/$_4$ inch) timber joist
3 120 x 120 mm (4^3/$_4$ x 4^3/$_4$ inch) timber cross beam
4 50 x 25 x 3 mm (2 x 1 x ^{1}/$_8$ inch) timber angle brace
5 90 x 90 mm (3^1/$_2$ x 3^1/$_2$ inch) timber brace
6 60 x 90 mm (2^3/$_8$ x 3^1/$_2$ inch) timber furring strip
7 60 x120 mm (2^3/$_8$ x 4^3/$_4$ inch) timber column
8 Reinforced concrete floor slab

13.06
South Facade
Window Plan Detail
1:10
1 12 mm (^{1}/$_2$ inch) plywood interior wall lining
2 Insulation between 60 x 60 mm (2^3/$_8$ x 2^3/$_8$ inch) cedar furring strips
3 15 mm (^{5}/$_8$ inch) thick waterproof fibre cement board
4 Waterproof membrane
5 3 mm (^{1}/$_8$ inch) thick asphalt shingles exterior cladding
6 Double silicon seal between shingles and corner angle
7 Cedar wall framing between fixed and opening windows
8 60 x 120 mm (2^3/$_8$ x 4^3/$_4$ inch) cedar framing
9 Cypress window frame
10 Aluminium angle trim
11 Double glazed hinged window
12 Mesh insect screen
13 Pull knob to insect screen
14 Box casing with stainless steel countersunk screw to fixed window

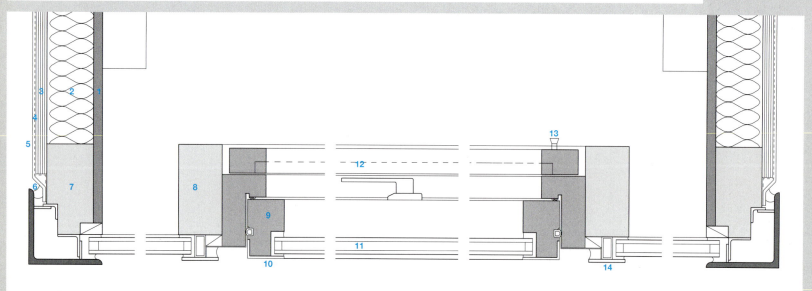

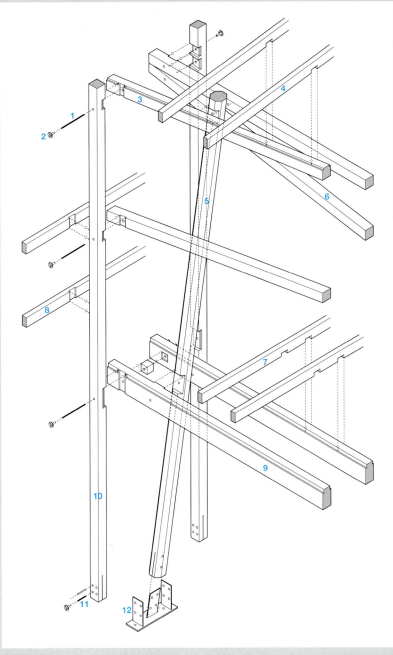

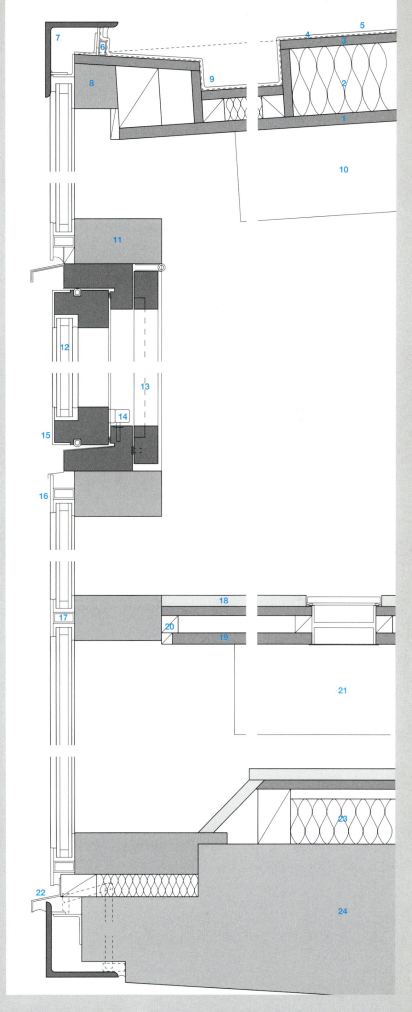

13.07
Cedar Structure
Detail
Not to scale
  1 12 mm (1/2 inch) diameter stainless steel bolt
  2 Stainless steel hybrid washer
  3 120 x 120 mm (43/4 x 43/4 inch) timber cross beam
  4 90 x 120 mm (31/2 x 43/4 inch) timber rafter
  5 50 x 25 x 3 mm (2 x 1 x 1/8 inch) timber angle brace
  6 90 x 90 mm (31/2 x 31/2 inch) timber brace
  7 60 x 120 mm (23/8 x 43/4 inch) timber joist
  8 60 x 90 mm (23/8 x 31/2 inch) timber furring strip
  9 120 x 180 mm (43/4 x 7 inch) timber cross beam
  10 120 x 120 mm (43/4 x 43/4 inch) timber column

  11 12 mm (1/2 inch) diameter drift pin
  12 16 x 110 x 550 mm (5/8 x 42/5 x 7 inch) steel plate shoe connector

13.08
Glazed Facade
Section Detail
1:5
  1 12 mm (1/2 inch) plywood ceiling
  2 Insulation
  3 15 mm (5/8 inch) thick waterproof fibre cement board
  4 Waterproof roofing membrane
  5 3 mm (1/8 inch) thick asphalt roofing shingles
  6 10 x 15 x 11.2 mm (3/8 x 5/8 x 1/2 inch) hollow aluminium section spacer
  7 100 x 100 x 11.2 mm (4 x 4 x 1/2 inch) steel angle edge beam
  8 Cedar roof framing
  9 Concealed parapet gutter
  10 60 x 120 mm (23/8 x 43/4 inch) cedar rafter
  11 60 x 120 mm (23/8 x 43/4 inch) cedar facade framing

  12 Fixed glazing
  13 Insect mesh screen
  14 Magnetic window catch
  15 Aluminium angle trim
  16 Galvanized aluminium window trim
  17 15 x 30 x 1.5 mm (5/8 x 11/5 x 1/16 inch) aluminium square section mullion
  18 15 mm (5/8 inch) cedar floorboards
  19 Plywood flooring substrate
  20 Cedar floor framing
  21 60 x 120 mm (23/8 x 43/4 inch) timber joist
  22 Flashing
  23 Rigid insulation
  24 Reinforced concrete floor slab

House to Catch the Mountain
Kamakura, Japan

Client
Private

Project Team
Takaharu Tezuka, Yui Tezuka

Structural Engineer
OHNO Japan

Lighting Designer
Masahide Kakudate Lighting Architect
& Associates

Landscape
Masako Yamazaki, Hiromi Iwao

This house is situated in Kamakura, the historic ancient capital of Japan, 50 kilometres (31 miles) south-west of Tokyo. It is surrounded to the north, east and west by mountains and to the south by the open water of Sagami Bay.

As its name suggests, 'House to Catch the Mountain' seeks to engage with the mountain, to become a part of the spirit of the place. The living spaces on the upper floor face a tree covered ridge at the base of the mountain which forms part of the property. From the terrace that wraps around the east and south facades of the living space, a bridge connects to the bottom of a small stair cut into the side of the mountain which leads up to the top of the ridge. The journey culminates in a viewing platform overlooking the sea.

Throughout the house, both inside and out, sliding walls are used to screen or to open up private spaces, including bedrooms and bathrooms on the ground floor, and the study, play room and guest room on the upper floor. Sliding walls are also a feature of the external envelope, most spectacularly on the first floor where the entire east and south glazed walls slide and stack away, opening the whole floor up to views of the mountain. Here, a single slender column supports the ambitiously cantilevered roof. Similarly, the external walls of the bedrooms and bathroom on the ground floor also slide away. This built-in flexibility is a deliberate and functional reference to traditional Japanese domestic architecture in which sliding screens are a defining feature.

1 The house seen from the bridge that leads to a viewing platform at the top of the ridge above. A spiral stair connects the two east facing terraces.
2 In the living space on the first floor, a single column supports the roof where two walls of glass doors slide away to open the entire space up to the mountain.
3 The street facade is a tripartite composition of a strip of clerestory windows over tall cupboards in the rooms on the first floor, a band of timber-faced plywood cladding, and a row of translucent sliding glass doors to the garage.
4 A stone lined bathroom with walk in shower and sunken bath occupies the north-east corner of the ground floor.

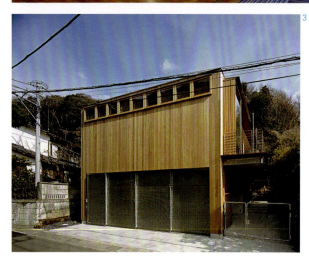

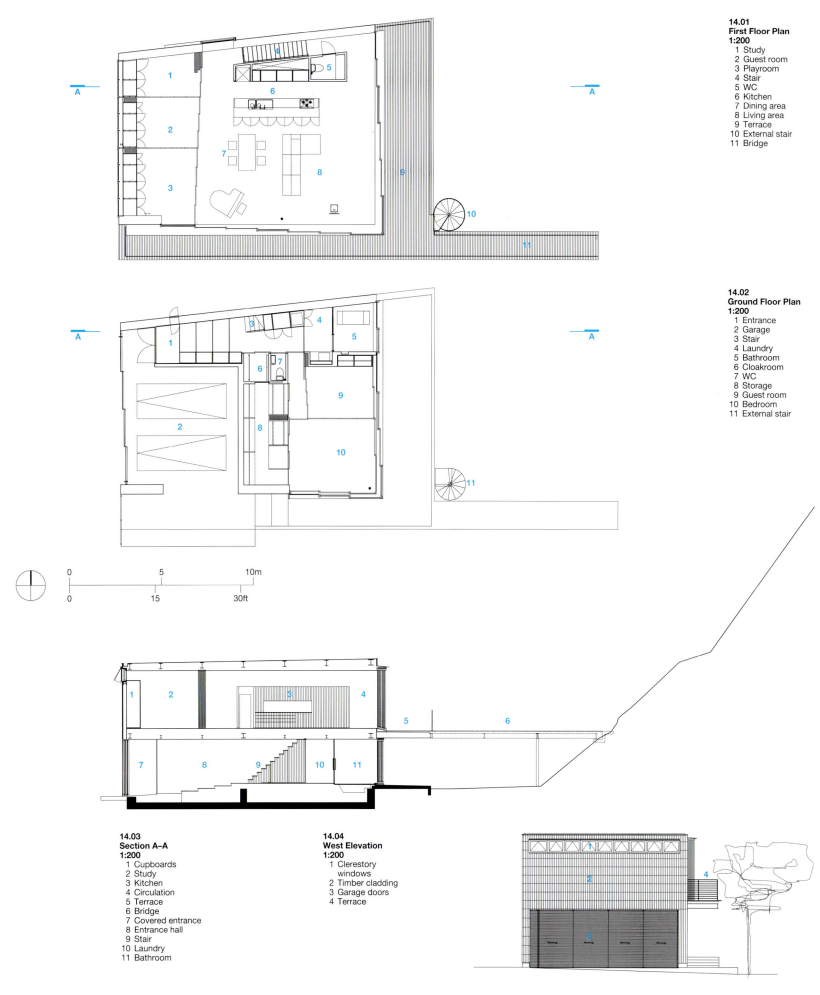

14.01
First Floor Plan
1:200
1 Study
2 Guest room
3 Playroom
4 Stair
5 WC
6 Kitchen
7 Dining area
8 Living area
9 Terrace
10 External stair
11 Bridge

14.02
Ground Floor Plan
1:200
1 Entrance
2 Garage
3 Stair
4 Laundry
5 Bathroom
6 Cloakroom
7 WC
8 Storage
9 Guest room
10 Bedroom
11 External stair

0　　　　　　5　　　　　　10m

0　　　　　　15　　　　　　30ft

14.03
Section A–A
1:200
1 Cupboards
2 Study
3 Kitchen
4 Circulation
5 Terrace
6 Bridge
7 Covered entrance
8 Entrance hall
9 Stair
10 Laundry
11 Bathroom

14.04
West Elevation
1:200
1 Clerestory
  windows
2 Timber cladding
3 Garage doors
4 Terrace

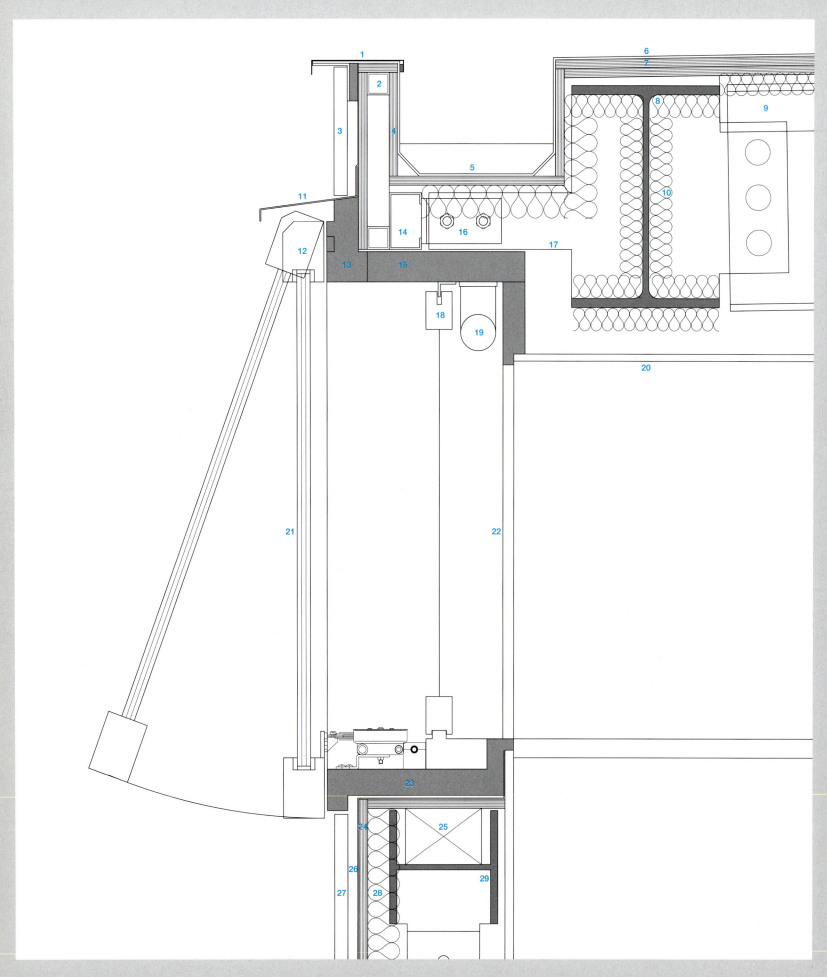

14.05
**West Facade Roof
and Window Section
Detail**
1:5
1 Polyvinyl
chloride-coated metal
flashing
2 30 x 30 mm (1¹/₅ x
1¹/₅ inch) steel square
section
3 20 mm (³/₄ inch)
thick apitong-faced
plywood external wall
cladding
4 12 mm (¹/₂ inch)
structural plywood
5 Stainless steel
rainwater gutter
6 Waterproof
membrane
7 Double layer of
plywood roofing
substrate with
waterproof fibre
reinforced plastic
coating
8 200 x 294 x 12 mm
(8 x 11¹/₂ x ¹/₂ inch)
universal steel beam
9 150 x 300 x 9 mm
(6 x 12 x ³/₈ inch)
universal steel beam
10 60 mm (2³/₈ inch)
thick sprayed urethane
thermal insulation
11 Aluminium coated
steel sheet flashing
12 Top hung pine
timber window frame
13 Glued laminated
pine flashing support
14 75 x 45 (3 x 1³/₄
inch) steel C-section
welded to gusset plate
15 Glued laminated
pine window head
16 Steel plate
connected to steel
gusset plate with two
12 mm (¹/₂ inch)
diameter bolts
17 Steel gusset plate
18 Insect mesh screen
19 Roller blind
20 Painted
plasterboard ceiling
21 Double glazing to
top hung window
22 Pine frame to
window reveal
23 Pine window sill
24 12 mm (¹/₂ inch)
structural plywood
25 Timber framing
26 Waterproof
membrane over
structural plywood
with ventilated cavity
27 20 mm (¹/₂ inch)
thick apitong-faced
plywood external wall
cladding
28 Sprayed urethane
thermal insulation
29 Steel sill support

14.06
**East Facade Roof
and Sliding Doors at
First Floor Section
Detail**
1:10
1 150 x 300 x 9 mm
(6 x 12 x ³/₈ inch)
universal steel beam
2 Double layer of
plywood roofing
substrate with
polyvinyl chloride-
coated metal
waterproof layer
3 Polyvinyl
chloride-coated metal
flashing
4 30 x 30 mm (1¹/₅ x
1¹/₅ inch) steel square
section
5 45 x 45 mm (1³/₄ x
1³/₄ inch) steel angle
6 20 mm (³/₄ inch)
apitong-faced
plywood external wall
cladding
7 Ventilation gap
8 Waterproof
membrane over
structural plywood
with ventilated cavity
9 300 x 300 x 15 mm
(12 x 12 x ⁵/₈ inch)
universal steel beam
10 60 mm (2³/₈ inch)
sprayed urethane
thermal insulation
11 Steel bracket to top
of door assembly
12 60 mm (2³/₈ inch)
sprayed urethane
thermal insulation
13 Stainless steel
flashing over
waterproof membrane
over structural
plywood
14 Silicon sealant
15 Glued laminated
pine lintel
16 Painted
plasterboard ceiling
17 Timber sliding door
frame
18 Curtains
19 Double glazing to
sliding door

14.07
**East Facade Sliding
Doors at Ground
Floor Section Detail**
1:10
1 Sliding glass,
pine-framed louvre
doors
2 Double glazing to
sliding door
3 15 mm (⁵/₈ inch)
thick ulin timber floor
boards
4 12 mm (¹/₂ inch)
thick plywood flooring
substrate
5 Air based
underfloor heating air
outlet chamber box
6 Dust collection box
7 90 x 90 mm (3¹/₂ x
3¹/₂ inch) floor joist
8 Sliding pine louvre
door frame
9 Timber sliding door
frame
10 Glu-lam pine
window sill
11 Concrete sill base
12 Concrete screed
13 Reinforced
concrete floor slab
14 45 mm (1³/₄ inch)
sprayed urethane
thermal insulation
15 Reinforced
concrete footing beam

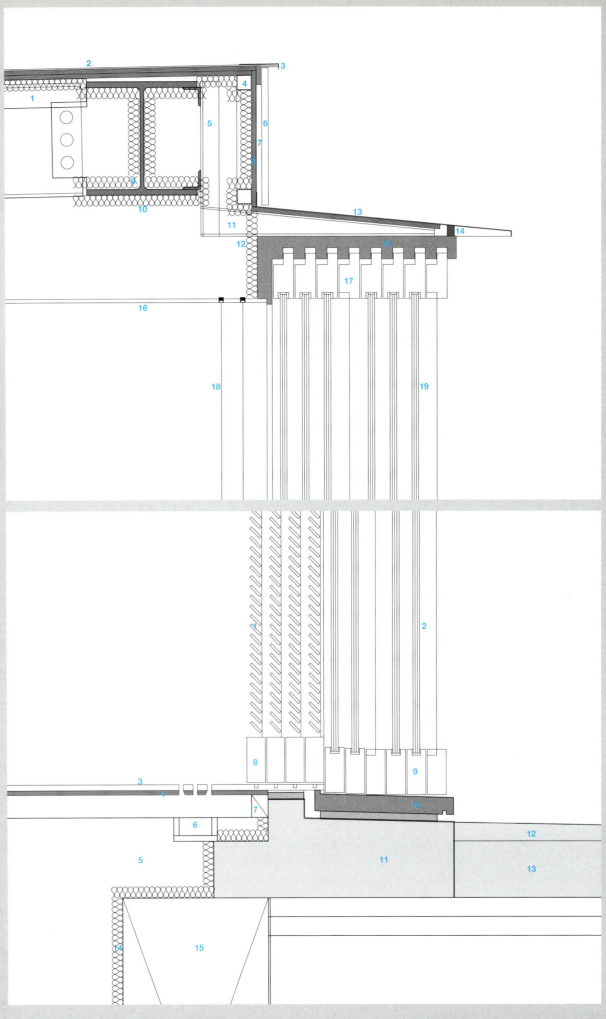

65

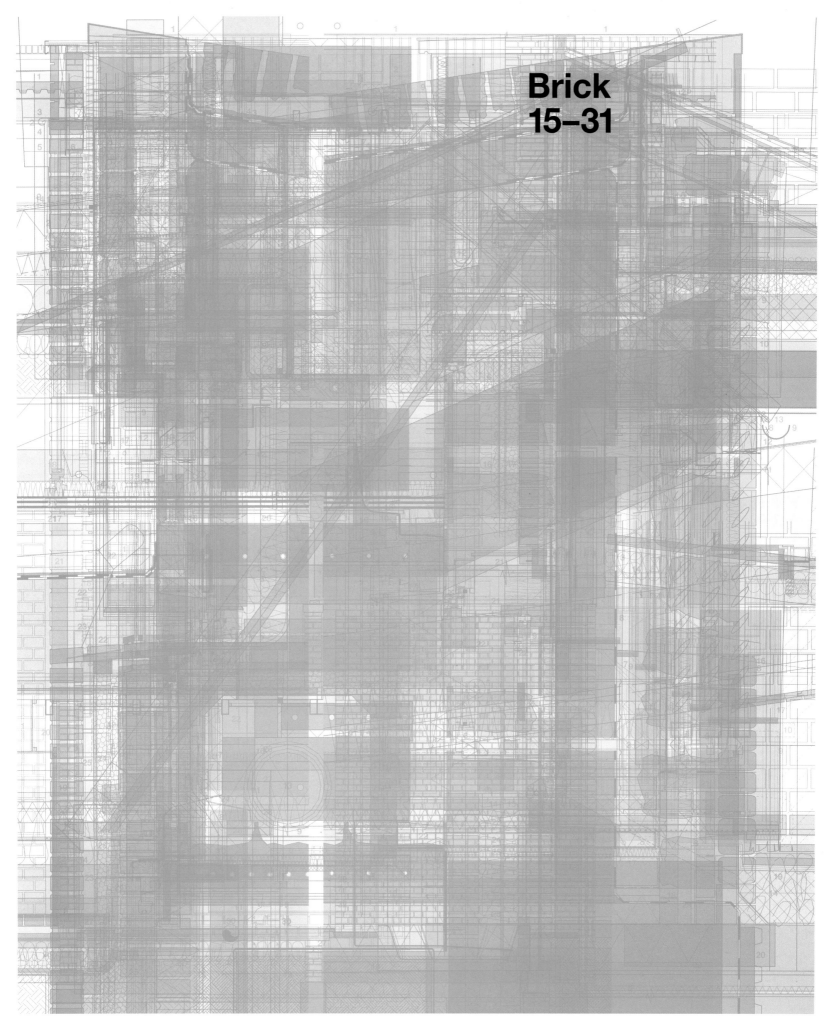

Brick
15–31

Villa Frenay
Lelystad, The Netherlands

Client
Frenay family

Project Team
Carina Nilsson, Bas ten Brinke

Structural Engineer
van Rossum Almere

Main Contractor
Ubink Almere

Villa Frenay is located in a new housing subdivision on the outskirts of Lelystad which, like much of the country, is built on reclaimed land that is approximately five metres (16 feet) below sea level. The architects were asked to design a detached house with two outbuildings (a garage and a sauna) on a flat polder site adjacent to a canal.

The long, single-storey grey brick building is designed to take advantage of its waterfront location through a broad covered terrace along the south facade, onto which all of the primary spaces have access, including the living spaces and hobby room as well as the master bedroom, bathroom and dressing room. The living spaces, consisting of an open plan living and dining space divided by a brick fireplace, turn the corner at the eastern end of the building, opening onto their own uncovered timber terrace which spans the all-glass east facade and a long, stepped, Corten lined water feature. The water feature is cut into the landscape, originating at the sauna and emptying into the canal at the corner of the terrace. On the other side of a central circulation zone are the children's bedrooms, plus a bathroom, utility room and entrance facing north across the garden towards the garage and sauna.

External walls, constructed from flat grey bricks, are modulated with large expanses of glazing. An entire wall of sliding doors extends to the south wall and a huge corner window is a feature of the dining and living space in the south-east corner, maximizing views over the terrace, water feature, canal and the rural landscape beyond. To break the monotony of the flat polder landscape, the roof over the living spaces has been lifted up and is dramatically pierced by the rectangular brick prism of the chimney.

1 The glazed corner of the living and dining spaces (right) opens onto a timber terrace. The terrace, in turn, overlooks the stepped waterfall which traverses the site from north to south, emptying into the canal (left).
2 The timber sauna building is accessed via a timber terrace and through a door set flush in the timber-clad wall. Inside the sauna itself, a large floor-to-ceiling window is aligned with the stepped water feature.
3 On the east wall, one side features a large corner window while the other has been removed to create the covered south terrace.
4 The south terrace features vertical timber louvres to give privacy to the bedroom, bathroom and dressing room, and a large roof overhang for shade.
5 The open plan living space (left) and dining space (right) is bisected by an elegant fireplace and chimney.

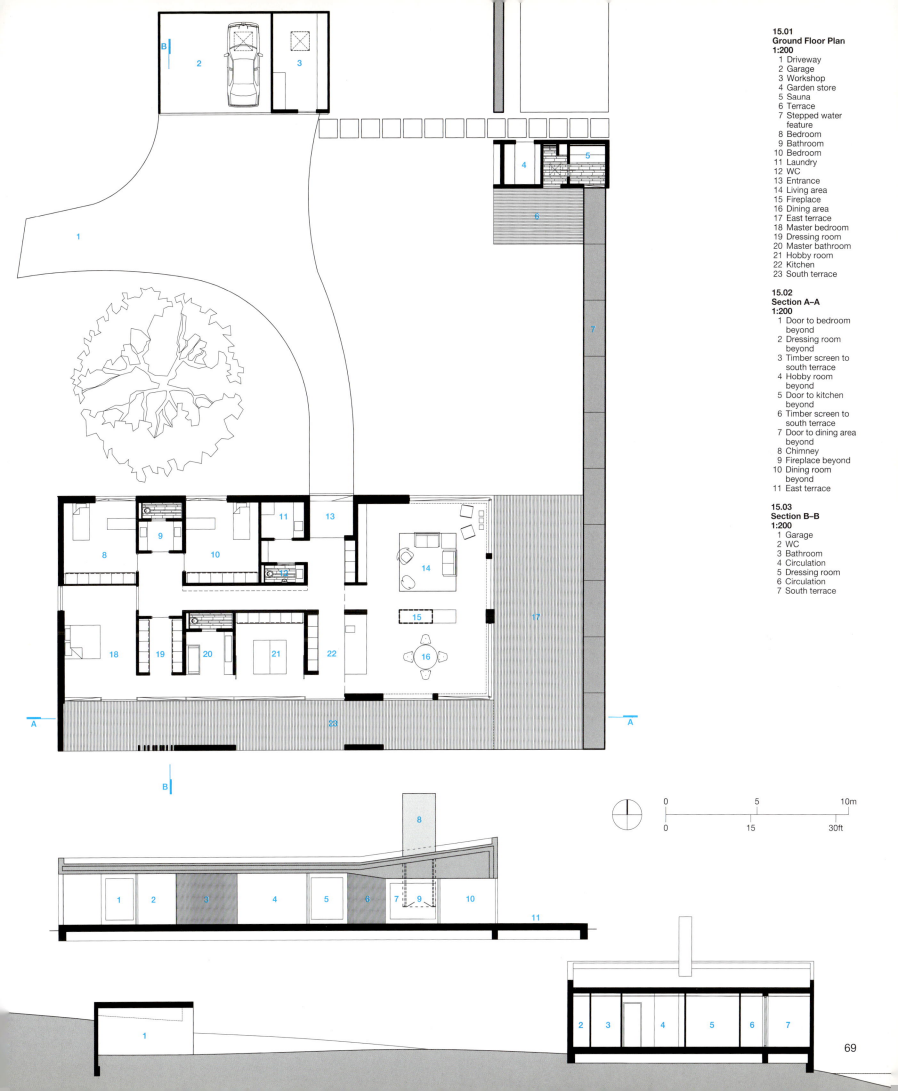

15.01
Ground Floor Plan
1:200
1 Driveway
2 Garage
3 Workshop
4 Garden store
5 Sauna
6 Terrace
7 Stepped water
  feature
8 Bedroom
9 Bathroom
10 Bedroom
11 Laundry
12 WC
13 Entrance
14 Living area
15 Fireplace
16 Dining area
17 East terrace
18 Master bedroom
19 Dressing room
20 Master bathroom
21 Hobby room
22 Kitchen
23 South terrace

15.02
Section A–A
1:200
1 Door to bedroom
  beyond
2 Dressing room
  beyond
3 Timber screen to
  south terrace
4 Hobby room
  beyond
5 Door to kitchen
  beyond
6 Timber screen to
  south terrace
7 Door to dining area
  beyond
8 Chimney
9 Fireplace beyond
10 Dining room
   beyond
11 East terrace

15.03
Section B–B
1:200
1 Garage
2 WC
3 Bathroom
4 Circulation
5 Dressing room
6 Circulation
7 South terrace

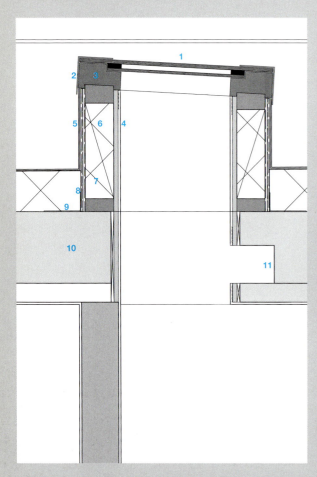

**15.04
Skylight Section
Detail
1:10**
 1 Thermally insulated
double glazing to
skylight
 2 Aluminium capping
 3 67 x 114 mm (2⁵/8 x
4¹/2 inch) hardwood
frame
 4 12 mm (¹/2 inch)
thick painted
plasterboard wall lining
 5 Bituminous
waterproof membrane
 6 46 x 71 mm (1³/4 x
2³/4 inch) timber
framing
 7 76 mm (3 inch)
thick rigid insulation
 8 12 mm (¹/2 inch)
waterproof plywood
 9 Galvanized steel
angle
 10 240 mm (9¹/2 inch)
thick concrete slab
roof
 11 Painted recess in
concrete slab formed
from 12 mm (¹/2 inch)
MDF for recessed light
fixtures

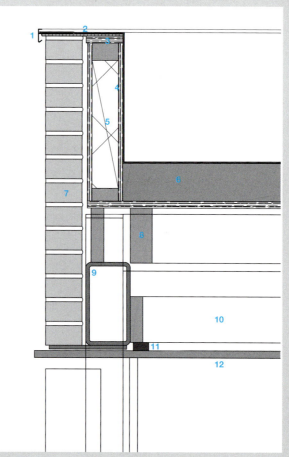

**15.05
Roof Parapet Section
Detail
1:10**
 1 Aluminium trim to
roof parapet
 2 6 mm (¹/4 inch)
thick cementitious
board screw-fixed to
timber upstand frame
 3 18 mm (³/4 inch)
thick waterproof
plywood
 4 Waterproof
plywood roofing
substrate
 5 76 mm (3 inch)
thick rigid insulation
between timber
framing
 6 Roofing membrane
on insulating substrate
 7 Single skin brick
external cladding
 8 59 x 146 mm (2³/8 x
5³/4 inch) timber
beams
 9 100 x 200 mm (4 x
8 inch) rectangular
steel section lintel
 10 59 x 96 mm (2³/8 x
3³/4 inch) timber
battens at 600 mm
(23¹/2 inch) centres
 11 42 x 22 mm (1⁵/8 x
⁷/8 inch) timber
counter battens at 400
mm (15³/4 inch)
centres
 12 Timber soffit lining
to terrace

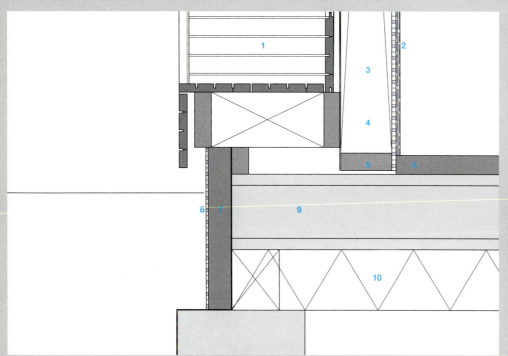

**15.06
Wood Store to
External Wall of
Sauna Section Detail
at Floor
1:10**
 1 22 mm (⁷/8 inch)
thick horizontal timber
cladding, external
flooring and deck
overhang
 2 Birch veneer with
semi-transparent
varnish finish to
internal walls
 3 Rigid insulation
 4 Timber framed
prefabricated wall
panel
 5 Timber bottom
plate wall framing
 6 50 mm (2 inch)
thick cement screed to
interior floor
 7 65 mm
(2¹/2 inch) rigid
insulation
 8 7 mm (³/8 inch)
thick painted
cementitious boarding
to subfloor
 9 200 mm (8 inch)
thick hollow core
concrete slab
 10 Rigid insulation

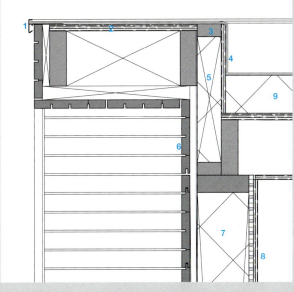

15.07
Wood Store to External Wall of Sauna Section Detail at Roof
1:10
1 Aluminium roof trim
2 Double layer of plywood roofing substrate
3 34 x 46 mm ($1^3/8$ x $1^3/4$ inch) timber framing at 400 mm ($15^3/4$ inch) centres
4 12 mm ($1/2$ inch) waterproof ply roofing substrate
5 76 mm (3 inch) thick rigid insulation between timber framing

6 22 mm ($7/8$ inch) thick horizontal timber cladding to external walls and soffit
7 Rigid insulation in timber framed prefabricated wall panel
8 Birch veneer with semi-transparent varnish finish to internal walls
9 Bituminous waterproof membrane on rigid insulation over 18 mm ($3/4$ inch) waterproof ply roofing substrate

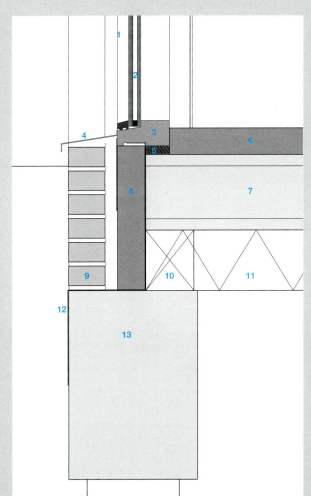

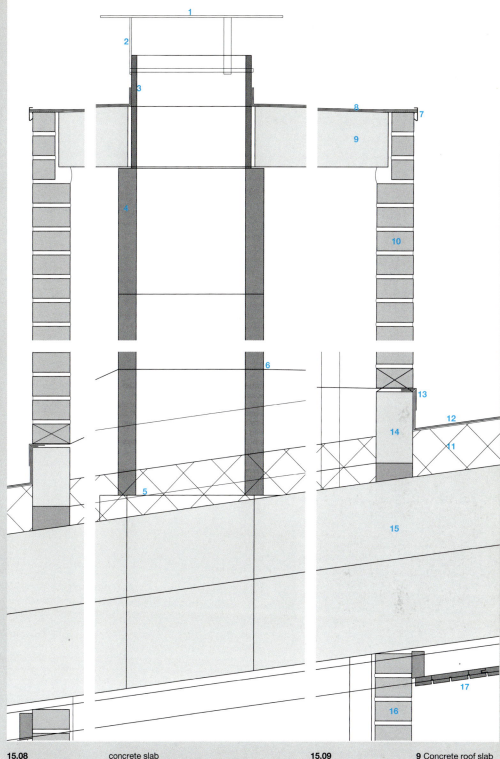

15.08
Fixed Glazing and Footing Section Detail
1:10
1 Line of burglar-proof sliding glass doors beyond
2 Double glazed fixed window with insulated glass
3 67 x 140 mm ($2^5/8$ x $5^1/2$ inch) Western red cedar window frame
4 Anodized aluminium window sill
5 Insulated frame support
6 70 mm ($2^3/4$ inch) thick concrete screed interior floor
7 200 mm (8 inch) thick hollow core

concrete slab
8 76 mm (3 inch) rigid insulation
9 Breather brick to single skin brick external wall
10 Timber bearer to subfloor
11 Rigid insulation
12 Damp-proof membrane
13 Reinforced concrete foundation

15.09
Chimney Section Detail
1:10
1 3 mm ($1/8$ inch) black steel vermin-proof chimney cover
2 3 x 30 mm ($1/8$ x $1^1/5$ inch) steel feet support to chimney cover
3 300 mm (12 inch) diameter steel chimney sleeve
4 300 mm (12 inch) brick flue
5 500 x 500 mm ($19^3/4$ x $19^3/4$ inch) concrete support
6 Lead flashing
7 Aluminium roof trim
8 Double layer of bituminous waterproof membrane

9 Concrete roof slab
10 100 mm (4 inch) thick single skin brick to chimney stack
11 Rigid insulation
12 Double layer of bituminous waterproof membrane
13 Lead flashing to chimney stack
14 100 mm (4 inch) limestone chimney base
15 Reinforced concrete roof slab
16 100 mm (4 inch) thick single skin brick internal chimney surround
17 22 mm ($7/8$ inch) thick timber ceiling

Villa Rotonda
Goirle, The Netherlands

Client
Private

Project Team
Pieter Bedaux, Thomas Bedaux, Koen de Witte, Kees Paulussen, Rien Lagerwerf, Cees de Rooij

Structural Engineer
H4D Raadgevende Ingenieurs

Main Contractor
Houtepen Aannemersbedrijf

This house in the south of the Netherlands has been designed in response to its location near a busy and noisy road. The design cleverly manages this difficult condition with the need for a quiet, comfortable, home with as much access to natural light and open views across the landscape as possible. These potentially conflicting requirements resulted in a house that is light and open to the garden at the back of the site and almost entirely closed towards the busy road. The street facade is composed of a solid grey brick wall punctured by a solitary window. This protective carapace wraps around the house to the north and west creating a literal, visual and acoustic barrier. At the north-west corner, the wall appears to rise up out of a reflection pool that wraps around the corner of the house creating a shallow moat that marks the transition between the private interior and the public street.

At the centre of the plan, and accommodated within a seemingly traditional brick, gabled, pitched slate roof structure, are the double height living space, kitchen, dining, laundry and cloakroom on the ground floor and bedroom, bathroom and storage on the first floor above. A wall of full height glazing overlooks the completely private garden and swimming pool to the south. Enclosing the garden, two wings extend from the front of the site, flanking the central volume. The west wing houses a study, sitting room, master bathroom and bedroom, with an open air covered jacuzzi terminating this flat roofed wing. To the east, the garage and covered dining terrace complete the protective U-shaped plan.

1 The south facing garden facade of the pitched-roof central volume is entirely glazed, providing the living, dining and kitchen spaces with views over the garden.
2 The study enjoys views over the

The low, flat-roofed wings and paved terraces on either side embrace the central lawn and swimming pool.

reflection pool via a full height frameless window. The still, moat-like water, along with the brick blade walls, separate the house from the busy road beyond.
3 From the road the house appears solid and secure behind the defensive screen of the outer brick wall (right).
4 A single window punctures the protective solidity of

the brick wall on the street facade, allowing a glimpse into the entrance hall and through to the double height living space.
5 A view from the entrance hall reveals

the reflection pool where it embraces the north-west corner of the site.

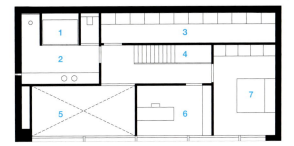

16.01
First Floor Plan
1:200
1 Sauna
2 Bathroom
3 Storage cupboards
4 Stair
5 Void over living
  area
6 Study
7 Bedroom

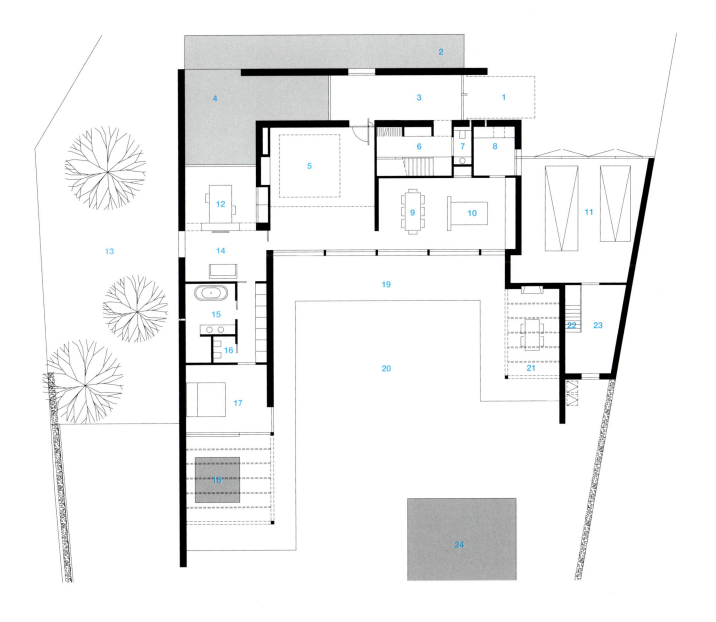

16.02
Ground Floor Plan
1:200
1 Entrance canopy
2 Reflection pool
3 Entrance hall
4 Reflection pool
5 Living area
6 Cloakroom
7 WC
8 Laundry
9 Dining area
10 Kitchen
11 Garage
12 Study
13 Garden
14 Sitting room
15 Bathroom
16 WC
17 Bedroom
18 Jacuzzi
19 Terrace
20 Lawn
21 Covered terrace
22 Stair to basement
   technical plant
23 Storage
24 Swimming pool

0   5   10m

0   15   30ft

16.03
External and Internal Door Section Detail
1:10
 1 140 mm (5¹/₂ inch) thick engineered clay block wall
 2 130 mm (5¹/₈ inch) thick rigid thermal insulation
 3 40 mm (1¹/₂ inch) ventilated cavity
 4 Timber door frame
 5 Thermally insulated timber external door
 6 Low emissivity fixed double glazing
 7 Brick soldier course
 8 18 mm (³/₄ inch) thick painted MDF internal wall lining
 9 50 mm (2 inch) thick thermal insulation and vapour barrier
 10 18 mm (³/₄ inch) thick painted plywood
 11 Timber wall framing
 12 140 x 140 x 10 mm (5¹/₂ x 5¹/₂ x ³/₈ inch) square hollow steel section
 13 Custom wrought iron door hinge
 14 Three 15 mm (⁵/₈ inch) thick laminated plywood doors with satin paint finish

16.04
Pitched Roof and Glazed Wall Section Detail
1:10
 1 Flat profile ceramic roof tiles
 2 22 x 32 mm (⁷/₈ x 1¹/₄ inch) timber battens
 3 Prefabricated roof structure
 4 120 mm (4³/₄ inch) insulation
 5 15 mm (⁵/₈ inch) plywood
 6 Timber nailer at eaves
 7 Timber framing to insulated roof panel
 8 Zinc gutter on steel supports
 9 Waterproof membrane
 10 Timber soffit lining
 11 Timber mounting frame for window
 12 Enamelled aluminium window frame
 13 Timber framing for ceiling construction
 14 Timber battens
 15 Skimmed and painted 15 mm (⁵/₈ inch) plasterboard
 16 Rainwater discharge to downpipe in wall cavity
 17 Remote controlled, enamelled metal blinds

16.05
Flat Roof and Glazed Wall Section Detail
1:10
 1 Zinc parapet capping on plywood substrate
 2 Timber framing
 3 Roofing membrane
 4 Zinc parapet capping turned down external face
 5 70 mm (2³/₄ inch) insulation
 6 Aerated concrete upstand
 7 140–180 mm (5¹/₂–7 inch) insulation laid to fall to downpipe
 8 200 mm (8 inch) thick reinforced concrete roof slab
 9 Zinc parapet capping with rolled edge
 10 230 x 170 mm (9 x 6³/₄ inch) laminated timber frame for external screens
 11 Waterproof membrane
 12 Timber mounting frame for window
 13 18 mm (³/₄ inch) MDF pelmet
 14 Aluminium window frame with trickle vent
 15 Low emissivity double glazing
 16 Stone window sill
 17 Ventilation brick
 18 Waterproof membrane
 19 100 mm (4 inch) thick cement and sand screed
 20 100 mm (4 inch) thick brick outer leaf
 21 130 mm (5¹/₈ inch) insulation
 22 100 mm (4 inch) thick brick inner leaf
 23 Concrete floor slab

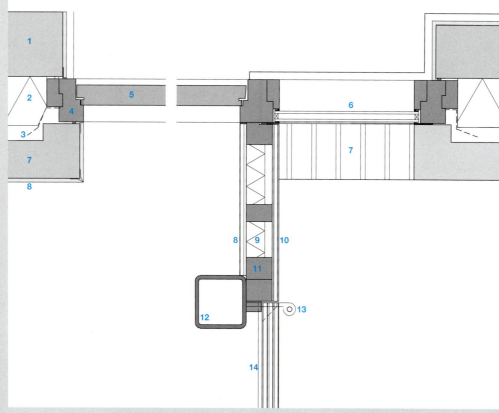

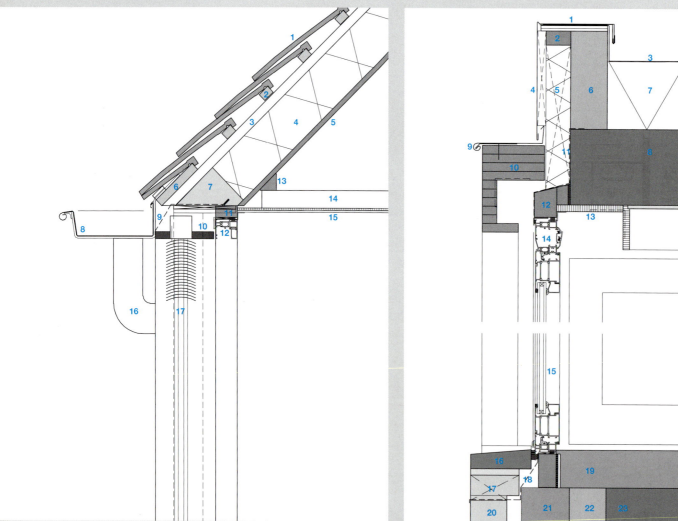

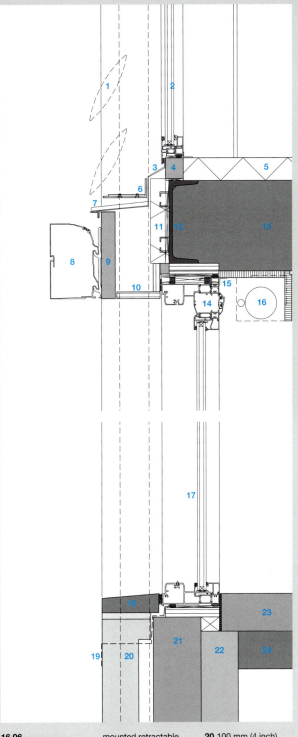

16.06
South Facade Glazing Section Detail
1:10
1 External metal louvre blinds
2 Aluminium window frame with low emissivity double glazing
3 Folded aluminium window sill
4 Timber mounting frame for window
5 Cement and sand screed with integrated floor heating
6 Folded metal frame for metal blinds
7 Folded aluminium window sill
8 Proprietary wall mounted retractable awning
9 Laminated timber fascia
10 18 mm (3/4 inch) plywood soffit lining
11 50 mm (2 inch) thick insulation
12 Steel C-channel
13 240 mm (91/2 inch) reinforced concrete floor slab
14 Aluminium trickle vent to window
15 Aluminium-framed sliding door
16 Remote controlled roller blind
17 Low emissivity double glazing
18 Stone window sill
19 Waterproof membrane
20 100 mm (4 inch) thick brick outer leaf
21 130 mm (51/8 inch) insulation
22 100 mm (4 inch) thick brick inner leaf
23 100 mm (4 inch) thick cement and sand screed with integrated floor heating
24 Concrete floor slab

16.07
External Wall Section Detail
1:10
1 Zinc parapet capping on plywood substrate
2 100 mm (4 inch) thick brick outer leaf
3 130 mm (51/8 inch) thick insulation
4 Aerated concrete parapet upstand
5 Roofing membrane
6 140–180 mm (51/2–7 inch) insulation laid to fall to downpipe
7 Reinforcement to brick lintel
8 Timber framing
9 200 mm (8 inch) reinforced concrete floor slab
10 Waterproof membrane
11 Acoustically attenuated trickle vent
12 Brick soldier course
13 Timber mounting frame for window
14 Remote controlled roller blind
15 18 mm (3/4 inch) MDF pelmet
16 Low emissivity double glazing
17 Folded aluminium window sill
18 Subsill flashing
19 Ventilation brick
20 Timber mounting frame
21 Stone window sill
22 Plaster finish to internal wall
23 Waterproof membrane
24 100 mm (4 inch) thick brick outer leaf
25 130 mm (51/8 inch) insulation
26 100 mm (4 inch) thick brick inner leaf
27 20 x 100 mm (3/4 x 4 inch) MDF skirting board
28 100 mm (4 inch) thick cement and sand screed with integrated floor heating

16.08
Sliding Louvre Wall Section Detail
1:10
1 Zinc parapet capping
2 Roofing membrane
3 18 mm (3/4 inch) plywood roofing substrate
4 Laminated timber frame for sliding louvre panels
5 59 x 146 mm (23/8 x 53/4 inch) timber beam
6 15 mm (5/8 inch) plywood soffit with paint finish
7 Guiderail for louvre panels
8 Sliding aluminium louvre panels
9 Stone paving

Kings Grove House
London, England, UK

Client
Private

Project Team
Mary Duggan, Joe Morris

Structural Engineer
Lyons O'Neill

Main Contractor
ME Construction

The Kings Grove House site in south London was once occupied by plaster moulding workshops and sheds and was designated as industrial land. The old buildings were demolished in 2004 and planning permission for domestic use was secured in 2006. The plot sits between the rear gardens of two parallel Victorian terraces containing a variety of early Victorian architecture of varying heights and typologies, typical of many south London streets.

The site is accessed via a parting in the street between two semi-detached properties, once forming an access lane to the industrial yard. The building is located towards the north of the site to create a large entrance courtyard to the south. Views and light are maximized with fully glazed facades to the north and south. The open plan ground floor connects the front courtyard to the rear terrace, while the first floor contains two bedrooms and a bathroom. To counteract the deep plan, a central void topped with clear glazing offers unobstructed views of the sky.

Brick was employed both internally and externally in order to maintain a material connection to the traditional Victorian surroundings, albeit through a thoroughly contemporary interpretation. The facades are simple compositions of brick and glazing with subtle flush details. One of the most important elements of the design is the unique, project specific glazing system, fabricated in a sapele timber frame with a brass trim. Silicone-bonded low-emissivity double glazed units are precisely detailed to brick dimensions. Finer architectural elements are rendered in brass, including taps and door handles, while oak joinery and flooring add a layer of familiarity and robustness that are congruous with robust family living.

1 The south facade features pivoting glass windows and doors that open the living spaces on the ground floor up to the garden courtyard. Planting beds are laid in the horizontal plane of the solid brick vertical elements, while door openings encounter stretcher bond brick paving that is a continuation of that used in the facades.
2 The dining area and kitchen are illuminated by a large window that opens onto a small courtyard to the north and by a central skylight-topped void. The texture of the brick walls contrast with the pale oak used for the kitchen units and the first floor balcony wall.
3 Set amidst a dense urban landscape of Victorian domestic buildings, with their ubiquitous London stock brick facades, the house appears comfortable and timeless.
4 The living area at the front of the house is a gentle essay in relaxed formality. The hard, practical surfaces are softened by the reflected light that fills the house.

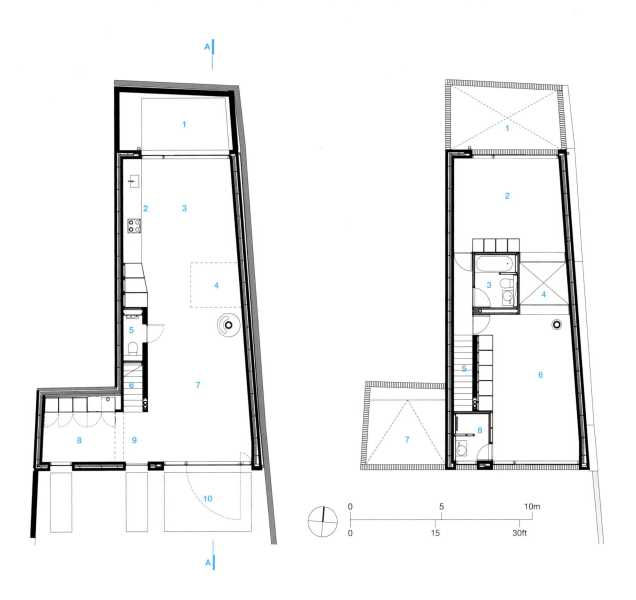

17.01
Ground Floor Plan
1:200
1 Rear terrace
2 Kitchen
3 Dining area
4 Central void
5 Cloakroom
6 Stair
7 Living area
8 Study
9 Entrance
10 Courtyard

17.02
First Floor Plan
1:200
1 Terrace below
2 Bedroom
3 Bathroom
4 Central void
5 Stair
6 Master bedroom
7 Roof to study below
8 Ensuite bathroom

17.03
Section A-A
1:100
1 Rear terrace
2 Bedroom
3 Dining area
4 Central void
5 Master bedroom
6 Living area
7 Entrance courtyard

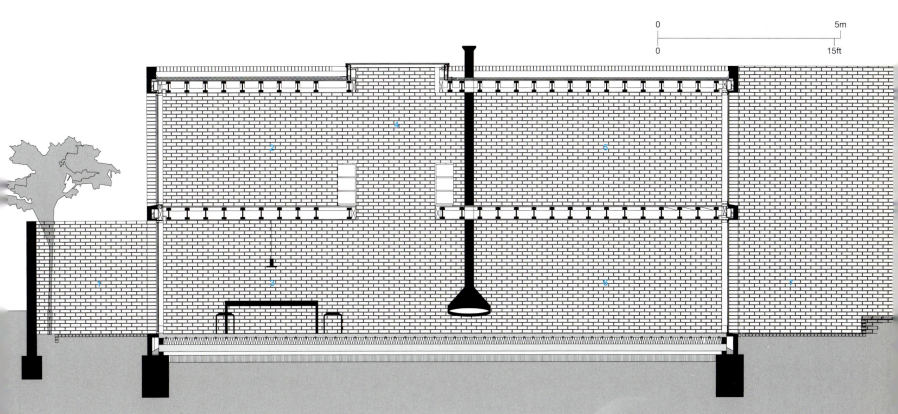

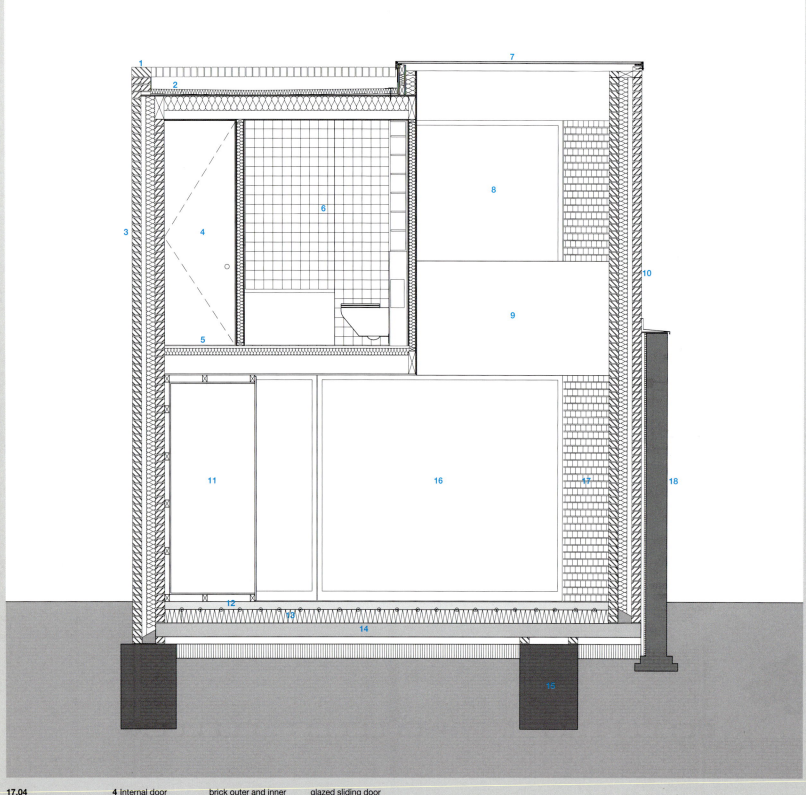

17.04
Detail Cross Section Through Central Void
1:50

1 Brick soldier course to roof parapet
2 Single ply roofing membrane on rigid insulation and marine grade ply
3 External wall from brick outer and inner courses in stretcher bond with flush mortar joints and 100 mm (4 inch) cavity insulation
4 Internal door
5 European oak timber flooring with environmental oil finish over underfloor heating system and underfloor insulation
6 Bathroom
7 Fixed double glazed unit over central void
8 Sliding window to bedroom
9 Timber balustrade to central void
10 External wall from
brick outer and inner courses in stretcher bond with flush mortar joints and 100 mm (4 inch) cavity insulation
11 Full height kitchen joinery
12 Concrete floor with power-floated finish over underfloor heating
13 Rigid insulation
14 Reinforced concrete slab
15 Reinforced concrete footing
16 Full height double
glazed sliding door
17 Fair faced brick internal wall
18 Brick footing and pier

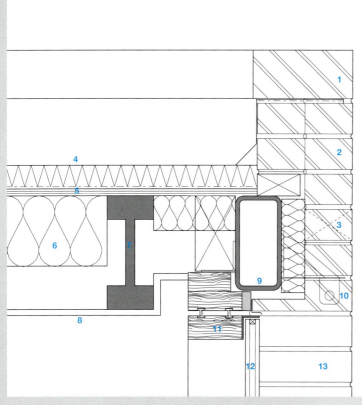

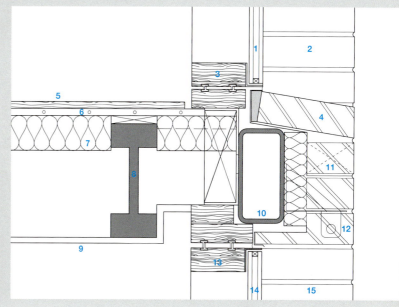

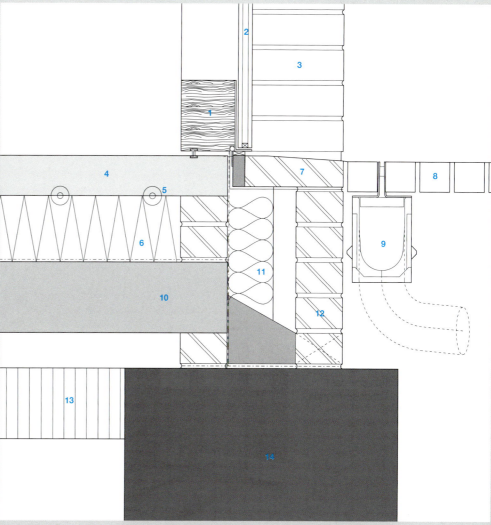

17.05
Brick External Wall Parapet Detail
1:10
1 Brick soldier course to roof parapet
2 Brick outer and inner courses in stretcher bond with flush mortar joints and 100 mm (4 inch) cavity insulation
3 50 mm (2 inch) vent brick
4 Single ply roofing membrane on rigid insulation
5 Marine ply substrate
6 Ceiling insulation
7 Engineered timber I-beam joists at 400 mm (15 3/4 inch) centres
8 Painted plasterboard ceiling
9 200 x 100 mm (8 x 4 inch) rectangular hollow section steel portal frame
10 Brick support system
11 Sapele hardwood window frame and reveal
12 Double glazed window unit with brass edge detail
13 Brick external window reveal

17.06
Window Head and Sill at First Floor Detail
1:10
1 Double glazed window unit with brass edge detail
2 Brick external window reveal
3 Sapele hardwood window frame and reveal
4 Special brick sill on tie support
5 180 x 15 mm (7 x 5/8 inch) European oak timber flooring with environmental oil finish
6 Underfloor heating system
7 Underfloor insulation
8 Engineered timber I-beam joists at 400 mm (15 3/4 inch) centres
9 Painted plasterboard ceiling
10 200 x 100 mm (8 x 4 inch) rectangular hollow section steel portal frame
11 50 mm (2 inch) vent brick
12 Brick support system
13 Sapele hardwood window frame and reveal
14 Double glazed window unit with brass edge detail
15 Brick external window reveal

17.07
External Wall and Footing Detail
1:10
1 Sapele hardwood window frame and reveal
2 Double glazed window unit with brass edge detail
3 Brick external window reveal
4 100 mm (4 inch) thick concrete floor with power-floated finish, surface hardener and seal
5 Underfloor heating system
6 Rigid insulation
7 Special brick sill on tie support
8 Brick pavers laid on edge
9 Brick slot drain and channel
10 Reinforced concrete slab
11 100 mm (4 inch) cavity insulation
12 Single skin brick foundation pier
13 Clay heave boards
14 Reinforced concrete footing

Seafield House
Isle of Man, UK

Client
Private

Project Team
Jay Gort, Fiona Scott, Mellis Haward

Structural Engineer
Structural Engineering Services

Quantity Surveyor
Berrie, Millar & Cox

Main Contractor
G J Ingham & Sons

Stonemason
Dennis Quayle

Positioned on the rocky, windswept topography of the Scarlett peninsula on the south coast of the Isle of Man, this house is constructed from silver-grey limestone, known locally as Castletown stone which was sourced from the Pooil Vaaish quarry just a few miles from the site. The house forms part of a collection of buildings and gardens on a large estate, which will be added to by the architects according to a strategic masterplan.

The building contains two discrete apartments, one for guests and another for an au pair, each requiring its own entrance and particular relationship to the main house. Inside, both apartments have a simple open plan layout of living and kitchen areas leading onto double bedrooms and bathroom. The upper apartment for guests is entered using the external staircase, leading into a double height living and dining area opening onto a large seaward-facing balcony. The ground floor au pair apartment enjoys views across neighbouring fields, the estate grounds and towards the sea.

The thick cavity construction external walls are comprised of a blockwork inner leaf with an outer face of 225 millimetre (8¾ inch) thick stone. These walls support a concrete beam and block floor and a timber and steel roof clad in Welsh slate. The dark colour and the roughness of the traditionally laid stonework is contrasted with the crisp pre-cast concrete window and door surrounds.

1 Glazed doors open from the upper apartment onto a broad balcony that also serves to shelter the patio area below. The protective stone walls that surround the garden merge into those of the house.
2 The living area in the upper apartment has a large north-west facing skylight as well as large glazed doors leading out onto the south-west facing terrace. Timber boards and white painted plasterboard create a simple but nuanced meeting of planes.
3 Emerging from the stone perimeter wall, the building's cuboid form tapers up into an asymmetric Welsh slate roof pitch that leans into the prevailing south-west Irish Sea winds.
4 The crisply finished, light coloured cast concrete window surrounds contrast dramatically with the local dark stone walls.

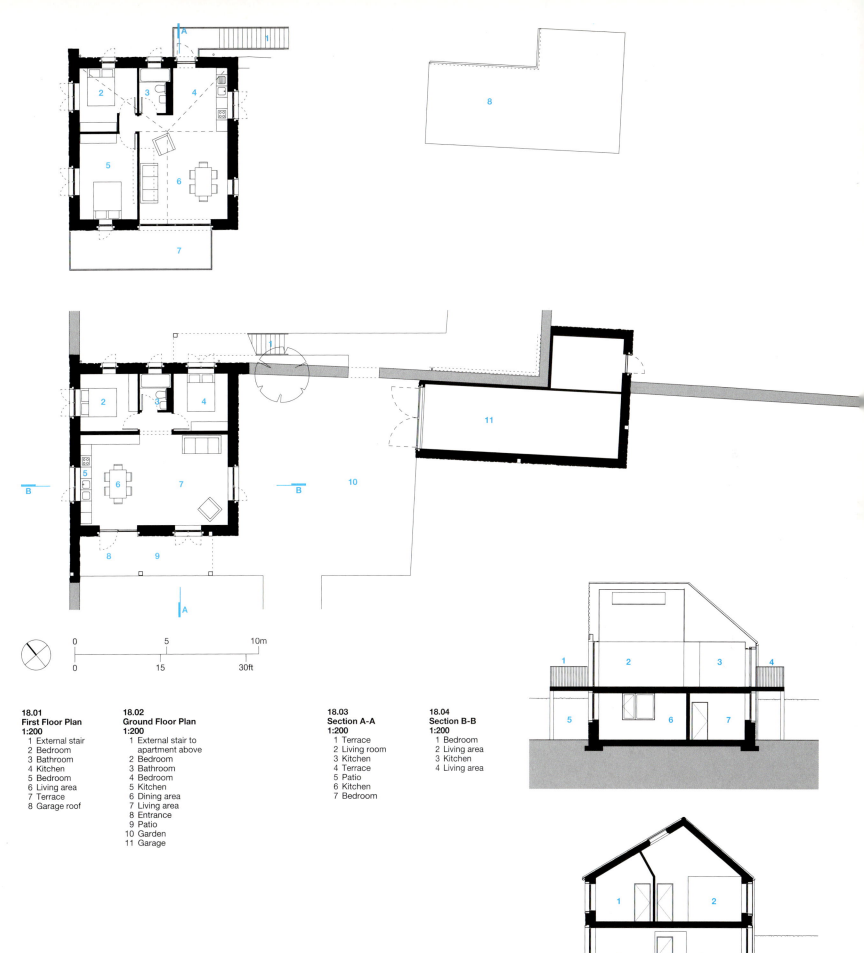

0   5   10m

0   15   30ft

18.01
First Floor Plan
1:200
1 External stair
2 Bedroom
3 Bathroom
4 Kitchen
5 Bedroom
6 Living area
7 Terrace
8 Garage roof

18.02
Ground Floor Plan
1:200
1 External stair to
  apartment above
2 Bedroom
3 Bathroom
4 Bedroom
5 Kitchen
6 Dining area
7 Living area
8 Entrance
9 Patio
10 Garden
11 Garage

18.03
Section A-A
1:200
1 Terrace
2 Living room
3 Kitchen
4 Terrace
5 Patio
6 Kitchen
7 Bedroom

18.04
Section B-B
1:200
1 Bedroom
2 Living area
3 Kitchen
4 Living area

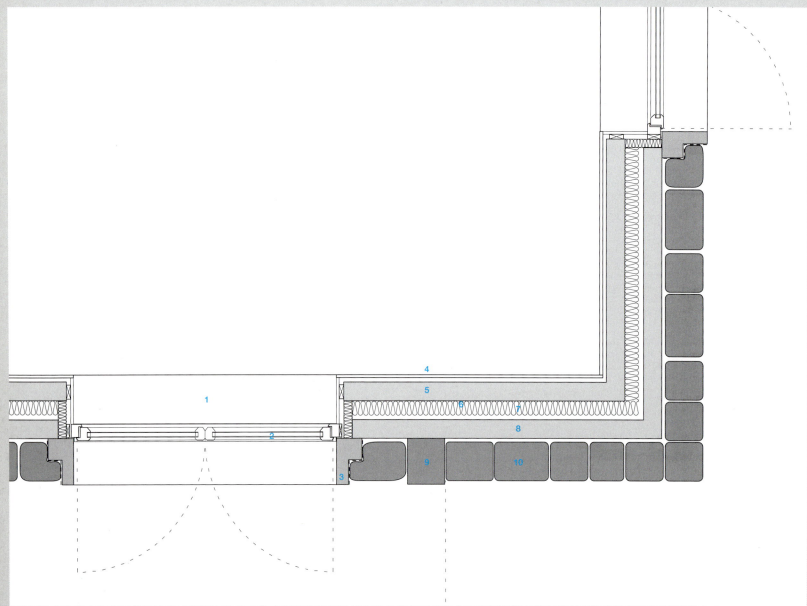

18.05
External Wall Plan Detail
1:20
 1 Timber door threshold
 2 Side-hung, aluminium-framed double glazed doors
 3 Reinforced pre-cast concrete door surround with 5 mm (1/5 inch) shadow gaps
 4 15 mm (5/8 inch) painted plasterboard on dabs
 5 100 mm (4 inch) thick high-density blockwork inner leaf to cavity wall
 6 Waterproof membrane
 7 75 mm (3 inch) rigid insulation in 100 mm (4 inch) cavity
 8 100 mm (4 inch) thick high-density blockwork outer leaf to cavity wall
 9 Pre-cast concrete column
 10 225 mm (83/4 inch) thick roughly coursed stone cladding

18.06
Roof Ridge, External Wall, Sliding Door and Floor Section Detail
1:20
 1 Welsh slate roof tiles
 2 Preservative treated timber roofing battens
 3 Breathable membrane
 4 Timber rafters and steel purlins
 5 150 mm (6 inch) insulation between rafters
 6 Preservative treated timber ceiling battens
 7 Painted plasterboard ceiling
 8 Mortar joint as necessary to fill gap between roof edge and stone wall
 9 225 mm (83/4 inch) thick roughly coursed stone cladding
 10 100 mm (4 inch) thick high-density blockwork outer leaf to cavity wall
 11 75 mm (3 inch) rigid insulation in 100 mm (4 inch) cavity

12 Waterproof membrane
13 100 mm (4 inch) thick high-density blockwork inner leaf to cavity wall
14 15 mm (5/8 inch) painted plasterboard on dabs
15 Damp-proof membrane
16 Stone slip over concrete lintel
17 Reinforced pre-cast concrete lintel
18 Insulated steel lintel to blockwork opening
19 Aluminium-framed sliding, folding doors
20 Stainless steel balustrade with 10 x 40 mm (3/8 x 11/2 inch) steel fin uprights
21 Ceramic floor tiles to terrace
22 In-situ concrete floor slab to terrace
23 Damp proof membrane
24 Reinforced pre-cast concrete door surround with 5 mm (1/5 inch) shadow gap at joints
25 Side-hung, UPVC

double glazed doors
26 20 mm (3/4 inch) thick timber floorboards
27 75 mm (3 inch) thick screed with underfloor heating
28 50 mm (2 inch) rigid insulation
29 Pre-cast concrete beam and block floor beam
30 Insulation packed into cavity closer
31 Steel channel
32 15 mm (5/8 inch) painted plasterboard on dabs

18.07
Roof, Eaves, Window and Floor Slab Section Detail
1:20
 1 Welsh slate roof tiles
 2 Preservative treated timber roofing battens
 3 Breathable membrane
 4 150 mm (6 inch) insulation between rafters
 5 Preservative treated timber ceiling battens
 6 Timber rafters
 7 Painted plasterboard ceiling
 8 Zinc flashing
 9 Half round black UPVC gutter
 10 Insulated steel lintel to blockwork opening
 11 Reinforced pre-cast concrete window surround with 5 mm (1/5 inch) shadow gap at joints
 12 Reinforced pre-cast concrete lintel
 13 Side-hung, UPVC double glazed window
 14 Timber sill
 15 Reinforced pre-cast

concrete sill, with slope to drain
16 Damp-proof membrane
17 Painted plasterboard wall
18 100 mm (4 inch) thick high-density blockwork inner leaf to cavity wall
19 Waterproof membrane
20 75 mm (3 inch) rigid insulation in 100 mm (4 inch) cavity
21 100 mm (4 inch) thick high-density blockwork outer leaf to cavity wall
22 225 mm (83/4 inch) thick roughly coursed stone cladding
23 20 mm (3/4 inch) thick timber floorboards
24 75 mm (3 inch) thick screed with underfloor heating
25 50 mm (2 inch) rigid insulation
26 150 mm (6 inch) reinforced concrete floor slab
27 Waterproof membrane

28 Compacted hardcore and blinding sand
29 Hardcore backfill to wall cavity
30 Reinforced concrete footing

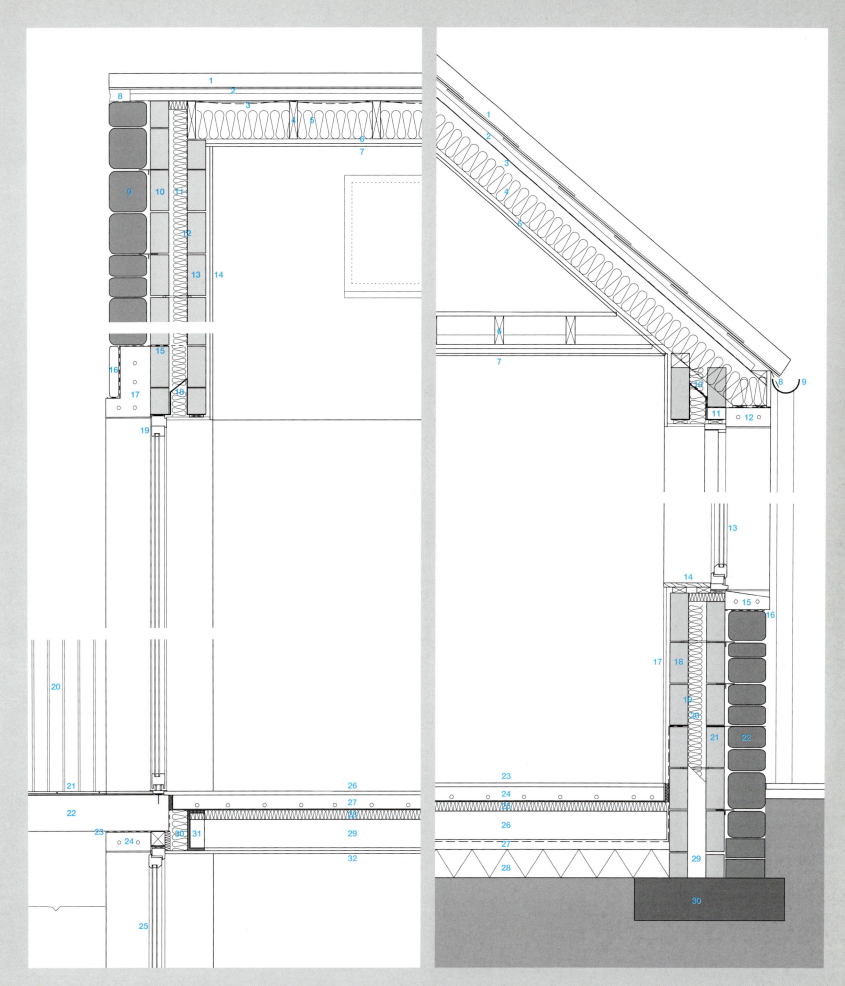

House 712
Gualba, Spain

Client
Private

Project Team
David Lorente, Josep Ricart, Xavier
Ros, Roger Tudó, Montse Fornés,
Anna Bonet

Quantity Surveyor
Iñaki González de Mendiguchia

Main Contractor
Construcciones Jufraed

Located on the outskirts of a small town in the forested mountains to the north-east of Barcelona, the house occupies a 400 square metre (4,305 square foot) triangular site. An extremely tight budget provided both programmatical and design constraints that informed the architectural solution. The clients provided a brief for a three bedroom home with the usual living, cooking and bathing facilities as well as a place to work from home. The result provided all of the required accommodation within the simplest envelope possible.

Following the geometry of the site, the triangular floor plan allows all of the spaces to have direct access to natural light and ventilation, without wasting space on circulation, which is limited to a triangular area at the centre of the plan. Material choices too have come under scrutiny. Perforated bricks are used throughout Spain as a cheap building material that is ordinarily covered up under an applied stucco finish. Instead, the ubiquitous red bricks are celebrated and used as the final finish for the exterior walls.

Other materials and construction systems were chosen so that the house could be built without any need for specialist trades or consultants. For example the glazing solution for the entire house is confined to a single model of proprietary timber-framed double doors, while the concrete floor and roof rely on standard load bearing construction. The load bearing interior walls and the ceilings are painted white. Services are treated in the same practical fashion with vertical service conduits left exposed and horizontal runs concealed in the polished concrete floor slab.

1 Each of the three facades in this triangular house is identical. Four sets of double doors on each side serve to obfuscate the interior layout but at the same time lend order to the architectural expression.
2 Ordinarily, perforated bricks are laid with the perforated face into the cavity, however here the texture of the perforated face is used as an architectural feature.
3 Specialist bricks for forming the acute angles at the corners of the traingular form were avoided. Instead, the standard bricks turn the corner in an interlocking brick dove joint.
4 The office (left) and one of the three bedrooms (right) feature white painted brickwork and a polished concrete floor slab.

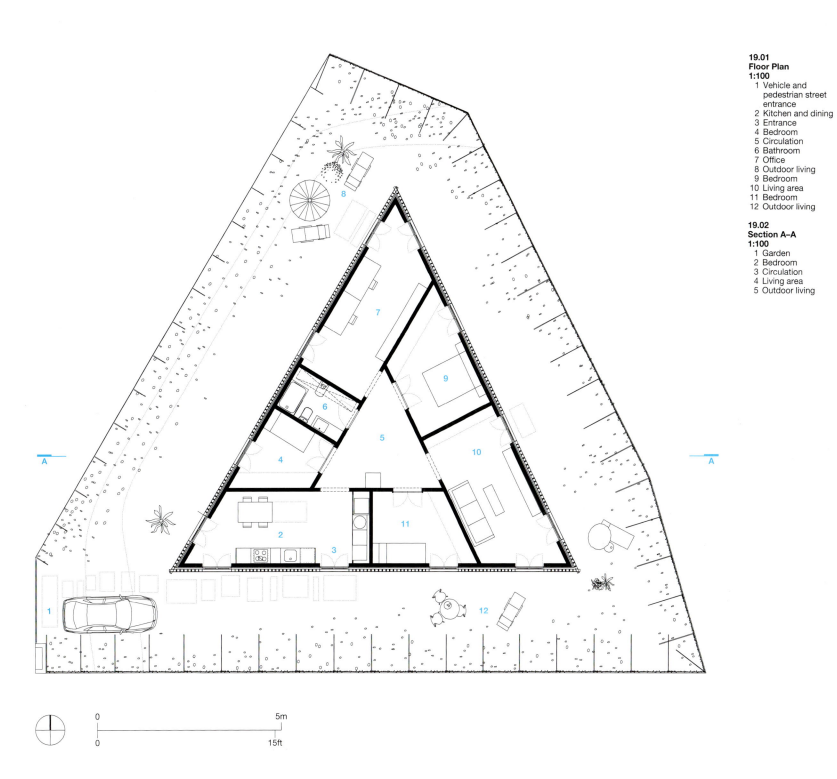

19.01
Floor Plan
1:100
1 Vehicle and
   pedestrian street
   entrance
2 Kitchen and dining
3 Entrance
4 Bedroom
5 Circulation
6 Bathroom
7 Office
8 Outdoor living
9 Bedroom
10 Living area
11 Bedroom
12 Outdoor living

19.02
Section A–A
1:100
1 Garden
2 Bedroom
3 Circulation
4 Living area
5 Outdoor living

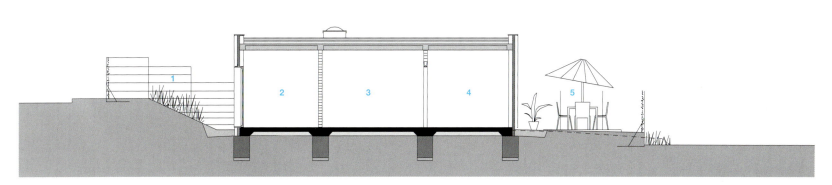

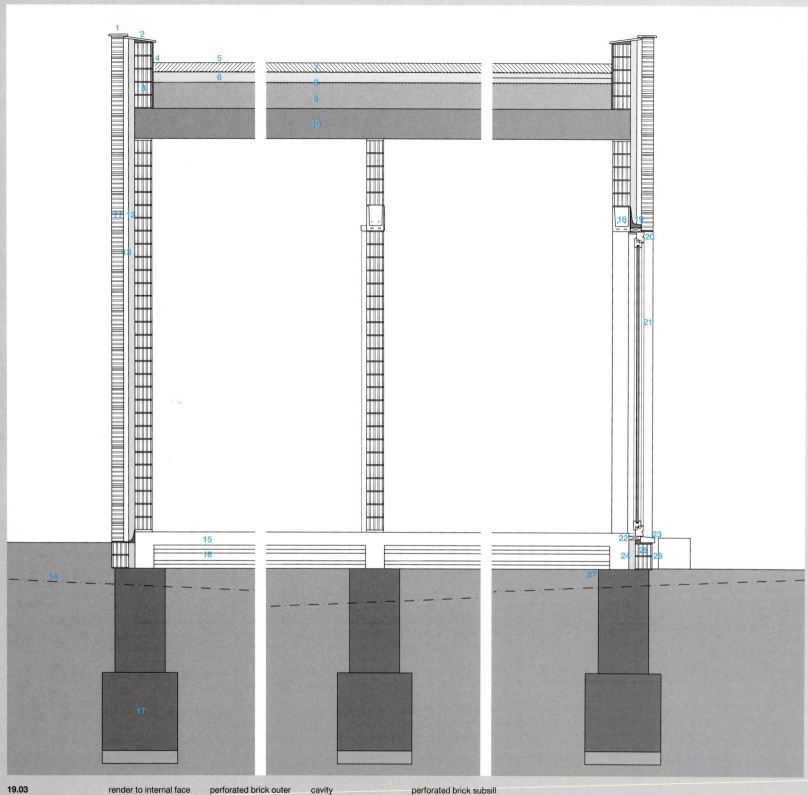

**19.03
Building Section
Detail
1:20**
1 150 x 15 mm (6 x
5/8 inch) glazed
ceramic tile parapet
capping
2 250 x 15 mm (10 x
5/8 inch) glazed
ceramic tile parapet
capping on mortar
bed, sloped to drain
towards roof
3 135 mm (5¼ inch)
structural masonry wall
4 Waterproof cement

render to internal face
of parapet
5 Gravel to flat roof
6 80 mm (3 inch) rigid
insulation
7 Felt separation
layer
8 Bituminous
waterproof membrane
9 70–200 mm (2¾–8
inch) lightweight
aerated concrete
sloped to drain
10 Reinforced
concrete roof slab
11 93 x 285 x 135 mm
(3⅝ x 11¼ x 5¼ inch)

perforated brick outer
leaf of external wall
12 50 mm (2 inch) rigid
insulation
13 42 mm (1⅝ inch)
ventilated cavity
14 Natural ground line
15 Concrete floor slab
16 50 mm (2 inch)
expanded polystyrene
insulation
17 x 600 mm (23½ x
23½ inch) concrete
footing
18 Ceramic U-channel
lintel
19 Mortar to base of

cavity
20 95 mm (3¾ inch)
painted timber reveal
21 Timber-framed
double glazed door
with 4 mm (1/10 inch)
glass, 8 mm (3/8 inch)
argon cavity and 8 mm
(3/8 inch) glass
22 92 x 30 mm (3⅝ x
1⅕ inch) timber cover
piece to subsill cavity
23 Ceramic tile sill
24 Waterproof
membrane
25 93 x 285 x 135 mm
(3⅝ x 11¼ x 5¼ inch)

perforated brick subsill
26 Waterproof and
breathable paint finish
to plinth
27 Liquid rubber
waterproofing paint to
slab and footing
junction

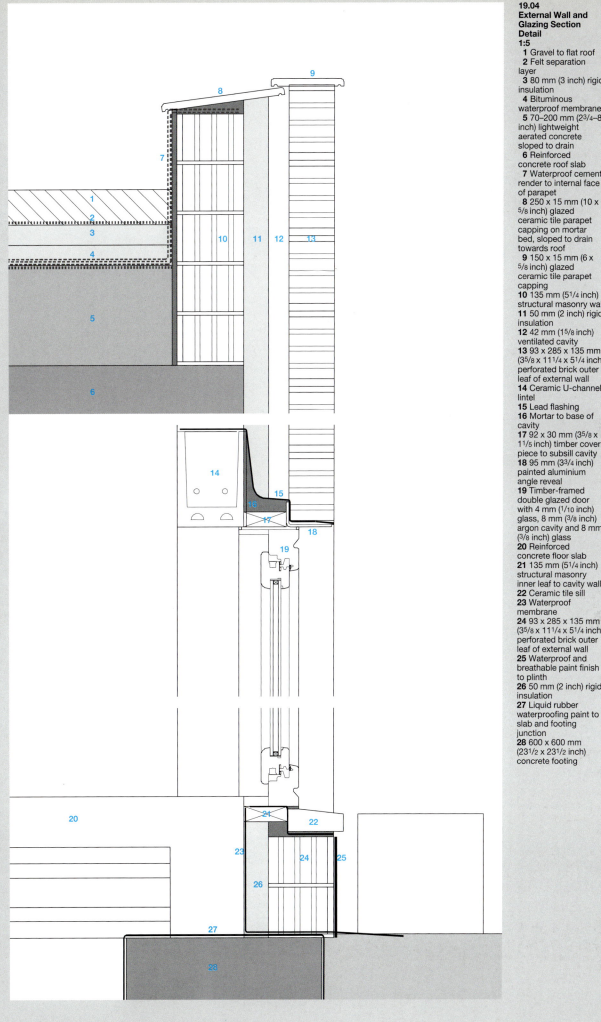

1 Gravel to flat roof
2 Felt separation
layer
3 80 mm (3 inch) rigid
insulation
4 Bituminous
waterproof membrane
5 70–200 mm (2³/₄–8
inch) lightweight
aerated concrete
sloped to drain
6 Reinforced
concrete roof slab
7 Waterproof cement
render to internal face
of parapet
8 250 x 15 mm (10 x
⁵/₈ inch) glazed
ceramic tile parapet
capping on mortar
bed, sloped to drain
towards roof
9 150 x 15 mm (6 x
⁵/₈ inch) glazed
ceramic tile parapet
capping
10 135 mm (5¹/₄ inch)
structural masonry wall
11 50 mm (2 inch) rigid
insulation
12 42 mm (1⁵/₈ inch)
ventilated cavity
13 93 x 285 x 135 mm
(3⁵/₈ x 11¹/₄ x 5¹/₄ inch)
perforated brick outer
leaf of external wall
14 Ceramic U-channel
lintel
15 Lead flashing
16 Mortar to base of
cavity
17 92 x 30 mm (3⁵/₈ x
1¹/₅ inch) timber cover
piece to subsill cavity
18 95 mm (3³/₄ inch)
painted aluminium
angle reveal
19 Timber-framed
double glazed door
with 4 mm (1/10 inch)
glass, 8 mm (3/8 inch)
argon cavity and 8 mm
(3/8 inch) glass
20 Reinforced
concrete floor slab
21 135 mm (5¹/₄ inch)
structural masonry
inner leaf to cavity wall
22 Ceramic tile sill
23 Waterproof
membrane
24 93 x 285 x 135 mm
(3⁵/₈ x 11¹/₄ x 5¹/₄ inch)
perforated brick outer
leaf of external wall
25 Waterproof and
breathable paint finish
to plinth
26 50 mm (2 inch) rigid
insulation
27 Liquid rubber
waterproofing paint to
slab and footing
junction
28 600 x 600 mm
(23¹/₂ x 23¹/₂ inch)
concrete footing

Dwelling-Workhouse HDT
Gelderland, The Netherlands

Client
HDT family

Project Team
Peter Groot, Martin-Paul Neys, Erwin
Schot, Cor Tiemens, Marten Kuijpers

Structural Engineer
Thomassen Bouwtechnisch
Adviesbureau

Main Contractor
Kuijpers Bouw Heteren

Located near Nijmegen in the far east
of the Netherlands near the German
border, the house is sited in a small
development of residential lots which
forms a transitional zone between an
industrial estate and a larger
established housing development. In
order to negotiate with the prosaic
context, the house presents itself as a
hard dark brick box that acts as an
architectural carapace. However on
closer inspection, the facades of this
villa have been gently pushed and
folded towards the centre of the form,
softening the effect of the grey brick
walls, and creating a variety of
naturally lit, intimate, domestic scale
spaces both inside and out.

Designed for a family of five, the
villa provides both private spaces and
shared spaces that offer plenty of
opportunity for family life and
communication. At the centre of a
plan split over four levels are two
courtyard patios that push into the
overall form. These are divided on the
ground floor by a circulation zone, and
on each side by a variety of stairs,
both steep and shallow, that provide
access to various levels and spaces.
Arranged on either side of this central
circulation zone, two butterfly-shaped
plan forms to the north and south
accommodate the living spaces and
bedrooms and bathrooms
respectively.

Inside, dark stone floors serenely
tumble across the various levels, with
a variety of finishes throughout the
house, including timber joinery, white
painted walls, black-framed glazing
and concrete ceiling panels providing
interest, contrast and variety to a wide
range of domestic spaces.

1 The main living
spaces are located to
the north and include a
family room and living
area with a large
corner window (centre)
and the kitchen and
dining space with its
glass concertina doors
that open directly onto
the garden (right).
2 The street facade,
constructed from dark
grey stretcher bonded
brick, is punctuated by
four carefully placed
and sized openings. A
timber garage door is
cut into the slope to
give access to the
basement level garage.
The same timber is
used for the unusually
tall front door which
hints at the double
height entrance hall
beyond.
3 The family room is
accessed via a shallow
stair from the kitchen
and dining space.
From there, a longer
stair leads up to the
mezzanine living area.
4 The dark stone
floors and black-
framed joinery contrast
with the white plaster
walls. The free flowing
sequence of spaces
are flooded with
natural light from the
courtyard windows.
5 The master bedroom
and bathroom overlook
the children's play area
and one of the
courtyards.

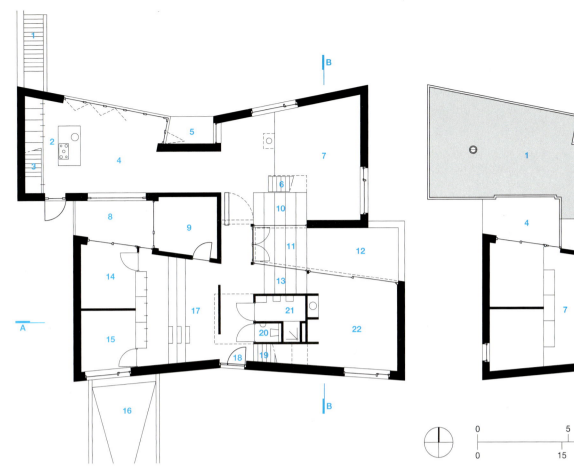

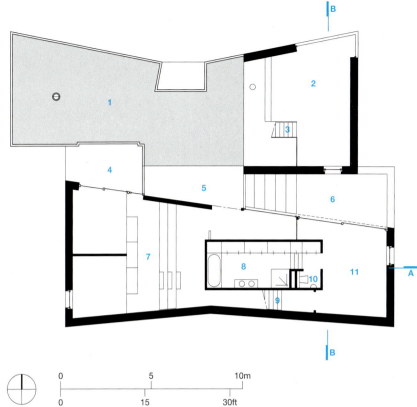

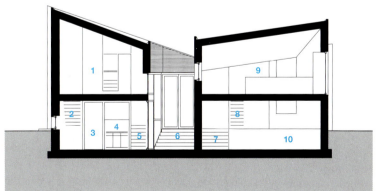

20.01 **Ground Floor Plan** **1:200** 1 Exterior stair to basement 2 Kitchen 3 Stair to basement 4 Dining area 5 Patio 6 Stair up to mezzanine living area 7 Family room 8 Patio 9 Bedroom 10 Stair down to family room 11 External stair 12 Patio	13 Stair down to office 14 Bedroom 15 Bedroom 16 External ramp to basement garage 17 Play area 18 Entrance 19 Stair up to master bedroom 20 WC 21 Bathroom 22 Office	**20.02** **First Floor Plan** **1:200** 1 Roof to kitchen and dining area 2 Mezzanine living area 3 Stair up to mezzanine living area 4 Patio below 5 Hallway below 6 Patio below 7 Play area below 8 Master bathroom 9 Stair up from entrance 10 WC 11 Master bedroom	**20.03** **Section A–A** **1:200** 1 External door to kitchen 2 Door to utility room 3 Garage 4 Bedroom 5 Play area 6 Door to bedroom 7 Entrance hall 8 Bathroom 9 Stair to office beyond 10 Office 11 Skylight 12 Master bathroom 13 Master bedroom	**20.04** **Section B–B** **1:200** 1 Master bedroom 2 Stair between entrance and master bedroom 3 Office 4 Office storage 5 Stair between entrance and office 6 Patio 7 Stair between family room and dining area 8 Stair between dining area and mezzanine living area 9 Mezzanine living area 10 Family room

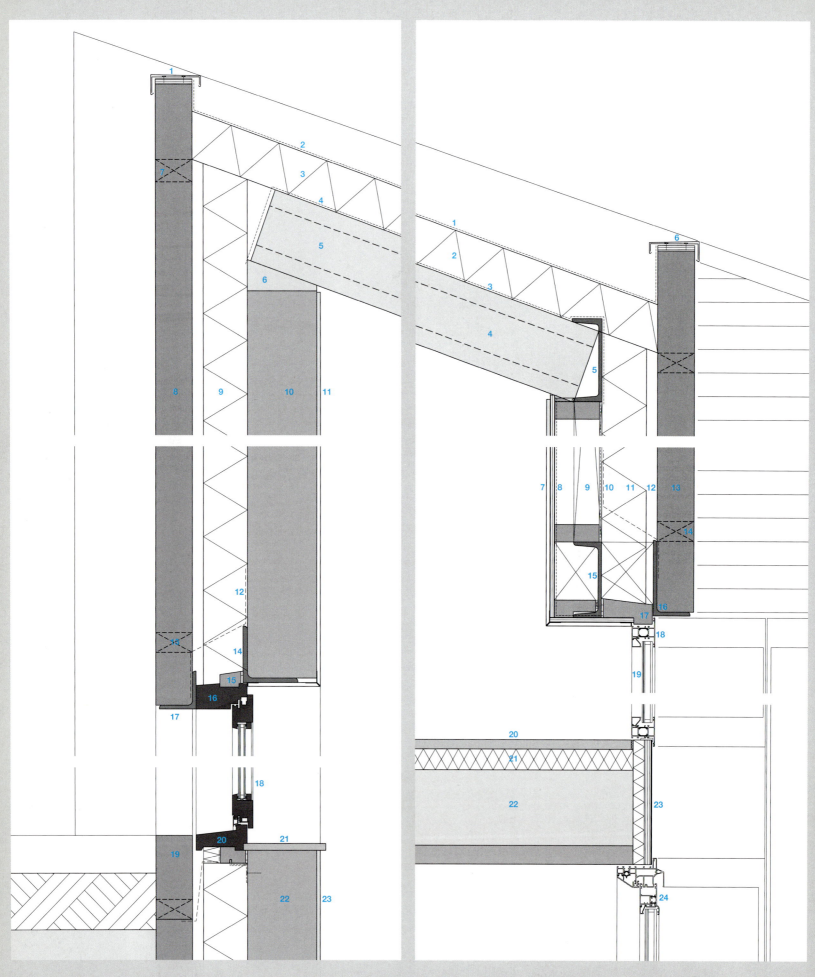

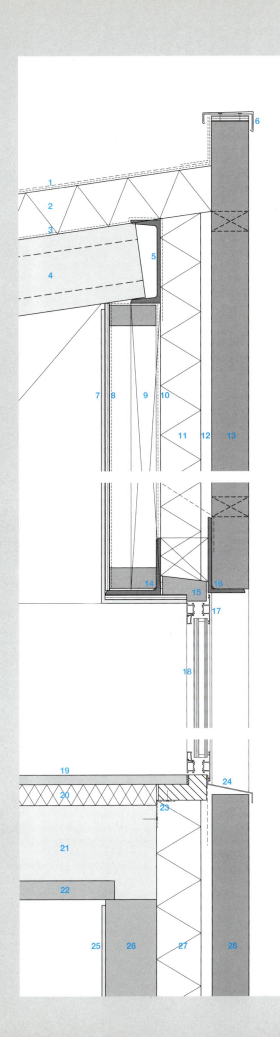

20.05
Roof and External
Wall Section Detail 1
1:10
 1 2 mm (1/8 in) thick zinc parapet capping on plywood substrate
 2 Bituminous layer
 3 120 mm (43/4 inch) thick thermal insulation
 4 Vapour barrier
 5 Pre-cast concrete ceiling panel
 6 Concrete fill between wall and ceiling
 7 Vent brick
 8 100 mm (4 inch) brickwork to external wall
 9 100 mm (4 inch) thermal insulation
 10 180 mm (7 inch) blockwork inner leaf of cavity wall
 11 Plaster finish
 12 Flashing
 13 Vent brick
 14 150 x 150 x 10 mm (6 x 6 x 3/8 inch) steel angle
 15 Timber mounting frame
 16 Black-painted timber window frame
 17 75 x 200 x 9 mm (3 x 8 x 3/8 inch) steel angle
 18 Low emissivity double glazing comprised of 8 mm (3/8 inch) glass, 20 mm (3/4 inch) argon-filled cavity and 5 mm (1/5 inch) glass
 19 100 mm (4 inch) brickwork to external wall
 20 Black-painted

timber window sill
 21 Timber window sill
 22 180 mm (7 inch) blockwork inner leaf of cavity wall
 23 Plaster finish

20.06
Roof and External
Wall Section Detail 2
1:10
 1 Bituminous layer
 2 120 mm (43/4 inch) thick thermal insulation
 3 Vapour barrier
 4 Pre-cast concrete ceiling panel
 5 Steel beam
 6 2 mm (1/8 in) thick zinc parapet capping on plywood substrate
 7 12.5 mm (1/2 inch) skimmed and painted plasterboard on plywood substrate
 8 Vapour barrier
 9 Steel wall framing
 10 Waterproof membrane
 11 100 mm (4 inch) thermal insulation
 12 30 mm (11/5 inch) ventilated cavity
 13 100 mm (4 inch) brickwork to external wall
 14 Vent brick
 15 75 x 200 x 9 mm (3 x 8 x 3/8 inch) steel angle
 16 200 x 100 x 10 mm (8 x 4 x 3/8 inch) colour coated steel angle
 17 Timber mounting frame
 18 Aluminium window frame
 19 Double glazing comprised of 8 mm

(3/8 inch) low emissivity glass, 20 mm (3/4 inch) argon-filled cavity and 5 mm (1/5 inch) laminated safety glass
 20 25 mm (1 inch) thick stone flooring
 21 Cement and sand screed
 22 250 mm (10 inch) thick reinforced concrete floor slab
 23 Insulated aluminium sandwich panel
 24 Aluminium window frame

20.07
Roof and External
Wall Section Detail 3
1:10
 1 Bituminous layer
 2 120 mm (5 inch) thick thermal insulation
 3 Vapour barrier
 4 Pre-cast concrete ceiling panel
 5 Steel beam
 6 2 mm (1/8 inch) thick zinc parapet capping on plywood substrate
 7 12.5 mm (1/2 inch) skimmed and painted plasterboard on plywood substrate
 8 Vapour barrier
 9 Steel wall framing
 10 Waterproof membrane
 11 100 mm (4 inch) thermal insulation
 12 30 mm (11/5 inch) ventilated cavity
 13 100 mm (4 inch) brickwork to external wall
 14 150 x 150 x 10 mm (6 x 6 x 3/8 inch) steel angle

 15 Timber mounting frame
 16 200 x 100 x 10 mm (8 x 4 x 3/8 inch) colour coated steel angle
 17 Aluminium window frame
 18 Double glazing comprised of 8 mm (3/8 inch) low emissivity glass, 20 mm (3/4 inch) argon-filled cavity and 5 mm (1/5 inch) laminated safety glass
 19 25 mm (1 inch) thick stone flooring
 20 Cement and sand screed
 21 250 mm (10 inch) thick reinforced concrete floor slab
 22 Pre-cast concrete ceiling panel
 23 Steel angle
 24 Folded aluminium window sill
 25 Plaster interior wall finish
 26 180 mm (7 inch) blockwork inner leaf of cavity wall
 27 100 mm (4 inch) thermal insulation
 28 100 mm (4 inch) brickwork to external wall

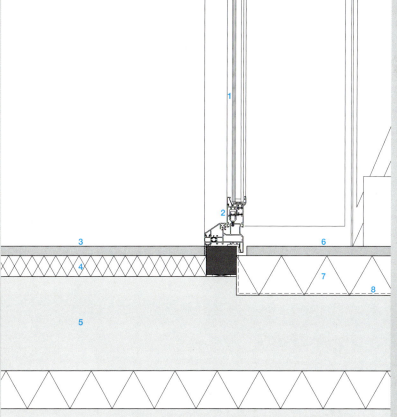

20.08
Glazed Door Sill and
Floor Slab Section
Detail
1:10
 1 Double glazing comprised of 8 mm (3/8 inch) low emissivity glass, 20mm (3/4 inch) argon-filled cavity and 5 mm (1/5 inch) laminated safety glass
 2 Aluminium window frame
 3 25 mm (1 inch) thick interior stone flooring
 4 Cement and sand screed
 5 250 mm (10 inch) thick reinforced concrete floor slab
 6 25 mm (1 inch) thick exterior stone paving
 7 Cement and sand screed
 8 Bituminous layer

Gingerbread House
London, England, UK

Client
Laura Dewe Mathews

Project Team
Laura Dewe Mathews

Structural Engineer
Tall Engineers

Main Contractor
J & C Meadows (IMS Building
Solutions)

This house, in Hackney in east London, was designed by the architect for her own occupation. The site was originally part of the garden of a Victorian end-of-terrace house which was first built on in the 1880s to create a box factory to provide wooden boxes for the perfume and jewellery industries. The site changed hands and uses a number of times over the following 100 years, before being purchased by Laura Dewe Mathews with a view to building a light and spacious one bedroom house.

The design is, in part, inspired by the old box factory, with the architect assembling yet another box inside the original envelope of the factory. The house employs a cross-laminated timber superstructure, placed inside the existing perimeter brickwork walls and rising up out of them. Externally the palette is limited to three materials – the original brickwork, rounded Western red cedar shingles and galvanized steel flashings, window frames and window reveals. This unusual mix of materials creates a frisson between the softness of handcrafted timber and the ruggedness of brick and steel which is at once charming and disarming.

To avoid impinging on neighbours' rights to light and privacy, all of the windows are placed on the north facing street facade. Additional light is brought into the house via large roof lights. Internally, the highly insulated cross-laminated timber super structure has been left exposed, the walls are lined with plywood panels, kitchen surfaces are stainless steel and the floors feature a smooth resin finish. The result is a small yet generously proportioned house that retains the simplicity and openness of the original workshop while achieving a sense of separation from the street immediately adjacent.

1 The patches of grey brick are the only remnants of the old box factory that once stood on the site. The new London stock bricks are infilled to create the new boundary wall, out of which the new shingle-clad structure rises. A timber door cut into the wall (left) provides access to the courtyard entrance.
2 The rounded shingles, known as 'fancy butts' were selected to soften the sharp silhouette of the stylized building form. Any suggestion of 'cuteness' however is balanced through the use of sharp galvanized steel window reveals.
3 The only opportunity for windows in the new house is in the street facade which looks directly onto the pavement in this busy part of east London. These two large windows bring light into the stair and first floor bedroom.
4 A large rooflight brings natural light into the kitchen and dining area which is lined with pale plywood panels and looks out onto the decked entrance courtyard.

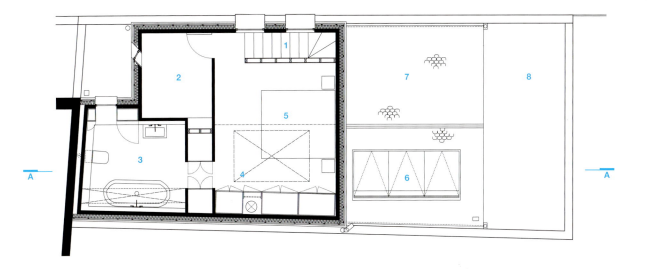

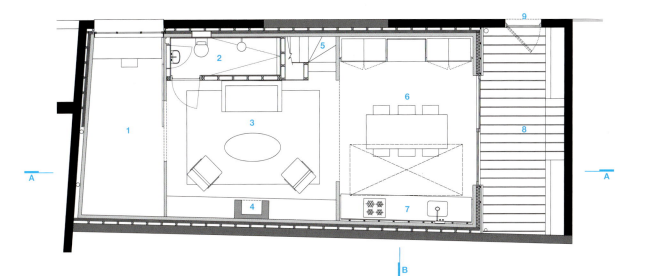

21.01
First Floor Plan
1:100
1 Stair
2 Study
3 Bathroom
4 Skylight over bedroom shown dotted
5 Bedroom
6 Skylight over kitchen
7 Kitchen to roof below
8 Courtyard below

21.02
Ground Floor Plan
1:100
1 Office
2 Shower room
3 Living area
4 Fireplace
5 Stair
6 Dining area
7 Kitchen
8 Courtyard
9 Street entrance

21.03
Section A-A
1:100
1 Bathroom
2 Bedroom
3 Office
4 Door to shower room
5 Living area
6 Stair
7 Kitchen and dining area
8 Street entrance
9 Courtyard

21.04
Section B-B
1:100
1 Wall to bedroom beyond
2 Skylight over kitchen
3 Kitchen
4 Living area beyond
5 Joinery to dining room

0   5m
0   15ft

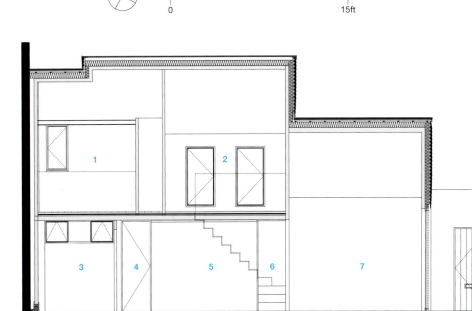

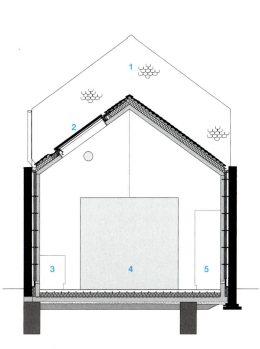

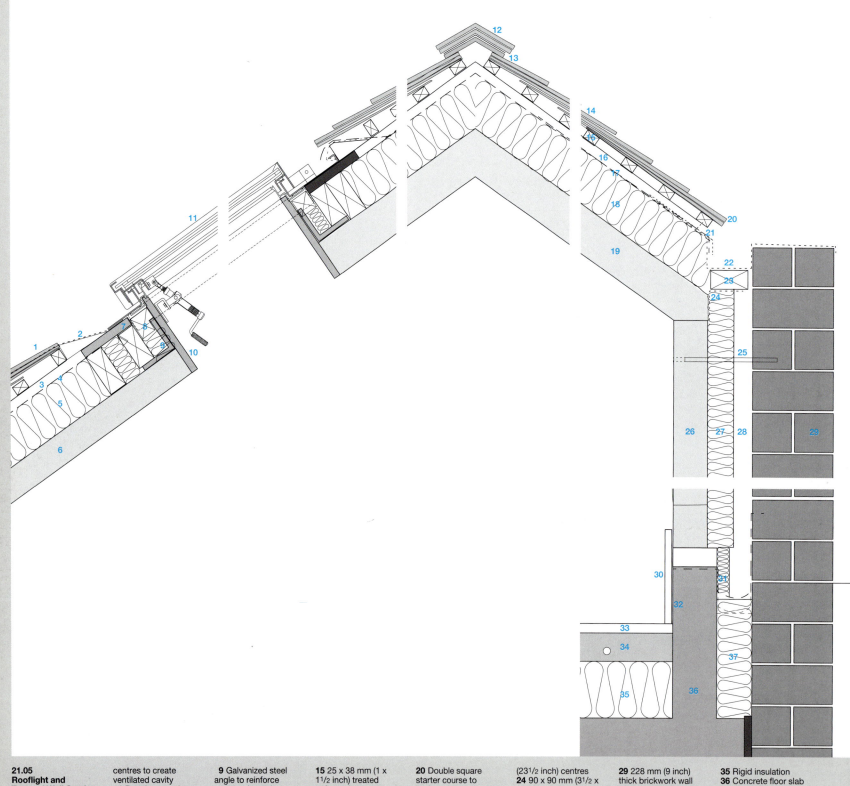

**21.05
Rooflight and
External Wall Section
Detail
1:10**

1 Round profile cedar
shingles fixed with
stainless steel nails on
25 x 38 mm (1 x 1½
inch) treated softwood
counter battens at 125
mm (5 inch) centres
2 Lead flashing
3 25 x 38 mm (1 x
1½ inch) treated
softwood battens at
400 mm (15¾ inch)

centres to create
ventilated cavity
4 Breather membrane
5 120 mm (4¾ inch)
rigid insulation
6 Solid, structural
cross-laminated timber
panel
7 25 mm (1 inch)
waterproof plywood
packer to fix roof light
frame into
8 Timber packer to
bring lining board out
to correct position,
packed with local
insulation

9 Galvanized steel
angle to reinforce
structural opening
10 Painted MDF roof
light reveal lining
11 Triple glazed,
openable roof light
12 203 mm (8 inch)
prefabricated cedar
ridge cap
13 Roll vent ventilation
system
14 Round profile cedar
shingles fixed with
stainless steel nails at
125 mm (5 inch)
centres

15 25 x 38 mm (1 x
1½ inch) treated
softwood counter
battens at 125 mm (5
inch) centres
16 25 x 38 mm (1 x
1½ inch) treated
softwood battens at
400 mm (15¾ inch)
centres to create
ventilated cavity
17 Breather membrane
18 120 mm (4¾ inch)
rigid insulation
19 Solid, structural
cross-laminated timber
panel

20 Double square
starter course to
project over gutter by
minimum of 38 mm
(1½ inch)
21 Insect mesh
22 3 mm (⅛ inch)
thick concealed
galvanized steel box
gutter with continuous
flashing and capping
to brick wall
23 Softwood batten to
support gutter fixed
back to laminated
timber with metal
brackets at 600 mm

(23½ inch) centres
24 90 x 90 mm (3½ x
3½ inch) galvanized
brackets installed at
500 mm (19¾ inch)
centres to enable fall in
gutter
25 Remedial wall tie
26 Solid, structural
cross-laminated timber
panel
27 70 mm (2¾ inch)
rigid insulation
28 50 x 50 mm (2 x 2
inch) treated softwood
battens to create
ventilated cavity

29 228 mm (9 inch)
thick brickwork wall
30 Painted softwood
skirting screw-fixed
into timber behind
31 30 mm (1⅕ inch)
rigid insulation glued to
damp-proof course
32 Damp-proof course
to form 75 mm (3 inch)
gutter in cavity
33 Power floated
concrete screed floor
finish
34 Insulated concrete
screed with underfloor
heating

35 Rigid insulation
36 Concrete floor slab
and upstand curb
37 80 mm (3 inch) rigid
insulation

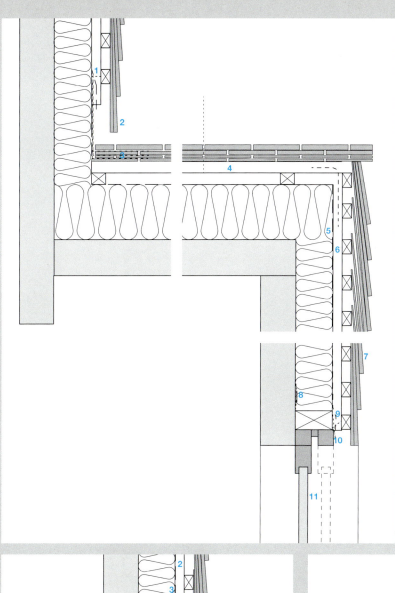

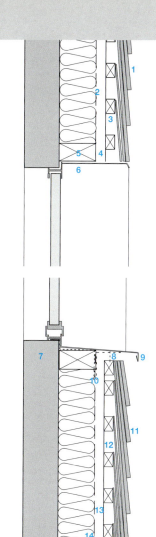

21.06
Shingle Roof and Wall Junction Section Detail
1:10
1 Insect mesh at bottom of 25 mm (1 inch) ventilated cavity
2 Double square profile starter course to sit off roof shingles by 25 mm (1 inch)
3 Metal soakers under each course of shingles
4 Ventilation to continue up into roof cavity
5 Breather membrane with bottom edge passing over top of door frame
6 25 x 38 mm (1 x 1½ inch) treated softwood battens at 400 mm (15¾ inch) centres to create ventilated cavity
7 Cedar shingles at 95 mm (3¾ inch) centres
8 Galvanized steel strap reinforcement to cross laminated timber structure
9 Damp-proof course stapled in place
10 Insect mesh at bottom of ventilated cavity
11 Powder coated aluminium-framed glass sliding doors

22.07
Window Head and Sill Section Detail to Shingle Wall
1:10
1 Cedar shingles at 95 mm (3¾ inch) centres
2 Breather membrane
3 25 x 38 mm (1 x 1½ inch) treated softwood counter battens at 95 mm (3¾ inch) centres
4 25 x 38 mm (1 x 1½ inch) treated softwood battens at 400 mm (15¾ inch) centres to create ventilated cavity
5 100 x 50 mm (4 x 2 inch) treated softwood window sub-frame
6 Galvanized steel reveal to window head
7 Solid, structural cross-laminated timber panel
8 25 mm (1 inch) ventilation gap and insect mesh
9 Custom formed 3 mm (⅛ inch) galvanized sill with drip detail to project over shingles by 38 mm (1½ inch)
10 Damp-proof course stapled in place
11 Cedar shingles at 95 mm (3¾ inch) centres
12 25 x 38 mm (1 x 1½ inch) counter battens at 95 mm (3¾ inch) centres
13 25 mm (1 inch) cavity to provide ventilation, formed by 25 x 38 mm (1 x 1½ inch) battens at 400 mm (15¾ inch) centres
14 Breather membrane

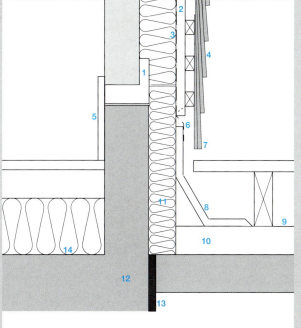

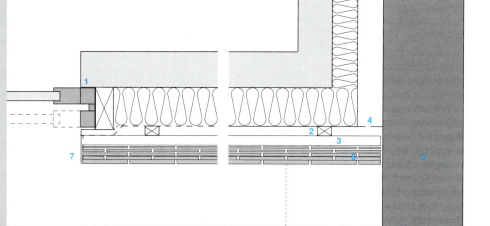

22.08
Shingle Wall and Raised Decking Section Detail
1:10
1 Timber sole plate
2 25 x 38 mm (1 x 1½ inch) battens at 400 mm (15¾ inch) centres to create ventilated cavity
3 Breather membrane
4 Round profile cedar shingles
5 Softwood skirting fitted without screws to avoid puncturing damp proof course
6 Insect mesh
7 Double starter course in square shingle to sit off decking by 30 mm (1⅕ inch) and actual drainage level by approx 185 mm (7¼ inch)
8 20 mm (¾ inch) double layer mastic asphalt with timber kerb
9 Concrete screed painted with black waterproof paint

compound
10 75 mm (3 inch) thick screed laid to fall towards yard drain
11 80 mm (3 inch) rigid insulation
12 Reinforced concrete floor slab and upstand
13 Movement joint in slab
14 Damp proof course

22.09
Door Opening in Shingle Wall Plan Detail
1:10
1 Damp proof course stapled in place
2 25 x 38 mm (1 x 1½ inch) battens at 400 mm (15¾ inch) centres to create ventilated cavity
3 25 x 38 mm (1 x 1½ inch) counter battens at 95 mm (3¾ inch) centres
4 Breather membrane

with end to turn out along brickwork with excess trimmed back after shingle installation
5 Existing 250 mm (10 inch) brickwork wall
6 Shingles fitted tight up against brickwork, with membrane sandwiched between
7 Galvanized steel sheet window reveal with shingles butted against edge

**The Shadow House
London, England, UK**

Client
Sophie Goldhill, David Liddicoat

Project Team
Sophie Goldhill, David Liddicoat

Structural Engineer
Peter Kelsey Associates

The Shadow House is located on an 83 square metre (893 square feet) scrap of land in the Camden Square conservation area, just north of Kings Cross in north London. The site was previously home to a derelict parking garage abutting a terrace of well-preserved late-Victorian houses. Previous owners had made repeated, unsuccessful attempts to secure permission to build a new house on the site, which indicated that the architect's dealings with the local planning authority were likely to be protracted and delicate.

The design was, as a result, developed in close conversation with the council's officers. The maximum envelope was determined by its relationship to its neighbours, and an early scheme for an entirely timber-built structure was put aside in favour of the conservation lobby's opinion that the house should instead reflect its tough, industrial-era context. Liddicoat & Goldhill's response was to propose a slim engineering brick with a black glazed finish. This is contrasted with sheer, frameless glazing, and with accents of white Statuarietto marble, echoing the plaster reveals and porticoes of the surrounding Victorian architecture.

The tight budget led to a small but liberating – rather than restricting – palette of primary materials. The substructure comprises reinforced concrete ground beams and piles, while the superstructure is in load bearing masonry. Larch glu-lam beams are laid directly into the brickwork to support the roof and floor structures. Floor finishes are in polished concrete, while larch panels form back-lit ceilings to the living area and bedroom, and line the deep internal reveals to form inviting window seats. The composition is completed in off-white fitted cabinetry.

1 Designed to present a sober face in this traditional London neighbourhood, none the less, a note of luxury and celebration is evident in the two slabs of bookmatched Statuarietto marble which are featured on the street facade, and also appear throughout the house as a contrast to the black brick walls.
 2 The entry door (left) and windows to the library above feature the same Statuarietto marble in their reveals. The slightly sunken snug living area (right) enjoys views into the entrance courtyard.

3 Pale polished concrete floors and untreated larch beams contrast with the dark bricks to give the interior a cool elegance. Robust light switches and power outlets, as well as their associated wiring and conduits are neatly surface mounted to the brick walls throughout the house.

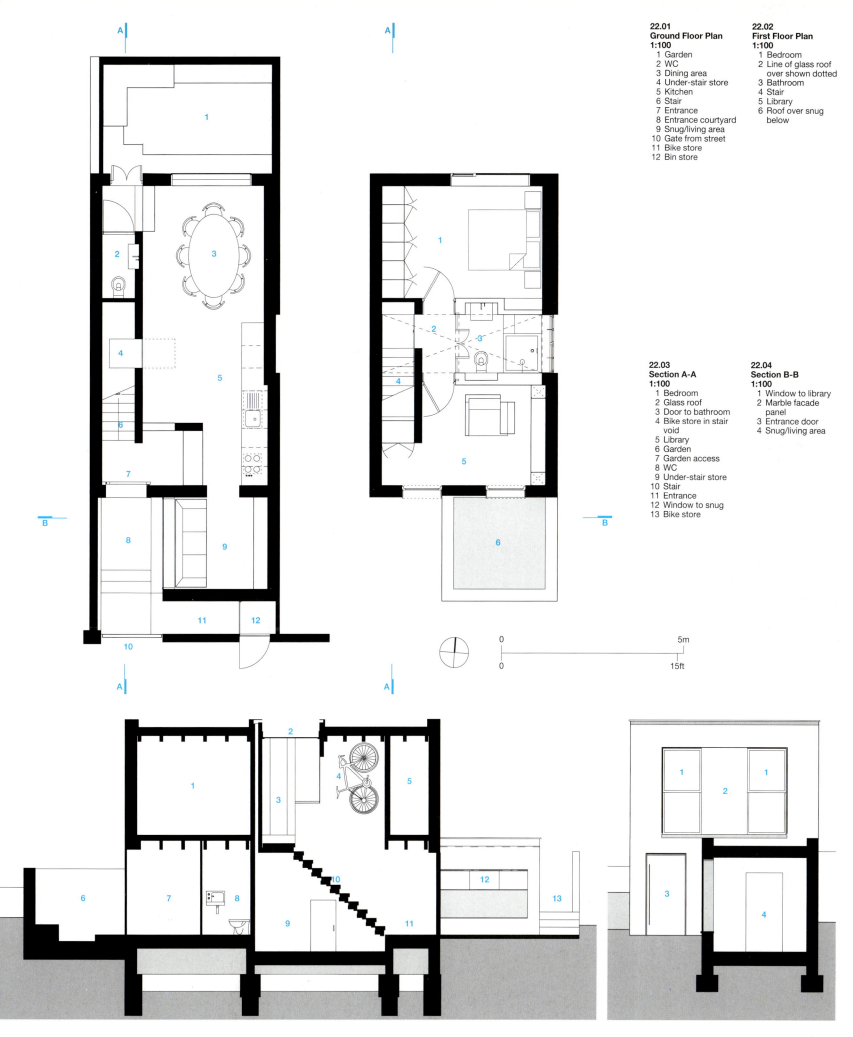

22.01
Ground Floor Plan
1:100
1 Garden
2 WC
3 Dining area
4 Under-stair store
5 Kitchen
6 Stair
7 Entrance
8 Entrance courtyard
9 Snug/living area
10 Gate from street
11 Bike store
12 Bin store

22.02
First Floor Plan
1:100
1 Bedroom
2 Line of glass roof over shown dotted
3 Bathroom
4 Stair
5 Library
6 Roof over snug below

22.03
Section A-A
1:100
1 Bedroom
2 Glass roof
3 Door to bathroom
4 Bike store in stair void
5 Library
6 Garden
7 Garden access
8 WC
9 Under-stair store
10 Stair
11 Entrance
12 Window to snug
13 Bike store

22.04
Section B-B
1:100
1 Window to library
2 Marble facade panel
3 Entrance door
4 Snug/living area

0   5m

0   15ft

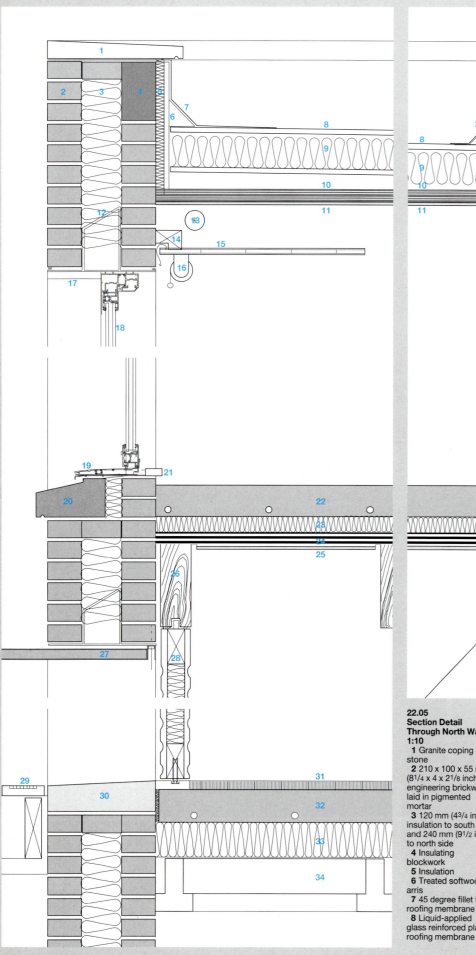

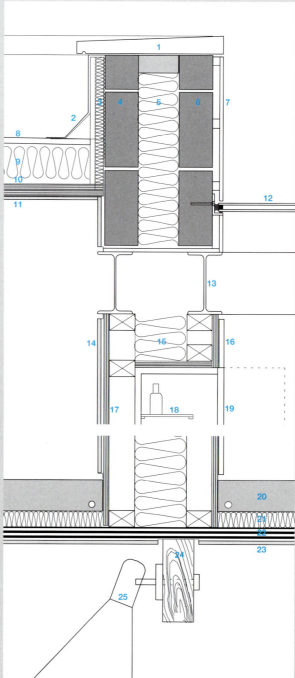

22.06
Section Detail Through Roof Parapet Wall and Skylight 1
1:10
1 Granite coping stone
2 45 degree fillet to roofing membrane
3 Insulation
4 Concrete blockwork
5 120 mm (4³/4 inch) insulation to south side and 240 mm (9¹/2 inch) to north side
6 Concrete blockwork
7 Powder-coated aluminium fascia
8 Glass reinforced plastic roofing membrane
9 Insulation
10 Waterproof plywood deck
11 Skimmed and painted plasterboard
12 Self-cleaning double glazed window unit comprised of 10 mm (³/8 inch) toughened glass, 16 mm (⁵/8 inch) argon filled cavity and 6 mm (1/4 inch) laminated glass
13 178 x 102 x 19 mm (7 x 4 x ³/4 inch) steel beam
14 Skimmed and painted plasterboard
15 Insulation
16 12 mm (1/2 inch) textured glazed ceramic tiles
17 Plywood sheathing
18 Concealed glass shelves
19 Flush mirror-fronted doors
20 Polished power-floated white concrete screed floor
21 Insulation
22 Waterproof plywood deck
23 Skimmed and painted plasterboard
24 Limewaxed 180 x 90 mm (7 x 3¹/2 inch) glu-lam larch joist
25 Spotlight

22.05
Section Detail Through North Wall
1:10
1 Granite coping stone
2 210 x 100 x 55 mm (8¹/4 x 4 x 2¹/8 inch) engineering brickwork, laid in pigmented mortar
3 120 mm (4³/4 inch) insulation to south side and 240 mm (9¹/2 inch) to north side
4 Insulating blockwork
5 Insulation
6 Treated softwood arris
7 45 degree fillet to roofing membrane
8 Liquid-applied glass reinforced plastic roofing membrane
9 Insulation
10 Waterproof plywood
11 Skimmed and painted plasterboard
12 Stainless steel insulated lintel
13 Concealed dimmable low-energy lamp
14 Timber batten, rebated to form picture rail
15 Limewaxed Siberian larch tri-ply soffit panel
16 Roller blind
17 Bookmatched white Statuarietto marble reveal lining
18 Aluminium window frame
19 Aluminium sill
20 Granite sub sill
21 Aluminium sill
22 Power-floated white concrete screed
23 Insulation
24 Waterproof plywood deck
25 Skimmed and painted plasterboard
26 Limewaxed 180 x 90 mm (7 x 3¹/2 inch) glu-lam larch joists
27 Cantilevered aluminium canopy
28 Sliding door
29 Teak decking
30 Granite sill
31 Coconut coir doormat
32 75 mm (3 inch) concrete screed
33 Insulation
34 Beam and block suspended floor deck

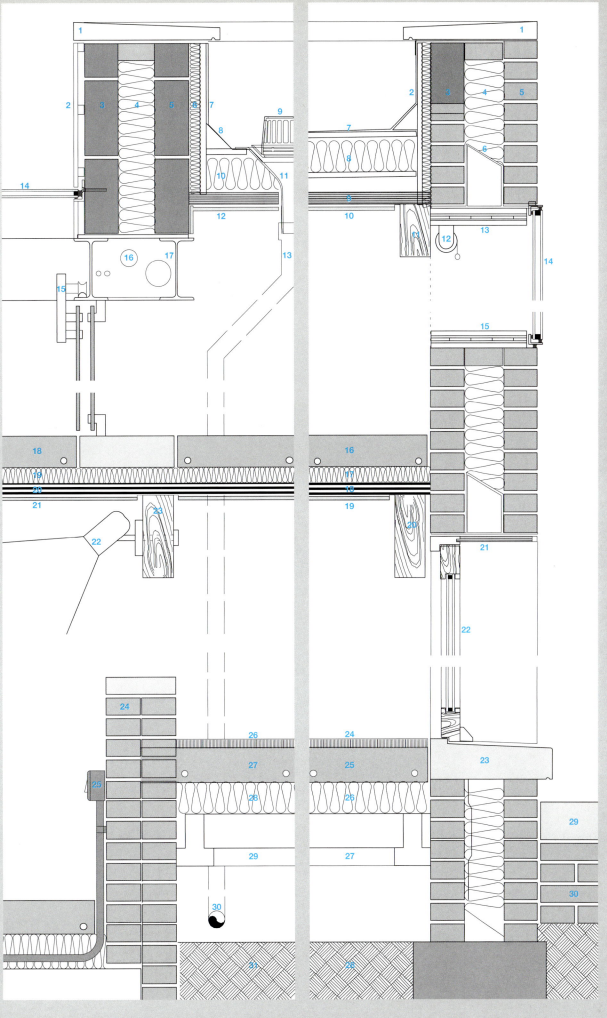

22.07
Section Detail Through Roof Parapet Wall and Skylight 2
1:10

1 Granite coping stone
2 Powder-coated aluminium fascia
3 Concrete blockwork
4 Insulation
5 Concrete blockwork
6 Insulation
7 Glass reinforced plastic roofing membrane
8 45 degree fillet to roofing membrane
9 Aluminium rainwater outlet
10 Insulation
11 Aluminium rainwater spigot
12 Skimmed and painted plasterboard
13 Line of rainwater downpipe beyond
14 Self-cleaning double glazed window unit comprised of 10 mm ($^3/_8$ inch) toughened glass, 16 mm ($^5/_8$ inch) argon filled cavity and 6 mm $^1/_4$ inch) laminated glass
15 Sliding door gear hung from steel flange
16 Services void
17 178 x 102 x 19 mm (7 x 4 x $^3/_4$ inch) steel beam
18 Polished power-floated white concrete screed
19 Insulation
20 Waterproof plywood deck
21 Skimmed and painted plasterboard
22 Spotlight
23 Limewaxed 180 x 90 mm (7 x 3$^1/_2$ inch) glu-lam larch joist
24 210 x 100 x 55 mm (8$^1/_4$ x 4 x 2$^1/_8$ inch) engineering brickwork, laid in pigmented mortar
25 Surface-mounted electrical services in galvanized conduit
26 Coconut coir doormat
27 75 mm (3 inch) concrete screed
28 Insulation
29 Beam and block suspended floor deck
30 Suspended drainage
31 Ground

22.08
North External Wall Section Detail
1:10

1 Granite coping stone
2 45 degree fillet to roofing membrane
3 Insulating blockwork
4 Insulation
5 210 x 100 x 55 mm (8$^1/_4$ x 4 x 2$^1/_8$ inch) engineering brickwork, laid in pigmented mortar
6 Stainless steel insulated lintel
7 Glass reinforced plastic roofing membrane
8 Insulation
9 Waterproof plywood deck
10 Skimmed and painted plasterboard
11 Limewaxed 180 x 90 mm (7 x 3$^1/_2$ inch) glu-lam larch joist
12 Concealed roller blind
13 Limewaxed Siberian larch tri-ply reveal board
14 Double glazed unit structurally silicone-bonded into galvanized steel angle frame
15 Limewaxed Siberian larch tri-ply sill
16 Polished power-floated white concrete screed
17 Insulation
18 Waterproof plywood deck
19 Skimmed and painted plasterboard
20 Limewaxed 180 x 90 mm (7 x 3$^1/_2$ inch) glu-lam larch joist
21 Painted plywood reveal
22 Glazed Douglas fir-framed door
23 Granite sill
24 Coconut coir doormat
25 75 mm (3 inch) concrete screed
26 Insulation
27 Beam and block suspended floor deck
28 Ground
29 Granite step
30 210 x 100 x 55 mm (8$^1/_4$ x 4 x 2$^1/_8$ inch) engineering brickwork, laid in pigmented mortar

Marsino Arquitectos Asociados

Diamante House
Diamante, Argentina

Client
Jorge Marsino and Cecilia Prado

Project Team
Jorge Marsino, María Inés Buzzoni,
Claudio Santander

Structural Engineer
Luis Gaitan

Main Contractor
Horacio Kapp

Located on top of a hill in Diamante, a
small town in north-eastern Argentina,
this red brick house has been
designed to take advantage of views
over the great Paraná River.
Constructed for a mature couple
returning to their homeland, the
requirements were for a house that
was compact, that was energy
efficient and that was sufficiently
flexible to accommodate their visiting
grown-up children.

The simple T-shaped floor plan
zones the programme into server and
served spaces, giving priority to open
views towards the river for the living
and dining area, as well as the study
and the bedrooms, all of which are
arranged along the south-west wing
– the 'top' of the T. The second wing
accommodates the functional spaces
such as the kitchen, garage and
laundry.

Beyond its main function of
providing protection, the roof defines
and generates a number of external
living and transition spaces that are
connected to the interior. These
outdoor spaces vary in character, size
and form depending on their
relationship to the interior, and to their
orientation. For example, the living
space opens on two sides, to the
north-east to an intimate, protected
dining terrace, and to the south-west
to an open terrace with views towards
the river. This same terrace narrows as
it extends towards the bedrooms and
bathrooms, where a brick screen
introduces privacy to the sleeping and
bathing spaces while maintaining
visual and physical access to the view.
Traditional red brickwork, commonly
used in vernacular buildings
throughout Argentina, is employed
here for both solid and screen walls,
creating an impression of depth,
texture, light and shade.

1 The south-west
wing of the house
features brick screens
to the living and dining
area and the study
(left) and to the
bedrooms and
bathrooms (right).
2 The house is
situated on a rocky cliff
above the Paraná River
which runs through
Brazil, Paraguay and
Argentina for some
4,880 kilometres (3,030
miles).
3 The entrance, at the
junction of the
T-shaped plan,
presents a more
private closed facade
and includes a covered
pedestrian entrance
courtyard under a
triangular roof
overhang (centre) and
direct vehicle access
to the garage (right).
4 The various screens
that define the terraces
and lend privacy and
shade to the living
spaces are
constructed from
rough red bricks laid in
alternate horizontal
and vertical courses.

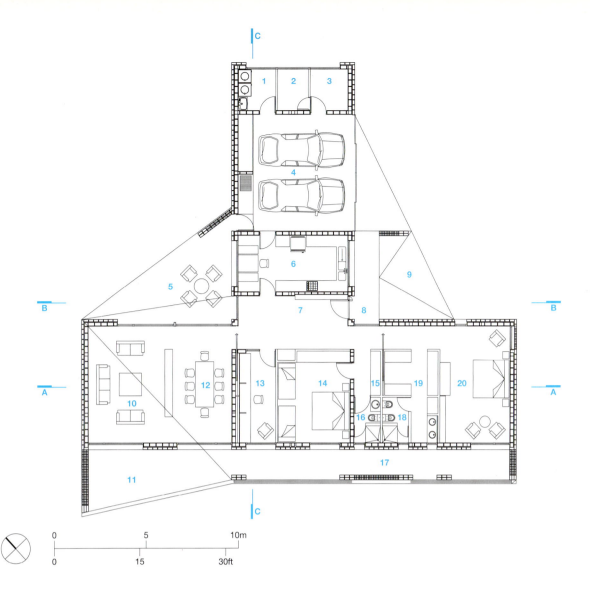

23.01
Ground Floor Plan
1:200
1 Laundry
2 Storage
3 Storage
4 Garage
5 Outdoor dining
terrace
6 Kitchen
7 Entrance hall
8 Entrance
9 Covered entrance
terrace
10 Living area
11 Terrace
12 Dining area
13 Study
14 Bedroom
15 Linen store
16 Bathroom
17 Screened terrace
18 Bathroom
19 Dressing area
20 Master bedroom

0   5   10m
0   15   30ft

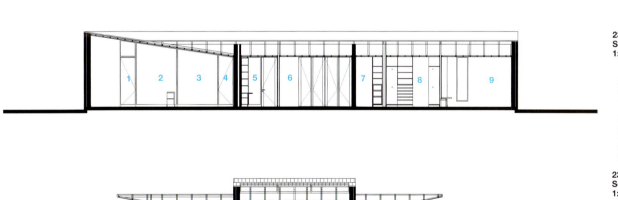

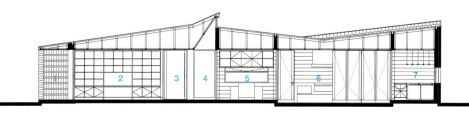

23.02
Section A–A
1:200
1 Door to dining
terrace
2 Living area
3 Dining area
4 Door to dining
terrace
5 Study
6 Bedroom
7 Linen store
8 Dressing area
9 Master bedroom

23.03
Section B–B
1:200
1 Dining terrace
2 Door to kitchen
3 Entrance hall
4 Covered entrance
terrace

23.04
Section C–C
1:200
1 Screened terrace
2 Study
3 Door to living area
4 Entrance hall
5 Kitchen
6 Garage
7 Laundry

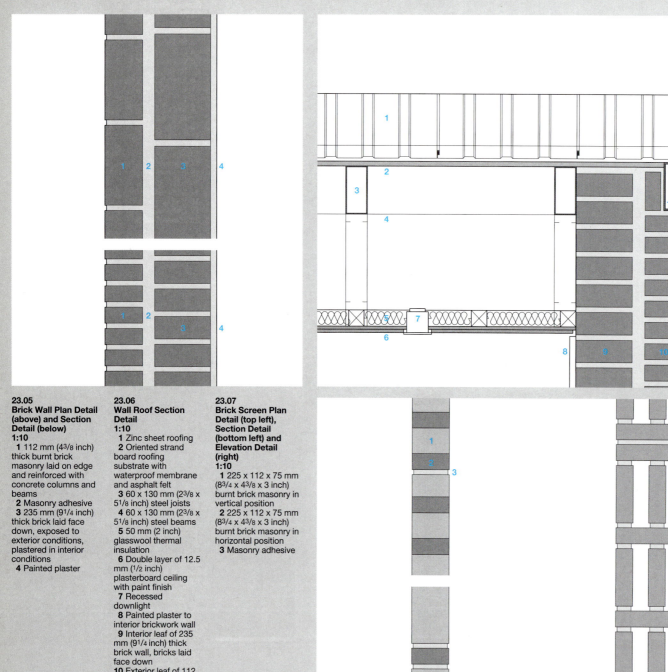

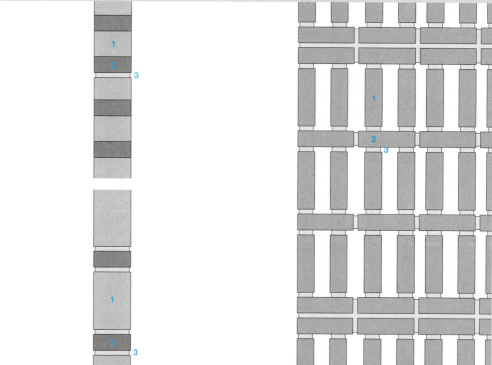

23.05
Brick Wall Plan Detail (above) and Section Detail (below)
1:10
1 112 mm (4³/8 inch) thick burnt brick masonry laid on edge and reinforced with concrete columns and beams
2 Masonry adhesive
3 235 mm (9¹/4 inch) thick brick laid face down, exposed to exterior conditions, plastered in interior conditions
4 Painted plaster

23.06
Wall Roof Section Detail
1:10
1 Zinc sheet roofing
2 Oriented strand board roofing substrate with waterproof membrane and asphalt felt
3 60 x 130 mm (2³/8 x 5¹/8 inch) steel joists
4 60 x 130 mm (2³/8 x 5¹/8 inch) steel beams
5 50 mm (2 inch) glasswool thermal insulation
6 Double layer of 12.5 mm (¹/2 inch) plasterboard ceiling with paint finish
7 Recessed downlight
8 Painted plaster to interior brickwork wall
9 Interior leaf of 235 mm (9¹/4 inch) thick brick wall, bricks laid face down
10 Exterior leaf of 112 mm (4³/8 inch) thick burnt brick masonry wall, bricks laid on edge and reinforced with concrete columns and beams
11 70 x 180 mm (2³/4 x 7 inch) steel C-beam with black paint finish

23.07
Brick Screen Plan Detail (top left), Section Detail (bottom left) and Elevation Detail (right)
1:10
1 225 x 112 x 75 mm (8³/4 x 4³/8 x 3 inch) burnt brick masonry in vertical position
2 225 x 112 x 75 mm (8³/4 x 4³/8 x 3 inch) burnt brick masonry in horizontal position
3 Masonry adhesive

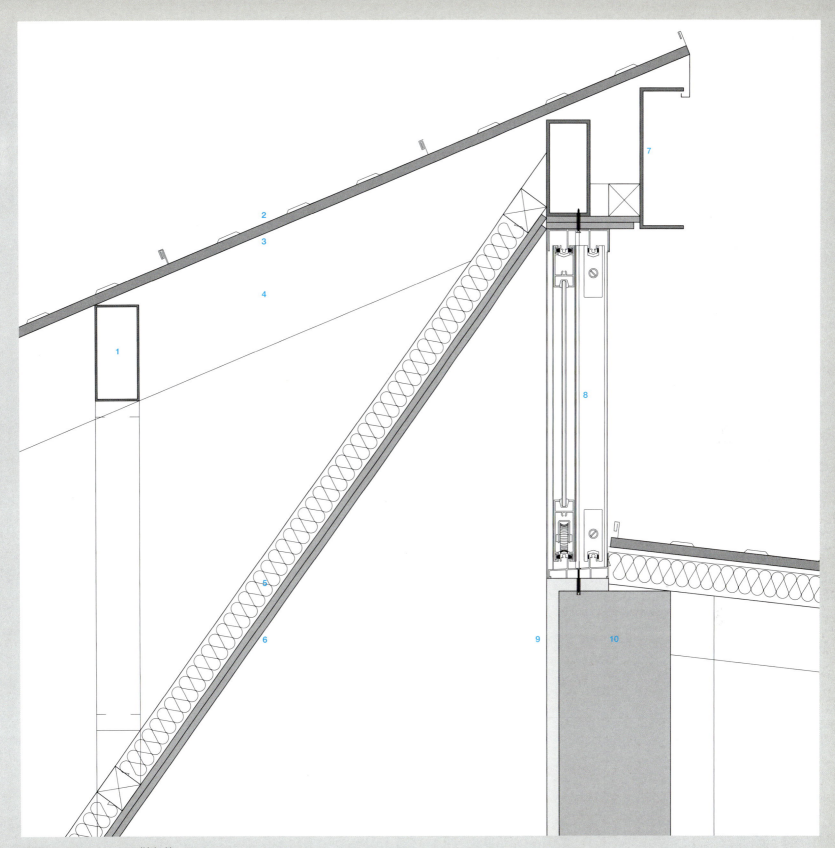

23.08
Clerestory Window
Section Detail
1:5
1 60 x 130 mm (2³/₈ x
5¹/₈ inch) steel joists
2 Zinc sheet roofing
3 Oriented strand
board roofing
substrate with
waterproof membrane
and asphalt felt
4 60 x 130 mm (2³/₈ x
5¹/₈ inch) steel beam
5 50 mm (2 inch)
glasswool thermal
insulation
6 Double layer of 12.5

mm (¹/₂ inch)
plasterboard ceiling
with paint finish
7 70 x 180 mm (2³/₄ x
7 inch) steel C-beam
with black paint finish
8 Anodized
aluminium-framed
double glazed sliding
clerestory window
9 Painted plaster to
interior wall
10 Brickwork wall

House Van Aelten-Oosterlinck
Opwijk, The Netherlands

Client
Private

Project Team
Marie-José Van Hee, Mattias
Deboutte, Wim Voorspoels, Dietlinde
Verhaeghe

Structural Engineer
BAS – Dirk Jaspaert

Main Contractor
Fiebra-Maes

The house is located in the town of
Opwijk, 24 kilometres (15 miles) north
of Brussels. The project comprises a
house for a family with three children
as well as spaces for a child
psychiatry practice run by one of the
clients. The building faces onto a
small square in the centre of town and
obliquely onto a winding road to the
south. The massing allows the spire of
the small church of St Paul's to be
seen in the distance.

The brick facade facing the square
is modulated by a partially recessed,
partially flush window that brings light
into the consulting room on the
ground floor, a deep recessed terrace
that is accessed from a bathroom and
the laundry, and a cantilevered glazed
volume on the first floor that contains
a landing to the internal stair. This four
storey composition that fills the
south-east end of the site is both civic
and abstract in nature, with the size
ameliorated by a mansard roof and a
concealed basement level.

The house is entered from the south
through a tall lobby that leads to the
consulting rooms and through a
separate opening to the house itself.
From here, an oversized circulatory
zone acts as a play space for the
children. The dining and kitchen
spaces are located in a wedge-
shaped space that is lit from above by
six circular skylights in the concrete
roof. This extends into a monopitch-
roofed living area that leads to both
the internal courtyard to the south and
the garden to the west.

The bedrooms and bathrooms
rotate around the upper storeys above
the practice consulting rooms and are
separated vertically by half-levels
reached by a timber stair that winds
through the house. Details and
materials throughout are simple and
robust, including the characteristic
brickwork which exemplifies the
straightforward simplicity of the
architectural expression.

1 The four openings to
the street facade bring
light into the bathroom
on the second floor
(top), the stair (left), the
bathroom and laundry
(right) and to the
psychiatry consulting

rooms on the ground
floor (bottom).
2 The west facade is
punctuated by bands
of windows to the
practice waiting room
on the ground floor
and bedrooms above.

The entrance to both
the consulting rooms
and the house is
protected by the roof
of the carport (left).
3 At the centre of the
house, a courtyard is
the focus of the living,

dining and kitchen
spaces (left) and the
children's play area
(right).
4 A small inner
courtyard acts as a
buffer zone between
the children's play area

and the office at the
front of the building.

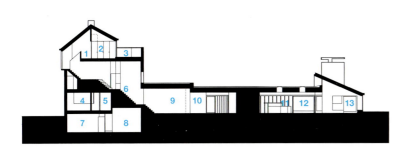

24.01
Section A–A
1:500
1 Stair
2 Bedroom
3 Terrace
4 Practice room
5 Practice store
6 Stair
7 Recreation room
8 Basement store
9 Entrance
10 Play area
11 Kitchen
12 Dining room
13 Living area

24.02
Second Floor Plan
1:200
1 Terrace
2 Bedroom
3 Bedroom
4 Stair
5 Bathroom
6 Void over terrace

24.03
First Floor Plan
1:200
1 Terrace
2 Linen store
3 Laundry
4 Terrace
5 Stair
6 Technical room
7 Bedroom
8 WC
9 Bathroom

24.04
Ground Floor Plan
1:200
1 Garden
2 Living area
3 Circulation
4 WC
5 Bathroom
6 Garden store
7 Dining area
8 Kitchen
9 Pantry
10 Courtyard
11 Play area
12 Courtyard
13 Office
14 Practice store
15 Practice room
16 House entrance
17 Stair to upper levels
18 Stair to basement
19 WC
20 Practice entrance
21 Practice waiting room
22 Bike store
23 Parking

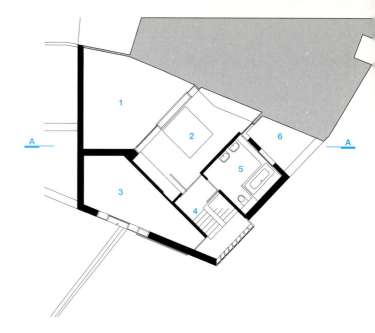

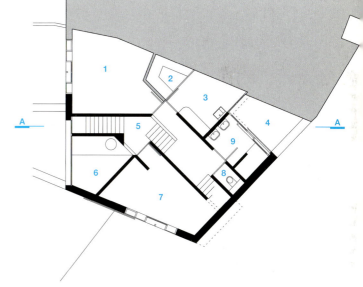

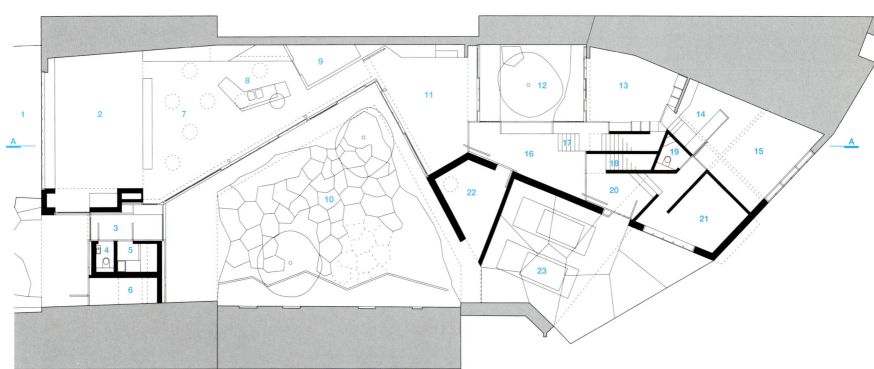

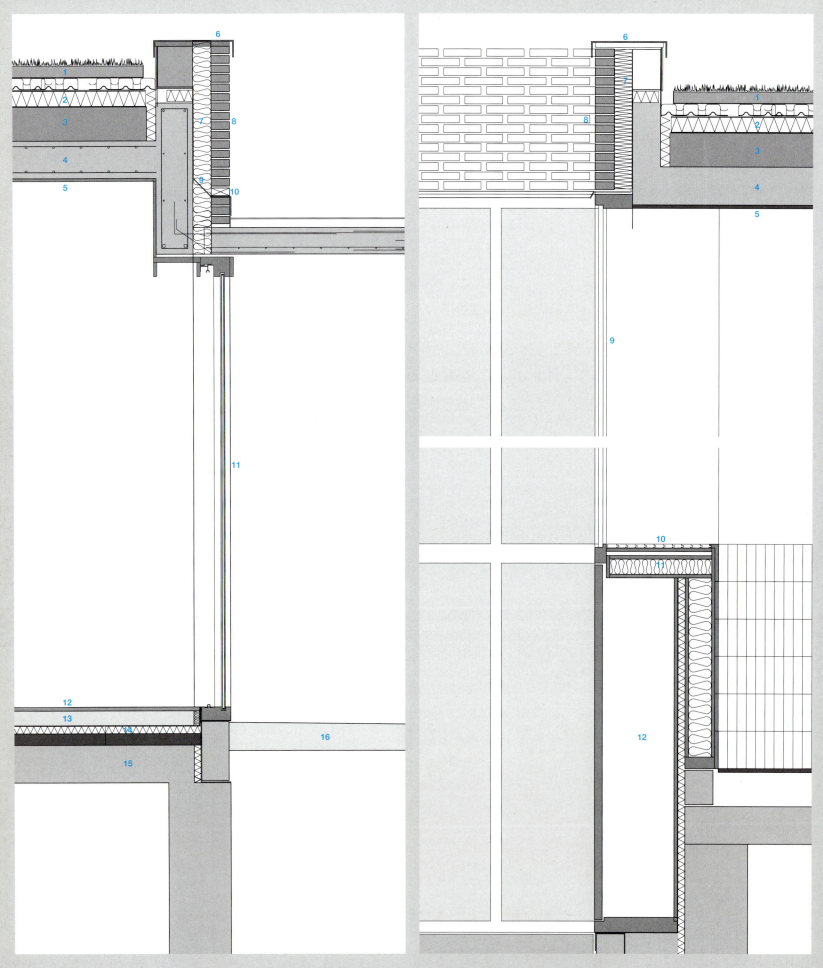

24.05
**Typical Wall Section
Detail 1**
1:20
1 210 mm (8¼ inch)
green roof comprised
of planted layer,
drainage medium and
geotextile membrane
2 Rigid thermal
insulation
3 180 mm (7 inch)
lean concrete laid with
2% slope to drain
4 200 mm (8 inch)
reinforced concrete
roof slab and 400 mm
(15¾ inch) downstand
beam
5 Painted
plasterboard ceiling
6 Folded stainless
steel capping to 400
mm (15¾ inch) deep
parapet
7 Thermal insulation
8 Brickwork to
external wall
9 Flashing
10 Ventilation brick
11 Timber framed
double glazed door
12 Timber floorboards
13 Concrete screed
14 Rigid insulation
15 Reinforced
concrete floor slab
16 Concrete paving

24.06
**Typical Wall Section
Detail 2**
1:20
1 210 mm (8¼ inch)
green roof comprised
of planted layer,
drainage medium and
geotextile membrane
2 Rigid thermal
insulation
3 180 mm (7 inch)
lean concrete laid with
2% slope to drain
4 200 mm (8 inch)
reinforced concrete
roof slab and 400 mm
(15¾ inch) downstand
beam
5 Painted
plasterboard ceiling
6 Folded stainless
steel capping to 400
mm (15¾ inch) deep
parapet
7 Thermal insulation
8 Brickwork to
external wall
9 Timber framed
double glazed door
10 Timber tongue-and-
groove cladding
11 Thermal insulation
12 Basement
ventilation void

24.07
**Roof and Skylight
Section Detail**
1:20
1 Folded stainless
steel eaves capping
2 Timber shingles
3 Steel beam
4 Timber joists
5 Ceramic tiles to
eaves soffit
6 External leaf of
brick cavity wall
7 Internal leaf of
concrete block cavity
wall
8 Ventilation brick
9 Flashing
10 Thermal insulation
11 Skylight
12 Concealed lighting
fixture
13 200 mm (8 inch)
reinforced concrete
roof slab and 400 mm
(15¾ inch) upstand
beam
14 Sliding timber
shutter
15 Timber framed
double glazed sliding
door
16 Thermal insulation
17 Concrete blockwork
wall
18 Painted
plasterboard wall lining
19 Concrete screed
exterior floor surface
20 Timber floorboards

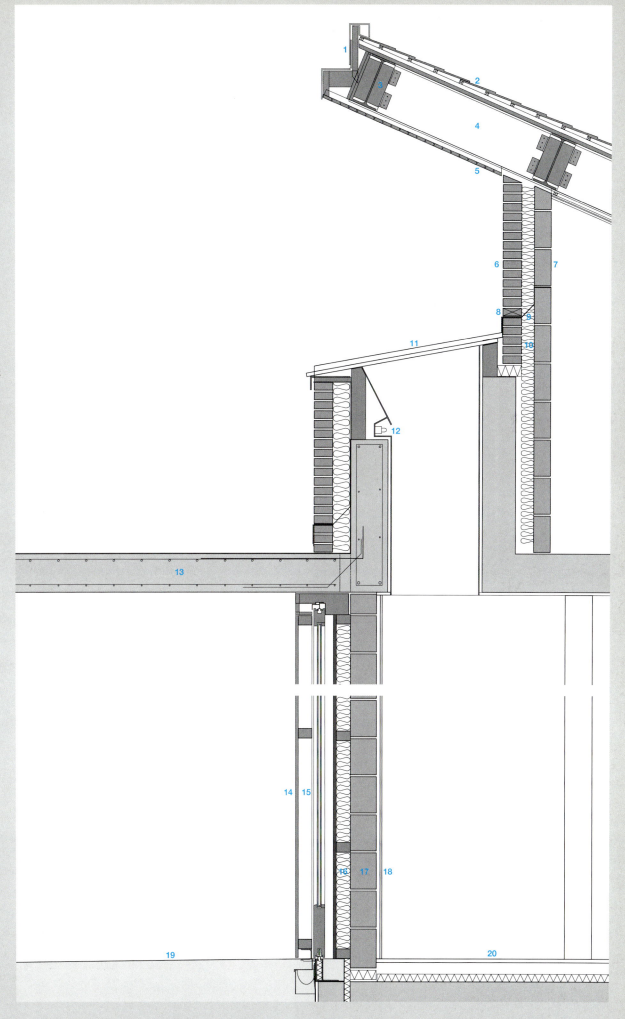

**V35K18 House
Leiden, The Netherlands**

Client
Martijn van Veelen

Project Team
Ralf Pasel, Frederik Künzel

Structural Engineer
Broersma Buro

This impressively compact house is one of 670 new houses that form part of MVRDV architect's masterplan for Leiden. Half of the new housing is being developed within the framework of private client agreements, including V35K18 House, and ten other houses also designed by Pasel Künzel, with the rest devoted to public housing. Set on the corner of a block of 18 houses, the residence provides a striking 'cornerstone' anchor to this newly developed urban area.

The residence is separated from the neighbouring house by a narrow three-storey high glazed slot which encloses a vertical and horizontal circulation zone extending the full height of the building. The timber staircase reaches from the entrance on the ground level right up to the second floor, with landings leading off into each level. The accommodation is arranged over three floors with the basement containing an office, storage and undercover parking, the first floor an open plan kitchen complete with a window looking into the stair void, as well as living and dining spaces. The top floor contains two double bedrooms with a shared bathroom separating them at the centre of the plan.

The exterior's distinct matt black brick facade is constructed from elegantly proportioned Hilversum bricks, bonded with black mortar. The flat facades are punctuated by large white framed floor to ceiling windows mounted flush with the brick facade. The windows are comprised of large panes of fixed glazing and solid openable ventilation panels. The interior features all-white walls and ceilings with a pale grey resin floor and pale oak for the staircase.

1 The black brick rectangular prism acts as a 'bookend' to the urban block. To the rear of the site, a simple timber screen conceals a courtyard garden and parking.
2 The large windows in the south facade provide light and ventilation to the two bedrooms on the top floor, the living and dining spaces on the first floor and the office on the ground floor.
3 The dining area on the first floor features glazing to the north and east facades.
4 The timber stair cascades in a single rise from the bedrooms on the top floor (right) all the way to the entrance on the ground floor, with a landing on the first floor opening onto the living spaces. Full height glazing to both ends of the stairwell bring light into the centre of the house.

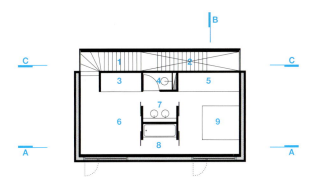

25.01
Second Floor Plan
1:200
1 Stair
2 Void over stair
  below
3 Wardrobe
4 WC
5 Wardrobe
6 Bedroom
7 Basins
8 Bath
9 Bedroom

25.02
First Floor Plan
1:200
1 Under-stair storage
2 Audio-visual
  cupboard
3 Living area
4 Stair
5 Void over entrance
  below
6 Kitchen
7 Dining area

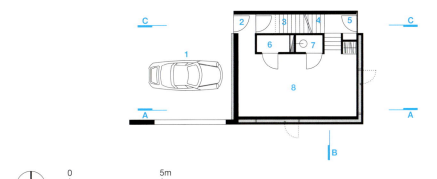

25.03
Ground Floor Plan
1:200
1 Parking
2 Entrance
3 Under-stair storage
4 Stair
5 Entrance
6 Storage
7 WC
8 Office

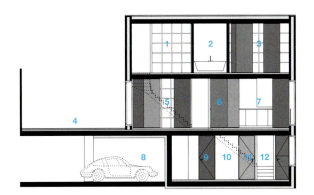
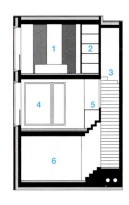
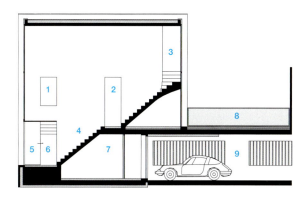

25.04
Section A–A
1:200
1 Bedroom
2 Bathroom
3 Bedroom
4 Courtyard
5 Living area
6 Dining area
7 Kitchen
8 Parking
9 Door to storage
10 Office
11 Door to WC
12 Stair

25.05
Section B–B
1:200
1 Bedroom
2 Wardrobe
3 Stair
4 Dining area
5 Kitchen
6 Office

25.06
Section C–C
1:200
1 Window to kitchen
2 Door to living area
3 Door to bedroom
4 Stair
5 Entrance
6 Door to office
7 Under-stair storage
8 Courtyard
9 Parking

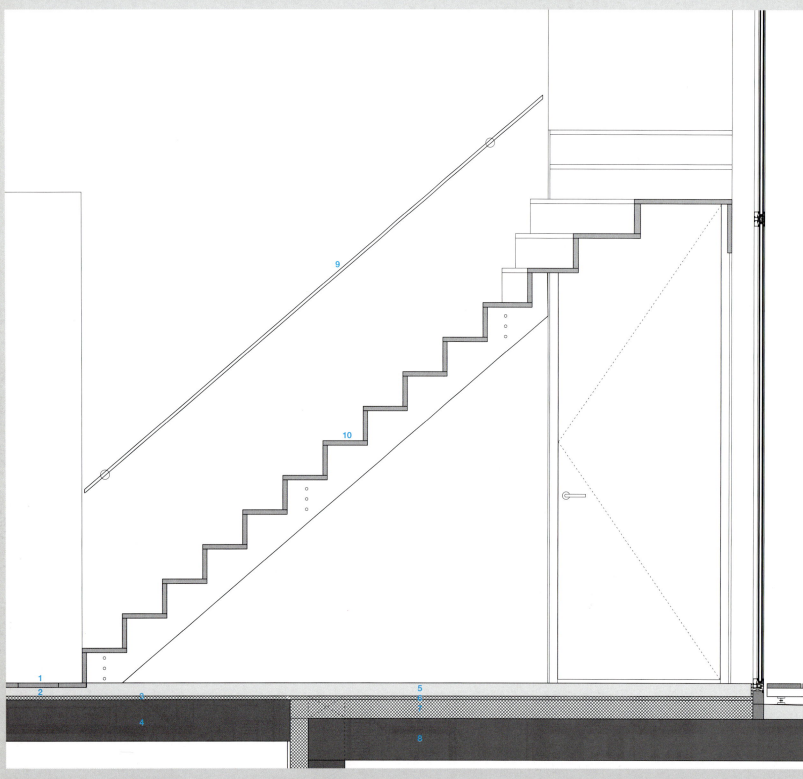

25.07
Staircase Section
Detail
1:20
 1 24 mm (⁷/8 inch)
thick timber parquet
flooring
 2 46 mm (1³/4 inch)
concrete screed
 3 20 mm (³/4 inch)
thick rigid insulation
with underfloor heating
 4 220 mm (8¹/2 inch)
reinforced concrete
floor slab
 5 70 mm (2³/4 inch)
concrete screed
 6 20 mm (³/4 inch)

thick rigid insulation
 7 100 mm (4 inch)
insulation
 8 220 mm (8¹/2 inch)
reinforced concrete
floor slab
 9 Stainless steel hand
rail
 10 24 mm (⁷/8 inch)
thick laminated oak
treads and risers
mounted on 10 mm
(³/8 inch) felt

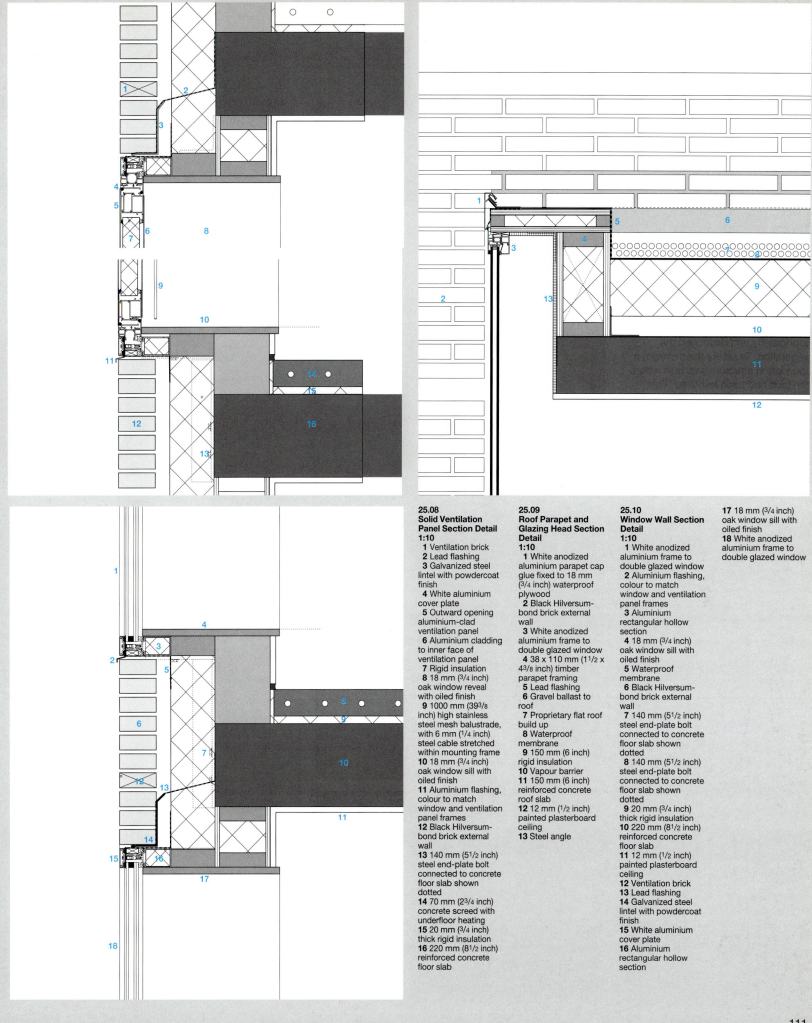

25.08
Solid Ventilation
Panel Section Detail
1:10
 1 Ventilation brick
 2 Lead flashing
 3 Galvanized steel
 lintel with powdercoat
 finish
 4 White aluminium
 cover plate
 5 Outward opening
 aluminium-clad
 ventilation panel
 6 Aluminium cladding
 to inner face of
 ventilation panel
 7 Rigid insulation
 8 18 mm (³/4 inch)
 oak window reveal
 with oiled finish
 9 1000 mm (39³/8
 inch) high stainless
 steel mesh balustrade,
 with 6 mm (1/4 inch)
 steel cable stretched
 within mounting frame
 10 18 mm (³/4 inch)
 oak window sill with
 oiled finish
 11 Aluminium flashing,
 colour to match
 window and ventilation
 panel frames
 12 Black Hilversum-
 bond brick external
 wall
 13 140 mm (5¹/2 inch)
 steel end-plate bolt
 connected to concrete
 floor slab shown
 dotted
 14 70 mm (2³/4 inch)
 concrete screed with
 underfloor heating
 15 20 mm (³/4 inch)
 thick rigid insulation
 16 220 mm (8¹/2 inch)
 reinforced concrete
 floor slab

25.09
Roof Parapet and
Glazing Head Section
Detail
1:10
 1 White anodized
 aluminium parapet cap
 glue fixed to 18 mm
 (³/4 inch) waterproof
 plywood
 2 Black Hilversum-
 bond brick external
 wall
 3 White anodized
 aluminium frame to
 double glazed window
 4 38 x 110 mm (1¹/2 x
 4³/8 inch) timber
 parapet framing
 5 Lead flashing
 6 Gravel ballast to
 roof
 7 Proprietary flat roof
 build up
 8 Waterproof
 membrane
 9 150 mm (6 inch)
 rigid insulation
 10 Vapour barrier
 11 150 mm (6 inch)
 reinforced concrete
 roof slab
 12 12 mm (1/2 inch)
 painted plasterboard
 ceiling
 13 Steel angle

25.10
Window Wall Section
Detail
1:10
 1 White anodized
 aluminium frame to
 double glazed window
 2 Aluminium flashing,
 colour to match
 window and ventilation
 panel frames
 3 Aluminium
 rectangular hollow
 section
 4 18 mm (³/4 inch)
 oak window sill with
 oiled finish
 5 Waterproof
 membrane
 6 Black Hilversum-
 bond brick external
 wall
 7 140 mm (5¹/2 inch)
 steel end-plate bolt
 connected to concrete
 floor slab shown
 dotted
 8 140 mm (5¹/2 inch)
 steel end-plate bolt
 connected to concrete
 floor slab shown
 dotted
 9 20 mm (³/4 inch)
 thick rigid insulation
 10 220 mm (8¹/2 inch)
 reinforced concrete
 floor slab
 11 12 mm (1/2 inch)
 painted plasterboard
 ceiling
 12 Ventilation brick
 13 Lead flashing
 14 Galvanized steel
 lintel with powdercoat
 finish
 15 White aluminium
 cover plate
 16 Aluminium
 rectangular hollow
 section

 17 18 mm (³/4 inch)
 oak window sill with
 oiled finish
 18 White anodized
 aluminium frame to
 double glazed window

**House in Figueiral
Benedita, Portugal**

Client
Luísa Fonseca Jorge

Project Team
Pedro Fonseca Jorge

Structural Engineer
Cristiano Vicente Isabel

Main Contractor
Manuel Mendes

This house in western Portugal, in a small town north of Lisbon, was designed for a site that required rehabilitation due to its previous incarnation as part of a small quarry which had created gouges in the topography and destroyed the vegetation. To rectify the damage, a foundation structure was built where the land had been removed. This structure, part retaining wall, part red brick facade, negotiates the differences in level across the site and introduces the lower level of accommodation which houses the private spaces including three bedrooms, two bathrooms as well as wardrobe and storage areas built along the retaining wall. A red brick wall with windows to the bedrooms and bathrooms faces out across the garden and beyond to the pine and cork trees in the nearby forest.

The communal spaces are placed on top of the foundation structure and are deconstructed into several discrete, but internally contiguous, volumes in order to manipulate the building's scale. Designed to reflect the region's vernacular architecture of simple gabled rural buildings, these volumes contain a garage, an office and the living areas. Raised above the original ground line, these spaces open up to a new garden, partly planted on the roof of the lower floor.

The brick walled and zinc roofed volumes have been placed to ensure appropriate levels of privacy and to introduce an experiential sequence to the house. The garage and the office are placed at the north-west end of the building and together create a protective space for the entrance. Once inside, the living room is at the centre of the plan, with the kitchen, dining and utility room on the other side of the central stair which leads down to the bedrooms on the lower level.

1 A brick podium containing the bedrooms and bathrooms supports the upper parts of the house, including the office (left) and living spaces (right) which are arranged as a series of linked pavilions.
2 The entrance courtyard is framed by the garage (left) and office (right). The entrance is located between the two structures.
3 Detail view of the joinery which features throughout the house.
4 Internal finishes are in the same red brick as the exterior. Views of the surrounding forest over the planted roof of the lower level are carefully framed by the arrangement of the windows.

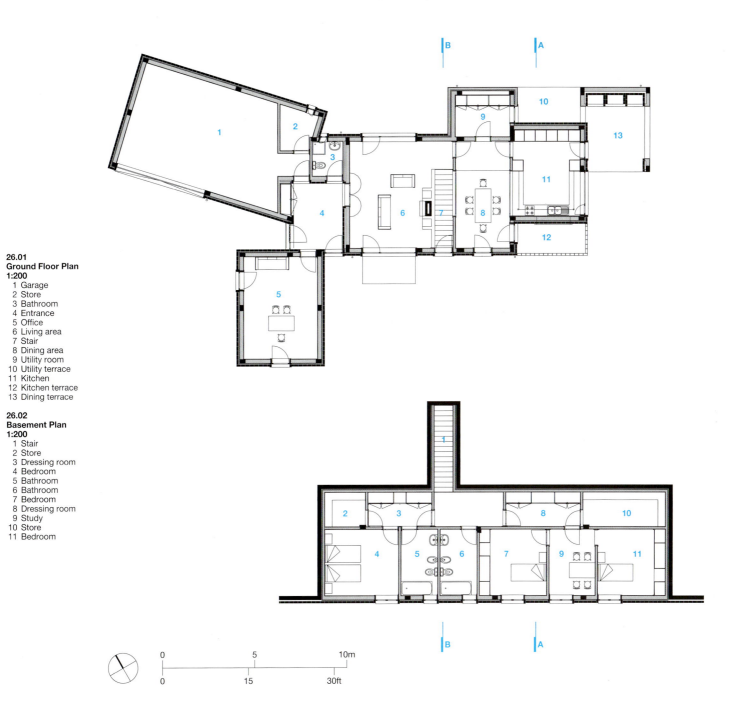

26.01
Ground Floor Plan
1:200
1 Garage
2 Store
3 Bathroom
4 Entrance
5 Office
6 Living area
7 Stair
8 Dining area
9 Utility room
10 Utility terrace
11 Kitchen
12 Kitchen terrace
13 Dining terrace

26.02
Basement Plan
1:200
1 Stair
2 Store
3 Dressing room
4 Bedroom
5 Bathroom
6 Bathroom
7 Bedroom
8 Dressing room
9 Study
10 Store
11 Bedroom

0   5   10m
0   15   30ft

26.03
Section A–A
1:200
1 Garden
2 Bedroom
3 Dressing room
4 Kitchen terrace
5 Kitchen
6 Utility terrace

26.04
Section B–B
1:200
1 Garden
2 Bathroom
3 Stair
4 Living area

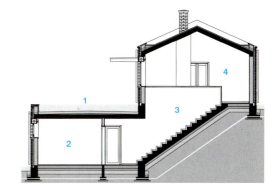

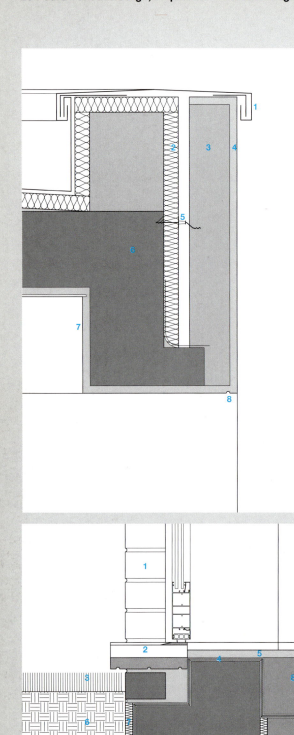

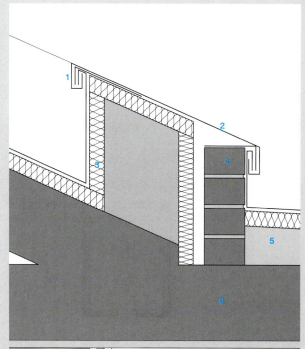

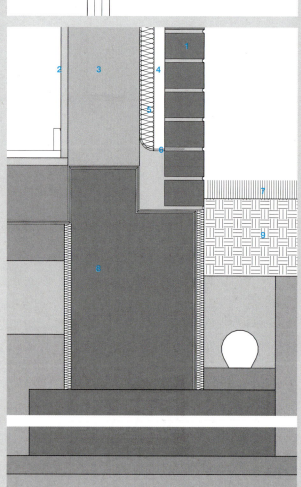

26.05
Flat Roof Parapet
Section Detail
1:10
 1 Zinc parapet capping
 2 Extruded polystyrene rigid insulation
 3 Hollow brickwork wall
 4 Lightweight cement stucco render finish
 5 Stainless steel structural tie
 6 Reinforced concrete roof slab and edge beam
 7 Stucco soffit lining
 8 Drip groove in stucco soffit

26.07
Pitched Roof Parapet
Section Detail
1:10
 1 Zinc clip
 2 Zinc roof sheeting
 3 Cork insulation
 4 Brick veneer parapet wall
 5 Lightweight concrete screed
 6 Reinforced concrete roof slab
 7 Lightweight cement stucco render finish to ceiling

26.06
Wall, Door and Floor
Section Detail
1:10
 1 Brickwork external wall
 2 Moleanos stone door sill
 3 Grass
 4 Waterproof membrane
 5 Lightweight concrete screed floor finish
 6 Soil
 7 Extruded polystyrene rigid insulation
 8 Concrete screed over reinforced concrete floor slab
 9 Geotextile membrane
 10 Reinforced concrete upstand beam
 11 Agricultural drain

26.08
Wall and Floor
Section Detail
1:10
 1 Brickwork external leaf of cavity wall
 2 Lightweight concrete stucco render to internal wall face
 3 Hollow blockwork internal leaf of cavity wall
 4 Ventilation cavity
 5 Extruded polystyrene rigid insulation
 6 Bituminous polymer membrane
 7 Grass
 8 Reinforced concrete upstand beam
 9 Soil

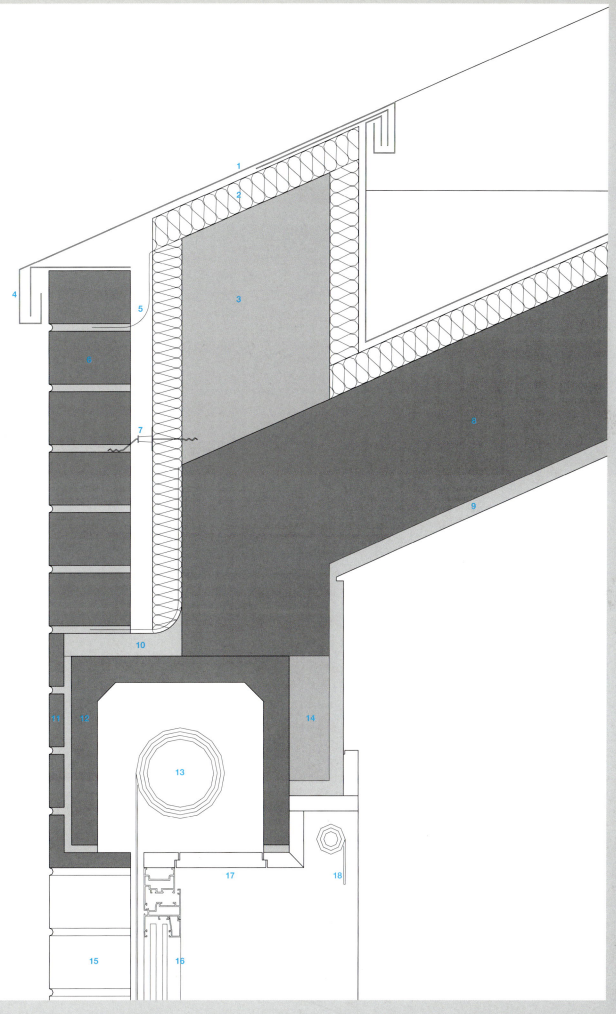

1 Zinc parapet
capping
2 Cork insulation
3 Hollow blockwork
parapet wall
4 Zinc clip
5 Bituminous polymer
membrane
6 Brick veneer
parapet wall
7 Stainless steel
structural tie
8 Reinforced
concrete roof slab
9 Lightweight cement
stucco render finish to
ceiling
10 Cement to base of
cavity
11 Brick facing over
shutter cavity
12 Pre-cast concrete
lintel and shutter
housing
13 External aluminium
roller blind
14 Hollow brick fill
15 Brickwork window
reveal
16 Aluminium framed
double glazed window
17 Timber reveal
18 Fabric roller blind

The Brick Kiln House
Maharashtra, India

Client
Private

Project Team
Sangeeta Merchant, Mangesh Jadhav,
Thomas Kariath, Mansoor Kudalkar,
Sanjeev Panjabi, Parag Satardekar

Structural Engineer
Gireesh Rajadhyaksha

Main Contractor
R.K. Construct

The Brick Kiln House is located in Munavali, a small village near Alibaug, a coastal town on the Arabian Sea, just 100 km (62 miles) south of Mumbai and a favourite getaway for affluent city dwellers. Throughout the district, the brick stacks of kilns from small scale brick production can be seen, and their striking presence in the Maharashtra landscape became the conceptual genesis of the design. The handmade, irregularly surfaced bricks, made from local red earth, feature throughout the house.

The 1.2 hectare (three acre) site includes beautiful groves of tamarind and mango trees, with the occasional fragrant frangipani. Sited to take advantage of the mature landscape, the two main wings of the house sit at right angles to one another, with an existing tree becoming a feature of the stone paved entrance hall at the junction of the two wings.

Every room has openings on two sides for cross ventilation in the tropical climate. Natural light is treated in a manner that is consistent with traditional country houses of the region, which have dark interiors to offer much needed respite from the scorching sun.

To achieve this, the tall brick walls are used to create private shaded courtyards. In marked opposition to urban life, these protective spaces allow for an intimate interface with the outdoors, both in the living areas and the private spaces, most notably in the bathroom at the termination of the north-south wing, with its sunken pool contained within a double height brick court. The sheer mass of the brick structure keeps the interior spaces comfortably cool. Sun, rain and wind freely enter the house and will mark it over the years, with the stacks of bricks gradually becoming covered with luminescent moss.

1 Surrounded by groves of mature tropical trees, the house is massed to reflect the random stacks of bricks and brick kilns common in the region.
2 The master bathroom on the first floor features an outdoor bath carved from black granite. The interior spaces of the teak-clad master suite are protected from the sun by the overhangs of the monopitch steel roof.
3 The walls and floor of the living area and the terrace are made from hand dressed and jointed basalt stone.
4 The living area doors slide away to extend the space into the garden and pool beyond. East-facing clerestory windows are shaded by the tree canopy.
5 The bathroom on the ground floor at the termination of the north-south wing is contained within double height walls of handmade red brick.

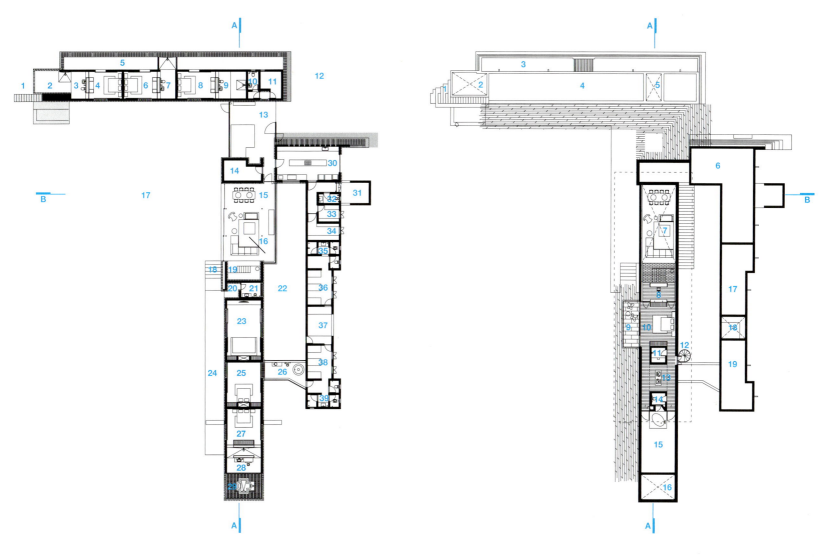

27.01
Ground Floor Plan
1:500
1 Brick steps
2 Shower courtyard
3 Bathroom
4 Bedroom
5 Courtyard
6 Bedroom
7 Bathroom
8 Bedroom
9 Bathroom
10 WC
11 Storage

12 Arrival court
13 Entrance hall
14 Storage
15 Dining area
16 Living area
17 Pool and garden
18 External stair
19 Stair to master
   bedroom suite
20 Bathroom lobby
21 WC
22 Courtyard
23 Media room
24 Verandah

25 Bedroom
26 Bathroom
27 Bedroom
28 Bathroom
29 Bathing court
30 Kitchen
31 Service courtyard
32 WC
33 Pantry
34 Wine store
35 Female staff
   bathroom
36 Female staff
   accommodation

37 Staff area
38 Male staff
   accommodation
39 Male staff
   bathroom

27.02
First Floor Plan
1:500
1 External brick stair
2 Skylight over
   bathroom
3 Courtyard
4 Roof to bedroom

wing
5 Skylight over
   bathroom
6 Roof to kitchen
7 Void over double
   height living and
   dining area
8 Study
9 Terrace
10 Master bedroom
11 Shower
12 External stair
13 Master bathroom
14 WC

15 Bathing terrace
16 Skylight over
   bathing court
   below
17 Roof to female
   staff area
18 Skylight over staff
   area
19 Roof to male
   staff area

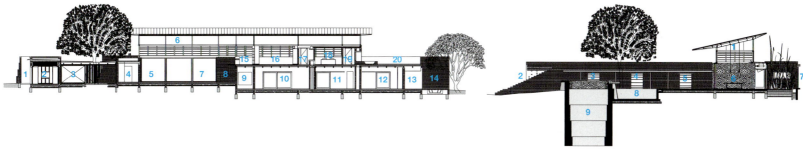

27.03
Section A–A
1:500
1 Courtyard
2 Bedroom
3 Entrance hall
4 Storage
5 Dining area
6 Roof over double
   height living space
7 Living area

8 Stair
9 WC
10 Media room
11 Bedroom
12 Bedroom
13 Bathroom
14 Bathing court
15 Study
16 Master bedroom
17 Shower
18 Master bathroom

19 WC
20 Bathing terrace

27.04
Section B–B
1:500
1 Roof over double
   height living space
2 Bathing courtyard
3 Bedroom
4 Bedroom

5 Bedroom
6 Living and dining
   area
7 Courtyard
8 Swimming pool
9 Existing well

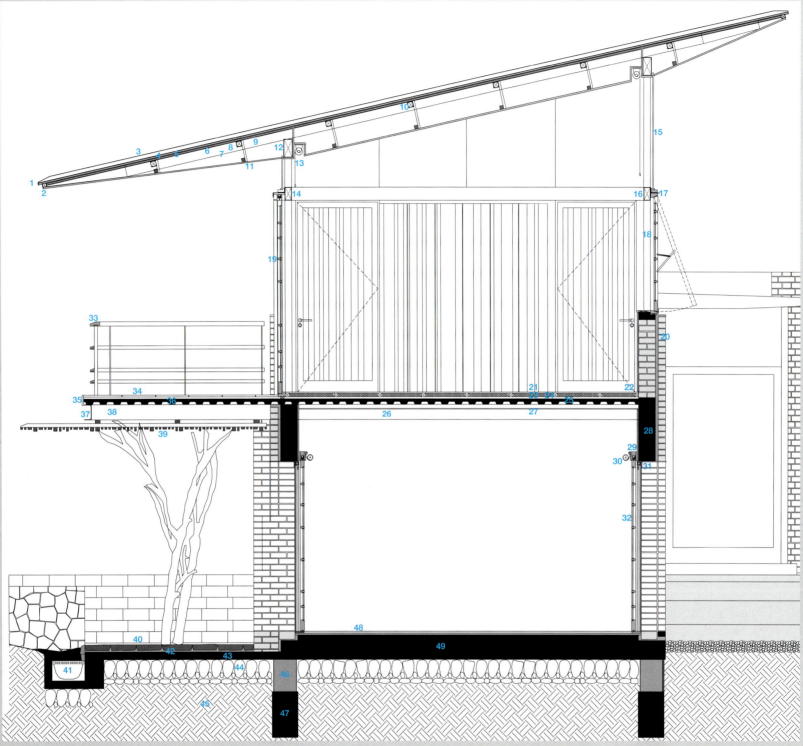

27.05
Master Bedroom and Living Area Section Detail
1:50

1 Zinc drip mould to roof overhang
2 Teak support member to roof overhang
3 Standing seam zinc roofing
4 Vapour barrier
5 3 mm (1/8 inch) bituminous sheet
6 19 mm (3/4 inch) thick waterproof plywood
7 50 mm (2 inch) thick thermal insulation

8 145 x 82 mm (53/4 x 31/4 inch) structural steel purlins at 1200 mm (471/4 inch) centres
9 Rigid insulation
10 50 x 50 mm (2 x 2 inch) steel cross beams at 1200 (471/4 inch) centres
11 19 mm (3/4 inch) waxed plywood soffit lining
12 120 x 240 mm (43/4 x 91/2 inch) structural mild steel box section beam
13 Roller blind
14 172 x 92 mm (63/4 x 35/8 inch) structural

mild steel box section beam
15 8 mm (3/8 inch) thick fixed, clear float glass clerestory glazing
16 50 x 100 mm (2 x 4 inch) salvaged teak window frame
17 Structural steel angle plate to window frame
18 Top hung teak framed window with salvaged teak mullions
19 Sliding teak framed door with 8 mm (3/8 inch) glass panels
20 Terracotta brick cladding of varying

thickness
21 18 mm (3/4 inch) salvaged teak tongue-and-grooved floorboards
22 Clear anodized aluminium L-angle skirting
23 25 mm (1 inch) thick screed
24 50 x 50 mm (2 x 2 inch) salvaged teak framing at 600 mm (231/2 inch) centres
25 Steel deck profile with 75 mm (3 inch) concrete with 12 mm (1/2 inch) diameter steel reinforcement at 95 mm (33/4 inch)

centres
26 100 x 200 mm (4 x 8 inch) structural steel box section
27 Waterproof plywood ceiling
28 230 x 500 mm (9 x 193/4 inch) reinforced concrete beam with 16 mm (5/8 inch) diameter reinforcement
29 Retractable mosquito screen
30 Bamboo roller blind
31 12 mm (1/2 inch) steel plate lintel finished with zinc chromate paint
32 Sliding teak framed door in C-channel

metal track with 8 mm (3/8 inch) glass panels
33 10 x 40 mm (3/8 x 11/2 inch) mild steel flat handrail
34 25 mm (1 inch) black limestone slabs with honed finished
35 25 mm (1 inch) timber fascia to balcony edge
36 Steel deck sheet with 75 mm (3 inch) concrete with 12 mm (1/2 inch) diameter steel reinforcement at 95 mm (33/4 inch) centres
37 100 x 200 mm (4 x 8 inch) steel C-profile

section
38 100 x 200 mm (4 x 8 inch) steel box section beam
39 Teak slats to underside of balcony
40 100 mm (4 inch) hand dressed and random jointed basalt paving
41 450 x 250 mm (173/4 x 10 inch) gutter with grating covered with 20–30 mm (3/4 –11/5 inch) basalt gravel
42 25 mm (1 inch) levelling screed
43 100 mm (4 inch) concrete bed

44 300 mm (12 inch) rubble packing
45 Compacted earth
46 350 mm (133/4 inch) brick plinth wall plastered with waterproof compound
47 350 x 600 mm (133/4 x 231/2 inch) concrete beam
48 8 mm (3/8 inch) tongue-and-groove timber floor
49 300 mm (12 inch) reinforced concrete floor slab

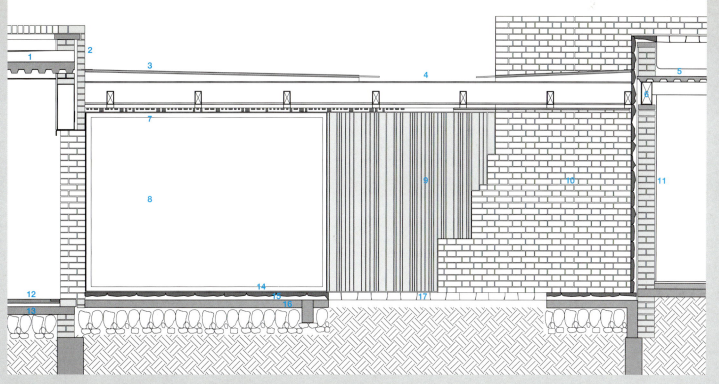

27.06
Entrance Hall Section
Detail
1:50
  1 Steel deck profile
permanent formwork
with 75 mm (3 inch)
thick concrete
  2 Terracotta brick wall
from bricks of varying
thickness
  3 8 mm (3/8 inch)
clear float glass roof
on steel framing
  4 Gap in roof for
existing tree trunk and
canopy
  5 Steel deck profile

permanent formwork
with 75 mm (3 inch)
thick concrete
  6 172 x 92 mm (63/4 x
35/8 inch) mild steel
box section beam
  7 Pergola ceiling
screen of salvaged
teak of varying widths
  8 Fixed glass wall to
entrance
  9 Pivoting entrance
door of 18 mm (3/4
inch) thick vertical
planks of salvaged
teak of varying widths
  10 Terracotta brick wall
from bricks of varying

thickness
  11 Basalt-clad brick
wall between entrance
hall and store room
  12 25 mm (1 inch)
thick black limestone
slabs with honed finish
  13 100 mm (4 inch)
thick plain concrete
floor slab
  14 100 mm (4 inch)
thick, hand dressed
and jointed basalt rock
floor
  15 25 mm (1 inch)
thick levelling screed
laid to fall
  16 100 mm (4 inch)

thick plain concrete
floor slab
  17 Opening in stone
floor for existing tree

27.07
Ground Floor Bathing
Court Section Detail
1:50
  1 Boxed out air
conditioning duct
  2 Shower head
  3 100 x 200 mm (4 x
8 inch) mild steel box
section beam
  4 12 mm (1/2 inch)
thick marine plywood
mounted on angle
cleats
  5 12 mm (1/2 inch)
thick terrazzo to
shower base and walls
  6 100 mm (4 inch)
thick plain concrete
floor slab
  7 300 mm (12 inch)
deep rubble packing
  8 Compacted earth
  9 Wall mounted spout
  10 Basin
  11 Wall hung WC
  12 25 mm (1 inch)
thick black limestone
slabs with honed finish
  13 8 mm (3/8 inch)
clear float glass roof
on timber framing
  14 12 mm (1/2 inch)
thick terrazzo to
sunken bathtub
  15 Terracotta brick
floor from bricks of
varying thickness
  16 Terracotta brick
external wall from
bricks of varying
thickness

119

**Hundertacht House
Bonn, Germany**

Client
Villa Faupel

Project Team
Uwe Schröder, Stefan Dahlmann, Till
Robin Kurz

Structural Engineer
Ertl und Partner

Located at the foot of Venusberg Hill is Kessenich is one of the oldest districts of Bonn, a primarily residential area of tree-lined streets and free standing villas, many of which date from the mid nineteenth century. On the southern outskirts of the city, the neighbourhood looks over parkland towards Venusberg and beyond to the forested acres of Kottenforst, part of the Rhineland Nature Park.

Hundertacht House is defined by a strict geometric system, and a severely reduced material palette that has been rigorously imposed on both the exterior and interior of the house. Through a process of reduction and simplification, both formal architectural expression and materiality reflect the traditional architecture of its suburban context.

Facing the street, a three storey high, entirely symmetrical flat white rendered facade is punctured only by three windows on the top storey and a door in the centre of the ground floor. Three datum lines of dark brown clinker bricks mark the floor levels and parapet at identical intervals. This highly controlled composition sits on a pedestal of brick that identifies the change in level from the lower street frontage to the higher rear garden side of the site. Here, each of the three above-ground levels is expressed as a white rectangular box, each layer smaller than the one below, the roof of each becoming a terrace to the one above. The same set of symmetrical openings, two windows flanking a central door, appear on each level, regardless of the interior programmatical differences.

Four walled and paved courtyards constructed from the same clinker bricks extend the rule of symmetry out into the garden. From the entrance courtyard on the street, the brick walls and floor continue through the centre of the ground floor, extending into three identical external spaces, one each on the sides and one to the rear, cut into the lawn.

1 To the street, a brick-lined courtyard forms a transitional space between the road and the interior.
2 Seen from the west, the house steps down in three levels creating a terrace for the studio on the top floor and the bedrooms on the first floor. The ground floor makes the connection to the garden via a brick-lined sunken courtyard, the height of the courtyard walls corresponding to the height of the brick podium at the front of the site.
3 Solid oak is used for all of the internal and external joinery details.
4 The brick walls extend from the exterior courtyards on each side of the house, through the living room at the centre of the ground floor, maintaining the expression of the datum line throughout. The living room opens to the dining room (left) and kitchen (right) though folding timber shutters.

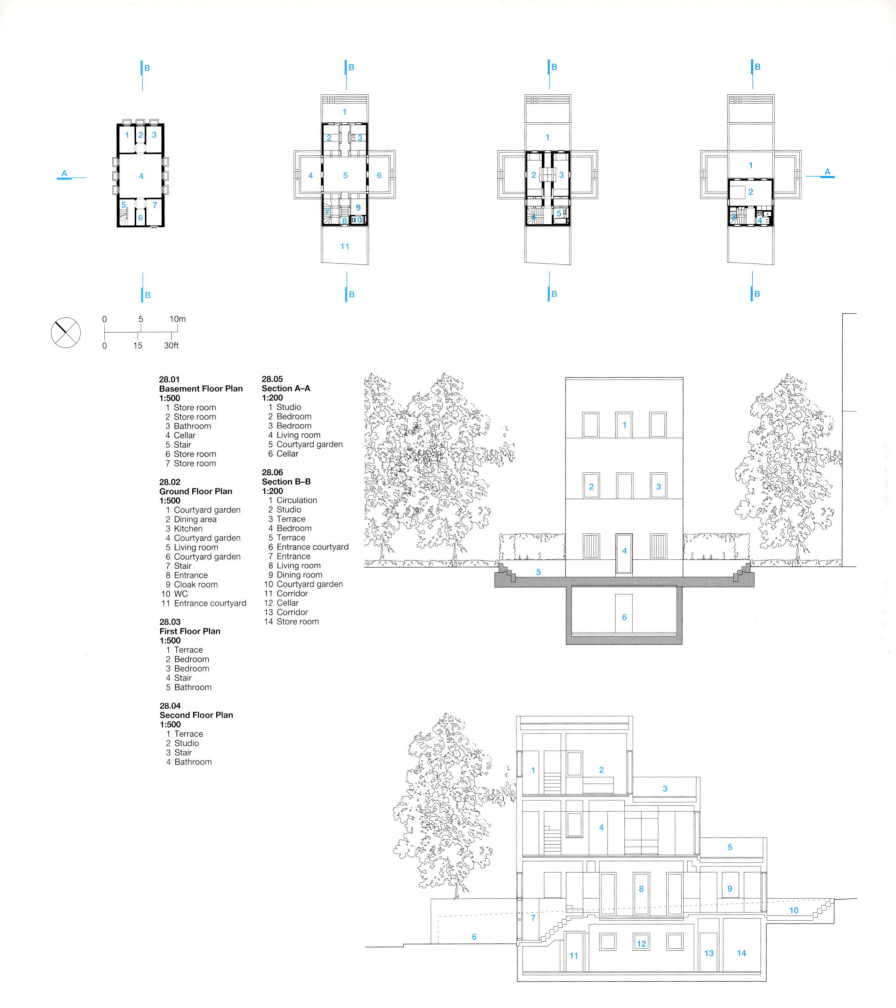

28.01
Basement Floor Plan
1:500
1 Store room
2 Store room
3 Bathroom
4 Cellar
5 Stair
6 Store room
7 Store room

28.02
Ground Floor Plan
1:500
1 Courtyard garden
2 Dining area
3 Kitchen
4 Courtyard garden
5 Living room
6 Courtyard garden
7 Stair
8 Entrance
9 Cloak room
10 WC
11 Entrance courtyard

28.03
First Floor Plan
1:500
1 Terrace
2 Bedroom
3 Bedroom
4 Stair
5 Bathroom

28.04
Second Floor Plan
1:500
1 Terrace
2 Studio
3 Stair
4 Bathroom

28.05
Section A–A
1:200
1 Studio
2 Bedroom
3 Bedroom
4 Living room
5 Courtyard garden
6 Cellar

28.06
Section B–B
1:200
1 Circulation
2 Studio
3 Terrace
4 Bedroom
5 Terrace
6 Entrance courtyard
7 Entrance
8 Living room
9 Dining room
10 Courtyard garden
11 Corridor
12 Cellar
13 Corridor
14 Store room

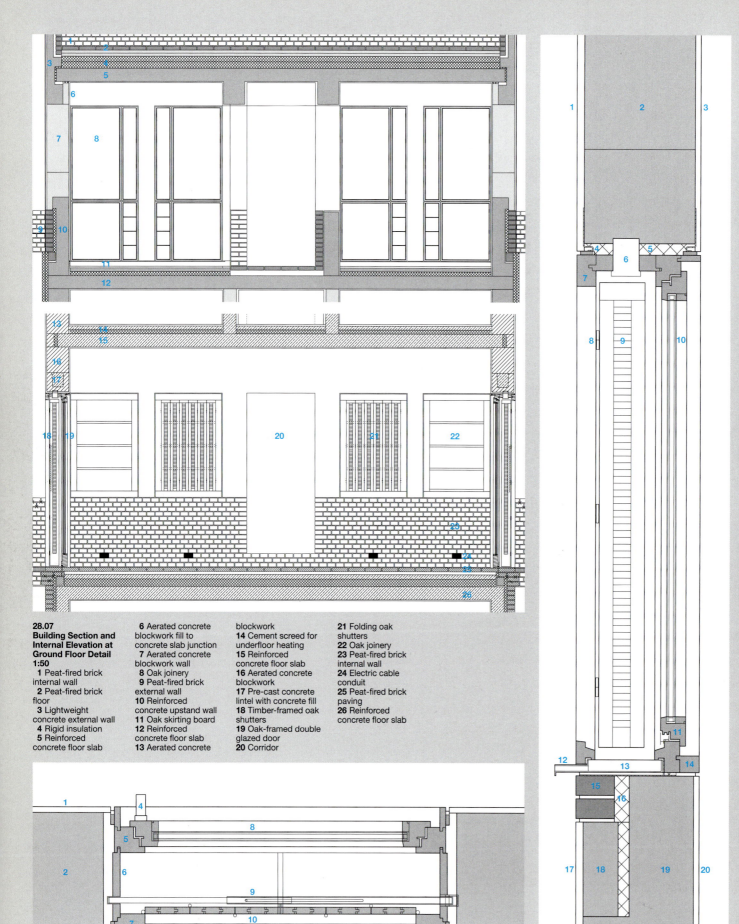

28.08
Living Room Window Section Detail
1:10
 1 Lime-based cement render to external wall face
 2 Aerated concrete block wall
 3 Gypsum plaster to internal wall face
 4 Aluminium render corner profile
 5 Insulation
 6 Light fixture
 7 Oak frame to window shutter
 8 Stainless steel straps to shutters
 9 Folding oak window shutter
 10 Oak-framed double glazed window
 11 Oak window frame
 12 Black anodized aluminium window sill with drip profile
 13 Black anodized aluminium drainage channel
 14 Oak window sill
 15 Peat-fired brick external wall
 16 Insulation
 17 Lime-based cement render to external wall face
 18 Reinforced concrete upstand wall
 19 Aerated concrete block wall
 20 Gypsum plaster to internal wall face

28.09
Living Room Window Plan Detail
1:10
 1 Gypsum plaster to internal wall face
 2 Aerated concrete block wall
 3 Lime-based cement render to external wall face
 4 Casement window handle
 5 Oak window frame
 6 Oak window reveal
 7 Oak frame to window shutter
 8 Oak-framed double glazed window
 9 Stainless steel shutter straps
 10 Folding oak window shutter
 11 Shutter handle

28.07
Building Section and Internal Elevation at Ground Floor Detail
1:50
 1 Peat-fired brick internal wall
 2 Peat-fired brick floor
 3 Lightweight concrete external wall
 4 Rigid insulation
 5 Reinforced concrete floor slab
 6 Aerated concrete blockwork fill to concrete slab junction
 7 Aerated concrete blockwork wall
 8 Oak joinery
 9 Peat-fired brick external wall
 10 Reinforced concrete upstand wall
 11 Oak skirting board
 12 Reinforced concrete floor slab
 13 Aerated concrete blockwork
 14 Cement screed for underfloor heating
 15 Reinforced concrete floor slab
 16 Aerated concrete blockwork
 17 Pre-cast concrete lintel with concrete fill
 18 Timber-framed oak shutters
 19 Oak-framed double glazed door
 20 Corridor
 21 Folding oak shutters
 22 Oak joinery
 23 Peat-fired brick internal wall
 24 Electric cable conduit
 25 Peat-fired brick paving
 26 Reinforced concrete floor slab

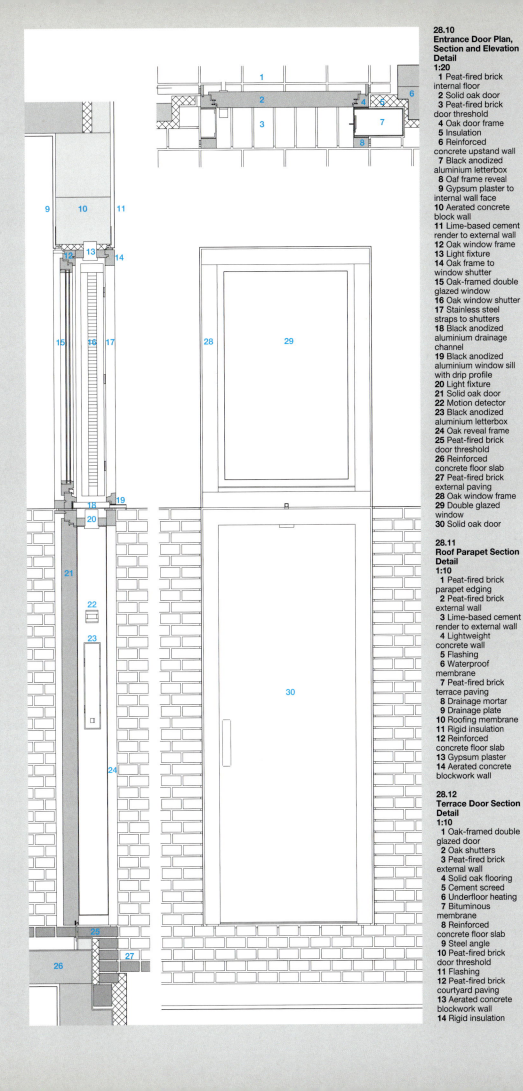

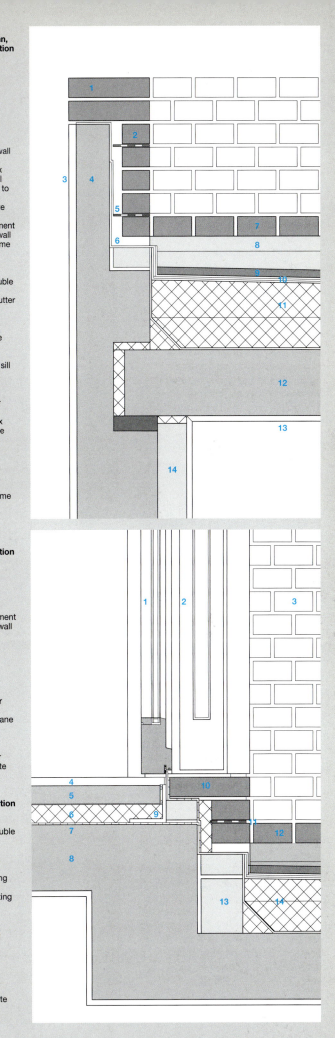

28.10
Entrance Door Plan, Section and Elevation Detail
1:20
1 Peat-fired brick internal floor
2 Solid oak door
3 Peat-fired brick door threshold
4 Oak door frame
5 Insulation
6 Reinforced concrete upstand wall
7 Black anodized aluminium letterbox
8 Oaf frame reveal
9 Gypsum plaster to internal wall face
10 Aerated concrete block wall
11 Lime-based cement render to external wall
12 Oak window frame
13 Light fixture
14 Oak frame to window shutter
15 Oak-framed double glazed window
16 Oak window shutter
17 Stainless steel straps to shutters
18 Black anodized aluminium drainage channel
19 Black anodized aluminium window sill with drip profile
20 Light fixture
21 Solid oak door
22 Motion detector
23 Black anodized aluminium letterbox
24 Oak reveal frame
25 Peat-fired brick door threshold
26 Reinforced concrete floor slab
27 Peat-fired brick external paving
28 Oak window frame
29 Double glazed window
30 Solid oak door

28.11
Roof Parapet Section Detail
1:10
1 Peat-fired brick parapet edging
2 Peat-fired brick external wall
3 Lime-based cement render to external wall
4 Lightweight concrete wall
5 Flashing
6 Waterproof membrane
7 Peat-fired brick terrace paving
8 Drainage mortar
9 Drainage plate
10 Roofing membrane
11 Rigid insulation
12 Reinforced concrete floor slab
13 Gypsum plaster
14 Aerated concrete blockwork wall

28.12
Terrace Door Section Detail
1:10
1 Oak-framed double glazed door
2 Oak shutters
3 Peat-fired brick external wall
4 Solid oak flooring
5 Cement screed
6 Underfloor heating
7 Bituminous membrane
8 Reinforced concrete floor slab
9 Steel angle
10 Peat-fired brick door threshold
11 Flashing
12 Peat-fired brick courtyard paving
13 Aerated concrete blockwork wall
14 Rigid insulation

VM Residence
Sint-Martens-Latem, Belgium

Client
Private

Project Team
Kristof Geldmeyer, Pascal Bilquin,
Humberto Nóbrega, Nicolas
Schuybroek

Structural Engineer
Faeye Studiebureau

Landscape
Jan Van Paemel

Located in East Flanders to the west
of the city of Gent, Sint-Martens-
Latem is a low density suburban
settlement of large private villas
surrounded by dense gardens,
pockets of forest and narrow streets
lined with ash, oak and maple trees.
The house is located on a double
block with the main L-shaped volume
at the corner of the site, opening the
internal spaces to the light and giving
views to the south. Long brick walls
and stacked volumes follow the
north-east and north-west boundaries,
enclosing the private garden from the
adjacent streets and defining the
outdoor spaces as physical
extensions of the internal areas.

The main entrance is located at the
junction of the two wings under the
cantilevered first floor volume.
Internally the house is organized in
two directions over two levels. On the
ground floor, living areas flow around
the double height, top lit main
entrance hall, creating the sense of
one continuous and dynamic space
with multidirectional views towards
the garden. The living area, which
occupies a split level, offers views of
both the natural and built landscape,
including the garden, the pool, and the
pool house with its outdoor cooking
and dining terrace. The upper level
accommodates the private sleeping
and bathing spaces where the
dialogue with the landscape continues
through large openings that flood the
main circulation areas and the private
spaces with southern light.

The architectural dialogue between
mass and void is expressed through
the finely detailed and textured grey
brick volumes which are contrasted
with the large openings. The concept
continues in the interior where the
presence of the soft grey brick
accentuates the pureness and
sobriety of the architecture.

1 The view from the pool house, over the pool (left) towards the living area on the ground floor and the master bedroom suite above. The architectural composition of mass, void and plane is executed with exemplary rigour.
2 Two perpendicular wings of accommodation are wrapped around a large garden, with a stone terrace creating a transitional zone between the two.
3 The double height entrance hall is crowned with a skylight, bringing light into the centre of the house. Grey brick walls on the ground floor are contrasted with white plaster for the upper level walls.
4 The living room steps down from the dining space, emphasizing the importance of the relationship between the interior and the landscape.
5 The master bathroom on the first floor looks into a glass-walled open-air courtyard patio.

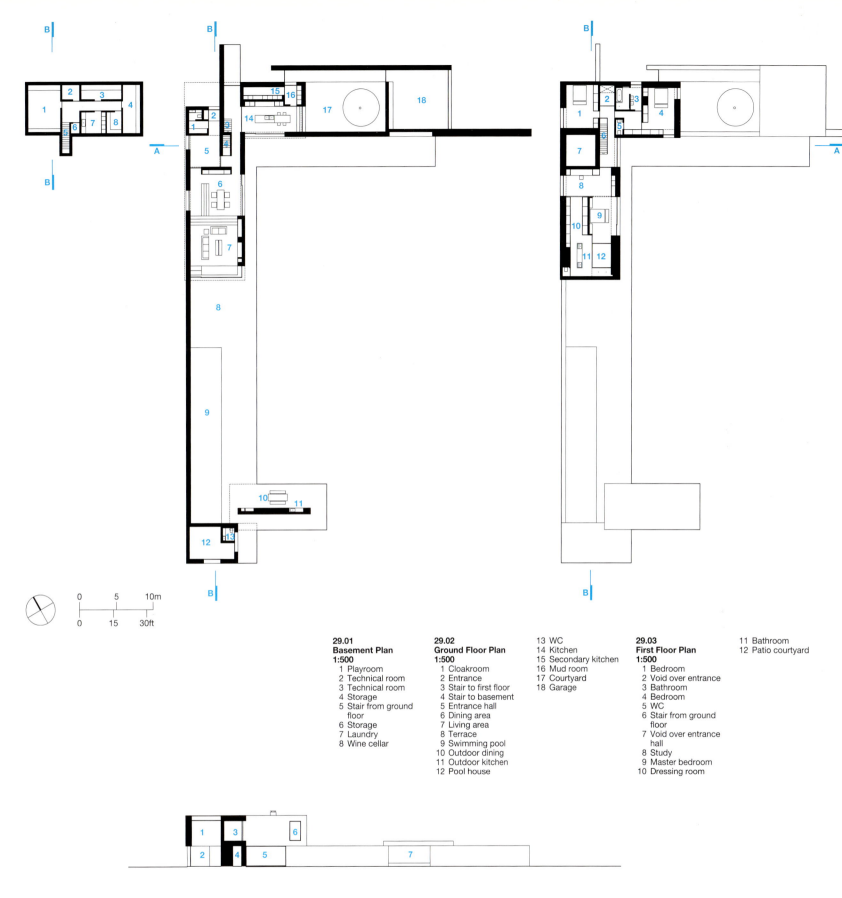

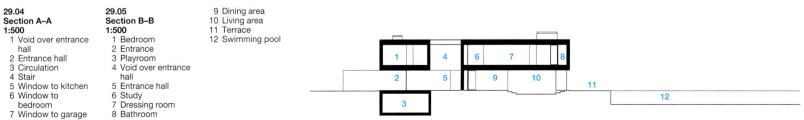

29.01
Basement Plan
1:500
1 Playroom
2 Technical room
3 Technical room
4 Storage
5 Stair from ground
  floor
6 Storage
7 Laundry
8 Wine cellar

29.02
Ground Floor Plan
1:500
1 Cloakroom
2 Entrance
3 Stair to first floor
4 Stair to basement
5 Entrance hall
6 Dining area
7 Living area
8 Terrace
9 Swimming pool
10 Outdoor dining
11 Outdoor kitchen
12 Pool house

13 WC
14 Kitchen
15 Secondary kitchen
16 Mud room
17 Courtyard
18 Garage

29.03
First Floor Plan
1:500
1 Bedroom
2 Void over entrance
3 Bathroom
4 Bedroom
5 WC
6 Stair from ground
  floor
7 Void over entrance
  hall
8 Study
9 Master bedroom
10 Dressing room

11 Bathroom
12 Patio courtyard

29.04
Section A–A
1:500
1 Void over entrance
  hall
2 Entrance hall
3 Circulation
4 Stair
5 Window to kitchen
6 Window to
  bedroom
7 Window to garage

29.05
Section B–B
1:500
1 Bedroom
2 Entrance
3 Playroom
4 Void over entrance
  hall
5 Entrance hall
6 Study
7 Dressing room
8 Bathroom

9 Dining area
10 Living area
11 Terrace
12 Swimming pool

125

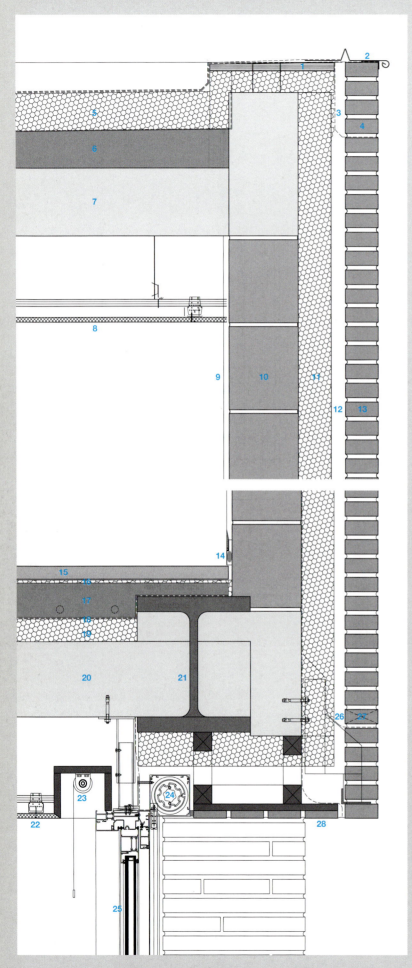

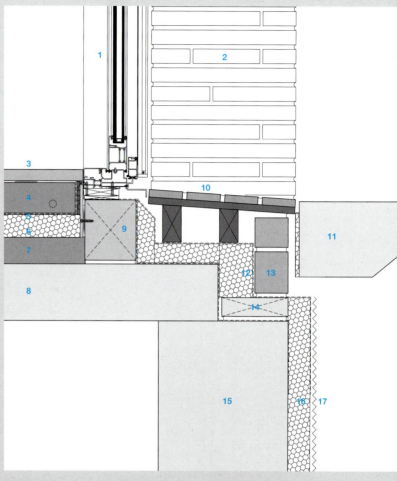

29.06
Wall and Window
Head Section Detail
1:10
 1 18 mm (3/4 inch)
waterproof plywood
parapet
 2 Zinc capping
 3 Waterproof
membrane
 4 Ventilation brick
 5 100 mm (4 inch)
rigid insulation
 6 Concrete topping
screed laid to fall
 7 200 mm (8 inch)
reinforced concrete
roof slab
 8 Suspended,
painted plasterboard
ceiling
 9 Painted plaster
internal wall finish
10 190 mm (7 1/2 inch)
blockwork wall
11 90 mm (3 1/2 inch)
rigid insulation
12 30 mm (1 1/5 inch)
cavity
13 Horizontal
handmade bricks of
various sizes
14 Aluminium profile
with reinforced mesh
to form invisible plinth
15 35 mm (1 3/8 inch)
solid Douglas fir
floorboards
16 Acoustic membrane
17 Cement screed with
underfloor heating
18 Vapour barrier
19 60 mm (2 3/8 inch)
thermal insulation
20 200 mm (8 inch)
reinforced concrete
floor slab
21 Steel beam
22 Suspended painted
plasterboard ceiling

23 Internal sun
protection screen
concealed in painted
MDF pelmet
24 External sun
protection screen
25 Aluminium framed
double glazed window
26 Waterproof
membrane
27 Ventilation brick
28 Soffit of handmade
brick strips glued to
high density building
board on timber
framing

29.07
Window Sill and Floor
Section Detail
1:10
 1 Aluminium framed
double glazed window
 2 Horizontal
handmade bricks of
various sizes
 3 30 mm (1 1/5 inch)
Pietra Serena
sandstone floor
 4 Cement screed with
underfloor heating
 5 Vapour barrier
 6 60 mm (2 3/8 inch)
thermal insulation
 7 Concrete screed
 8 200 mm (8 inch)
reinforced concrete
roof slab
 9 Insulated brick
10 Sill of handmade
brick strips glued to
high density building
board on timber
framing
11 Concrete slab to
terrace with polished
finish
12 Waterproof
membrane
13 90 mm (3 1/2 inch)
blockwork wall
14 Insulated brick
15 350 mm (13 3/4 inch)
waterproof concrete
wall
16 60 mm (2 3/8 inch)
thermal insulation
17 Drainage mat

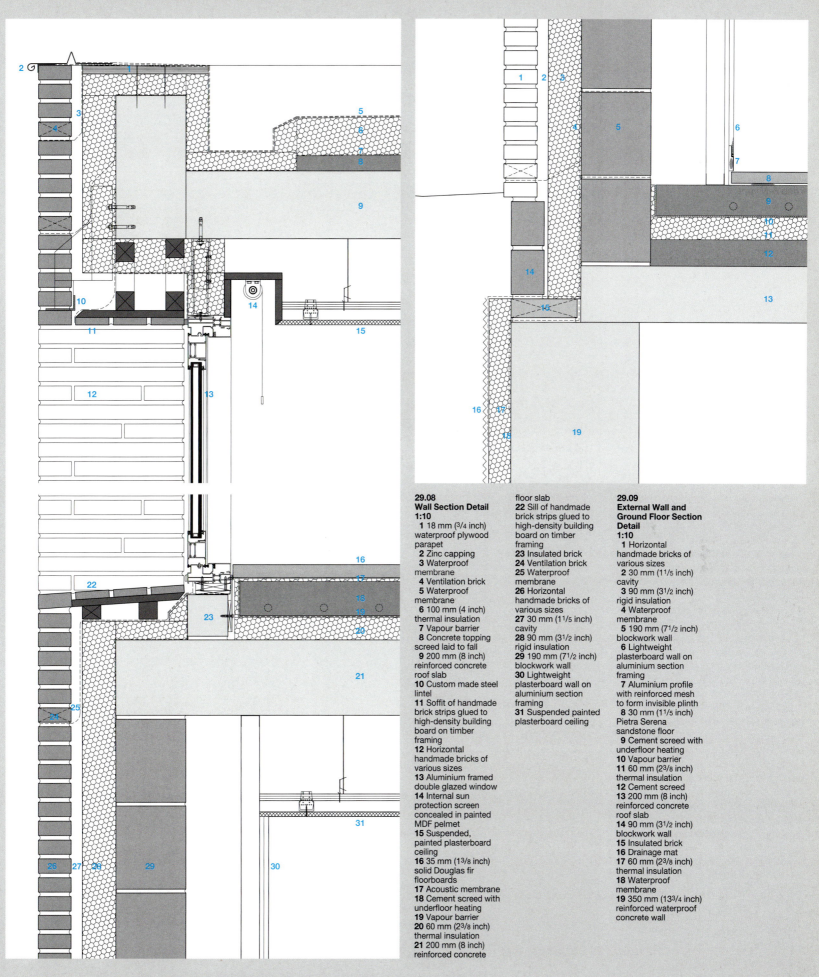

29.08
Wall Section Detail
1:10
1 18 mm (³/₄ inch) waterproof plywood parapet
2 Zinc capping
3 Waterproof membrane
4 Ventilation brick
5 Waterproof membrane
6 100 mm (4 inch) thermal insulation
7 Vapour barrier
8 Concrete topping screed laid to fall
9 200 mm (8 inch) reinforced concrete roof slab
10 Custom made steel lintel
11 Soffit of handmade brick strips glued to high-density building board on timber framing
12 Horizontal handmade bricks of various sizes
13 Aluminium framed double glazed window
14 Internal sun protection screen concealed in painted MDF pelmet
15 Suspended, painted plasterboard ceiling
16 35 mm (1³/₈ inch) solid Douglas fir floorboards
17 Acoustic membrane
18 Cement screed with underfloor heating
19 Vapour barrier
20 60 mm (2³/₈ inch) thermal insulation
21 200 mm (8 inch) reinforced concrete

floor slab
22 Sill of handmade brick strips glued to high-density building board on timber framing
23 Insulated brick
24 Ventilation brick
25 Waterproof membrane
26 Horizontal handmade bricks of various sizes
27 30 mm (1¹/₅ inch) cavity
28 90 mm (3¹/₂ inch) rigid insulation
29 190 mm (7¹/₂ inch) blockwork wall
30 Lightweight plasterboard wall on aluminium section framing
31 Suspended painted plasterboard ceiling

29.09
External Wall and Ground Floor Section Detail
1:10
1 Horizontal handmade bricks of various sizes
2 30 mm (1¹/₅ inch) cavity
3 90 mm (3¹/₂ inch) rigid insulation
4 Waterproof membrane
5 190 mm (7¹/₂ inch) blockwork wall
6 Lightweight plasterboard wall on aluminium section framing
7 Aluminium profile with reinforced mesh to form invisible plinth
8 30 mm (1¹/₅ inch) Pietra Serena sandstone floor
9 Cement screed with underfloor heating
10 Vapour barrier
11 60 mm (2³/₈ inch) thermal insulation
12 Cement screed
13 200 mm (8 inch) reinforced concrete roof slab
14 90 mm (3¹/₂ inch) blockwork wall
15 Insulated brick
16 Drainage mat
17 60 mm (2³/₈ inch) thermal insulation
18 Waterproof membrane
19 350 mm (13³/₄ inch) reinforced waterproof concrete wall

Astley Castle
Warwickshire, England, UK

Client
The Landmark Trust

Project Team
Stephen Witherford, Christopher
Watson, William Mann, Freddie
Phillipson, Jan Liebe, Daniela Bueter,
Joerg Maier, Lina Meister

Structural Engineer
Price & Myers

Main Contractor
William Anelay

Astley Castle has been in continuous occupation since the twelfth century. In its more recent past, it was requisitioned during the Second World War, then partially restored in the 1950s as a hotel before reaching its lowest ebb when it was gutted by a fire in 1978. Vandalism, unauthorized removal of building materials and collapse worsened its condition until in 2007 it was listed as one of the sixteen most endangered sites in Britain by English Heritage. In 2005, the owner, The Landmark Trust, proposed to reinstate occupancy of Astley Castle and an architectural competition was held.

The winning scheme, by Witherford Watson Mann, was simultaneously pragmatic and poetic. New accommodation has been built within the oldest part of the castle, while wings from the fifteenth and seventeenth centuries have been retained as walled external courts to maintain the open character of the ruin rather than attempting to recreate its completeness. The inverted layout, with living quarters on the first floor and bedrooms and bathrooms on the ground floor, occupies approximately half the footprint of the extensive ruins. However the new construction extends over the courtyards to tie together and stabilize the retained building fragments.

Old walls are capped and edged in new lime mortar brick diaphragm walls the full depth of the originals. The rehabilitated building benefits from significantly improved energy efficiency without prejudicing the character of the listed building through the use of highly insulated, thermally massive construction. The masonry and carpentry are simple, economical and contemporary, yet they would be recognizable to the original medieval, and many subsequent, builders of Astley Castle.

1 The south facade of the castle features significant new brickwork infill walls to the bedrooms (left) and dining courtyard (right). Built from flat Danish bricks with concrete lintels to the openings, the brickwork extends over vulnerable parts of the ruins, following the lines of the original stonework.
2 From the north it can be seen that surviving parts of the original structure have been delicately reframed as a record of Astley's long history.
3 New oak-framed windows to the first floor living area (left) look out over the partially enclosed dining courtyard (right) where the original chimney has been brought back into use.
4 Two windows in the large living space give views over the parkland and St Mary's Church (centre). The other looks into two courtyards formed from the shell of the ruined castle.
5 The new oak staircase is structurally independent with a single pocket connection between it and the existing masonry wall.

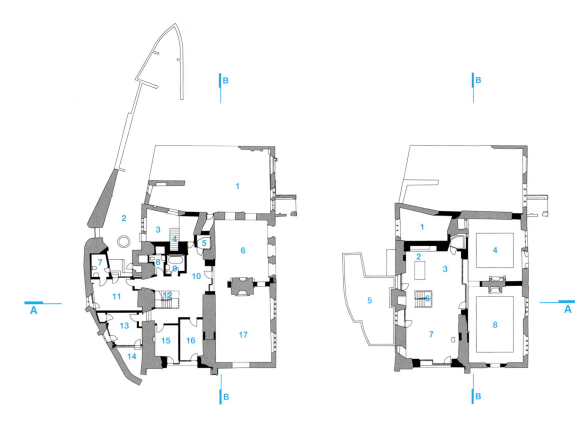

30.01
Ground Floor Plan
1:500
1 Garden courtyard
2 Well courtyard
3 Courtyard
4 Stair to basement
5 Lift
6 Entrance courtyard
7 Bathroom
8 WC
9 Bathroom
10 Entrance hall
11 Bedroom

12 Stair
13 Bedroom
14 Courtyard
15 Bedroom
16 Bedroom
17 Dining courtyard

30.02
First Floor Plan
1:500
1 Void over
  courtyard
2 Kitchen
3 Dining area
4 Void over entrance
  courtyard
5 Roof to bedroom
  and bathroom
  wing below
6 Stair
7 Living area

8 Void over dining
  courtyard

30.03
Section A–A
1:500
1 Bedroom
2 Stair
3 Entrance hall
4 Basement
5 Living area
6 Dining courtyard

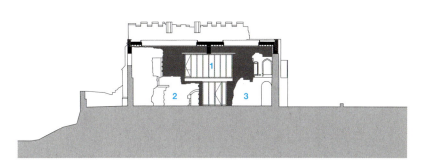

30.04
Section B–B
1:500
1 Window to living
  and dining areas
2 Dining courtyard
3 Entrance courtyard

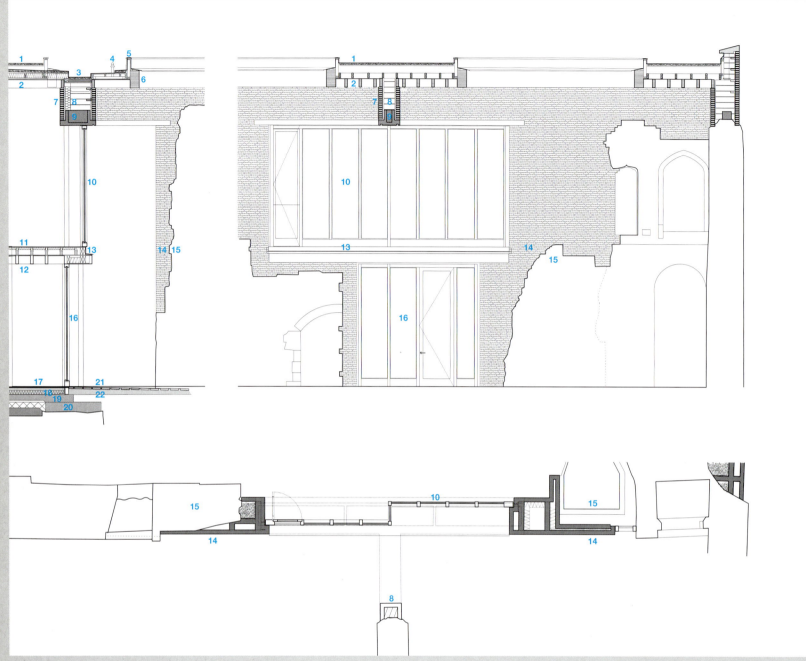

30.05
East Courtyard Facade Section, Elevation and Plan Details
1:100
1 Bituminous roof covering with gravel ballast
2 220 x 75 mm (8$^{1}/_{2}$ x 3 inch) laminated softwood roof joists at 400 mm (15$^{3}/_{4}$ inch) centres, with 19 mm ($^{3}/_{4}$ inch) birch plywood sheathing, insulation, softwood firrings and plywood roof deck
3 Valley gutter formed in roof build-up
4 Safety access system
5 Lead roof edge flashing
6 450 x 250 mm (17$^{3}/_{4}$ x 8$^{3}/_{4}$ inch) laminated softwood primary roof beams

7 Diaphragm brick wall from face brickwork
8 Clay block diaphragms at 865 mm (34 inch) centres, bonded into facing bricks every six courses
9 Precast concrete T-lintel with in situ structural topping
10 Glazed oak screen with opening casement
11 22 mm ($^{7}/_{8}$ inch) engineered oak floorboards, raised over underfloor heating and insulation
12 220 x 75 mm (8$^{1}/_{2}$ x 3 inch) laminated pine floor joists at 400 mm (15$^{3}/_{8}$ inch) centres
13 Lead flashing
14 Diaphragm brick wall from face brickwork coursed into existing stone wall
15 Existing stone wall

16 Glazed oak screen with front door
17 300 x 150 x 25 mm (12 x 6 x 1 inch) terracotta tiles in herringbone bond
18 Insulation and underfloor heating
19 Reinforced concrete slab
20 Reinforced concrete footing over existing wall foundation
21 Reclaimed brick paving
22 Sand-cement bedding

30.06
Stair Section A–A
1:50
1 40 x 125 mm (1$^{1}/_{2}$ x 5 inch) oak top rail
2 900 mm (35$^{1}/_{2}$ inch) high, 25 x 125 mm (1 x 5 inch) oak balusters
3 Finished first floor level
4 Top of joists
5 Underside of joists
6 40 x 125 mm (1$^{1}/_{2}$ x 5 inch) oak top rail
7 2 x 12 mm ($^{1}/_{8}$ x $^{1}/_{2}$ inch) oak ply with lapped joints
8 13 x 13 mm ($^{1}/_{2}$ x $^{1}/_{2}$ inch) steel balusters formed to support handrail where offset from stringer

30.07
Stair Section B–B
1:50
1 40 x 125 mm (1$^{1}/_{2}$ x 5 inch) oak top rail
2 900 mm (35$^{1}/_{2}$ inch)

high, 25 x 125 mm (1 x 5 inch) oak balusters
3 Top of joists
4 40 x 125 mm (1$^{1}/_{2}$ x 5 inch) oak top rail
5 2 x 12 mm ($^{1}/_{8}$ x $^{1}/_{2}$ inch) oak ply with lapped joints
6 Three sided 20 x 6 mm ($^{3}/_{4}$ x $^{1}/_{4}$ inch) steel frame embedded flush in rear of tread with horizontal 20 x 6 mm ($^{3}/_{4}$ x $^{1}/_{4}$ inch) top member set flush into underside of tread, all to this flight only
7 Flight hung from first floor using bolts through underside of tread into end of 40 x 125 mm (1$^{1}/_{2}$ x 5 inch) oak hangers
8 Open risers
9 13 x 13 mm ($^{1}/_{2}$ x $^{1}/_{2}$ inch) steel balusters formed to support handrail where offset from stringer

30.08
Stair Section C–C
1:50
1 40 x 125 mm (1$^{1}/_{2}$ x 5 inch) oak top rail
2 900 mm (35$^{1}/_{2}$ inch) high, 25 x 125 mm (1 x 5 inch) oak balusters
3 40 x 125 mm (1$^{1}/_{2}$ x 5 inch) oak top rail
4 2 x 12 mm ($^{1}/_{8}$ x $^{1}/_{2}$ inch) oak ply with lapped joints
5 Flight hung from first floor using bolts through underside of tread into end of 40 x 125 mm (1$^{1}/_{2}$ x 5 inch) oak hangers
6 13 x 13 mm ($^{1}/_{2}$ x $^{1}/_{2}$ inch) steel balusters formed to support handrail where offset from stringer

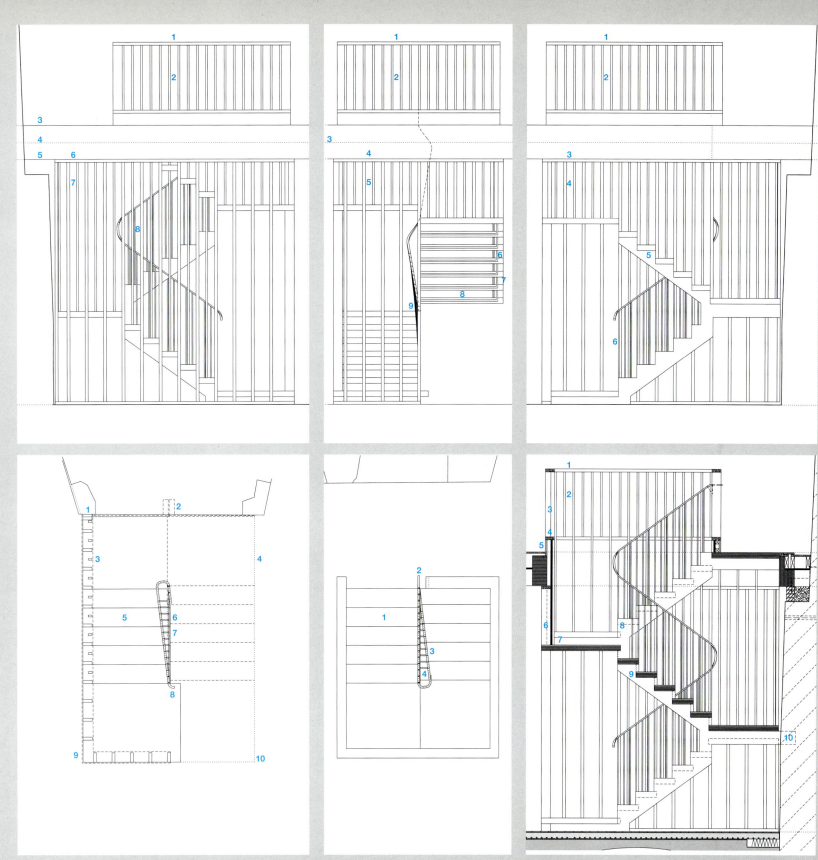

30.09
Stair Ground Floor Plan
1:50
1 Landing stops short of wall
2 Bracket into pocket in existing masonry
3 25 x 50 mm (1 x 2 inch) oak balusters
4 40 x 125 mm (1¹/₂ x 5 inch) oak framing
5 76 x 290 mm (3 x 11³/₈ inch) laminated oak treads
6 13 mm (¹/₂ inch) steel stringer with 12 mm (¹/₂ inch) oak ply either side with top and underside visible
7 13 x 13 mm (¹/₂ x ¹/₂ inch) steel balusters formed to support handrail where offset from stringer
8 25 mm (1 inch) wide steel handrail with wreathing
9 Footprint of 150 mm (6 inch) wide concrete foundation
10 Outline of stair above

30.10
Stair First Floor Plan
1:50
1 76 x 290 mm (3 x 11³/₈ inch) laminated oak treads
2 25 mm (1 inch) wide steel handrail with wreathing
3 13 mm (¹/₂ inch) steel stringer with 12 mm (¹/₂ inch) oak ply either side with top and underside visible
4 13 x 13 mm (¹/₂ x ¹/₂ inch) steel balusters formed to support handrail where offset from stringer

30.11
Stair Section D–D
1:50
1 40 x 125 mm (1¹/₂ x 5 inch) oak rail notched over studs and balusters
2 25 x 125 mm (1 x 5 inch) oak balusters reducing to 25 x 75 mm (1 x 3 inch) around beams and joists, alternating with notched studs
3 25 x 50 mm (1 x 2 inch) studs deepens to 25 x 125 mm (1 x 5 inch) above skirting rail
4 40 x 125 mm (1¹/₂ x 5 inch) oak rail notched over studs and balusters
5 25 mm (1 inch) oak skirting
6 2 x 12 mm (¹/₈ x ¹/₂ inch) oak ply with lapped joints
7 Rebate at end of steel stringer embedded into central oak stud with side fixings through pre-drilled holes
8 13 mm (¹/₂ inch) steel stringer with 12 mm (¹/₂ inch) oak ply either side with top and underside visible
9 Three sided 20 x 6 mm (³/₄ x ¹/₄ inch) steel frame embedded flush in rear of tread with horizontal 20 x 6 mm (³/₄ x ¹/₄ inch) top member set flush into underside of tread above, all to this flight only
10 Bracket into pocket in existing masonry

131

Brione House
Locarno, Switzerland

Client
Private

Project Team
Markus Wespi, Jérôme de Meuron

Structural Engineer
IFEC Consulenze

Main Contractor
Merlini + Ferrari

This strikingly austere stone house is located in Brione sopra Minusio, a small town in the canton of Ticino, Switzerland. Positioned on a forest covered mountainside, high above Locarno, the house has commanding views over the blue waters of Lake Maggiore. The house has been designed as a direct response to two critical site-specific conditions: the spectacular views and the desire to capture them, and the need to create privacy and solitude in a built up neighbourhood of closely spaced residences. The latter constraint led to the rejection of any typical architectural forms, including the usual arrangements of large windows and terraces.

Instead, the house presents itself as a solid, almost fortress-like stone structure, protectively anchored into the steep hillside. Two stone-clad volumes have been tucked into the site, one below the other to negotiate the steep slope. The lower volume acts as the main entrance and garage, accessed through a remotely operated timber gate that rises into a concealed slot. From the garage, lit from above through a slot of glazing at the end of the swimming pool, a stone stair rises in a continuous flight, arriving in the stone walled courtyard of the upper volume.

The courtyard offers an open portal to the swimming pool and leads into the living spaces via a glazed wall. From here, a separate stair built against the rear wall leads to the top level bedrooms and bathrooms, each bedroom with its own courtyard. The lack of windows is counteracted by a series of top-lit voids and courtyards and serves to concentrate the view when it is made available from the living spaces, and from the garden and pool. From here, the neighbours seem far away, the hillside drops away and panoramic views of the waters of Lake Maggiore are centre stage.

1 The roughness of the stone walls are contrasted with crisp pre-cast concrete elements including window and door lintels and the pool surround. The entrance courtyard (right) provides direct access to the pool via a flight of underwater steps.
2 In the garage, light dramatically slices into the space through a skylight at the end of the swimming pool above. The stair to the living spaces above (right) is cut into a dramatic wall of sloping concrete that forms the shell of the pool and the wall to the technical room.
3 Light is brought down into the house from above through a series of open voids and small courtyards.
4 The floor and walls, both inside and out, are constructed from granite, used in a traditional rough coursed arrangement for the walls and a more formal pattern of large flags for the floor.

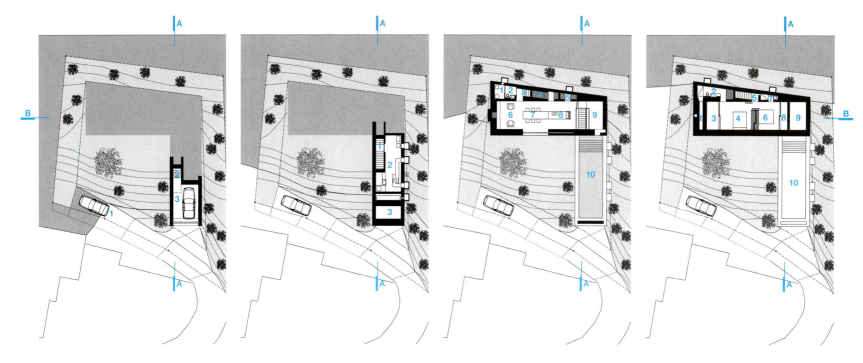

31.01
Basement Level 2
Floor Plan
1:500
1 Parking
2 Stairs
3 Garage

31.02
Basement Level 1
Floor Plan
1:500
1 Stair
2 Plant room
3 Void over garage

31.03
Ground Floor Plan
1:500
1 Store
2 WC
3 Stair
4 Firewood store
5 Pantry
6 Living area
7 Dining area
8 Kitchen
9 Courtyard
10 Swimming pool

31.04
First Floor Plan
1:500
1 Light well over
 living area
2 Bathroom
3 Courtyard
4 Bedroom
5 Stair
6 Bedroom
7 Shower room
8 Courtyard
9 Void over
 courtyard below
10 Swimming pool

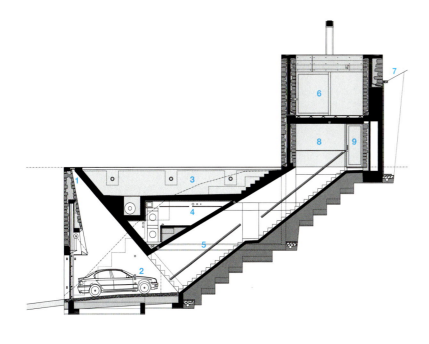

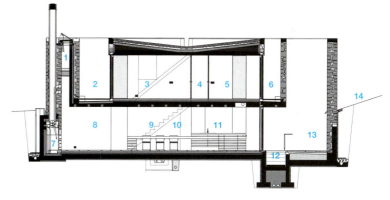

31.05
Section A–A
1:200
1 Light well to
 garage
2 Garage
3 Swimming pool
4 Plant room
5 Stair
6 Courtyard to
 bedroom

7 Ground line
8 Courtyard
9 Entrance

31.06
Section B–B
1:200
1 Light well
2 Courtyard
3 Bedroom
4 Wardrobes
5 Bedroom
6 Courtyard
7 Fireplace
8 Living area

9 Stair beyond
10 Dining area
11 Kitchen
12 Entrance stair
13 Courtyard
14 Ground line

**East Window Details
1:10**
1 8 mm (³/8 inch) thick vulcanized facade panels
2 230 x 310 mm (9 x 12¹/4 inch) pre-stressed concrete lintel
3 Natural stone cladding of varying sizes, maximum 250 mm (10 inch) thick, set in mortar over reinforced concrete roof structure
4 Grout bedding
5 250 mm (10 inch) reinforced concrete roof slab
6 Recess for sun shade electric motor
7 Steel bracing bar
8 Electrically operated external sun shade
9 Waterproof membrane
10 460 mm (18 inch) concrete beam
11 Limestone lintel
12 68 x 120 mm (2⁵/8 x 4³/4 inch) timber door frame to sliding glass door
13 Double glazing
14 22 mm (⁷/8 inch) aluminium shutter rail guides for sun shade
15 Sliding glazed window beyond shown dotted
16 Silicon fill to window surround
17 Modular stone paving
18 Waterproof membrane
19 290 mm (11³/8 inch) reinforced concrete floor slab
20 90 mm (3¹/2 inch) concrete screed with underfloor heating
21 40 mm (1¹/2 inch) bedding mortar
22 60 mm (2³/8 inch) rigid insulation
23 290 mm (11³/8 inch) reinforced concrete floor slab
24 Double glazed top hung window
25 Granite paving slabs
26 Mortar bed
27 140 mm (5¹/2 inch) concrete edge beam
28 Granite flooring slabs
29 150 mm (6 inch) screed bed with underfloor heating
30 45 mm (1³/4 inch) rigid insulation
31 250 mm (10 inch) reinforced concrete floor slab

**31.09
Typical External Wall
Section Detail
1:10**
1 Natural stone cladding of varying sizes, maximum 250 mm (10 inch) thick
2 Bedding mortar
3 Grout bedding
4 250 mm (10 inch) reinforced concrete roof slab
5 460 mm (18 inch) concrete beam
6 250 mm (10 inch) reinforced concrete wall
7 Waterproof membrane to 35 mm (1³/8 inch) cavity
8 Concrete bed
9 Natural stone cladding of varying sizes, maximum 250 mm (10 inch) thick, set in mortar over reinforced concrete wall structure
10 90 mm (3¹/2 inch) concrete screed with underfloor heating
11 40 mm (1¹/2 inch) bedding mortar
12 290 mm (11³/8 inch) reinforced concrete floor slab
13 Granite flooring slabs
14 150 mm (6 inch) screed bed with underfloor heating
15 45 mm (1³/4 inch) rigid insulation
16 250 mm (10 inch) reinforced concrete floor slab
17 Mortar fill to bottom of cavity
18 35 mm (1³/8 inch) protective mortar bed to slab edge
19 Gravel bed for rain water filtration
20 Filtration grid to exposed slab edge

**31.07
Garage and
Swimming Pool
Section Detail
1:50**
1 250 mm (10 inch) thick reinforced concrete structure and pool shell
2 Plant room
3 100 mm (4 inch) high rendered concrete pool edge
4 Swimming pool
5 Swimming pool filtration system
6 250 mm (10 inch) wide trafficable skylight
7 Natural stone cladding of varying sizes, maximum 250 mm (10 inch) thick, set in mortar over reinforced concrete wall structure
8 200 x 460 mm (8 x 18 inch) pre-stressed concrete lintel
9 Moisture resistant permanent formwork with integrated reinforcing to concrete wall structure
10 220 mm (8¹/2 inch) cavity for garage door track installation
11 Minimum 350 mm (13³/4 inch) thick rubble stone wall set in reinforced concrete wall structure
12 330 x 220 mm (13 x 8¹/2 inch) pre-stressed concrete lintel over garage door track mounting
13 Motor unit to automatic garage door
14 Emergency electric cable for automatic garage door
15 320 x 500 mm (12¹/2 x 19³/4 inch) pre-stressed concrete lintel with cast-in light recess
16 45 mm (1³/4 inch) thick timber grid automatic garage door
17 Emergency manual door release
18 Intercom speaker
19 On-off switch for garage door
20 Electric movement detector
21 Reinforced concrete footing
22 Entrance stair beyond shown dotted
23 150 mm (6 inch) deep stone paving in mortar bed to garage floor
24 Geotextile fabric
25 400 mm (15³/4 inch) deep gravel bed

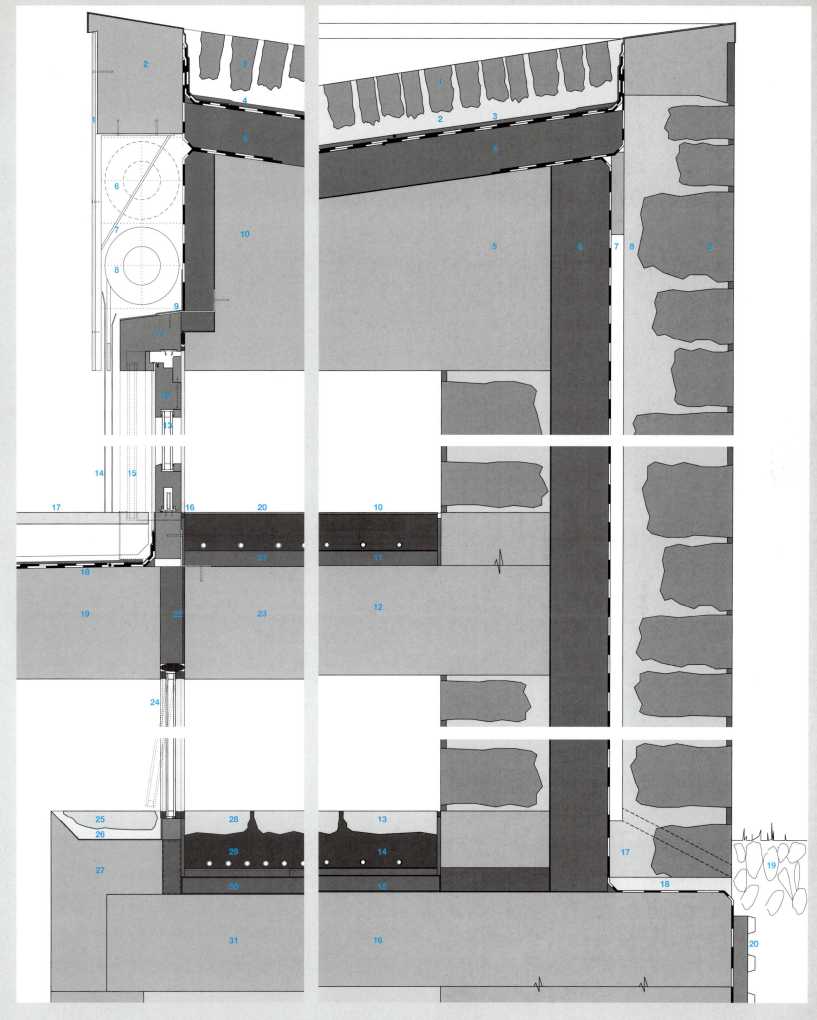

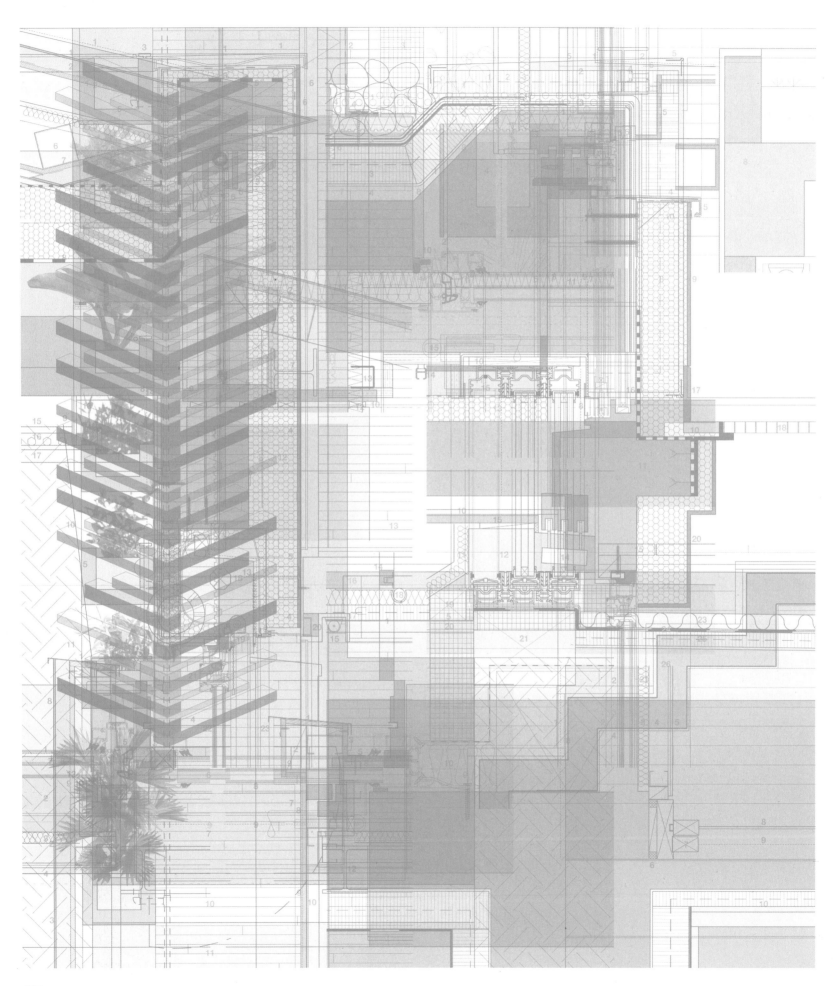

Concrete House
Madrid, Spain

Client
Private

Project Team
Joaquín Torres, Rafael Llamazares

Landscaping
Benavides Laperche

Main Contractor
Tudic

This large 1,500 square metre (16,145 square foot) house near Madrid sits low in an architecturally constructed landscape of lawns, manicured planes of planting, expansive stone terraces and water features. Constructed entirely of precision off-form concrete, its grey bulk is relieved by dispersing the accommodation over two levels and introducing large expanses of north and south facing glazing, as well as fragmenting the composition through a variety of solid, open, horizontal and vertical elements.

The upper floor is divided into three primary zones. Firstly the family spaces – two living areas, a dining area, the kitchen and children's recreation area are assembled in a stepped plan form arranged towards the north-east corner of the building to open onto the stone paved terrace. Secondly, private sleeping and bathing spaces consisting of four bedrooms, each with its own bathroom, dressing and sitting area, as well as an office, occupy the north-west corner of the plan and benefit from direct access to north or south facing terraces and patio gardens. These two zones are roughly bisected by an entrance sequence that begins with an extended stone path that runs alongside a reflection pool, through a covered entrance portico and terminates in an entrance lobby with a sky lit void. Lastly the outdoor relaxation zone is accessed directly from the living spaces and extends to the swimming pool via a mobile gazebo and pool terrace.

The lower level contains a large garage, accessed via a ramp cut into the site beside the house, as well as other service functions such as storage rooms, wine cellar, pantry store and staff break and change rooms. In addition, a guest accommodation suite and gym open up to an expansive lawn via large sliding glass doors.

1 The black steel frame of the pool gazebo is reflected in the swimming pool, emphasizing the layered off-form concrete and stone paved terraces that comprise the north facing outdoor living areas.
2 The pool and living terrace (left) are contrasted with an apron of clipped lawn that runs up to the guest suite and gymnasium on the lower floor (centre) and is overlooked by the bedrooms on the first floor (right).
3 A view of the entrance where the precision detailing is evident in the regular pattern of circular holes left in the concrete walls by the tie bolts in the shuttering.
4 The entrance hall looking back over the reflection pool towards the covered street entrance.
5 In the entrance hall, a sky lit, glass encased concrete blade wall rises through two floors and acts as a privacy screen to the master suite bathroom.

32.01
Basement Floor Plan
1:500
1 Pool plant
2 Void under pool
3 Landscaped ramp
4 Pit for vertical sliding window in living room above
5 Garage
6 Entrance to garage
7 Garden
8 Terrace
9 Store
10 Gym
11 Guest suite
12 Wine cellar
13 WC
14 Guest suite store
15 Stair to upper floor
16 Ramp
17 Staff changing room
18 Staff changing room
19 Sunken patio
20 Staff room
21 Laundry
22 Car parts store
23 Store
24 Kitchen store
25 Technical plant
26 Technical plant

32.02
Ground Floor Plan
1:500
1 Swimming pool
2 Pool terrace
3 Pool gazebo
4 Living terrace
5 Living area
6 Outdoor dining terrace
7 Living area
8 Dining area
9 Fireplace
10 Stair to basement
11 Staff office
12 Pantry
13 Kitchen
14 Bedroom terrace
15 Bedroom
16 Bedroom
17 Master suite living
18 Master suite bedroom
19 Children's recreation area
20 Ensuite bathroom
21 Ensuite bathroom
22 Master suite dressing room
23 Master suite dressing room
24 Master suite bathroom
25 Ensuite bathroom
26 Bedroom
27 Garden
28 Office
29 Reflection pool
30 Cloakroom
31 Entrance hall
32 Carport
33 Water feature
34 Covered entrance
35 Driveway

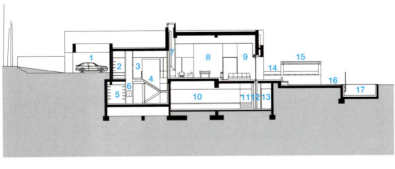

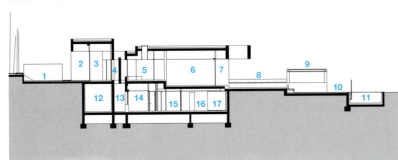

32.03
Section A–A
1:500
1 Carport
2 Kitchen
3 Hallway
4 Stair
5 Pantry
6 Dumb waiter
7 Fireplace
8 Living area
9 Living area
10 Garage
11 Stair and door to store
12 Pit for vertical sliding window in living area above
13 Pool plant
14 Terrace
15 Pool gazebo
16 Pool terrace
17 Swimming pool

32.04
Section B–B
1:500
1 Water feature and reflection pool
2 Covered entrance
3 Entrance hall
4 Light well
5 Master suite bathroom
6 Children's recreation area
7 Children's covered terrace
8 Terrace
9 Pool gazebo
10 Pool terrace
11 Swimming pool
12 Technical plant
13 Sunken patio
14 Laundry
15 Guest suite bathroom
16 Guest suite
17 Door to terrace

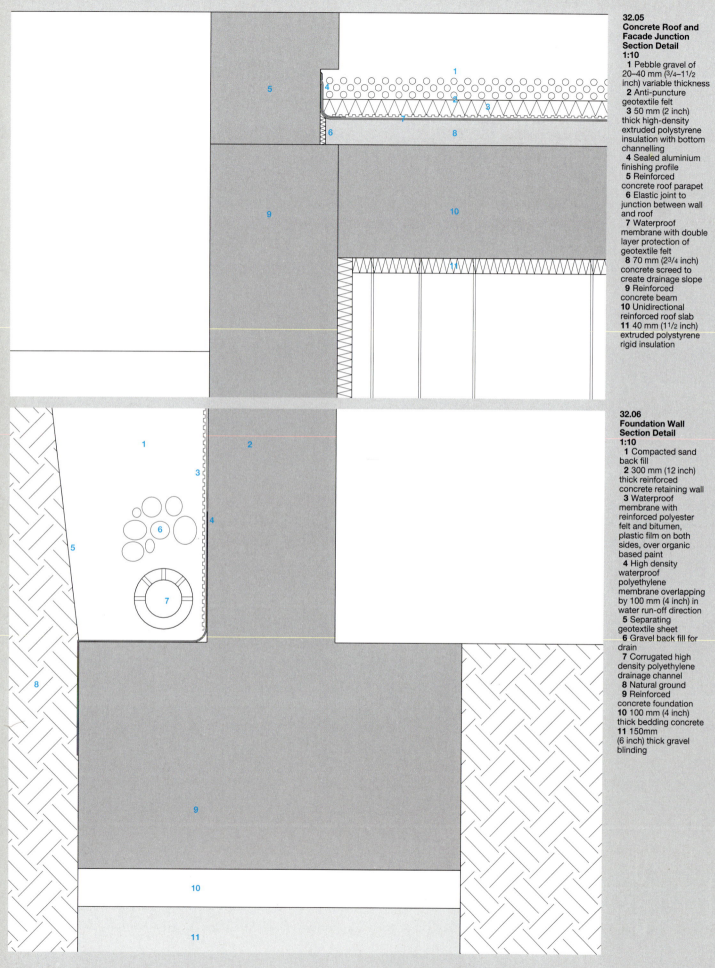

32.05
Concrete Roof and Facade Junction Section Detail
1:10
1 Pebble gravel of 20–40 mm ($3/4$–$11/2$ inch) variable thickness
2 Anti-puncture geotextile felt
3 50 mm (2 inch) thick high-density extruded polystyrene insulation with bottom channelling
4 Sealed aluminium finishing profile
5 Reinforced concrete roof parapet
6 Elastic joint to junction between wall and roof
7 Waterproof membrane with double layer protection of geotextile felt
8 70 mm ($23/4$ inch) concrete screed to create drainage slope
9 Reinforced concrete beam
10 Unidirectional reinforced roof slab
11 40 mm ($11/2$ inch) extruded polystyrene rigid insulation

32.06
Foundation Wall Section Detail
1:10
1 Compacted sand back fill
2 300 mm (12 inch) thick reinforced concrete retaining wall
3 Waterproof membrane with reinforced polyester felt and bitumen, plastic film on both sides, over organic based paint
4 High density waterproof polyethylene membrane overlapping by 100 mm (4 inch) in water run-off direction
5 Separating geotextile sheet
6 Gravel back fill for drain
7 Corrugated high density polyethylene drainage channel
8 Natural ground
9 Reinforced concrete foundation
10 100 mm (4 inch) thick bedding concrete
11 150mm (6 inch) thick gravel blinding

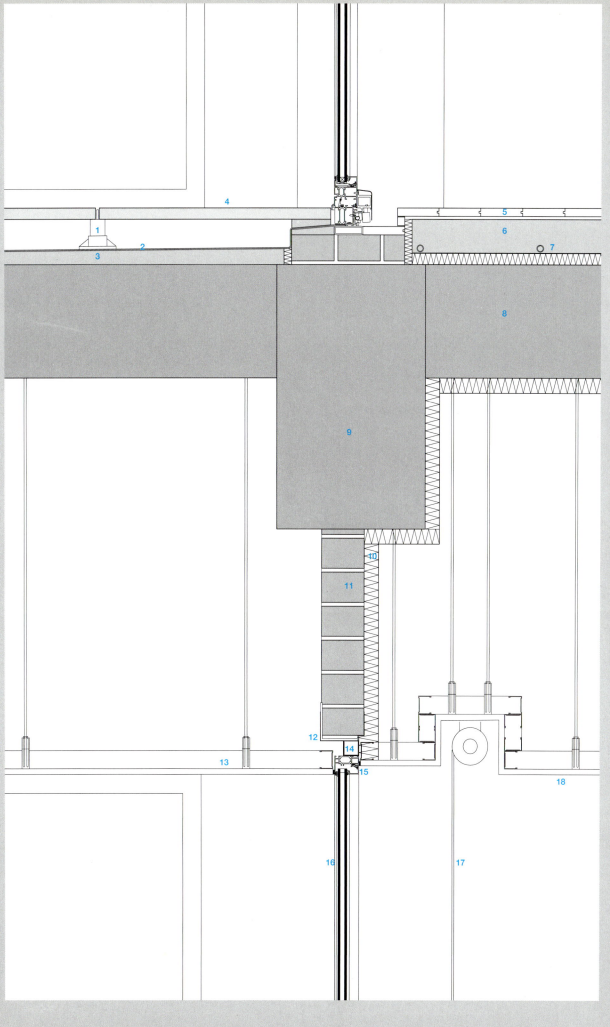

32.07
Window, Floor and Suspended Ceiling Junction Section Detail
1:10

1 Adjustable polystyrene support feet to stone terrace
2 Rubber waterproof membrane with geotextile felt
3 Enlargement of lightened concrete for slope formation approx. 50 mm (2 inch)
4 30 mm (1$^1/_5$ inch) thick natural stone pavers
5 Suspended scaffold of natural wood placed over felt sheet
6 70 mm (2$^3/_4$ inch) concrete screed to create drainage slope
7 Flexible pre-insulated underfloor heating conduits over 30 mm (1$^1/_5$ inch) insulation
8 Unidirectional reinforced concrete floor slab
9 Reinforced concrete beam
10 40 mm (1$^1/_2$ inch) thick extruded polystyrene rigid insulation
11 115 mm (4$^1/_2$ inch) thick perforated brick partition wall
12 100 x 100 x 5 mm (4 x 4 x $^1/_5$ inch) laminated steel structural support profile
13 Continuous suspended soffit lining of cementitious board with plastic paint finish
14 Galvanized steel hollow square section framing
15 Hidden lacquered aluminium window frame
16 Fixed double glazing
17 Roller blind
18 Suspended, painted plasterboard ceiling

**Earth House
Gyeonggi-do, South Korea**

Client
Byoung Soo Cho

Project Team
Hong-joon Yang, Woo-Hyun Kang,
Tae-Hyun Nam

Structural Engineer
C&O International

Main Contractor
CPLUS International

This extraordinarily simple dwelling was built to honour Yoon Dong-joo, a Korean poet whose work was concerned with nature, especially with the sky and the earth. As such, the building seeks to express and intensify the relationship between humans and nature.

Set within a 14.2 x 7.6 metre (46 x 25 foot) underground pit enclosed by thick concrete walls, the house is composed of six rooms and two earth-filled courtyards. Each room is the same size – one pyeong – derived from a traditional Korean unit of built space that relates to the size needed for an adult to lie down. Opening directly from the large main courtyard is a kitchen, a resting space (used for both living and sleeping) and a utility area. A bathroom with a wooden bath and toilet, the second resting space and the study open onto the smaller courtyard, in effect, a narrow light well.

Access to the house is via a stair cut into the ground and opening into the main courtyard. The entrance doors in the courtyard wall have raised thresholds and lowered head heights so that people entering the building are required to bend down and more obviously experience the process of entering the domestic space. Internal walls are made from rammed earth from the excavation. Sections from the trunk of a pine tree cut down on the site are set into the courtyard walls. As they decay they will provide opportunities for plants to grow. The building is heated and cooled using a geothermal cooling system with a radiant floor heating system under the rammed clay and concrete floor.

1 The house is all but invisible in its wooded site. Access to the main courtyard is from a concrete stairway cut into the ground.
2 Concrete retaining walls define the courtyard and the external walls of the house itself, and are also used for the primary roof. A small secondary roof shelters the entrance terrace.
3 The entry sequence from the courtyard crosses a row of stone slabs that sit on top of the rammed earth courtyard floor, then step up to a timber terrace, then to the raised threshold of the entrance door itself.
4 View from the terrace through the courtyard to the entrance stair. The slices of pine cast into the concrete walls provide points of focus and a memory of what once grew on the site. Over time they will decay, acting as a reminder that nothing is permanent.
5 The sleeping areas feature a practical storage and sitting area (right) and openings with deep reveals that can be used as window seats.

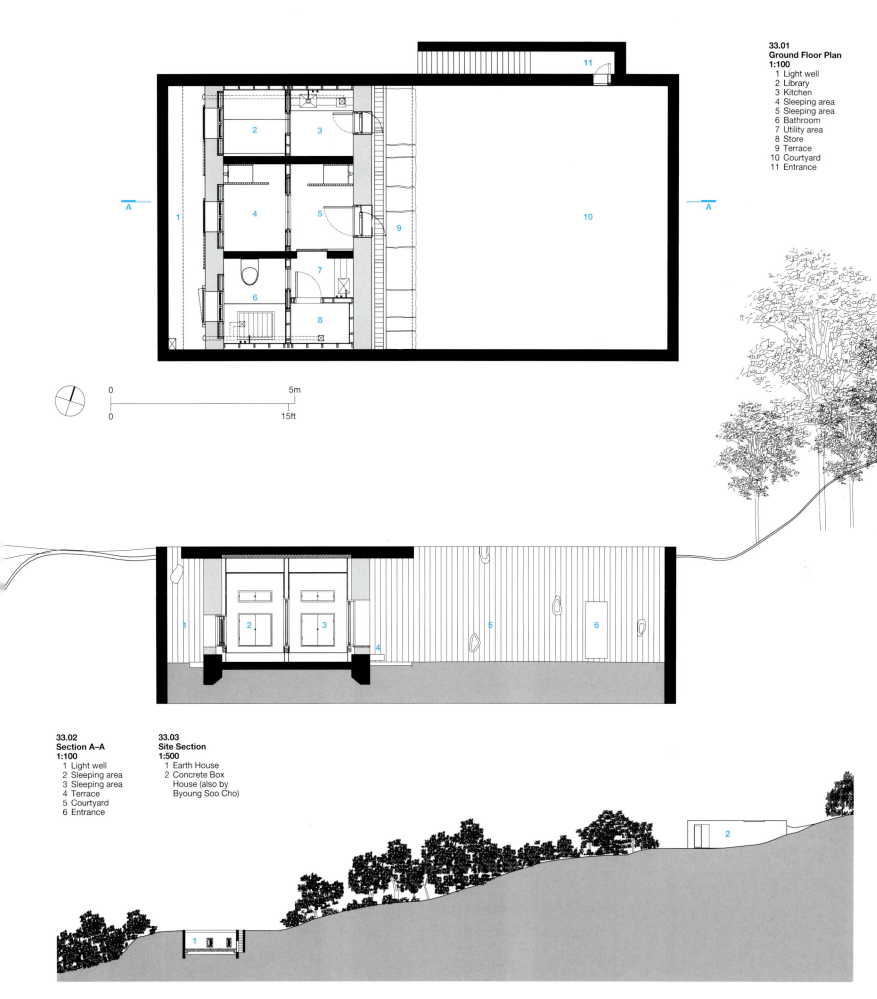

33.01
Ground Floor Plan
1:100
  1 Light well
  2 Library
  3 Kitchen
  4 Sleeping area
  5 Sleeping area
  6 Bathroom
  7 Utility area
  8 Store
  9 Terrace
 10 Courtyard
 11 Entrance

0
5m
0
15ft

33.02
Section A–A
1:100
  1 Light well
  2 Sleeping area
  3 Sleeping area
  4 Terrace
  5 Courtyard
  6 Entrance

33.03
Site Section
1:500
  1 Earth House
  2 Concrete Box
    House (also by
    Byoung Soo Cho)

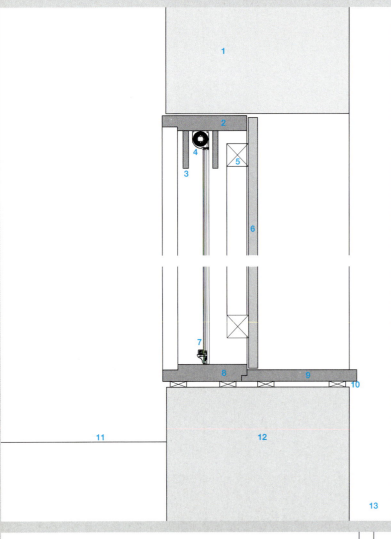

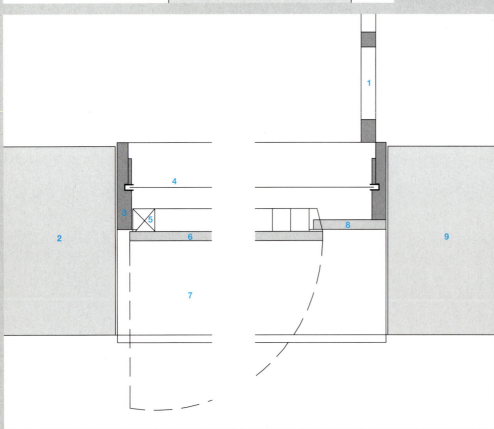

33.04
Window and External Shutter Door to Courtyard Wall Head and Sill Section Detail
1:10
 1 500 mm (19³/4 inch) thick rammed earth wall
 2 30 x 230 mm (1¹/5 x 9 inch) timber window frame and reveal
 3 15 x 100 mm (⁵/8 x 4 inch) timber pelmet
 4 Roller for retractable insect screen
 5 50 x 50 mm (2 x 2 inch) timber stiffener frame to shutter panel
 6 25 mm (1 inch) thick external timber door and shutter
 7 Retractable insect screen
 8 30 x 230 mm (1¹/5 x 9 inch) timber window frame and reveal
 9 30 x 300 mm (1¹/5 x 12 inch) timber tread plate
 10 20 mm (³/4 inch) timber packers and shadow gap
 11 Finished interior floor level
 12 500 mm (19³/4 inch) thick rammed earth wall
 13 Entry terrace

33.05
Window and External Shutter Door to Courtyard Wall Plan Detail
1:10
 1 Timber framed sliding internal partition
 2 500 mm (19³/4 inch) thick rammed earth wall
 3 30 x 230 mm (1¹/5 x 9 inch) timber window frame and reveal
 4 Retractable insect screen
 5 50 x 50 mm (2 x 2 inch) timber stiffener frame to shutter panel
 6 25 mm (1 inch) thick external timber door and shutter
 7 30 x 300 mm (1¹/5 x 12 inch) timber tread plate
 8 30 x 200 mm (1¹/5 x 8 inch) fixed timber panel
 9 500 mm (19³/4 inch) thick rammed earth wall

33.06
Window Section Detail to Light Well Wall Through Sliding Panels in Open Position
1:10
 1 500 mm (19³/4 inch) thick rammed earth wall
 2 160 x 60 mm (6¹/4 x 2³/8 inch) timber box frame and reveal with slider profile
 3 Sliding window in 30 mm (1¹/5 inch) pine window frame
 4 Traditional handmade Korean paper over pocket for sliding windows
 5 Finished interior floor level

33.07
Window to Light Well Wall Head and Sill Section Detail
1:10
 1 500 mm (19³/4 inch) thick rammed earth wall
 2 Steel lintel
 3 50 x 50 mm (2 x 2 inch) timber box frame with slider profile for insect screen
 4 Timber framed sliding insect screen
 5 160 x 60 mm (6¹/4 x 2³/8 inch) timber box frame and reveal with slider profile
 6 Sliding window in 30mm (1¹/5 inch) pine window frame

33.08
Window to Light Well Wall Head and Sill Plan Detail
1:10
 1 Timber framed sliding insect screen
 2 Steel stopper plate fixed to rammed earth wall
 3 Timber framed insect screen in open position shown dotted
 4 500 mm (19³/4 inch) thick rammed earth wall
 5 Rammed earth sill
 6 160 x 60 mm (6¹/4 x 2³/8 inch) timber box frame and reveal with slider profile
 7 Sliding window in open position shown dotted
 8 Traditional handmade Korean paper over pocket for sliding windows
 9 40 x 35 mm (1¹/2 x 1³/8 inch) timber frame to paper screen
 10 Sliding window in 30mm (1¹/5 inch) pine window frame

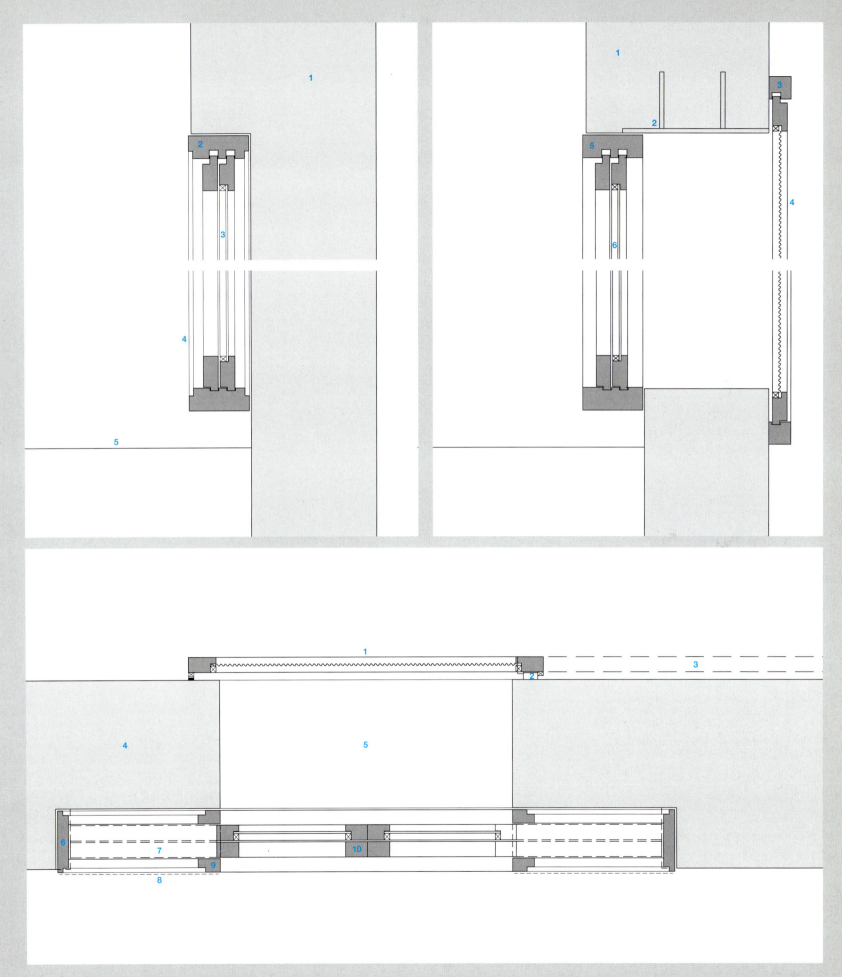

**Jelenovac Residence
Zagreb, Croatia**

Client
Private

Project Team
Tomislav Ćurković, Zoran Zidarić

Collaborator
Maja Markus

Structural Engineer
Projekt Konstrukcija

Main Contractor
Izgradnja

The house is situated in a densely wooded residential area on the northern outskirts of Zagreb in the foothills of the Medvednica massif, a designated nature reserve popular for winter sports. In a cluster of mostly traditional residential buildings, Jelenovac Residence stands out as a lone example of contemporary architecture. Located adjacent to a small public park, the house, which takes up the majority of its plot, appropriates views across the grassy park that slopes away from the house, to the forest beyond.

Built on a gentle slope, rubble stonework is used as both a perimeter wall and building podium, on which sits a bright white two-storey cubic structure punctuated by deep set, crisp black openings. This grey, black and white composition, rough where it touches the ground and smooth above, is in stark contrast with both the built and natural context and proposes a new aesthetic for residential architecture in Croatia.

The building is expressed as two unequal rectangular prisms, connected by a smaller volume in between. This hinge in the building allows it to follow the contours of the site and to take advantage of a variety of views. On the ground floor, all of the living spaces are in the larger volume, while in the smaller one are service spaces such as cloakroom, laundry and storage. Upstairs, the two volumes contain private spaces including bedrooms, bathrooms and a smaller sitting space with access to a south facing terrace. In the link volume, a sensuously curved dark wooden spiral staircase contrasts with the bright white orthogonal surfaces elsewhere in the house.

1 The front of the house is a balanced composition of smooth white render and textured dark grey stone. Black shutters to the punctured window openings complete the monochrome composition.
2 At the rear of the house, the lower dining area opens out onto the garden. Above is a wide terrace on top of the stone podium accessed from the mid level living spaces.
3 The walnut veneer-clad staircase spirals through the building contrasting in colour, texture and geometry with the pale white walls and blond timber floors.
4 The main living spaces open directly from the entrance foyer and stair hall (left). The kitchen and dining space are separated from the living space (right) by a change in level. All of the living spaces benefit from direct access to the stone walled terrace.

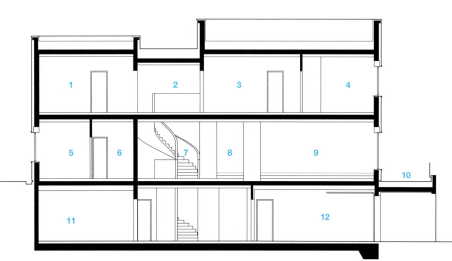

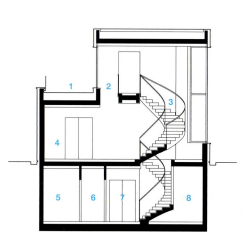

34.01
First Floor Plan
1:200
1 Bedroom
2 Ensuite bathroom
3 Sitting area
4 Terrace
5 Stair
6 Void
7 Ensuite bathroom
8 Master bedroom
9 Dressing room
10 Bathroom
11 Bedroom and
   study space
12 Bedroom and
   study space

34.02
Ground Floor Plan
1:200
1 Store
2 Laundry
3 Entrance
4 WC
5 Stair
6 Void
7 Kitchen
8 Dining area
9 Living area

34.03
Section A–A
1:200
1 Bedroom
2 Stair hall
3 Hallway
4 Bedroom and
   study space
5 Store
6 Entrance lobby
7 Stair hall
8 Kitchen
9 Dining area
10 Terrace
11 Technical store
12 Garage

34.04
Section B–B
1:200
1 Terrace
2 Void
3 Stair
4 Entrance lobby
5 Sauna
6 Hall
7 WC
8 Storage

0   5   10m

0   15   30ft

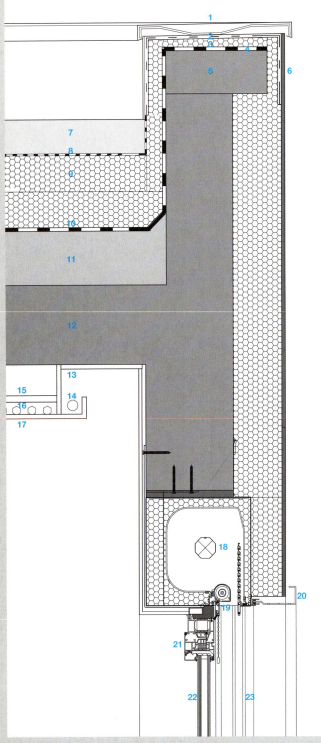

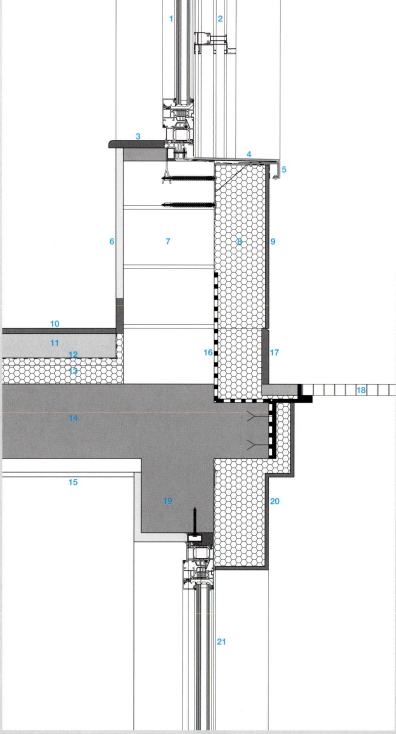

34.05
Roof Parapet,
External Wall and
Window Head
Section Detail
1:10

1 40 mm (1¹/₂ inch) aluminium parapet capping
2 50 mm (2 inch) flexible waterproofing and crack-isolation membrane
3 50 mm (2 inch) rigid insulation
4 Waterproof membrane
5 Concrete parapet
6 10 mm (³/₈ inch) cement render

7 100 mm (4 inch) gravel to roof
8 Geotextile membrane
9 250 mm (10 inch) thermal insulation
10 50 mm (2 inch) flexible waterproofing and crack-isolation membrane
11 170 mm (6³/₄ inch) concrete topping
12 220 mm (8¹/₂ inch) concrete roof slab
13 Painted plasterboard ceiling
14 Concealed light fixture
15 18 mm (³/₄ inch) oriented strand board

16 36 mm (1³/₈ inch) chilled ceiling system
17 12.5 mm (¹/₂ inch) insulated ceiling panel
18 Electrically operated metal security shutter
19 External blind
20 Aluminium window reveal
21 Aluminium window frame
22 Double glazing
23 Guide rails for security shutter

34.06
External Wall,
Window Head and Sill
Section Detail
1:10

1 Aluminium framed double glazing
2 Guide rails for security shutter
3 Painted MDF interior window sill
4 Aluminium window sill
5 Folded aluminium drip profile
6 20 mm (³/₄ inch) thick painted plaster to interior wall
7 200 mm (8 inch) brick wall

8 140 mm (5¹/₂ inch) rigid insulation
9 10 mm (³/₈ inch) cement render
10 14 mm (⁵/₈ inch) thick parquet flooring
11 70 mm (2³/₄ inch) concrete topping
12 Geotextile membrane
13 50 mm (2 inch) rigid insulation
14 220 mm (8¹/₂ inch) reinforced concrete floor slab
15 Suspended plasterboard ceiling
16 Waterproof membrane
17 Stone plinth to wall

base
18 Metal grid sun shade
19 Reinforced concrete downstand beam
20 10 mm (³/₈ inch) cement render
21 Aluminium framed double glazing

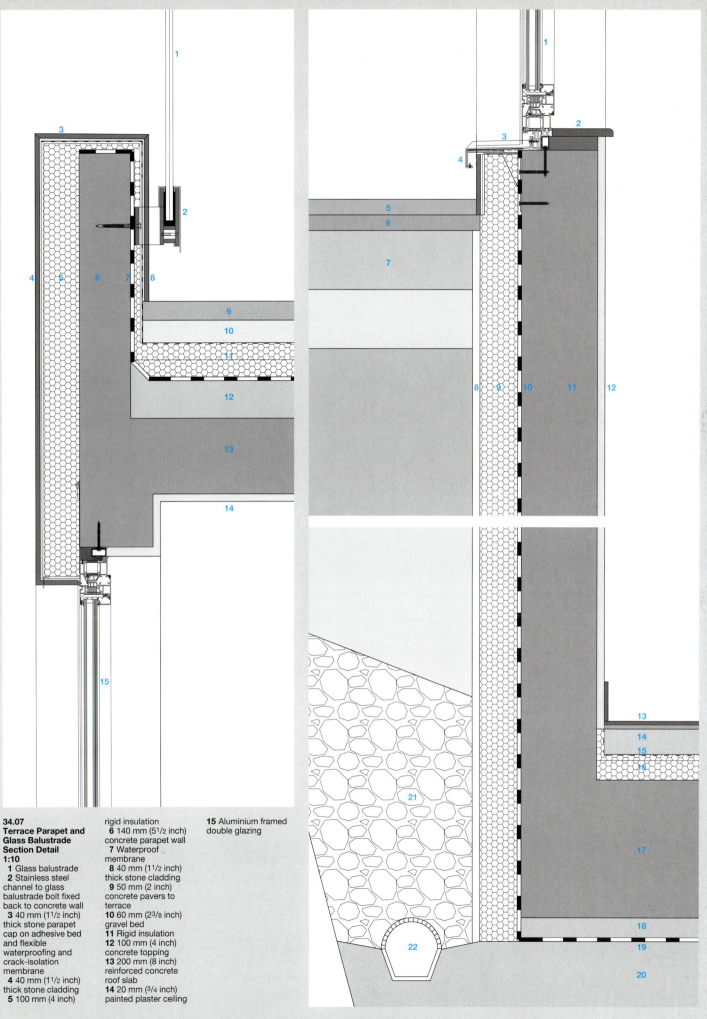

 1 Aluminium framed double glazing
 2 Painted MDF interior window sill
 3 Aluminium window sill
 4 Folded aluminium drip profile
 5 40 mm (1¹/2 inch) concrete paver
 6 40 mm (1¹/2 inch) cement mortar
 7 Reinforced concrete floor slab
 8 Cavity drain membrane
 9 100 mm (4 inch) rigid insulation
 10 Waterproof membrane
 11 200 mm (8 inch) reinforced concrete wall
 12 20 mm (³/4 inch) cement render to external wall
 13 20 mm (³/4 inch) ceramic floor tiles on tile adhesive bed
 14 Concrete screed
 15 Vapour barrier
 16 Extruded polystyrene rigid insulation
 17 350 mm (13³/4 inch) reinforced concrete floor slab
 18 50 mm (2 inch) waterproofing compound of light concrete
 19 Waterproof membrane
 20 300 mm (12 inch) gravel bed
 21 Hardcore backfill
 22 Drain

34.07
Terrace Parapet and Glass Balustrade Section Detail
1:10
 1 Glass balustrade
 2 Stainless steel channel to glass balustrade bolt fixed back to concrete wall
 3 40 mm (1¹/2 inch) thick stone parapet cap on adhesive bed and flexible waterproofing and crack-isolation membrane
 4 40 mm (1¹/2 inch) thick stone cladding
 5 100 mm (4 inch) rigid insulation
 6 140 mm (5¹/2 inch) concrete parapet wall
 7 Waterproof membrane
 8 40 mm (1¹/2 inch) thick stone cladding
 9 50 mm (2 inch) concrete pavers to terrace
 10 60 mm (2³/8 inch) gravel bed
 11 Rigid insulation
 12 100 mm (4 inch) concrete topping
 13 200 mm (8 inch) reinforced concrete roof slab
 14 20 mm (³/4 inch) painted plaster ceiling
 15 Aluminium framed double glazing

Villa 921
Iriomote Island, Okinawa, Japan

Client
Kenji Kunii

Project Team
Shoko Murakaji, Naoto Murakaji

Structural Engineer
Tatsumi Terado Structural Studio

Main Contractors
Hatiken Jitujyo, Iriomote Takashi

Villa 921 is located on Iriomote Island, the largest of Japan's beautiful Yaeyama Islands. Lacking an airstrip, the island is only accessible by ferry. Infrastructure for the population of only several thousand permanent residents is limited to a single coastal road connecting the hamlets on the northern and eastern shores, leaving the remaining 90 per cent of the island covered in dense jungle and mangrove swamps which form the protected Iriomote National Park.

The minimal, single storey house is designed to meet the simple needs of the clients who have lived on the island for many years. The modest 70 square metre (753 square feet) floor area is divided into three approximately equal zones with a kitchen and bathroom on one side, a bedroom on the opposite side, and a living and a dining space in the centre. Full width terraces to both the east and west are equipped with sliding glass doors to open the entire interior up to cooling breezes in the hot summers. Conversely, storm shutters can be deployed across both glazed facades to protect the house from seasonal typhoons.

The house is built primarily from reinforced concrete which has been used for both internal and external walls as well as the pitched roof. Unusually, gutters have been dispensed with to allow rainwater to run down the exterior walls to remove the salt residue which collects in this marine environment. The interior features plain white painted walls with timber floors and joinery to contrast with the concrete shell.

1 The entire west side of the house can be completely opened up through large glass sliding doors which open onto an elevated covered terrace with expansive views over the coastal farmland.
2 Deep eaves to the covered terrace keep the sun from the interior. Windbreak nets can be attached to the outer edge of the terrace roof to mitigate against regular typhoons.
3 The structure, essentially a concrete extrusion of roof, floor and north and south walls, is punctured by only one opening to the bedroom to take advantage of rural views to the south.
4 A narrow terrace to the east, also featuring a protective overhang and full height sliding glass doors, is further protected by a retained earth bank.
5 The interior features simple timber joinery including open shelves and built-in cupboards in the central living and dining space.

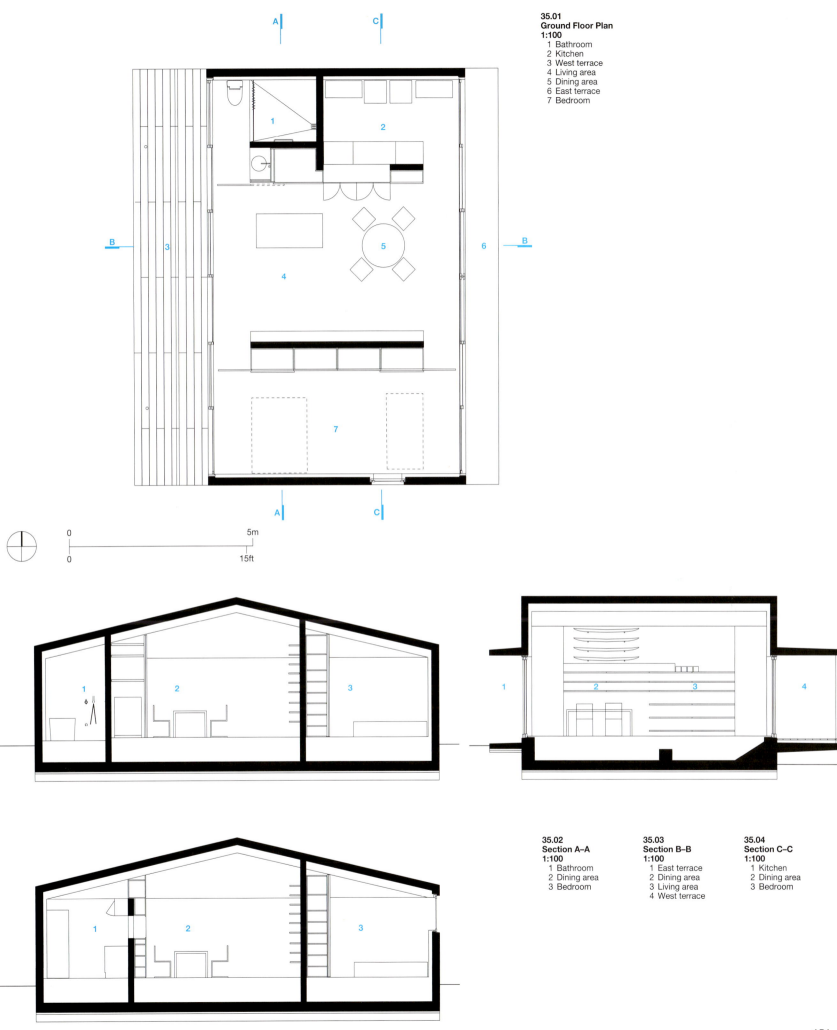

35.01
Ground Floor Plan
1:100
1 Bathroom
2 Kitchen
3 West terrace
4 Living area
5 Dining area
6 East terrace
7 Bedroom

0   5m

0   15ft

35.02
Section A–A
1:100
1 Bathroom
2 Dining area
3 Bedroom

35.03
Section B–B
1:100
1 East terrace
2 Dining area
3 Living area
4 West terrace

35.04
Section C–C
1:100
1 Kitchen
2 Dining area
3 Bedroom

151

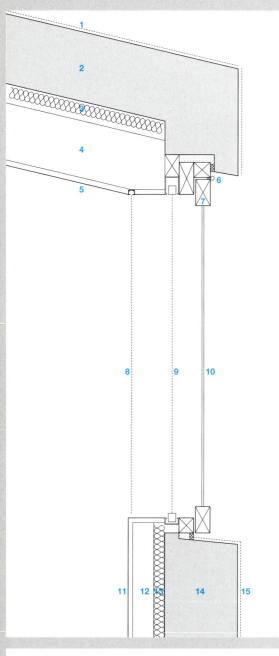

35.05
Window to Bedroom
Section Detail
1:10
 1 Waterproof coating
 2 180 mm (7 inch)
concrete roof
 3 50 mm (2 inch)
thick rigid styrofoam
insulation
 4 Timber framing
 5 12.5 mm (1/2 inch)
thick painted
plasterboard ceiling
 6 Silicone seal
 7 Hardwood door
frame with clear
varnish finish
 8 Curtain
 9 Sliding insect
screen
10 5mm (1/5 inch) thick
glass
11 12.5 mm (1/2 inch)
thick painted
plasterboard wall lining
12 Metal stud framing
13 50 mm (2 inch)
thick rigid styrofoam
insulation
14 180 mm (7 inch)
thick concrete wall
15 Waterproof coating

35.06
Window to Bedroom
Plan Detail
1:10
 1 Waterproof coating
 2 180 mm (7 inch)
concrete wall
 3 50 mm (2 inch)
thick rigid styrofoam
insulation
 4 12.5 mm (1/2 inch)
thick painted
plasterboard wall
 5 Metal stud framing
 6 Silicone seal
 7 Hardwood door
frame with clear
varnish finish
 8 5mm (1/5 inch) thick
glass
 9 Sliding insect
screen

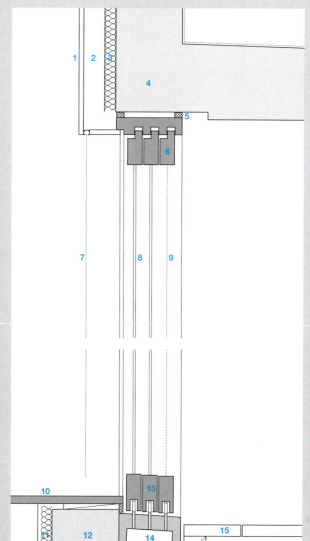

35.07
Sliding Glass Door
Section Detail
1:10
 1 12.5 mm (1/2 inch)
thick painted
plasterboard wall lining
 2 Metal stud framing
 3 50 mm (2 inch)
thick rigid styrofoam
insulation
 4 180 mm (7 inch)
concrete roof
 5 Silicone seal
 6 Hardwood door
frames with clear
varnish finish
 7 Curtain
 8 5 mm (1/5 inch)
thick glass to sliding
doors
 9 Sliding insect
screen
10 20 mm (3/4 inch)
thick teak floorboards
11 50 mm (2 inch)
thick rigid insulation
12 180 mm (7 inch)
concrete floor slab and
upstand beam
13 Hardwood door
frames with clear
varnish finish
14 Stainless sliding
track mechanism set in
mortar bed
15 30 mm (11/5 inch)
thick Japanese cedar
decking boards

35.08
Sliding Glass Door
Plan Detail
1:10
 1 Waterproof coating
 2 180 mm (7 inch)
concrete wall
 3 50 mm (2 inch)
thick rigid styrofoam
insulation
 4 Metal stud wall
framing
 5 12.5 mm (1/2 inch)
thick painted
plasterboard wall lining
 6 Silicone seal
 7 Hardwood door
frames with clear
varnish finish
 8 5 mm (1/5 inch)
thick glass to sliding
doors
 9 Sliding insect
screen
10 30 mm (11/5 inch)
thick Japanese cedar
decking boards

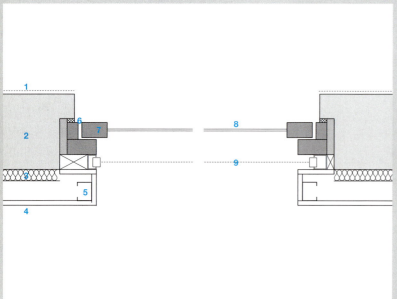

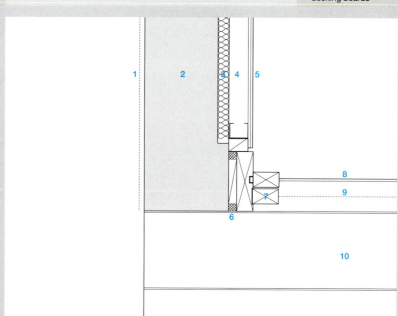

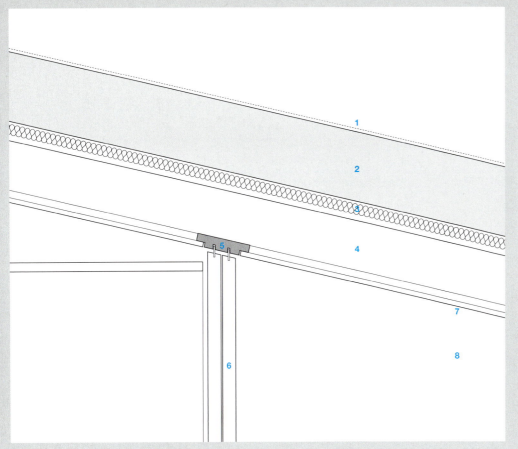

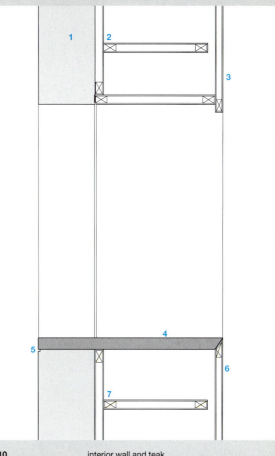

35.09
Interior Sliding Door Section Detail
1:10
 1 Waterproof coating
 2 180 mm (7 inch) concrete wall
 3 50 mm (2 inch) thick rigid styrofoam insulation
 4 Timber framing
 5 Hardwood sliding door frame with white paint finish and hardwood pins to sliding mechanism
 6 Plywood interior door with clear polyurethane coating

 7 12.5 mm (1/2 inch) thick painted plasterboard ceiling
 8 12.5 mm (1/2 inch) thick painted plasterboard wall lining

35.10
Kitchen Counter Section Detail
1:10
 1 150mm (6 inch) interior concrete wall with polyurethane finish
 2 Plywood joinery carcass with polyurethane finish
 3 Hinged kitchen cupboard door with downstand finger pull
 4 Teak kitchen counter with beeswax finish
 5 Cast in-situ shadow gap between concrete

interior wall and teak counter top
 6 Hinged kitchen cupboard door with mitred finger pull
 7 Plywood joinery carcass with polyurethane finish

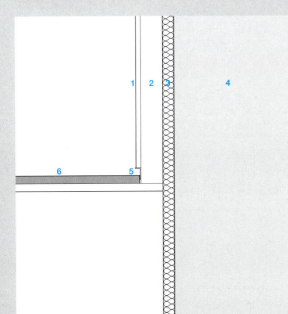

35.11
Interior Concrete Wall With Plasterboard Lining Section Detail
1:10
 1 12.5 mm (1/2 inch) thick painted plasterboard wall lining
 2 Metal stud wall framing
 3 50 mm (2 inch) thick rigid styrofoam insulation
 4 180 mm (7 inch) concrete wall
 5 15 x 30 x 2 mm (5/8 x 1 1/5 x 1/8 inch) aluminium angle shadow gap
 6 20 mm (3/4 inch) thick teak floorboards

35.12
Exposed Interior Concrete Wall Section Detail
1:10
 1 180 mm (7 inch) concrete wall with emulsion paint finish
 2 20 mm (3/4 inch) thick teak floorboards
 3 20 mm (3/4 inch) cast in-situ shadow gap

KW House
Esslingen, Germany

Client
Sabine Käß, Hans Walter

Project Team
Isolde Käß, Jan Hauschildt

Structural Engineer
Schneck-Schaal-Braun

Services Engineer
System Sonne

Landscape Architect
Reinboth

Located in a relatively new residential district of Esslingen, to the east of Stuttgart, KW House sits on the edge of an established orchard. Designed by the architects as their own house, the building appears as a compact concrete tower set into the green hill. Three stories face the road, from where the site slopes upwards towards the rear of the house where two stories overlook the orchard. On the ground floor an entrance hall provides access to an office, a bathroom, the laundry and storage space. An elegantly sparse concrete staircase leads to the first floor kitchen, dining and living area with direct access to the garden and a terrace built on top of the garage, via a full height corner window. The top floor accommodates three bedrooms and a family bathroom.

The load bearing grey concrete shell has a rough industrial finish that contrasts with the precisely positioned and detailed window openings. The emphatically linear fenestration punches through the concrete box, exposing the wall thickness at the corners. Equally precisely detailed are the metal shutters which roll down in front of the windows to provide security, privacy and protection from the sun when required.

Like the exterior, the interior is arranged and expressed with a minimum of materials, textures and colours. Flush door handles, a lack of skirtings and architraves, plain concrete ceilings and stairs, pale timber floors and white painted walls provide a calm and ascetic setting for family life.

1 The living spaces are located on the middle level of the house, which at the rear of the site, seen here, opens directly onto the garden via full height glazing that wraps around the corner of the concrete structure. The mute power of the concrete prism is balanced by the rural meadow setting.
2 The view from the street reveals the three storeys. The ribbon windows cut into the concrete shell come equipped with black steel security shutters which match the painted entry door and garage doors (right).
3 The interior displays the same reserved solemnity as the exterior. A view of the top floor hall between the bedrooms reveals the concrete floors, ceilings and stair and the white-painted walls employed throughout the house.

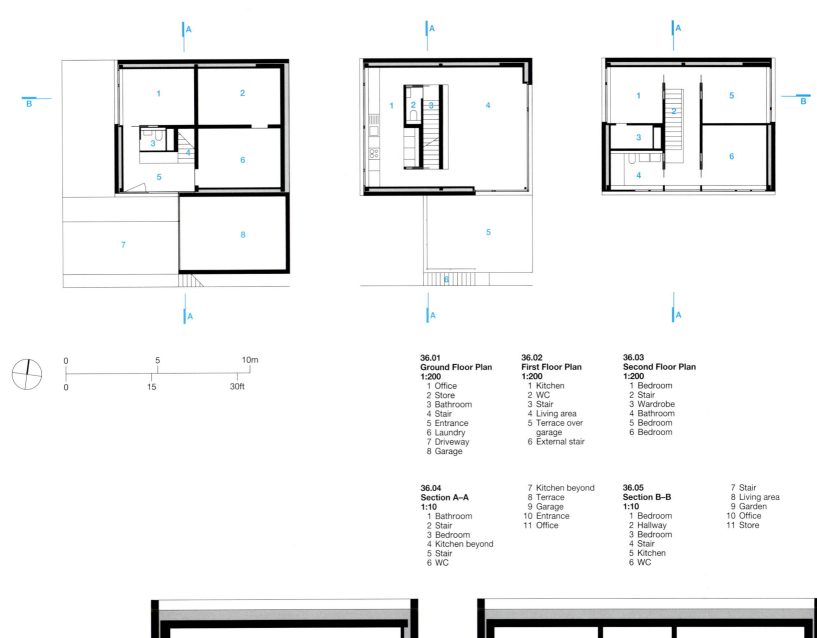

0 5 10m
0 15 30ft

36.01
Ground Floor Plan
1:200
1 Office
2 Store
3 Bathroom
4 Stair
5 Entrance
6 Laundry
7 Driveway
8 Garage

36.02
First Floor Plan
1:200
1 Kitchen
2 WC
3 Stair
4 Living area
5 Terrace over
  garage
6 External stair

36.03
Second Floor Plan
1:200
1 Bedroom
2 Stair
3 Wardrobe
4 Bathroom
5 Bedroom
6 Bedroom

36.04
Section A–A
1:10
1 Bathroom
2 Stair
3 Bedroom
4 Kitchen beyond
5 Stair
6 WC

7 Kitchen beyond
8 Terrace
9 Garage
10 Entrance
11 Office

36.05
Section B–B
1:10
1 Bedroom
2 Hallway
3 Bedroom
4 Stair
5 Kitchen
6 WC

7 Stair
8 Living area
9 Garden
10 Office
11 Store

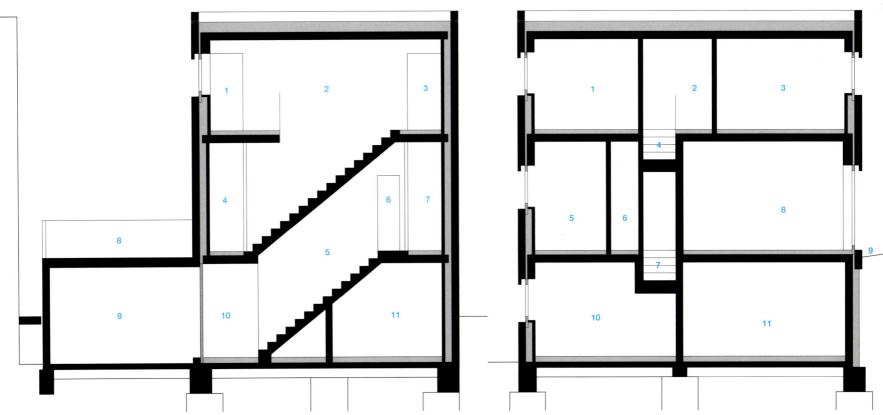

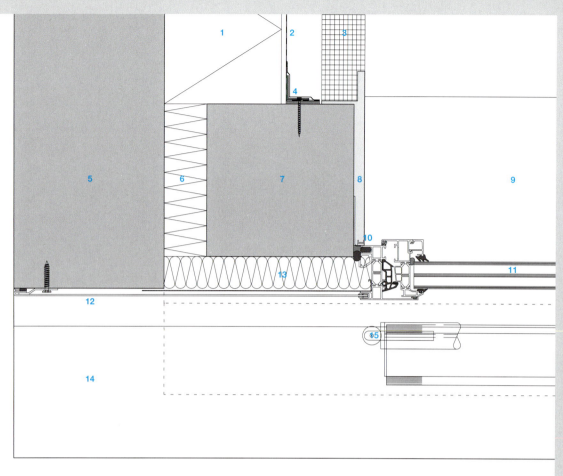

36.06
External Wall and Window Plan Detail 1
1:5
 1 160 mm (6¹/₄ inch) rigid insulation
 2 Vapour barrier
 3 60 mm (2³/₈ inch) thick painted gypsum block interior wall lining
 4 Support angle for window sill and vapour barrier
 5 200 mm (8 inch) thick reinforced cast in-situ concrete external wall
 6 60 mm (2³/₈ inch) insulation
 7 200 x 200 mm (8 x 8 inch) reinforced cast in-situ concrete column
 8 Painted plasterboard column facing
 9 Gypsum block interior window sill
10 Plaster stop bead
11 Basalt grey colour aluminium-framed triple glazed window
12 Basalt grey aluminium fascia panel screw-fixed to concrete wall
13 60 mm (2³/₈ inch) rigid insulation
14 Concrete window sill sloped towards external face to drain with silicone impregnation water proofing treatment
15 Cable tensioner to external security blind

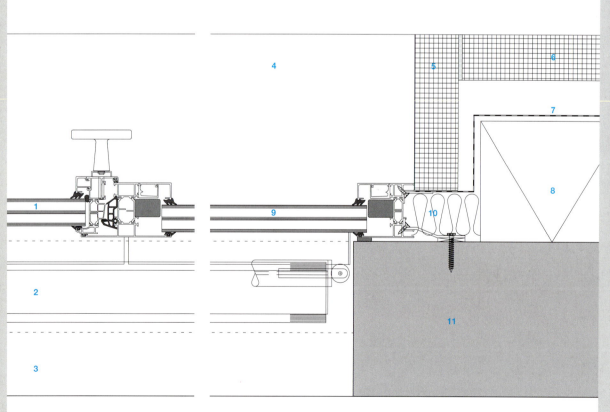

36.07
External Wall and Window Plan Detail 2
1:5
 1 Basalt grey colour aluminium-framed triple glazed fixed window
 2 External security blind
 3 Concrete window sill sloped towards external face to drain with silicone impregnation water proofing treatment
 4 Gypsum block interior window sill
 5 60 mm (2³/₈ inch) thick painted gypsum block window reveal
 6 60 mm (2³/₈ inch) thick painted gypsum block interior wall lining
 7 Vapour barrier
 8 160 mm (6¹/₄ inch) rigid insulation
 9 Basalt grey colour aluminium-framed triple glazed openable window
10 60 mm (2³/₈ inch) rigid insulation
11 200 mm (8 inch) thick reinforced cast in-situ concrete external wall

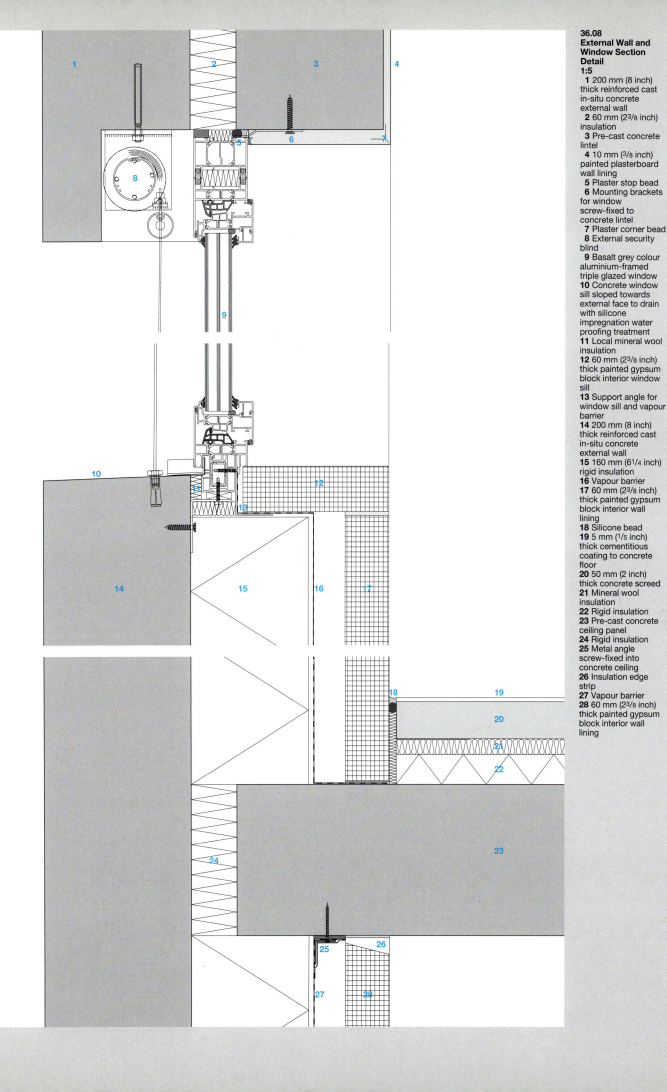

1 200 mm (8 inch) thick reinforced cast in-situ concrete external wall

2 60 mm (2³/₈ inch) insulation

3 Pre-cast concrete lintel

4 10 mm (³/₈ inch) painted plasterboard wall lining

5 Plaster stop bead

6 Mounting brackets for window screw-fixed to concrete lintel

7 Plaster corner bead

8 External security blind

9 Basalt grey colour aluminium-framed triple glazed window

10 Concrete window sill sloped towards external face to drain with silicone impregnation water proofing treatment

11 Local mineral wool insulation

12 60 mm (2³/₈ inch) thick painted gypsum block interior window sill

13 Support angle for window sill and vapour barrier

14 200 mm (8 inch) thick reinforced cast in-situ concrete external wall

15 160 mm (6¹/₄ inch) rigid insulation

16 Vapour barrier

17 60 mm (2³/₈ inch) thick painted gypsum block interior wall lining

18 Silicone bead

19 5 mm (¹/₅ inch) thick cementitious coating to concrete floor

20 50 mm (2 inch) thick concrete screed

21 Mineral wool insulation

22 Rigid insulation

23 Pre-cast concrete ceiling panel

24 Rigid insulation

25 Metal angle screw-fixed into concrete ceiling

26 Insulation edge strip

27 Vapour barrier

28 60 mm (2³/₈ inch) thick painted gypsum block interior wall lining

Riverbank House
Shizuoka, Japan

Client
Private

Project Team
Atsushi Kawamoto, Mayumi
Kawamoto

Structural Engineer
Daisuke Hasegawa & Partners

Main Contractor
Mabucki Industry

This striking wedge-shaped house is located in a small city in the west of Shizuoka, not far from Mount Fuji, in an area famous for the production of green tea. The house is built on a long, narrow strip of land located between a riverbank and a road in a residential neighbourhood. Although the site is not far from both a motorway and a railway line, the riverside site is quiet and peaceful and is surrounded by natural vegetation and fine views of fields and mountains in the distance.

In response to the tiny site area, the plan of the house takes the shape of two isosceles triangles. The larger triangle contains all of the living accommodation, with the smaller triangle docked to the north-west facade to create an entrance lobby. While necessarily compact, the open plan and generous terraces located in the point of the triangle contribute to airy, naturally lit living spaces. The entire first floor is devoted to the kitchen, dining and living area, with a simple stair dividing the open plan space. On the ground floor, the base of the triangle is divided between a single bedroom and a bathroom, with the remainder of the floor devoted to an office with direct access to a large terrace.

The north-west facing, cement-rendered facade is entirely windowless, with just the entrance portico and its translucent glass door pivoted out from the two-storey-high plain grey wall. In contrast, the south-east facade features large, full height sliding doors to the kitchen and bedroom on the first and ground floors respectively, as well as the two triangular terraces facing the riverbank.

1 The kitchen and bedroom on the first and ground floor respectively (left) and the terraces from the living area and office on the first and ground floors (right) face south-east over the river to the green bank beyond.
2 The north-west facade of this emphatically triangular building is an entirely blank wall of grey concrete, interrupted only by the white portico with its glazed entry door.
3 The first floor accommodates the open plan kitchen in the base of the triangle (right) and tapers towards the living area and a triangular terrace in the apex of the triangular plan.
4 A minimal white steel balustrade indicates the stair arriving in the first floor living area from the bedroom, bathroom and office on the ground floor.

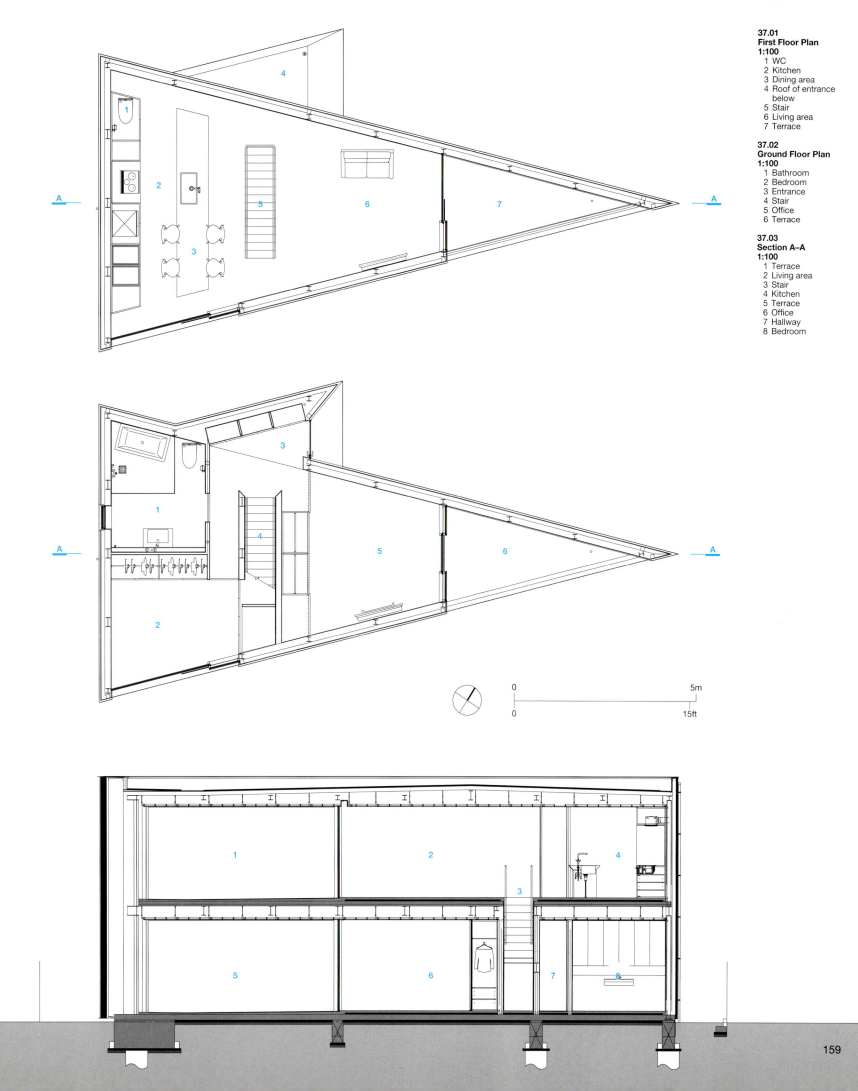

37.01
First Floor Plan
1:100
  1 WC
  2 Kitchen
  3 Dining area
  4 Roof of entrance
    below
  5 Stair
  6 Living area
  7 Terrace

37.02
Ground Floor Plan
1:100
  1 Bathroom
  2 Bedroom
  3 Entrance
  4 Stair
  5 Office
  6 Terrace

37.03
Section A–A
1:100
  1 Terrace
  2 Living area
  3 Stair
  4 Kitchen
  5 Terrace
  6 Office
  7 Hallway
  8 Bedroom

0
5m
0
15ft

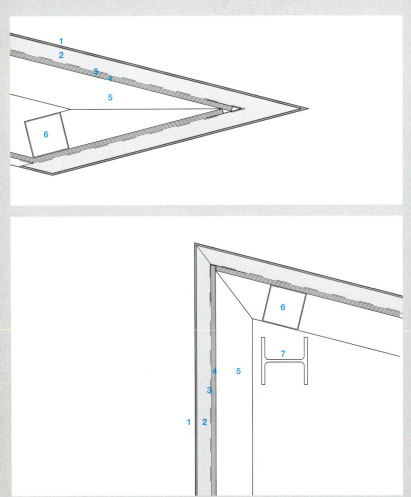

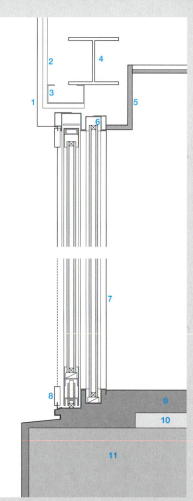

37.04
North-East Terrace Corner Plan Detail
1:10
1 Trowel finish resin mortar with water repellent paint finish
2 40 mm (1 1/2 inch) thick rigid foam insulation
3 Asphalt impregnated felt waterproof membrane
4 12 mm (1/2 inch) thick structural plywood
5 100 x 50 mm (4 x 2 inch) furring channels
6 100 x 100 mm (4 x 4 inch) steel square hollow section

37.05
North-West Kitchen Corner Plan Detail
1:10
1 Trowel finish resin mortar with water repellent paint finish
2 40 mm (1 1/2 inch) thick rigid foam insulation
3 Asphalt impregnated felt waterproof membrane
4 12 mm (1/2 inch) thick structural plywood
5 100 x 50 mm (4 x 2 inch) furring channels
6 100 x 100 mm (4 x 4 inch) steel square hollow section
7 Universal steel column

37.08
Glass Sliding Doors to Ground Floor Terrace Section Detail
1:10
1 Trowel finish resin mortar with water repellent paint finish
2 12 mm (1/2 inch) thick structural plywood
3 100 x 50 mm (4 x 2 inch) furring channels
4 Steel lintel
5 12.5 mm (1/2 inch) painted plasterboard interior wall lining
6 Steel window frame to sliding glass doors
7 Double glazed sliding window units with 6 mm (1/4 inch) glass
8 External fabric blind
9 Trowel finished concrete screed with water repellent paint finish
10 25 mm (1 inch) thick rigid insulation
11 Reinforced concrete floor slab

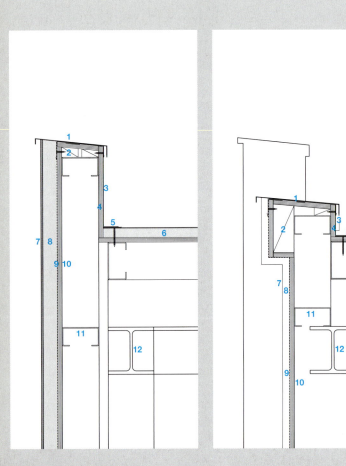

37.06
Parapet Section Detail Type 1
1:10
1 1.4 mm (1/16 inch) galvanized sheet steel parapet capping on structural plywood
2 Timber packing
3 1.5 mm (1/16 inch) bituminous sheet waterproof membrane
4 12 mm (1/2 inch) structural plywood
5 PVC coated steel corner angle
6 25 mm (1 inch) thick rigid urethane foam insulation
7 Trowel finish resin mortar with water repellent paint finish
8 40 mm (1 1/2 inch) rigid foam insulation
9 Asphalt impregnated felt waterproof membrane
10 12 mm (1/2 inch) thick structural plywood
11 100 x 50 mm (4 x 2 inch) furring channels
12 Universal steel beam

37.07
Parapet Section Detail Type 2
1:10
1 1.4 mm (1/16 inch) galvanized sheet steel parapet capping on structural plywood
2 Timber framing
3 1.5 mm (1/16 inch) bituminous sheet waterproof membrane
4 12 mm (1/2 inch) structural plywood
5 PVC coated steel corner angle
6 25 mm (1 inch) thick rigid urethane foam insulation
7 Trowel finish resin mortar with water repellent paint finish
8 40 mm (1 1/2 inch) rigid foam insulation
9 Asphalt impregnated felt waterproof membrane
10 12 mm (1/2 inch) thick structural plywood
11 100 x 50 mm (4 x 2 inch) furring channels
12 Universal steel beam

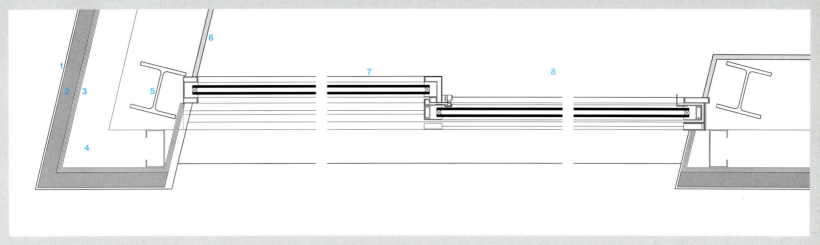

37.09
Glass Sliding Doors to Ground Floor Terrace Plan Detail 1:10
1 Trowel finish resin mortar with water repellent paint finish
2 40 mm (1 1/2 inch)

thick rigid foam insulation
3 12 mm (1/2 inch) thick structural plywood
4 100 x 50 mm (4 x 2 inch) furring channels
5 Universal steel column

6 12.5 mm (1/2 inch) painted plasterboard interior wall lining
7 Double glazed sliding window units with 6 mm (1/4 inch) glass
8 Trowel finished concrete screed with

water repellent paint finish

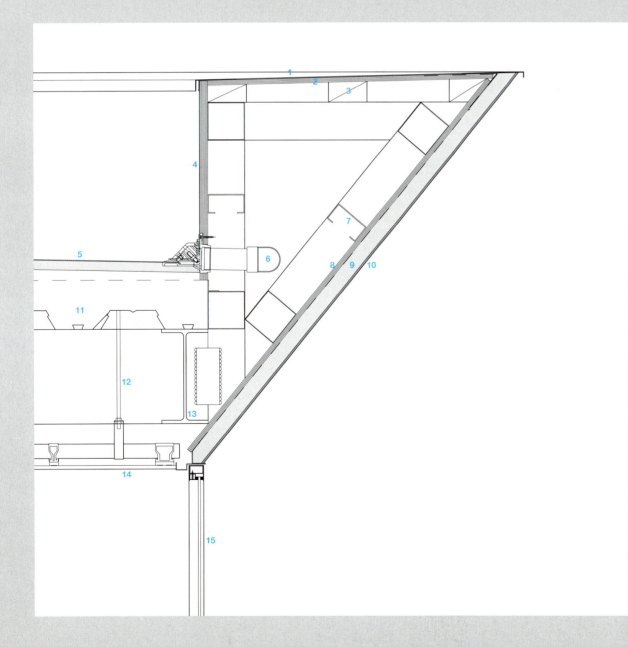

37.10
Entrance Door Section Detail 1:10
1 1.4 mm (1/16 inch) galvanized sheet steel parapet capping on structural plywood
2 12 mm (1/2 inch) thick structural plywood
3 Timber packing
4 1.5 mm (1/16 inch) bituminous sheet waterproof membrane on 12 mm (1/2 inch) structural plywood
5 1.5 mm (1/16 inch) bituminous sheet waterproof membrane on rigid urethane insulation over steel deck
6 Drainpipe
7 100 x 50 mm (4 x 2 inch) furring channels
8 12 mm (1/2 inch) structural plywood
9 40 mm (1 1/2 inch) thick rigid foam insulation
10 Trowel finish resin mortar with water repellent paint finish
11 Concrete roof slab on permanent formwork steel deck
12 Hangars for suspended ceiling
13 Steel beam and lintel
14 12.5 mm (1/2 inch) painted plasterboard interior ceiling
15 Glazed entrance door

House in Melides
Melides, Grândola, Portugal

Client
Private

Project Team
Tiago Tomás, Isabel Silvestre

Structural Engineer
Alves Rodrigues & Associados

Main Contractor
ACRIBIA

Landscape
Global 2 - Inês Norton

This house in Melides, located not far from the Atlantic coast in southern Portugal is a holiday house for a client who lives in Lisbon. Unusually in the commissioning of a work of residential architecture, the client made the decision to hold an architectural competition between three studios in order to assess both the possibilities the site offered, as well as the architectural solutions. The winning proposal by Pedro Reis is a dramatic formal composition that celebrates the drama of the natural landscape.

The building sits on top of a small steep hill that, while relatively protected by the surrounding rugged topography, has access to wide-ranging views. The house is comprised of two distinct rectangular volumes that overlap in the shape of an asymmetric cross. The upper volume contains the living spaces as well as a master bedroom suite and can be used as a self contained domestic unit. The lower volume, partly buried in the slope of the hill and supporting the upper volume, accommodates more bedrooms, bathrooms and service areas, and can be inhabited or expanded into as required.

The two volumes are expressed quite distinctly with the upper volume appearing as a light, white volume whose envelope gives way to full height walls of glazing, a louvred pergola to the terrace and notably a void cut through both the roof and the floor of the master bathroom, creating a void over the end of the outdoor swimming pool. In contrast, the lower volume is built from blocks of earth-coloured concrete that were cast on site. These blocks form the walls, the roof and the pool terrace, creating a monolithic rectangular prism that anchors the composition both visually and structurally.

1 The house appears to both emerge from, and hover over, the typically dry southern Iberian landscape. The earth-coloured volume with protective slit windows accommodates the private sleeping and bathing spaces (right), while the living, dining and kitchen spaces above enjoy large expanses of full height glazing.
2 The living spaces open up to a pergola-covered stone terrace overlooking the swimming pool (left) and the garden.
3 The western facade of the upper volume features an entire wall of sliding floor-to-ceiling glass doors opening onto the pool terrace (left).
4 The roof of the living area at the north end of the upper level is supported on slender columns, allowing three walls of full height glass to embrace the spectacular views.

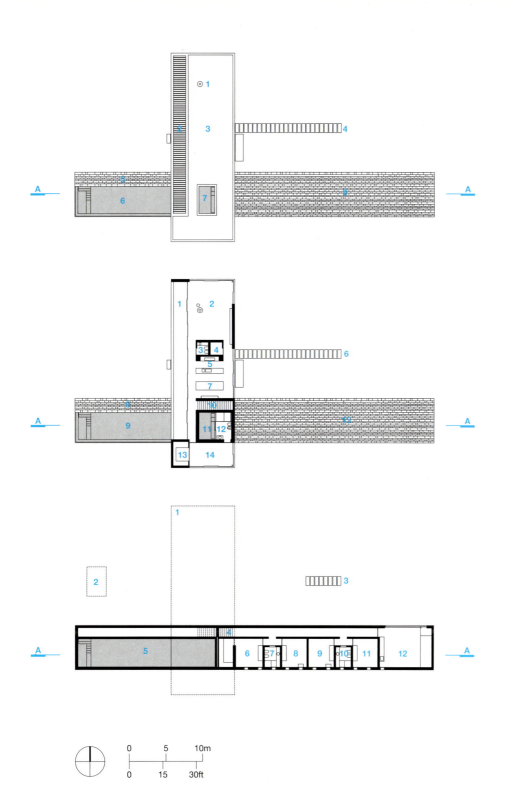

0 5 10m
0 15 30ft

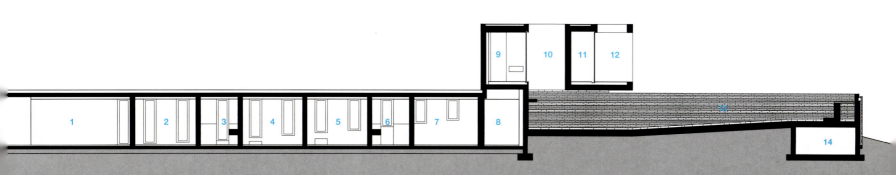

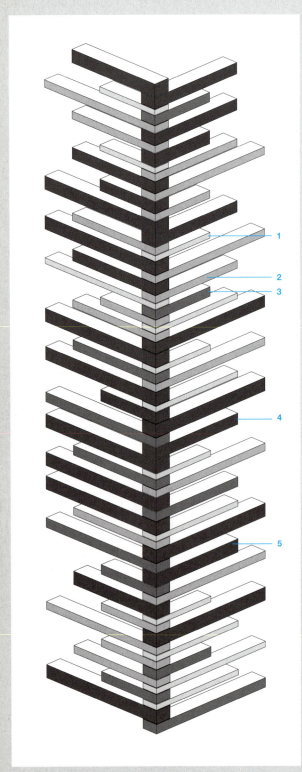

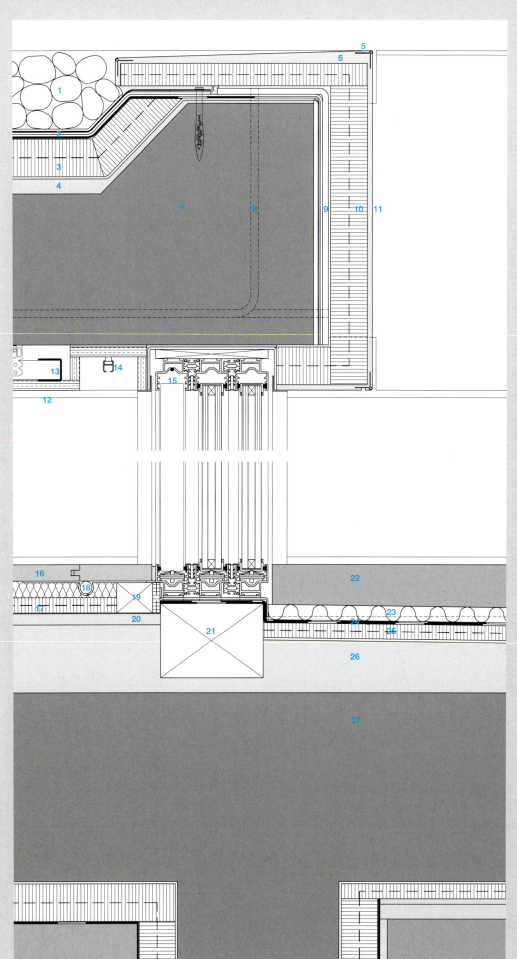

38.05
Bedroom Pavilion
Concrete Block
Corner Detail
1:100
1 30 mm (1¹/₅ inch)
type A earth-coloured
concrete block,
150–450 mm (6–17³/₄
inch) variable length
2 40 mm (1¹/₂ inch)
type B earth-coloured
concrete block,
150–600 mm (6–23¹/₂
inch) variable length
3 50 mm (2 inch) type
C earth-coloured
concrete block,
150–600 mm (6–23¹/₂

inch) variable length
4 60 mm (2³/₈ inch)
type D earth-coloured
concrete block,
300–600 mm (12–23¹/₂
inch) variable length
5 70 mm (2³/₄ inch)
type E earth-coloured
concrete block,
300–600 mm (12–23¹/₂
inch) variable length

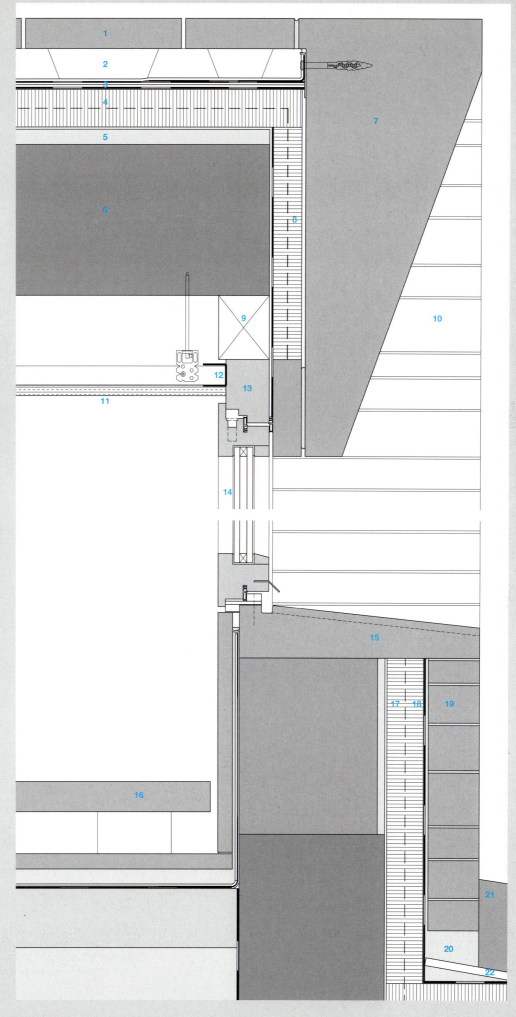

38.06
Living Pavilion West Wall Section Detail
1:5
 1 140 mm (5 1/2 inch) gravel ballast to flat roof
 2 13 mm (1/2 inch) thick double layer of bituminous roofing felt
 3 60 mm (2 3/8 inch) rigid insulation
 4 15 mm (5/8 inch) lean concrete screed
 5 Galvanized external corner plastering bead
 6 Cement render sloped to drain towards flat roof
 7 200 mm (8 inch) reinforced concrete roof slab with integral upstand
 8 Reinforcing bars
 9 Steel corner plate
 10 60 mm (2 3/8 inch) rigid insulation
 11 Cement render finish to external wall
 12 12.5 mm (1/2 inch) skimmed and painted plasterboard ceiling
 13 Aluminium ceiling framing
 14 Concealed curtain track
 15 Anodized aluminium window frame with double glazing
 16 22 mm (7/8 inch) timber floorboards
 17 22 mm (7/8 inch) rigid insulation glazing to sliding doors
 18 Underfloor heating
 19 42 mm (1 5/8 inch) solid timber floor framing
 20 15 mm (5/8 inch) lean concrete screed
 21 Timber blocking to window
 22 70 mm (2 3/4 inch) thick cast-in-place concrete pavers
 23 High density polyethylene drainage mat
 24 13 mm (1/2 inch) thick double layer of bituminous roofing felt
 25 22 mm (7/8 inch) rigid insulation
 26 90 mm (3 1/2 inch) thick lean concrete topping slab sloped to drain
 27 250 mm (10 inch) reinforced concrete floor slab

38.07
Bedroom Pavilion South Wall Section Detail
1:5
 1 40 mm (1 1/2 inch) earth-coloured concrete slabs to roof
 2 Rigid insulation
 3 13 mm (1/2 inch) thick double layer of bituminous roofing felt
 4 60 mm (2 3/8 inch) rigid insulation
 5 15 mm (5/8 inch) lean concrete screed
 6 200 mm (8 inch) reinforced concrete roof slab with integral upstand
 7 Earth-coloured concrete lintel
 8 40 mm (1 1/2 inch) rigid insulation
 9 Solid timber floor framing
 10 290 mm (11 3/8 inch) earth-coloured concrete block cladding
 11 12.5 mm (1/2 inch) skimmed and painted plasterboard ceiling
 12 Aluminium ceiling framing
 13 Timber window frame
 14 Fixed double glazing
 15 Earth-coloured concrete sill
 16 40 mm (1 1/2 inch) travertine flooring
 17 60 mm (2 3/8 inch) rigid insulation
 18 Waterproof membrane
 19 Earth-coloured concrete block wall
 20 Mortar bed
 21 Natural ground
 22 Drainage membrane

Stacking Green House
Ho Chi Minh City, Vietnam

Client
Private

Project Team
Vo Trong Nghia, Daisuke Sanuki,
Shunri Nishizawa

Main Contractors
Thuan Viet Company, Wind and Water
House JSC

On a site that is just four metres (13 feet) wide and twenty metres (66 feet) deep, a dozen layers of concrete planters create a vertical garden on the facade of this house in Ho Chi Minh City. Built for a couple and one of their mothers, the building's extreme proportions are typical of the narrow 'tube houses' common in Vietnam. Uncommonly, however, planters spaced according to the height of the plants, span the side walls to cover the front and rear facades in cascades of tropical plants.

Arranged over four storeys, the clever use of voids, skylights and small courtyards make this modest two bedroom home a comfortable and light-filled oasis in the middle of a chaotic tropical city. The ground floor extends to create a gated parking area, beyond which a bedroom, bathroom and private courtyard are placed, acting as a semi self-contained apartment. Above, the first floor is devoted to the living spaces, at the centre of which is a void that extends up to the roof, bringing light into the centre of the plan. The stair changes location at this floor, moving from the front to the back of the house. It rises up through the rear courtyard to the master bedroom and bathroom on the next level and terminates on the top floor where the study and prayer room have access to a planted roof garden. Essentially four open plan layers with few internal walls, the eponymous stacks of greenery, fitted with an automatic irrigation system, are visible throughout the house, filtering out visual, noise and air pollution from the quiet calm of the interior.

While this is just one small house in a sprawling capital city of endless cheaply built concrete structures, the architects hope that this potentially iconoclastic home will inspire others to redefine the image and architecture of Ho Chi Minh City through the reintroduction of a plethora of tropical greenery.

1 The street facade by day. A gated and partly covered parking area provides a transition zone between the street and the interior. The plants, arranged in 12 layers of planters across the facade, are spaced according to the height of the plants in each.
2 At night, the house glows behind its verdant wall of tropical greenery.
3 Bringing natural light into the living spaces on the first floor is carefully considered, with filtered light from the planted facades supplemented by direct light from a skylight at the centre of the plan.
4 The main stair rises up over the small courtyard on the ground floor, all the way through three levels to the roof garden on the top floor.
5 The planted roof garden includes a glazed slot next to the planters which is replicated in steel mesh in the floors below to provide direct access to the planted facade.

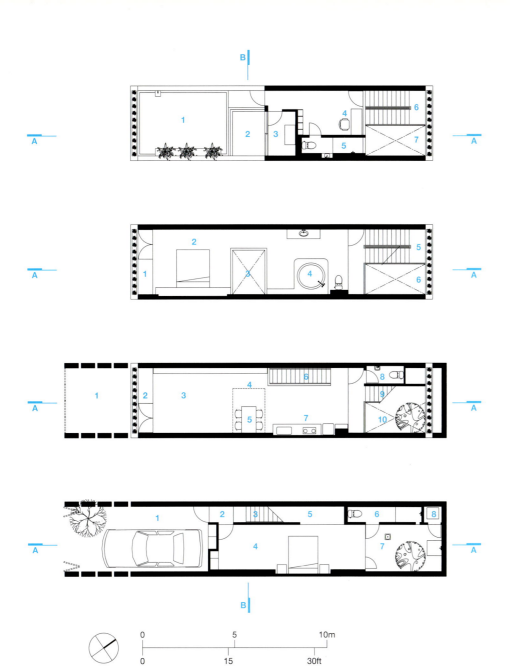

39.01
Third Floor Plan
1:200
1 Roof garden
2 Skylight
3 Prayer room
4 Study
5 Bathroom
6 Stair
7 Skylight

39.02
Second Floor Plan
1:200
1 Terrace
2 Bedroom
3 Void over living
  area
4 Bathroom
5 Stair
6 Void over
  courtyard

39.03
First Floor Plan
1:200
1 Garage roof
2 Terrace
3 Living area
4 Void over shown
  dotted
5 Dining area
6 Stair from ground
  floor
7 Kitchen
8 WC
9 Stair to upper
  floors
10 Courtyard below

39.04
Ground Floor Plan
1:200
1 Garage
2 Entrance
3 Stair
4 Bedroom
5 Wardrobe
6 Bathroom
7 Courtyard
8 Laundry

39.05
Section A–A
1:200
1 Solar hot water
  heater
2 Water tank
3 Skylight
4 Roof garden
5 Skylight
6 Prayer room
7 Study
8 Terrace
9 Bedroom
10 Void over living
  area
11 Bathroom
12 Stair
13 Terrace
14 Living and dining
  area
15 Kitchen
16 Parking
17 Bedroom
18 Wardrobe
19 Bathroom
20 Courtyard
21 Laundry

39.06
Section B–B
1:200
1 Door to study from
  roof garden
2 Prayer room
  beyond
3 Skylight over void
4 Bedroom
5 Void
6 Dining and kitchen
7 Entrance and stair
8 Bedroom
9 Door to courtyard

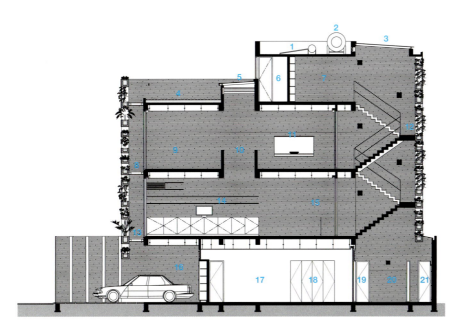

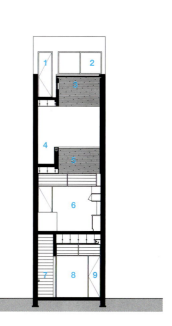

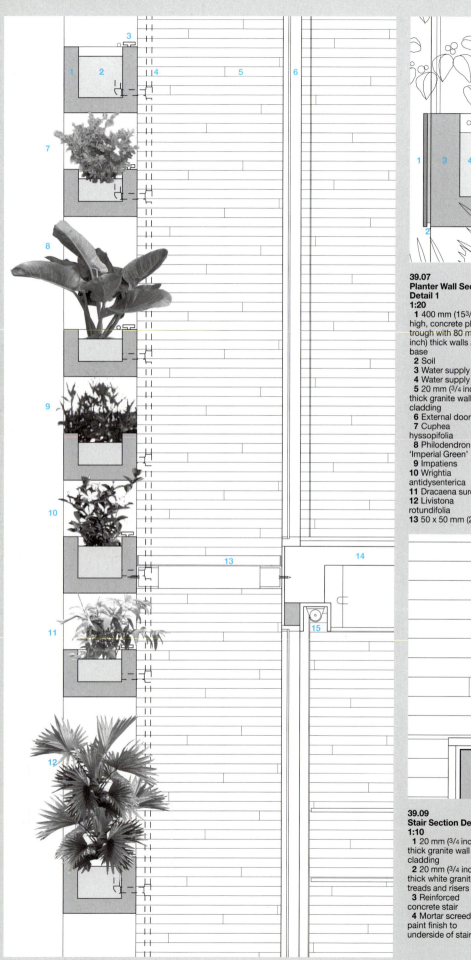

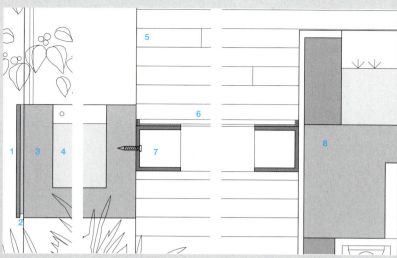

39.07
Planter Wall Section Detail 1
1:20
1 400 mm (15³/4 inch) high, concrete plant trough with 80 mm (3 inch) thick walls and base
2 Soil
3 Water supply valve
4 Water supply pipe
5 20 mm (³/4 inch) thick granite wall cladding
6 External door
7 Cuphea hyssopifolia
8 Philodendron 'Imperial Green'
9 Impatiens
10 Wrightia antidysenterica
11 Dracaena surculosa
12 Livistona rotundifolia
13 50 x 50 mm (2 x 2 inch) steel grating to terrace
14 Reinforced concrete floor slab and downstand beam
15 Interior roller blind

39.08
Planter Wall Section Detail 2
1:10
1 20 mm (³/4 inch) natural stone finish to planter trough
2 Water switch
3 400 mm (15³/4 inch) high, 400 mm (15³/4 inch) deep concrete plant trough with 80 mm (3 inch) thick walls and base
4 Soil
5 20 mm (³/4 inch) thick granite wall cladding
6 12 mm (¹/2 inch) tempered glass floor to terrace
7 120 x 120 x 10 mm (4³/4 x 4³/4 x ³/8 inch) steel frame to glass terrace fixed to concrete on either side with clamping screws
8 Concrete floor slab

39.09
Stair Section Detail
1:10
1 20 mm (³/4 inch) thick granite wall cladding
2 20 mm (³/4 inch) thick white granite treads and risers
3 Reinforced concrete stair
4 Mortar screed and paint finish to underside of stair

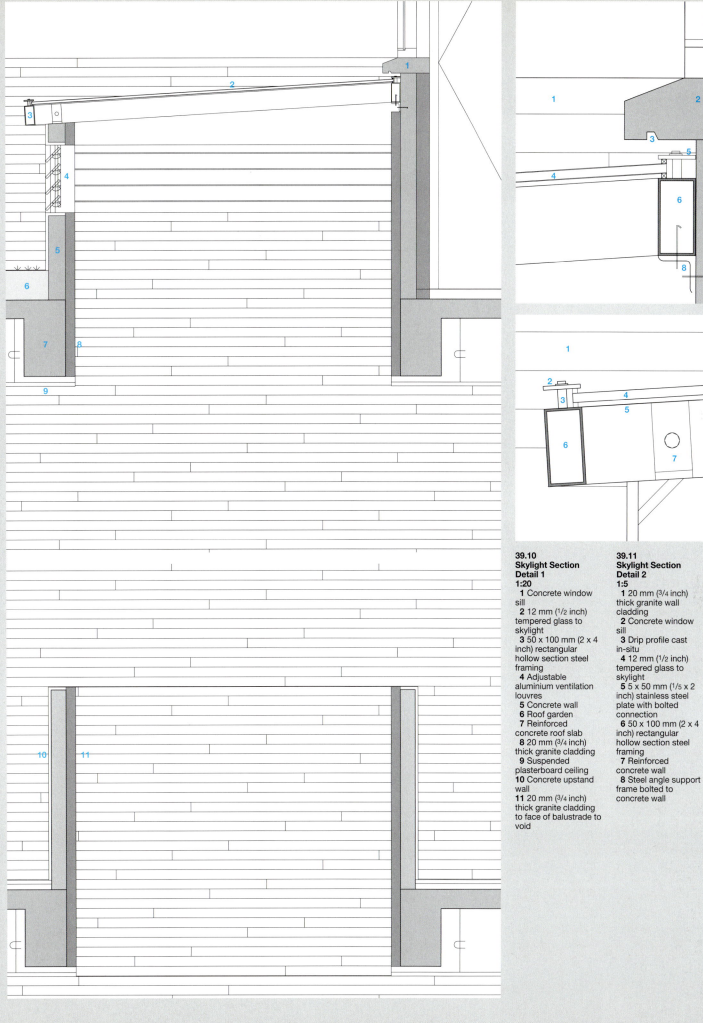

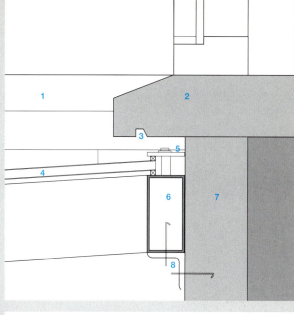

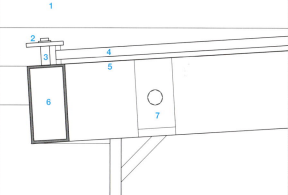

39.10
Skylight Section
Detail 1
1:20
1 Concrete window sill
2 12 mm (^{1}/2 inch) tempered glass to skylight
3 50 x 100 mm (2 x 4 inch) rectangular hollow section steel framing
4 Adjustable aluminium ventilation louvres
5 Concrete wall
6 Roof garden
7 Reinforced concrete roof slab
8 20 mm (^{3}/4 inch) thick granite cladding
9 Suspended plasterboard ceiling
10 Concrete upstand wall
11 20 mm (^{3}/4 inch) thick granite cladding to face of balustrade to void

39.11
Skylight Section
Detail 2
1:5
1 20 mm (^{3}/4 inch) thick granite wall cladding
2 Concrete window sill
3 Drip profile cast in-situ
4 12 mm (^{1}/2 inch) tempered glass to skylight
5 5 x 50 mm (^{1}/5 x 2 inch) stainless steel plate with bolted connection
6 50 x 100 mm (2 x 4 inch) rectangular hollow section steel framing
7 Reinforced concrete wall
8 Steel angle support frame bolted to concrete wall

39.12
Skylight Section
Detail 3
1:5
1 20 mm (^{3}/4 inch) thick granite wall cladding
2 5 x 50 mm (^{1}/5 x 2 inch) stainless steel plate with bolted connection
3 12 x 25 mm (^{1}/2 x 1 inch) steel pipe
4 12 mm (^{1}/2 inch) tempered glass to skylight
5 Silicon rubber sealant
6 50 x 100 mm (2 x 4 inch) rectangular hollow section steel framing
7 50 x 50 mm (2 x 2 inch) steel angle

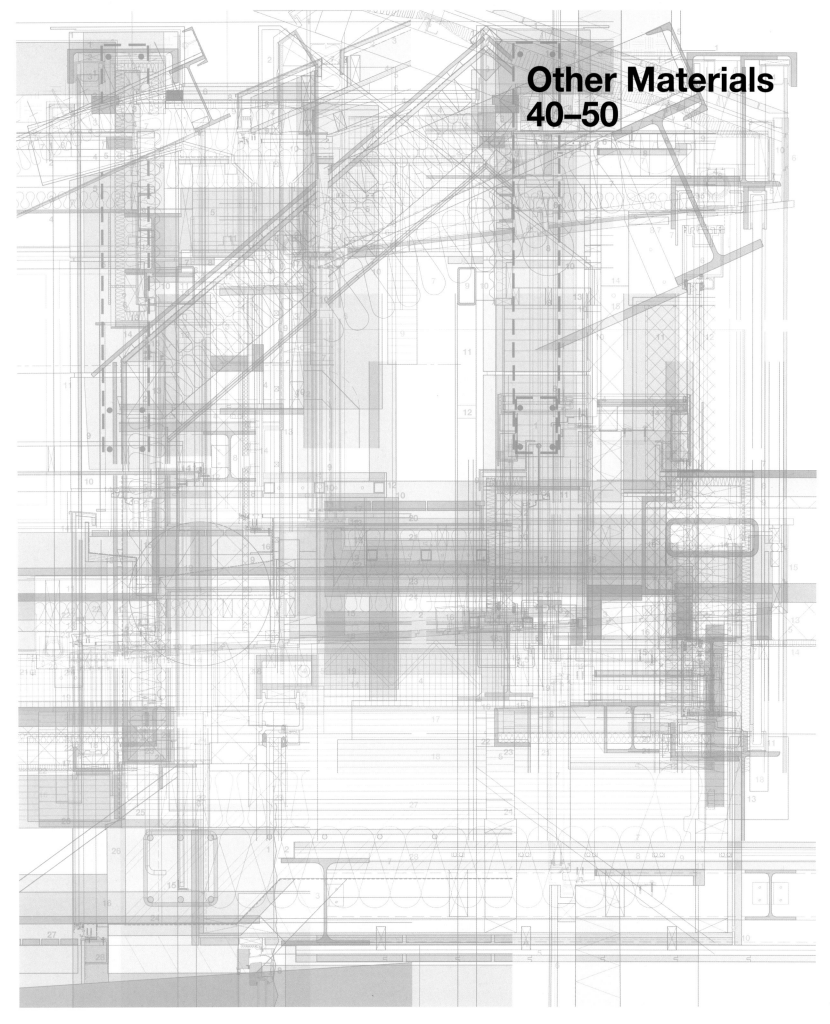

Living On The Edge House
Zoetermeer, The Netherlands

Client
Private

Project Team
Arjen Reas

Thatcher
Voogt Rietdekkers

Main Contractors
Adviesbureau Docter, C.L. de Boer
& Zn

This striking thatched house is located in a small city near The Hague in western Netherlands. It was designed for clients who work in the city but who wanted to move their family away from the noise and crowds while remaining within commuting distance. As such, the site is located on the edge, in that sub-urban place where the city and the countryside meet. The architects wanted to create a contemporary house that met the accommodation needs of their client but also made reference to, and reinterpreted, traditional Dutch building forms and materials. Thatching, once a common building material, is currently undergoing a resurgence in the Netherlands and is used to great aesthetic and functional effect here to create a house that evokes both rural and urban living.

A thick blanket of thatch covers the walls as well as the roof, the cladding beginning just above ground level and wrapping all four sides of the simple two storey gabled structure. The thatch is only interrupted by the double height projecting entry canopy on the south-west facade, the chimney at the other end of the house and by a series of deeply set vertical windows sliced into the roof and walls on both the north-west and south-east facades.

Inside, accommodation is arranged over three levels with four bedrooms and two bathrooms on the first floor within the pitch of the thatched roof. The basement accommodates a garage, generous storage spaces and direct access to the living spaces. On the ground floor, a kitchen, dining area, laundry and entrance hall occupy the south-west end of the plan with glazed doors either side of the fireplace at the other end of the plan folding open to connect the living area with the terrace and garden.

1 The thickness of the walls and roof is most apparent where the deep window reveals have been cut into the thatch. The windows shown here are to the kitchen, dining and living space on the ground floor and the bedroom, dressing room and master bedroom within the pitch of the roof above.
2 The house can be entered either through the two-storey high portico (centre) or via the basement garage which is accessed via a ramp cut into the site and flanked by white-rendered walls (right). An internal stair leads directly from the basement up into the centre of the ground floor.
3 A covered terrace runs the entire width of the house, opening from the living space onto views over the garden and beyond.
4 The living room features two large glazed doors on either side of the fireplace which open onto a covered terrace. The simple black and white interior has limestone floors throughout.

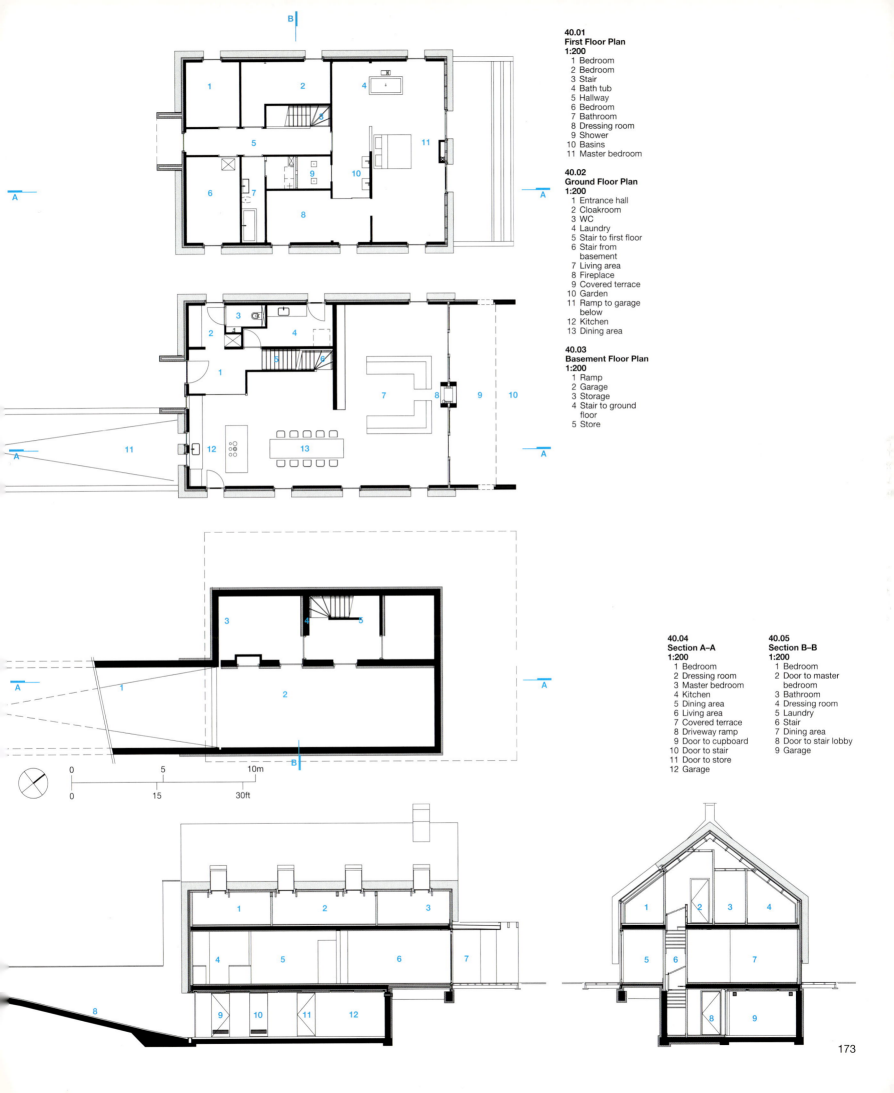

40.01
First Floor Plan
1:200
1 Bedroom
2 Bedroom
3 Stair
4 Bath tub
5 Hallway
6 Bedroom
7 Bathroom
8 Dressing room
9 Shower
10 Basins
11 Master bedroom

40.02
Ground Floor Plan
1:200
1 Entrance hall
2 Cloakroom
3 WC
4 Laundry
5 Stair to first floor
6 Stair from
 basement
7 Living area
8 Fireplace
9 Covered terrace
10 Garden
11 Ramp to garage
 below
12 Kitchen
13 Dining area

40.03
Basement Floor Plan
1:200
1 Ramp
2 Garage
3 Storage
4 Stair to ground
 floor
5 Store

40.04
Section A–A
1:200
1 Bedroom
2 Dressing room
3 Master bedroom
4 Kitchen
5 Dining area
6 Living area
7 Covered terrace
8 Driveway ramp
9 Door to cupboard
10 Door to stair
11 Door to store
12 Garage

40.05
Section B–B
1:200
1 Bedroom
2 Door to master
 bedroom
3 Bathroom
4 Dressing room
5 Laundry
6 Stair
7 Dining area
8 Door to stair lobby
9 Garage

173

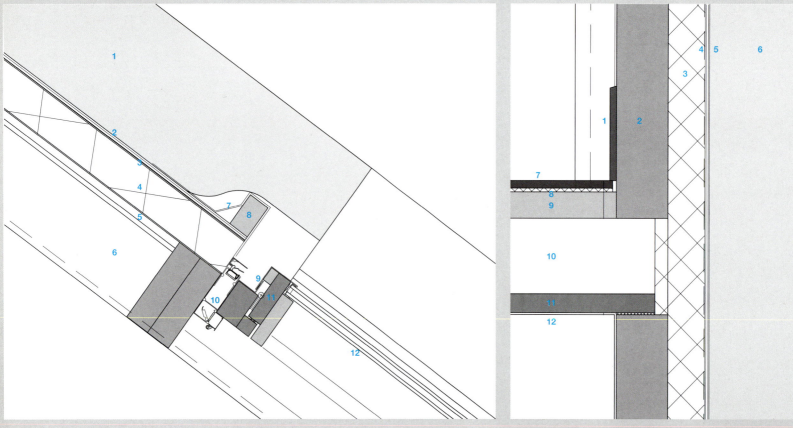

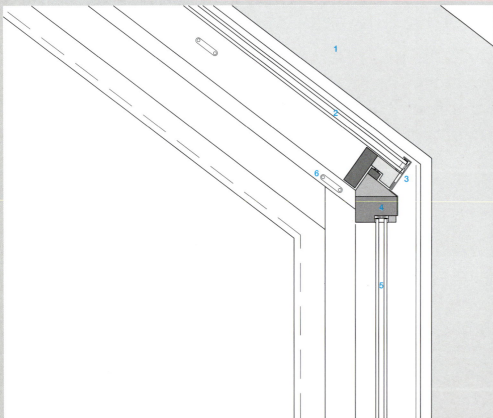

40.06
Roof Window Head and Thatch Junction Section Detail
1:10
 1 350 mm (13³/₄ inch) thick Chinese thatch
 2 Waterproof plywood roofing substrate
 3 Waterproof membrane
 4 122 mm (4³/₄ inch) rigid insulation
 5 Painted plasterboard ceiling
 6 246 mm (9³/₄ inch) steel joist
 7 Waterproof membrane
 8 Timber framing
 9 Aluminium profile
 10 Trickle vent
 11 Timber window frame
 12 Insulated double glazing

40.07
Wall and Floor Detail at First Floor
1:10
 1 Painted MDF skirting board
 2 140 mm (5¹/₂ inch) timber wall framing
 3 100 mm (4 inch) rigid insulation
 4 Waterproof membrane
 5 Waterproof plywood roofing membrane
 6 350 mm (13³/₄ inch) thick Chinese thatch)
 7 Limestone flooring
 8 Insulation
 9 Concrete screed with underfloor heating
 10 Reinforced concrete floor slab
 11 Timber battens
 12 Painted plasterboard ceiling

40.08
Roof Window Opening and Fixed Junction Section Detail
1:10
 1 350 mm (13³/₄ inch) thick Chinese thatch)
 2 Insulated double glazing
 3 Aluminium profile
 4 Timber window frame
 5 Insulated double glazing
 6 Spring mechanism for opening window

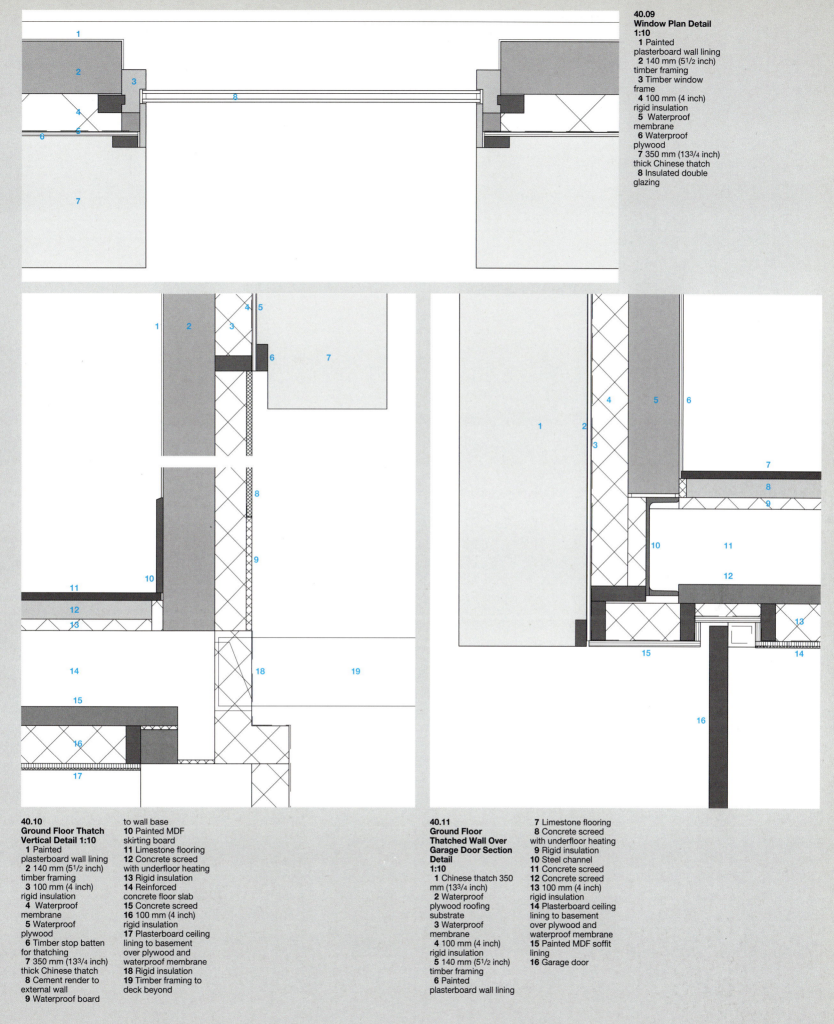

40.09
Window Plan Detail
1:10
1 Painted plasterboard wall lining
2 140 mm (5½ inch) timber framing
3 Timber window frame
4 100 mm (4 inch) rigid insulation
5 Waterproof membrane
6 Waterproof plywood
7 350 mm (13¾ inch) thick Chinese thatch
8 Insulated double glazing

40.10
Ground Floor Thatch Vertical Detail 1:10
1 Painted plasterboard wall lining
2 140 mm (5½ inch) timber framing
3 100 mm (4 inch) rigid insulation
4 Waterproof membrane
5 Waterproof plywood
6 Timber stop batten for thatching
7 350 mm (13¾ inch) thick Chinese thatch
8 Cement render to external wall
9 Waterproof board to wall base
10 Painted MDF skirting board
11 Limestone flooring
12 Concrete screed with underfloor heating
13 Rigid insulation
14 Reinforced concrete floor slab
15 Concrete screed
16 100 mm (4 inch) rigid insulation
17 Plasterboard ceiling lining to basement over plywood and waterproof membrane
18 Rigid insulation
19 Timber framing to deck beyond

40.11
Ground Floor Thatched Wall Over Garage Door Section Detail
1:10
1 Chinese thatch 350 mm (13¾ inch)
2 Waterproof plywood roofing substrate
3 Waterproof membrane
4 100 mm (4 inch) rigid insulation
5 140 mm (5½ inch) timber framing
6 Painted plasterboard wall lining
7 Limestone flooring
8 Concrete screed with underfloor heating
9 Rigid insulation
10 Steel channel
11 Concrete screed
12 Concrete screed
13 100 mm (4 inch) rigid insulation
14 Plasterboard ceiling lining to basement over plywood and waterproof membrane
15 Painted MDF soffit lining
16 Garage door

**Edgeland House
Austin, Texas, USA**

Client
Private

Project Team
Thomas Bercy, Calvin Chen, Dan Loe,
Ryan Michael, Brad Purrington,
Agustina Rodriguez

Structural Engineer
MJ Structures

Main Contractor
Bercy Chen Studio

Situated near the shores of the
Colorado River, Bercy Chen's
Edgeland House is visible only as a
narrow cut in the ground, and from
some angles is all but invisible. The
house is integrated into the slope of a
rehabilitated brownfield site,
positioned where the removal of a
disused oil pipeline had already left a
scar on the site. Designed for a writer
with an interest in human habitation at
the urban frontiers of abandoned
industrial zones, the house reimagines
the single-family house typology.

Approached from the north via a
concrete stair cut into the ground, two
green-roofed wings shelter each other
from the harsh Texas sun. One planted
roof shelters an open plan living
space, while on the other side of a
multi-faceted courtyard that runs
through the centre of the plan, the
other shelters the private sleeping and
bathing spaces. Both spaces are fully
glazed and look over the courtyard
and the wedge-shaped swimming
pool which occupies the pointed
'prow' of the cut in the land.

The design is influenced by the
native American pit house, one of the
oldest north American housing
typologies. Like traditional pit houses,
Edgeland House has been sunk two
metres (6 1/2 feet) into the ground, both
to reduce its visual presence in the
rehabilitated landscape, as well as
helping to achieve thermal stability by
using the earth's thermal mass. The
design also includes an insulating
green roof and hydronic heating to
maximize energy efficiency. Architects
collaborated with the Lady Bird
Johnson Wildflower Center, who
specialize in protecting and preserving
North America's native flora, to bring
40 lost native plant species back to the
site, supporting the local ecosystem.

1 The two green roofs
provide effective
thermal insulation,
helping to keep the
interior spaces cooler
in summer and warmer
in winter.
2 The view from the
top of the entrance
stair reveals the slice
of view that is revealed
through the courtyard
between the glazed
walls of the bedroom
pavilion (left) and the
living pavilion (right).
3 The tapering
cantilever of the roof of
the living pavilion
protects the living
spaces from the hot
south-west summer
sun.
4 The wedge shaped,
weir-edged swimming
pool employs a
high-tech diamond
electrode, chlorine-free
water purification
system and is used as
an additional thermal
mass tied to the
hydronic heating and
cooling system.
5 The open plan
kitchen, dining and
living space has a
white painted ceiling
that sails up to meet a
curtain of glazing
overlooking the
courtyard.

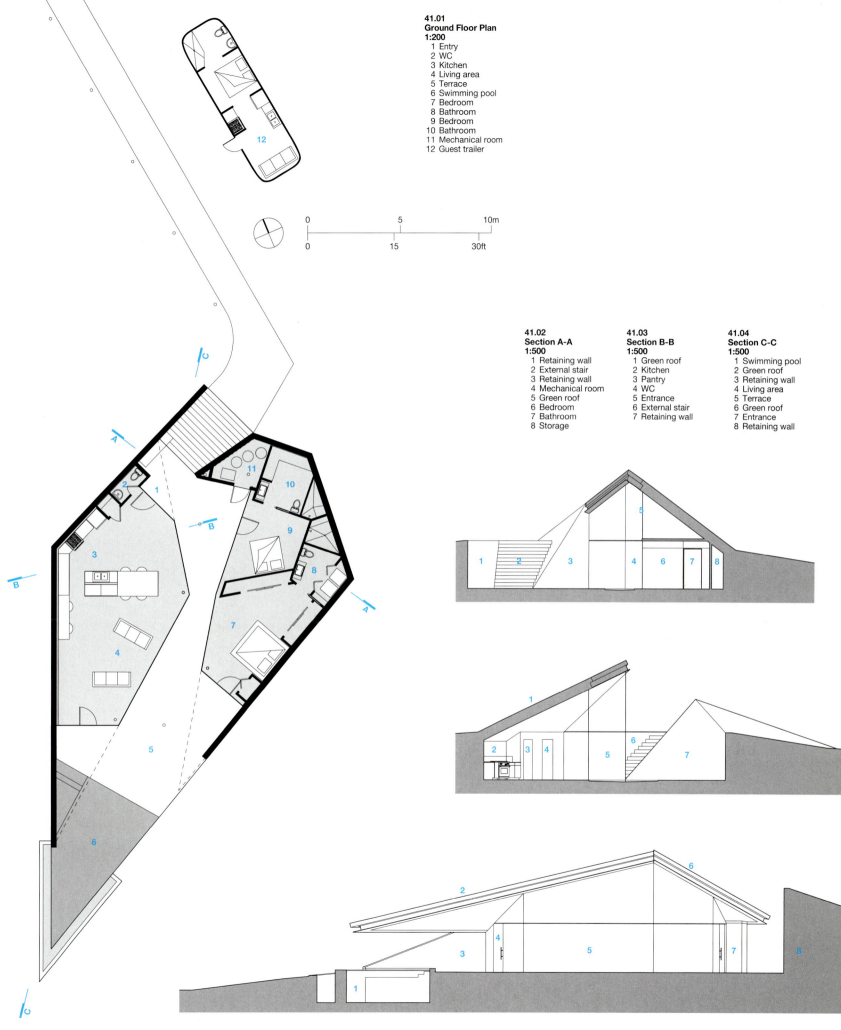

41.01
Ground Floor Plan
1:200
1 Entry
2 WC
3 Kitchen
4 Living area
5 Terrace
6 Swimming pool
7 Bedroom
8 Bathroom
9 Bedroom
10 Bathroom
11 Mechanical room
12 Guest trailer

0   5   10m
0   15   30ft

41.02
Section A-A
1:500
1 Retaining wall
2 External stair
3 Retaining wall
4 Mechanical room
5 Green roof
6 Bedroom
7 Bathroom
8 Storage

41.03
Section B-B
1:500
1 Green roof
2 Kitchen
3 Pantry
4 WC
5 Entrance
6 External stair
7 Retaining wall

41.04
Section C-C
1:500
1 Swimming pool
2 Green roof
3 Retaining wall
4 Living area
5 Terrace
6 Green roof
7 Entrance
8 Retaining wall

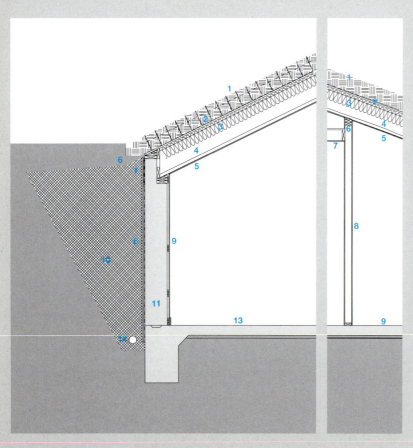

41.05
Typical External Wall Section to Living Wing Detail
1:50
1 Seasonally responsive green roof with native wildflowers
2 Waterproof membrane on 18 mm (3/4 inch) plywood decking
3 Spray foam insulation
4 Engineered timber I-joist
5 Painted plasterboard ceiling over hydronic ceiling loops
6 Gravel filled trench perimeter drain
7 Perforated plastic drain
8 Waterproof membrane
9 40 mm (1 1/2 inch) rigid insulation under painted plasterboard internal wall lining
10 Sand backfill to drainage layout and retaining wall
11 Reinforced concrete retaining wall
12 Perforated foundation drain
13 Reinforced concrete floor slab and footings

41.06
Typical Internal Wall Section Detail
1:50
1 Seasonally responsive green roof with native wildflowers
2 Waterproof membrane on 18 mm (3/4 inch) plywood decking
3 Spray foam insulation
4 Engineered timber I-joist
5 Painted plasterboard ceiling over hydronic ceiling loops
6 Timber framing to internal wall
7 Painted plasterboard ceiling
8 Painted plasterboard internal wall lining
9 Reinforced concrete floor slab and footings

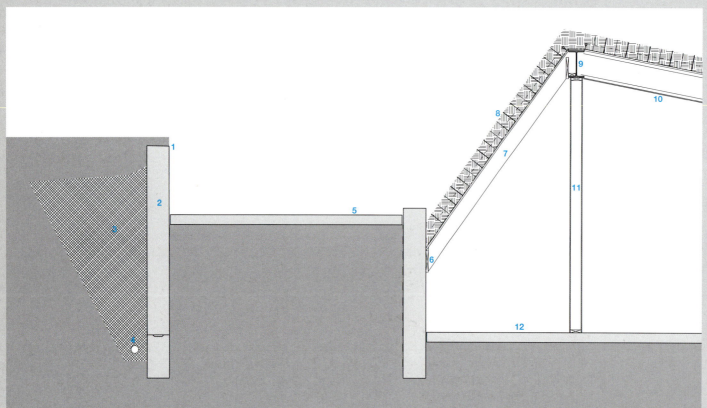

41.07
Retaining Wall and Green Roof at Stair Section Detail
1:50
1 6 mm (1/4 inch) thick bent steel cap to concrete retaining wall
2 Reinforced concrete retaining wall
3 Sand backfill to drainage layout and retaining wall
4 Perforated foundation drain
5 Concrete entry stair
6 50 x 300 mm (2 x 12 inch) timber blocking to retaining wall
7 50 x 200 mm (2 x 8 inch) composite timber roof joists
8 Seasonally responsive green roof with native wildflowers on 18 mm (3/4 inch) decking
9 Steel roof beam
10 Painted plasterboard ceiling over hydronic ceiling loops
11 Timber framed painted plasterboard internal wall
12 Reinforced concrete floor slab

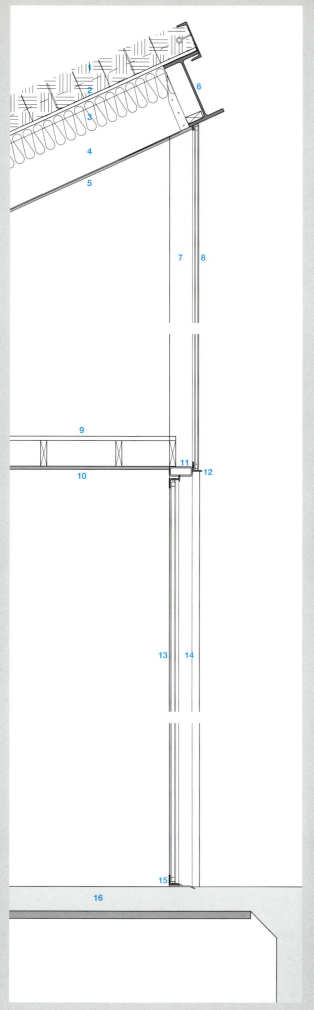

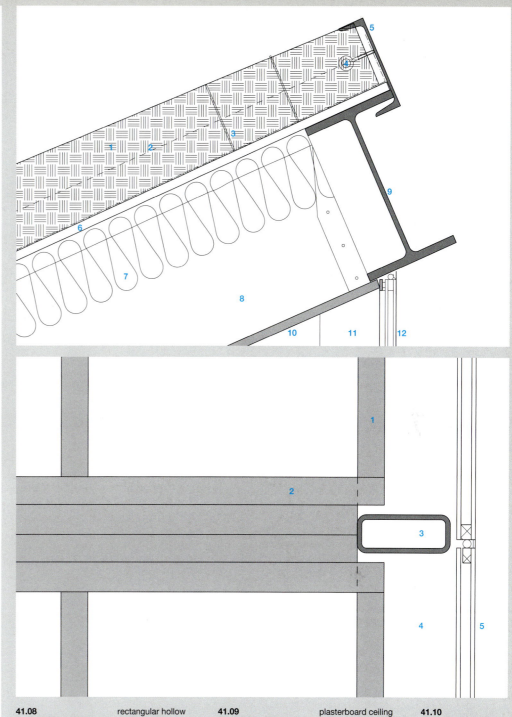

41.08
Typical Glass Wall Section Detail
1:20
1 Seasonally responsive green roof with native wildflowers
2 Waterproof membrane on 18 mm (3/4 inch) plywood decking
3 Spray foam insulation
4 Engineered timber I-joist
5 Painted plasterboard ceiling over hydronic ceiling loops
6 Universal steel edge beam
7 Steel mullion
8 25 mm (1 inch) thick, fixed low emissivity glazing
9 Plywood decking to mezzanine
10 Painted plasterboard ceiling on timber framing
11 150 x 150 x 6 mm (6 x 6 x 1/4 inch) steel

rectangular hollow section transom
12 40 x 40 mm (1 1/2 x 1 1/2 inch) steel angle glazing support
13 12 mm (1/2 inch) tempered glass door
14 Steel mullion
15 6 mm (1/4 inch) steel plate threshold
16 Reinforced concrete floor slab

41.09
Green Roof Edge Section Detail
1:10
1 Seasonally responsive green roof with native wildflowers
2 Permeable membrane for tensioning retaining strips for planted roof
3 150 mm (6 inch) geotextile grid structure for green roof containment
4 Galvanized eyelet welded to channel
5 200 x 343 mm (8 x 13 1/2 inch) steel C-section edge beam
6 Waterproof membrane on 18 mm (3/4 inch) plywood decking
7 Spray foam insulation
8 Engineered timber I-joist
9 Universal steel edge beam
10 Painted

plasterboard ceiling over hydronic ceiling loops
11 Steel mullion
12 25 mm (1 inch) thick, fixed low emissivity glazing

41.10
Floor Framing to Mezzanine Column Plan Detail
1:5
1 50 x 150 mm (2 x 6 inch) floor framing joists at 405 mm (16 inch) centres
2 Four layers of 50 x 150 mm (2 x 6 inch) joists
3 50 x 125 x 6 mm (2 x 5 x 1/4 inch) steel rectangular hollow section column centred on beam above
4 50 x 125 x 6 mm (2 x 5 x 1/4 inch) steel transom beyond
5 25 mm (1 inch) thick, fixed low emissivity glazing

**Slip House
London, England, UK**

Client
Carl Turner, Mary Martin

Project Team
Carl Turner, Tom Ebdon,
Alicja Borkowska, Zoe Fudge, Jake
Moulson, Ed Friel

Structural Engineer
Structure Workshop

Main Contractor
Neil Turner

Located in a traditional street of Victorian and Edwardian terraced houses in Brixton, Slip House brings a striking sculptural presence to this corner of south London. Designed by Carl Turner as his own home and studio, the house consists of three simple 'slipped' orthogonal boxes clad in translucent glass planks. Built across the full width of the site, the house is designed to be 'terraced', which will allow its future neighbours to be built right up to its north and south boundaries.

Arranged over three floors with an additional roof terrace level, a studio occupies the entire ground floor, with bedrooms and a bathroom on the first floor, and living spaces with views over the street and roofscapes on the second floor. All of the structural support is placed in the exterior walls leaving the interior free of columns or load bearing walls. The house, one of the most energy efficient ever built in the UK, features a wide range of energy saving systems including a solar assisted ground source heat pump, photovoltaic panels, a wildflower roof, rainwater harvesting, and mechanical ventilation with heat recovery within an airtight envelope.

The result is a house that is cheaper to run and more comfortable to live in than any of its Victorian neighbours, and indeed many of its contemporary counterparts. The house is both a universal prototype for dense, flexible, urban living, and a singular and personal design statement. The clean, cool interior spaces, the reductive colour and material palette, even the lack of furniture itself, along with the ice-like glazed exterior come together to create a liberating, sculptural and daring architectural expression.

1 A glass-clad box forms the upper two levels of the house containing the living spaces and an open roof terrace. The glass walls accentuate the sculptural quality of the house and provide an extreme contrast with the existing traditional streetscape.
2 At night the building shimmers and glows, revealing something of its structure through its skin. The gate from the street to the front courtyard has slots to allow the occupants to engage with the life of the street.
3 The living area on the second floor has a concrete stair that leads up to the roof terrace. Built-in birch ply furniture, simple white walls and concrete floors and ceilings are featured throughout the house.
4 Located between the two bedrooms, the bathroom can be opened up to the circulation space or closed through two large sliding wired glass walls.

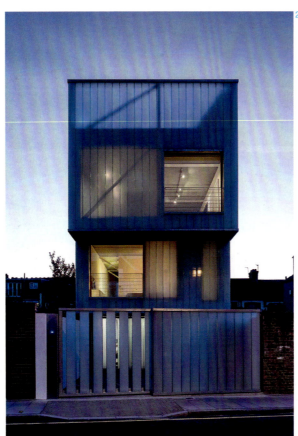

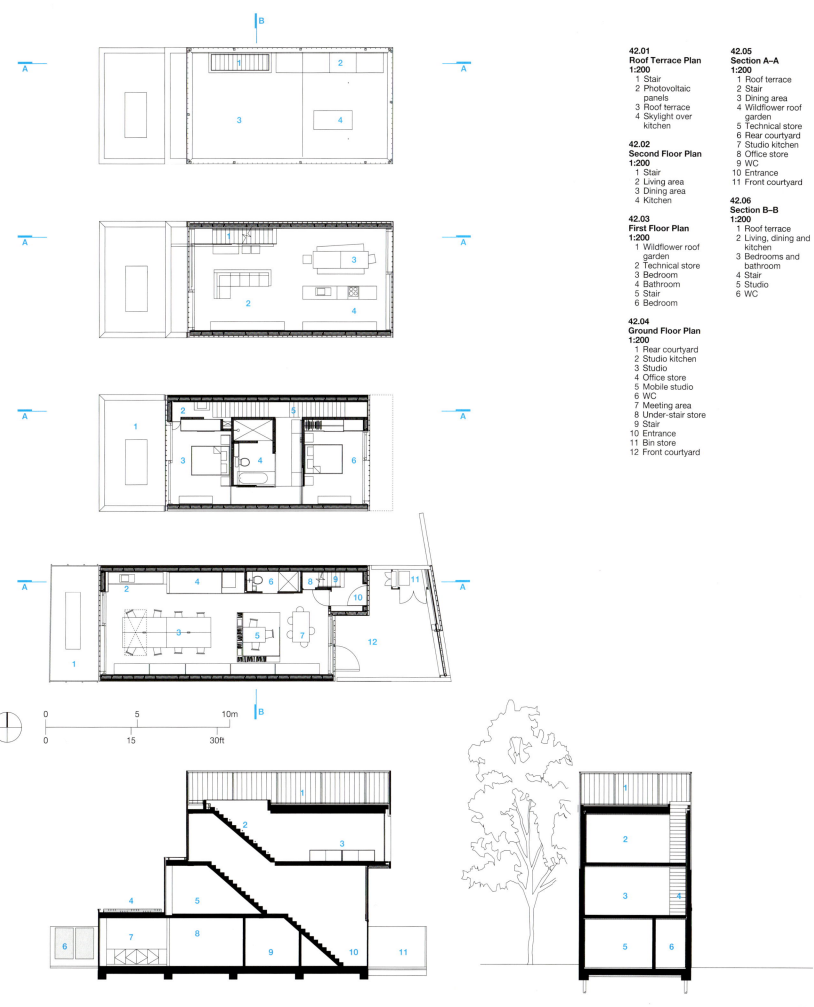

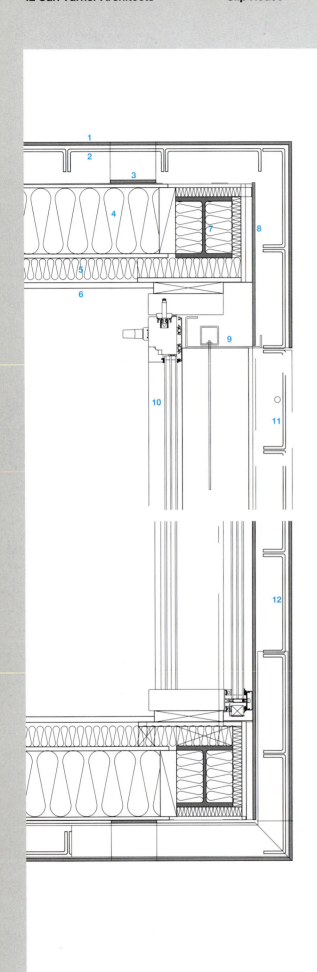

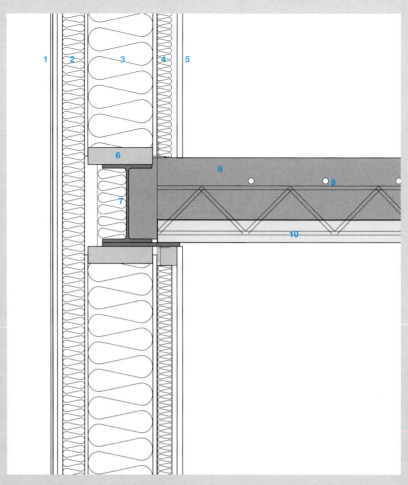

42.07
**External Wall and
Sliding Door Plan
Detail**
1:10
 1 Aluminium channel
for glazing system
 2 Translucent glass
channel external
cladding
 3 System fixing clip
 4 Prefabricated
structural insulated
panel comprised of
oriented strand board
panels sandwiched
around insulating foam
core
 5 Rigid insulation
 6 Skimmed and
painted plasterboard
wall lining
 7 Universal steel
beam packed with
local insulation
 8 Glass reinforced
plastic on oriented
strand board
 9 Folded steel cover
plate and window
reveal
10 Sliding triple glazed
window
11 Glass channel
cladding over window
opening
12 Translucent glass
channel external
cladding over fixed
glazing

42.08
**External Wall and
First Floor Section
Detail**
1:10
 1 Acrylic render on
render board external
cladding
 2 Rigid insulation
 3 Prefabricated
structural insulated
panel comprised of
oriented strand board
panels sandwiched
around insulating foam
core
 4 Rigid insulation
 5 Skimmed and
painted plasterboard
wall lining
 6 Timber framing
 7 Universal steel
beam
 8 Power floated
concrete screed
 9 Underfloor heating
10 Pre-cast concrete
ceiling panel

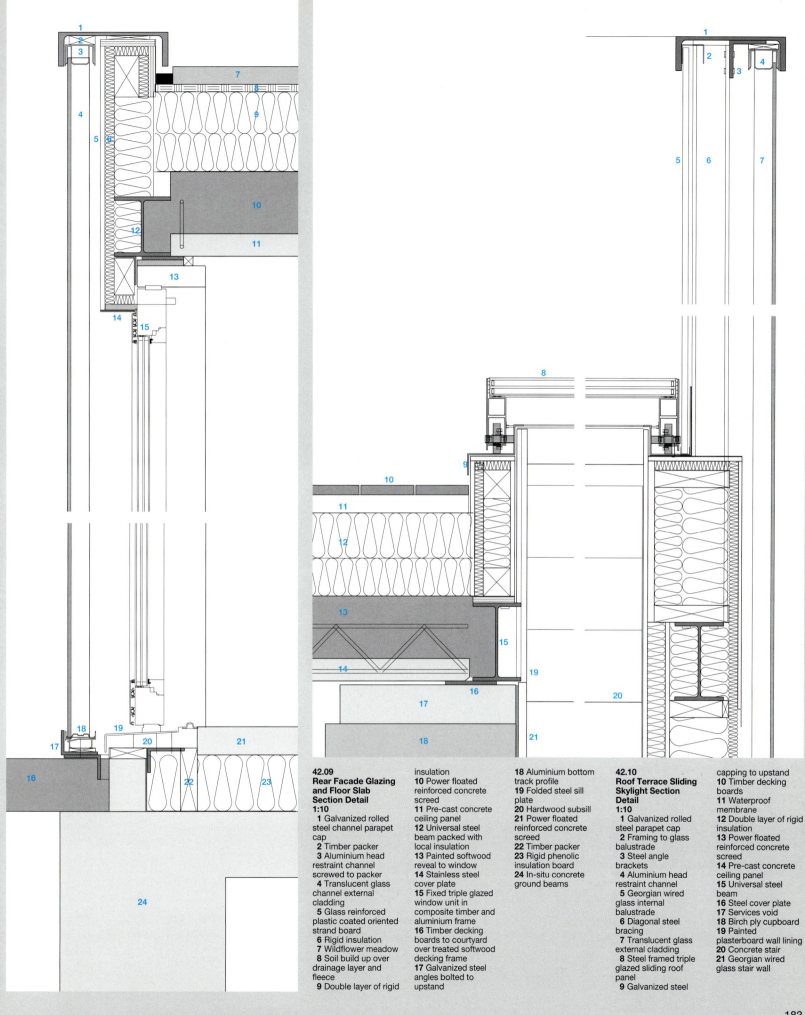

42.09
**Rear Facade Glazing
and Floor Slab
Section Detail**
1:10
1 Galvanized rolled
steel channel parapet
cap
2 Timber packer
3 Aluminium head
restraint channel
screwed to packer
4 Translucent glass
channel external
cladding
5 Glass reinforced
plastic coated oriented
strand board
6 Rigid insulation
7 Wildflower meadow
8 Soil build up over
drainage layer and
fleece
9 Double layer of rigid

insulation
10 Power floated
reinforced concrete
screed
11 Pre-cast concrete
ceiling panel
12 Universal steel
beam packed with
local insulation
13 Painted softwood
reveal to window
14 Stainless steel
cover plate
15 Fixed triple glazed
window unit in
composite timber and
aluminium frame
16 Timber decking
boards to courtyard
over treated softwood
decking frame
17 Galvanized steel
angles bolted to
upstand

18 Aluminium bottom
track profile
19 Folded steel sill
plate
20 Hardwood subsill
21 Power floated
reinforced concrete
screed
22 Timber packer
23 Rigid phenolic
insulation board
24 In-situ concrete
ground beams

42.10
**Roof Terrace Sliding
Skylight Section
Detail**
1:10
1 Galvanized rolled
steel parapet cap
2 Framing to glass
balustrade
3 Steel angle
brackets
4 Aluminium head
restraint channel
5 Georgian wired
glass internal
balustrade
6 Diagonal steel
bracing
7 Translucent glass
external cladding
8 Steel framed triple
glazed sliding roof
panel
9 Galvanized steel

capping to upstand
10 Timber decking
boards
11 Waterproof
membrane
12 Double layer of rigid
insulation
13 Power floated
reinforced concrete
screed
14 Pre-cast concrete
ceiling panel
15 Universal steel
beam
16 Steel cover plate
17 Services void
18 Birch ply cupboard
19 Painted
plasterboard wall lining
20 Concrete stair
21 Georgian wired
glass stair wall

183

Prospect House
Bath, Somerset, England, UK

Client
Private

Project Team
Alun Jones, Biba Dow

Structural Engineer
Momentum

Services Engineer
Buro Happold

Prospect House is located on Sion Hill, overlooking the historic city of Bath in south west England. The house is not completely new; rather it is a comprehensive reinterpretation of an existing house that was built in the mid 1980s. The original house was stylistically compromised and failed to make good use of the beautiful views available through windows that were too small and badly positioned. It was, however, decided that redesign was a better solution than demolition.

Internally the rooms have been carefully reordered. The main living space is on the upper level facing south with a balcony running along its length, accessed by a new concrete stair at the side of the building. The location of the kitchen in the north-west corner of the house has been ameliorated by the addition of a large, east-facing trapezoidal rooflight that projects the morning sun onto the kitchen table. To the east side of the house the architects have constructed a new building containing a garage at entrance level and a studio at the lower garden level, the two-level structure taking advantage of both an existing retaining wall and the natural slope of the site.

Once reconfigured, the whole house was wrapped in rigid insulation and an outer layer of dark brown standing-seam zinc sheet cladding. Windows are flush with the zinc, helping to make the envelope read as a taught skin. The intelligent retrofit, including the comprehensive use of high performance insulation, thermally efficient doors and windows, and a solar hot water system, have resulted in a spacious and comfortable home with a greatly enhanced thermal performance.

1 The two-level house traverses a steeply sloping site. The upper living level opens directly onto a paved entrance courtyard to the north-east (far right) and a balcony to the south-west, while the lower bedroom level opens onto a timber terrace and the lower parts of the terraced garden (left).
2 The west facing dining room takes advantage of a full height window to catch the evening sun.
3 The garage (left) and the entrance to the house (right) open onto a large paved courtyard at the upper level of the site.
4 In the living area a wood-burning stove provides heating, while the floor to ceiling south-west facing windows open onto the balcony that runs the full width of the living room.

43.01
Ground Floor Plan
1:200

1 Terraced garden
2 Kitchen
3 Boiler room
4 Laundry
5 WC
6 Entrance hall
7 Dining room
8 Stair down to
  bedroom level
9 Study
10 Living area
11 Balcony
12 Stair down to
   lower garden
13 Entrance courtyard
14 Garage

43.02
Lower Ground Floor
Plan
1:200

1 Terraced garden
2 Bedroom
3 Ensuite bathroom
4 Stair up to living
  level
5 Bathroom
6 Ensuite bathroom
7 Bedroom
8 Bedroom
9 Bedroom
10 Terrace
11 Exterior stair up to
   living level
12 Courtyard
13 Studio
14 Store room

0   5   10m

0   15   30ft

43.03
Section A–A
1:200
1 Balcony
2 Study
3 Dining room
4 Kitchen
5 Terrace

6 Bedroom
7 Hallway
8 Bedroom

43.04
Section B–B
1:200
1 Balcony
2 Living area
3 Stair void
4 Kitchen
5 Terrace

6 Bedroom
7 Hallway

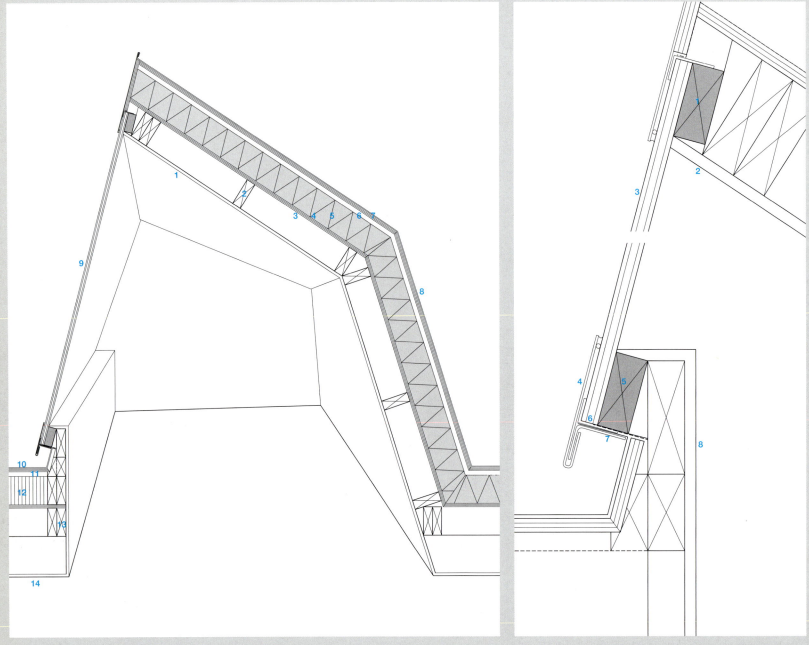

43.05
Kitchen Roof Light
Section Detail
1:20
1 Skimmed and painted plasterboard ceiling
2 Timber framing
3 18 mm (3/4 inch) waterproof plywood
4 Vapour barrier
5 150 mm (6 inch) styrofoam rigid insulation
6 Waterproof membrane
7 18 mm (3/4 inch) waterproof plywood
8 Standing-seam zinc roof sheeting
9 Aluminium-framed double glazed roof light
10 Standing-seam zinc roof sheeting
11 Ventilation void
12 150 mm (6 inch) styrofoam rigid insulation
13 Existing joists cut out to form shape of

roof light
14 Suspended ceiling attached to existing steelwork

43.06
Roof Light Glazing
Section Detail
1:5
1 Timber setting block fixed into softwood framing structure
2 Skimmed and painted plasterboard ceiling
3 Double glazed roof light unit comprised of 6.4 mm (1/4 inch) laminated glass and 10mm (3/8 inch) argon-filled cavity
4 Zinc flashing with continuous bonded silicone seal to glazing
5 Timber setting block fixed into softwood framing structure
6 Glazing bonded into aluminium angle

with continuous structural silicone
7 Aluminium angle fixed into setting block
8 Skimmed and painted plasterboard

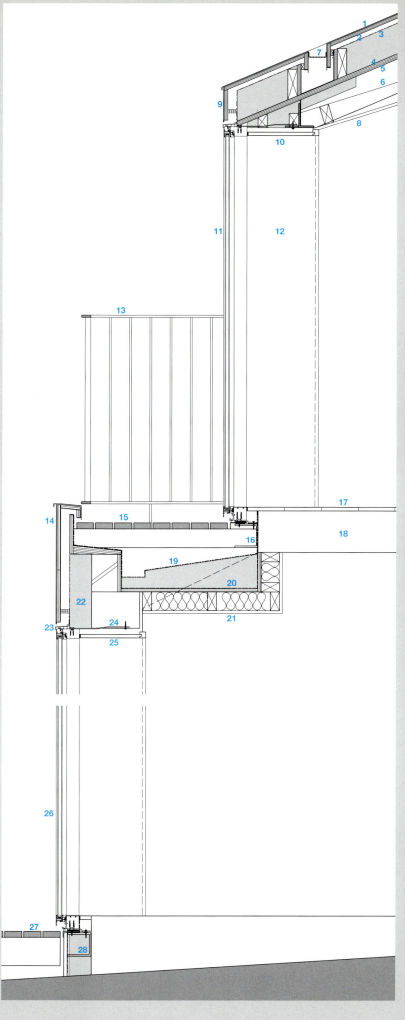

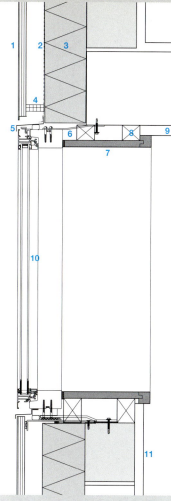

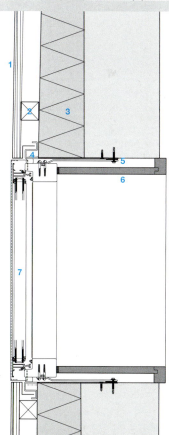

43.07
External Wall and Balcony Section Detail
1:20
1 Standing seam zinc roof sheeting on 18 mm (³/₄ inch) waterproof plywood
2 25 mm (1 inch) ventilation void with 25 mm (1 inch) timber battens
3 Roofing membrane over 150 mm (6 inch) styrofoam rigid insulation
4 Vapour barrier
5 18 mm (³/₄ inch) waterproof plywood screw-fixed to existing joists
6 Existing roof structure
7 Rainwater gutter with concealed downpipes in isolation zone at either end of fall
8 Skimmed and painted plasterboard ceiling
9 Zinc cladding to external wall
10 Painted MDF window reveal
11 Top hung double glazed window
12 Window reveal
13 Powder coated steel balustrade
14 Zinc cladding to external wall
15 Hardwood timber deck
16 Balcony joist hanger fixed to existing structure
17 Timber interior floor
18 Timber floor joist
19 Membrane over tapered insulation with integral gutter to feed downpipes at either end of balcony concealed in insulation zone
20 Vapour barrier on 18 mm (³/₄ inch) waterproof plywood
21 Local insulation, timber framing and painted plasterboard ceiling
22 Rigid insulation
23 Zinc flashing
24 Proprietary straps and fixings back to structure
25 Painted MDF window reveal
26 Top hung double glazed door
27 Hardwood timber deck
28 Steel support to glazed doors

43.08
Typical Window Section Detail 1
1:10
1 Standing seam zinc roof sheeting on 18 mm (³/₄ inch) waterproof plywood
2 Waterproof membrane
3 150 mm (6 inch) styrofoam rigid insulation
4 Cladding spacer
5 Zinc flashing
6 Proprietary straps and fixings back to structure
7 Painted MDF window reveal
8 Timber framing
9 Skimmed and painted plasterboard ceiling
10 Top hung double glazed window
11 Skimmed and painted plasterboard wall lining

43.09
Typical Window Section Detail 2
1:10
1 Standing seam zinc roof sheeting on 18 mm (³/₄ inch) waterproof plywood
2 25 mm (1 inch) timber battens
3 150 mm (6 inch) styrofoam rigid insulation
4 Zinc flashing
5 Proprietary straps and fixings back to structure
6 Painted MDF window reveal
7 Top hung double glazed window

**Beach Chalet
Humberston Fitties, Lincolnshire,
UK**

Client
Paul Tidswell, Linda Olgeirsson

Project Team
Jonathan Hendry, Daniel Sharp

Structural Engineer
Alan Wood & Partners

In 2009, the architects were asked to alter and extend an existing beach house located within the Humberston Fitties salt marsh conservation area in north-west England. Development of the Humberston Fitties began in the 1920s. During both world wars the area was used for military billeting and then in 1953, many of the informal chalets and huts were destroyed by the devastating floods that breached the Lincolnshire coastline. The area was declared a conservation area in 1996 to preserve its unique character. Planning permission was granted to alter and extend the existing chalet, with a condition that the structural timber frame was retained. However it became evident that the structure was in very poor condition and after a year-long battle with the planning department, the conservation officer and the Environment Agency, planning permission for a brand new chalet was finally granted.

The client wanted to create a dwelling that was not like a conventional home, in which the plan is organized as a series of rooms. In response to this the architects created a single, open space, in which four carefully positioned pieces of furniture have been placed. These items are a sleeping box, a bathing box with sleeping platform, a kitchen and a stove, which are clad in a variety of materials including mirror, timber, marble and linen to lend different spatial and atmospheric qualities for the domestic rituals of sleeping, bathing and eating. The floor and exterior walls up to a height of 2.4 metres (8 feet) are lined in timber. In places, the wall lining is adjusted in depth or height to provide storage for clothes, a television, the pantry or to sit at a computer. Externally, the form of the chalet is dictated by its predecessor. The two verandahs create covered transition spaces between the intimate domestic interior and the world outside.

1 On the south-west side of this modest holiday house, a cantilevered stainless steel roof provides protection to a timber verandah which is accessed from the living space via large sliding glass doors.
2 In contrast, the north-east verandah is supported by closely spaced timber columns to protect the entrance (right).
3 The roof and side walls of the house are clad in standing-seam stainless steel while the front and rear facades are finished in black bitumen paint.
4 The interior is as deliberately plain and simple as the exterior, employing a limited vocabulary of wood, mirror, linen and marble to great effect.

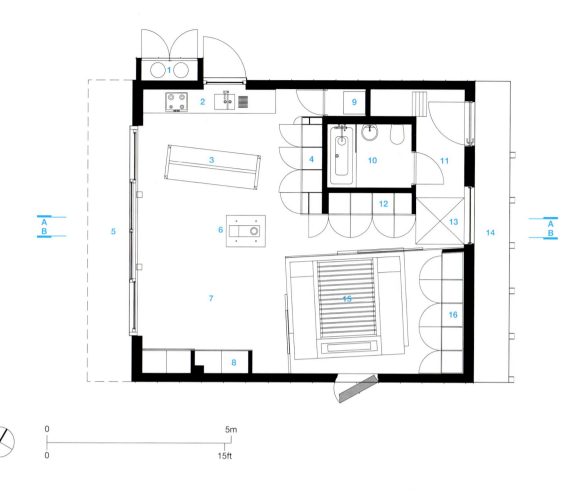

44.01
Floor Plan
1:100
1 Hot water storage tanks
2 Fixed kitchen
3 Mobile kitchen
4 Pantry
5 Verandah
6 Wood-burning stove
7 Living area
8 Audio-visual storage
9 Laundry
10 Bathroom
11 Entry
12 Storage
13 Skylight over
14 Verandah
15 Sleeping pod
16 Bedroom storage

0   5m

0   15ft

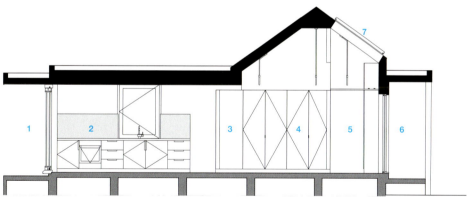

44.02
Section A–A
1:100
1 Verandah
2 Kitchen
3 Pantry
4 Storage
5 Entrance
6 Verandah
7 Skylight

44.03
Section B–B
1:100
1 Verandah
2 Skylight
3 Sliding door to sleeping box
4 Wood-burning stove
5 Audio-visual storage
6 Verandah

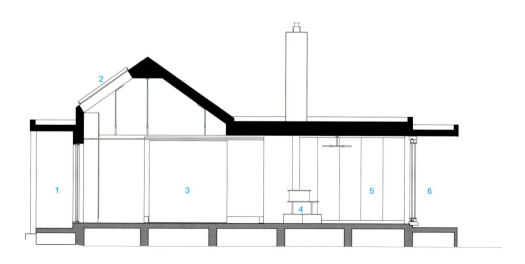

189

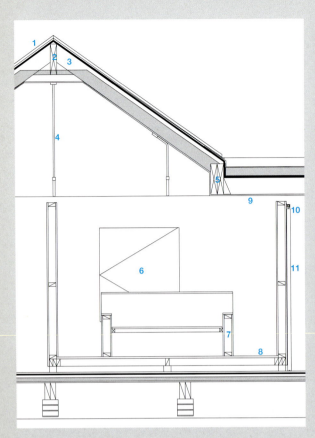

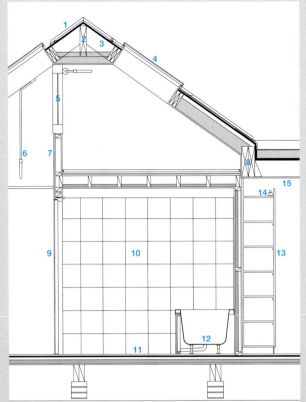

44.04
Sleeping Pod Section Detail
1:50
 1 Galvanized sheet metal roofing
 2 100 x 400 mm (4 x 15³/4 inch) glu-lam timber ridge beam
 3 200 x 50 mm (8 x 2 inch) treated softwood timber rafters at 400 mm (15³/4 inch) centres
 4 Custom made light fitting formed from bent galvanized steel conduit
 5 Two 100 x 400 mm (4 x 15³/4 inch) glu-lam timber beams
 6 Window beyond
 7 18 mm (³/4 inch) Douglas fir timber boards fixed to softwood timber sleeping pod frame
 8 18 mm (³/4 inch) Douglas fir timber floorboards
 9 Painted plasterboard ceiling
10 Mild steel sliding track supporting oak sleeping pod doors
11 Black linen stretched over 18 mm (³/4 inch) MDF sheet secretly hung from softwood timber stud frame

44.05
Bathroom Section Detail
1:50
 1 Galvanized sheet metal roofing
 2 100 x 400 mm (4 x 15³/4 inch) glu-lam timber ridge beam
 3 200 x 50 mm (8 x 2 inch) treated softwood timber rafters at 400 mm (15³/4 inch) centres
 4 Aluminium framed skylight
 5 Douglas fir framed window for indirect light to bathroom, oiled internally, painted externally with bitumen paint
 6 Custom made light fitting formed from bent galvanized steel conduit
 7 Internal wall with mirror bonded back to plywood sheet on non bathroom side and plasterboard with vapour check layer on bathroom side
 8 Two 100 x 400 mm (4 x 15³/4 inch) glu-lam timber beams
 9 Internal door from mirror bonded back to plywood sheet
10 Ceramic wall tiles
11 18 mm (³/4 inch) Douglas fir timber floorboards
12 Bath tub
13 Timber joinery
14 Warm white fluorescent striplighting
15 12.5 mm (¹/2 inch) painted plasterboard ceiling

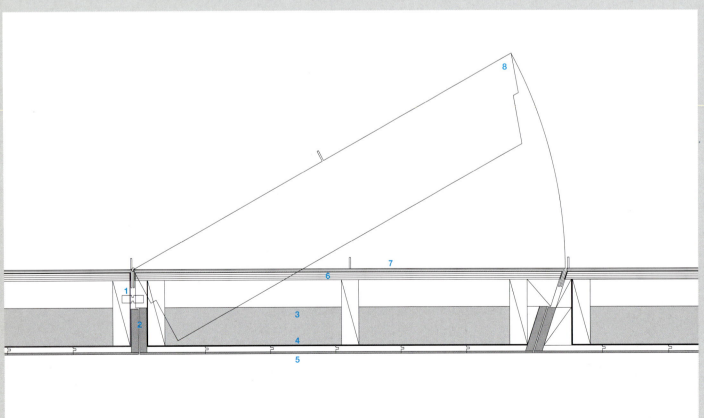

44.06
Ventilation Panel to External Wall Plan Detail
1:10
 1 Stainless steel invisible soss hinge
 2 Solid oak window reveal
 3 100 mm (4 inch) rigid insulation boards between timber studs
 4 Breather membrane
 5 Internal wall cladding from engineered oak tongue-and-groove boards
 6 18 mm (³/4 inch) waterproof plywood
 7 Terne coated stainless steel standing-seam external cladding
 8 Ventilation panel in open position

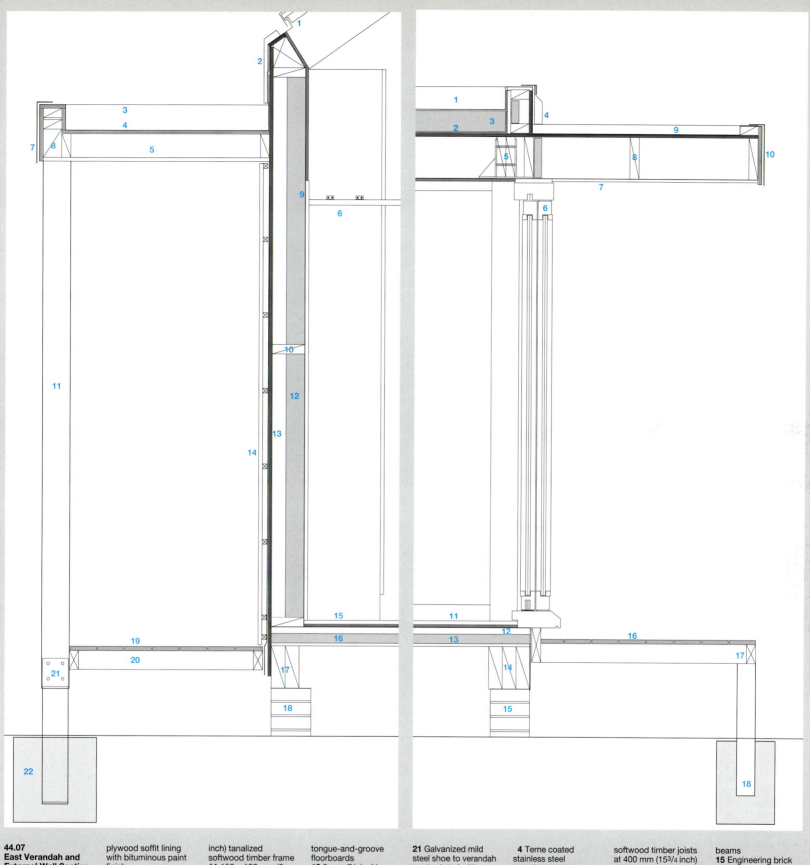

44.07
East Verandah and External Wall Section Detail
1:20
1 Aluminium framed skylight
2 Terne coated stainless steel standing-seam external wall and roof cladding
3 Three layer felt roof system
4 Plywood decking screw-fixed to timber joists
5 18 mm (3/4 inch) plywood soffit lining with bituminous paint finish
6 Lacquered mild steel track supporting sliding doors to sleeping box
7 Terne coated stainless steel fascia
8 150 x 100 mm (6 x 4 inch) softwood timber beam
9 12.5 mm (1/2 inch) skimmed and painted plasterboard with vapour check layer behind
10 175 x 50 mm (7 x 2 inch) tanalized softwood timber frame
11 150 x 150 mm (6 x 6 inch) Douglas fir post painted with bituminous paint
12 100 mm (4 inch) rigid insulation board between studs
13 Breather membrane
14 18 mm (3/4 inch) thick plywood cut into 600 mm (231/2 inch) strips screwed back to 25 x 25 mm (1 inch) treated softwood timber battens
15 Engineered oak tongue-and-groove floorboards
16 9 mm (3/8 inch) plywood subfloor panels fixed between joists and supporting insulation
17 225 x 75 mm (83/4 x 3 inch) treated softwood timber cross beams
18 Engineering brick piers
19 Rhodesian teak verandah decking
20 100 x 50 mm (4 x 2 inch) treated softwood joists
21 Galvanized mild steel shoe to verandah post painted with bituminous paint
22 450 mm (173/4 inch) concrete pad foundation

44.08
West Verandah and External Wall Section Detail
1:20
1 Three layer felt roof system
2 Breather membrane
3 140 mm (51/2 inch) rigid insulation
4 Terne coated stainless steel standing-seam cladding
5 Continuous mild steel support bracket and flitch plates
6 Douglas fir framed windows, oiled internally and painted externally with bituminous paint
7 18 mm (3/4 inch) plywood soffit lining with bituminous paint finish
8 225 x 50 mm (87/8 x 2 inch) treated softwood timber joists at 400 mm (153/4 inch) centres
9 Three layer felt roof system
10 Terne coated stainless steel fascia
11 Engineered oak tongue-and-groove flooring
12 Damp-proof membrane
13 60 mm (23/8 inch) rigid insulation between floor joists
14 225 x 75 mm (83/4 x 3 inch) treated softwood timber cross beams
15 Engineering brick piers
16 Rhodesian teak verandah decking boards
17 100 x 50 mm (4 x 2 inch) treated softwood joists
18 100 x 100 mm (4 x 4 inch) treated softwood decking post with bituminous paint finish cast into concrete pad foundation

191

**Bridge House
Ashbourne, South Australia,
Australia**

Client
Private

Project Team
Max Pritchard, Andrew Gunner

Structural Engineer
Sam Case for Pocius & Associates

Located an hour's drive from Adelaide, the capital city of the state of South Australia, this bridge-like house spans a creek that is dry for much of the year. The clients needed a building that would allow appreciation of the natural beauty of the site without damaging the water course or the delicate habitat of native plants and animals. These requirements had to be balanced against a tight budget which was comparable to that of an off-the-shelf prefabricated dwelling.

The house is a narrow orthogonal box with substantial quantities of glazing to each of the long sides to facilitate enjoyment of views in both directions. The 'bridge' is supported on two steel trusses that form the primary structure. The trusses were fabricated off site and then erected on site by two men and a crane over two days. Four small concrete piers, two on each side of the creek, anchor the trusses. The simple plan is symmetrical about its short axis with an open plan kitchen, dining and living area in the centre, with a bedroom and bathroom at one end and an office and utility room at the other.

Passive design devices including the east-west orientation, sun shading, cross ventilation and rain water collection have resulted in a highly energy efficient house that requires no mechanical heating or cooling, despite the hot climate. In the winter the low winter sun from the north heats the black insulated concrete floor, storing heat for re-radiating at night. Insulation to the underside of the slab, walls and roof combined with double glazed windows, aid the retention of heat while a wood-burning fire fuelled with sustainable fuel from the site, provides additional heat if required. Other sustainable strategies include the use of photovoltaic cells for electricity, solar hot water panels and a waste water treatment system.

1 The house bridges the creek with an effortless elegance, barely touching the earth. The simple rectangular prism establishes a dynamic dialogue between the natural environment and the orthogonal man made form.
2 On the north side of the building, sun shades made from steel framed expanded aluminium mesh protect the interior from the strong summer sun.
3 The building rests on four small concrete piers, minimizing contact with the ground. The colour of the corrugated sheet metal cladding was chosen to blend in with and complement the native plants and trees, such as the eucalyptus on the creek bank.
4 The living area, comprised of a single open plan kitchen, dining and living space, is at the centre of the plan.

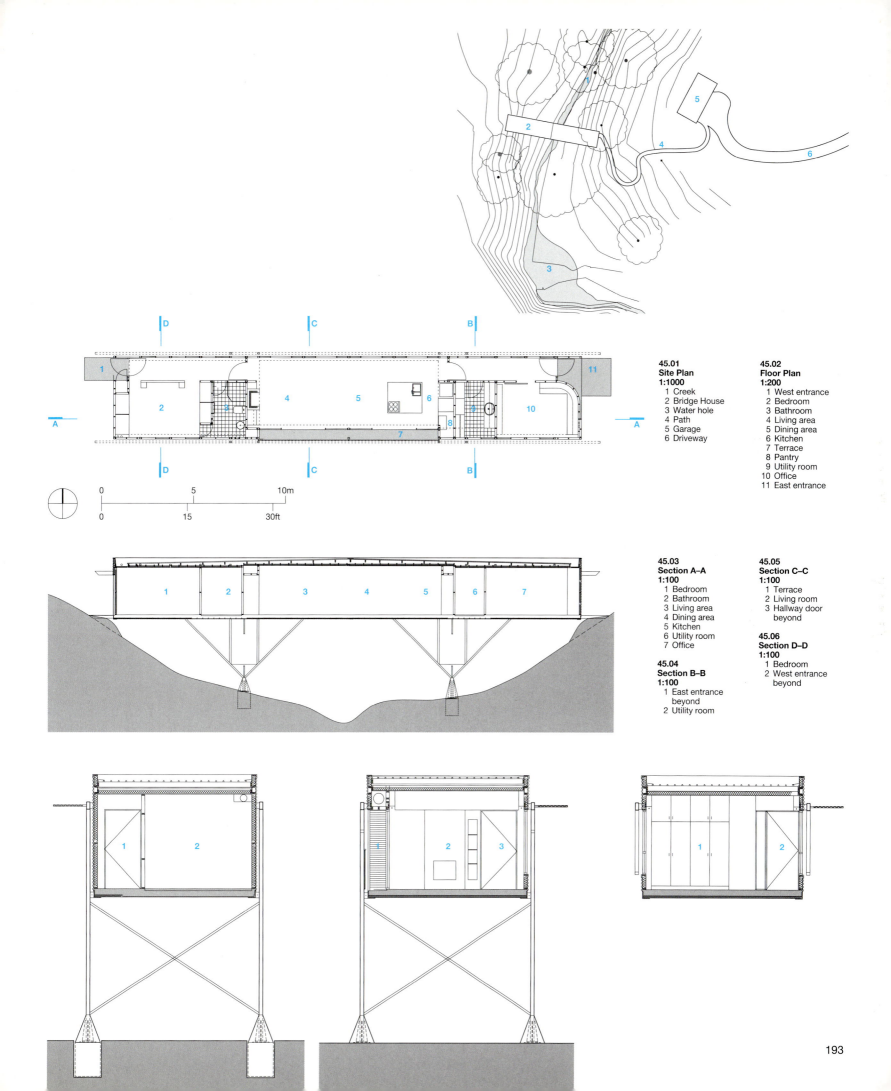

45.01
Site Plan
1:1000
1 Creek
2 Bridge House
3 Water hole
4 Path
5 Garage
6 Driveway

45.02
Floor Plan
1:200
1 West entrance
2 Bedroom
3 Bathroom
4 Living area
5 Dining area
6 Kitchen
7 Terrace
8 Pantry
9 Utility room
10 Office
11 East entrance

45.03
Section A–A
1:100
1 Bedroom
2 Bathroom
3 Living area
4 Dining area
5 Kitchen
6 Utility room
7 Office

45.04
Section B–B
1:100
1 East entrance
beyond
2 Utility room

45.05
Section C–C
1:100
1 Terrace
2 Living room
3 Hallway door
beyond

45.06
Section D–D
1:100
1 Bedroom
2 West entrance
beyond

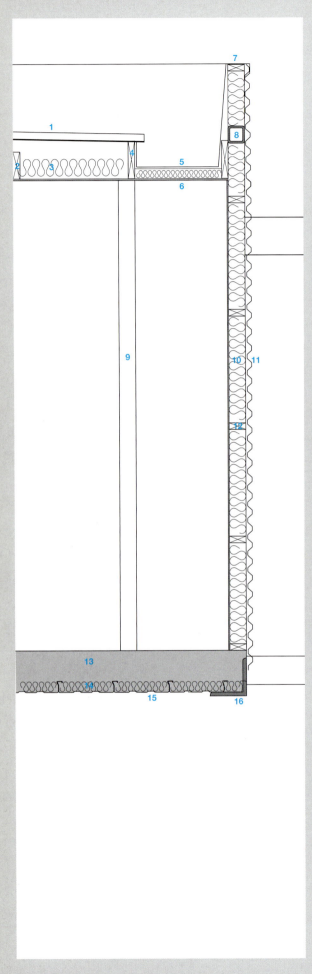

45.07
Section Detail
Through West
External Wall
1:20
1 Corrugated sheet metal roofing over laminated foil condensation barrier
2 140 x 35 mm (5^1/$_2$ x 1^3/$_8$ inch) timber ceiling joists at 450 mm (17^3/$_4$ inch) centres
3 Mineral wool insulation
4 140 x 45 mm (5^1/$_2$ x 1^3/$_4$ inch) timber rafters at 1200 mm (47^1/$_4$ inch) centres
5 Zincalume pre-formed gutter
6 Skimmed and painted plasterboard interior wall lining
7 Sheet metal parapet capping in colour to match cladding
8 100 x 100 mm (4 x 4 inch) hollow steel section wall framing
9 Timber framing to cupboards
10 Mineral wool insulation
11 Corrugated sheet metal external wall cladding over laminated foil condensation barrier
12 Timber wall framing
13 160 mm (6^1/$_4$ inch) thick concrete floor slab
14 50 mm (2 inch) thick rigid foam insulation
15 Metal decking permanent formwork
16 200 x 200 (8 x 8 inch) steel angle

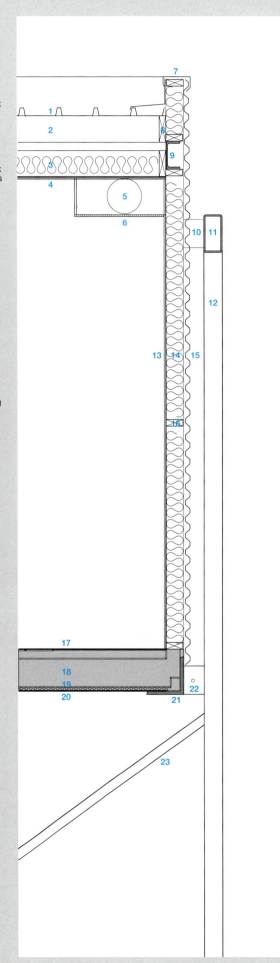

45.08
Section Detail
Through Utility Room
External Wall
1:20
1 Corrugated sheet metal roofing over laminated foil condensation barrier
2 140 x 45 mm (5^1/$_2$ x 1^3/$_4$ inch) timber rafters at 1200 mm (47^1/$_4$ inch) centres
3 Mineral wool insulation
4 Skimmed and painted plasterboard ceiling
5 Duct from wood burner in living area
6 15 mm (5$/$$_8$ inch) MDF box to conceal duct
7 Sheet metal parapet capping in colour to match cladding
8 140 x 35 mm (5^1/$_2$ x 1^3/$_8$ inch) timber wall plate
9 150 mm (6 inch) pre-formed channel
10 150 x 100 mm (6 x 4 inch) steel spacer
11 200 x 100 mm (8 x 4 inch) rectangular hollow section
12 100 x 100 mm (4 x 4 inch) square hollow section diagonal strut
13 Skimmed and painted plasterboard interior wall lining
14 Mineral wool insulation
15 Corrugated sheet metal external wall cladding over laminated foil condensation barrier
16 Timber wall framing
17 Floor tiles on concrete screed
18 160 mm (6^1/$_4$ inch) thick concrete floor slab
19 10 mm (^{3}/$_8$ inch) rigid foam insulation
20 Metal decking permanent formwork
21 200 x 200 (8 x 8 inch) steel angle
22 12 mm (^{1}/$_2$ inch) steel cleats to anchor strut to facade
23 65 x 65 mm (2^1/$_2$ x 2^1/$_2$ inch) square hollow section cross bracing

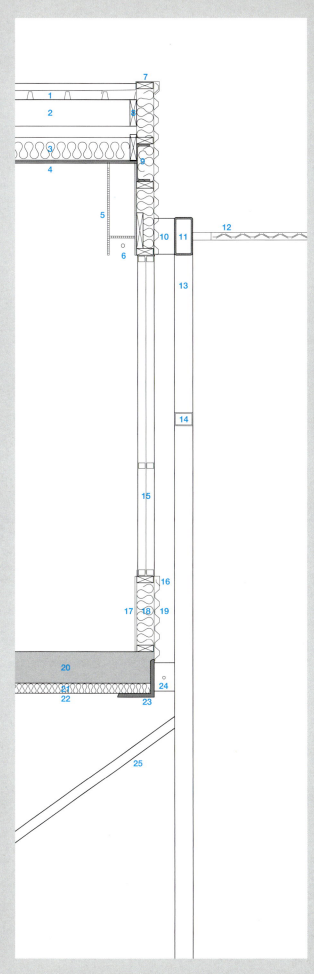

45.09
Section Detail
Through Bedroom
West External Wall
1:20

1 Corrugated sheet metal roofing over laminated foil condensation barrier
2 140 x 45 mm (5^1/$_2$ x 1^3/$_4$ inch) timber rafters at 1200 mm (47^1/$_4$ inch) centres
3 Mineral wool insulation
4 Skimmed and painted plasterboard ceiling
5 15 mm (^{5}/$_8$ inch) MDF pelmet
6 Light fixture
7 Sheet metal parapet capping in colour to match cladding
8 140 x 35 mm (5^1/$_2$ x 1^3/$_8$ inch) timber wall plate
9 150 mm (6 inch) pre-formed channel
10 150 x 100 mm (6 x 4 inch) steel spacer
11 200 x 100 mm (8 x 4 inch) rectangular hollow section
12 900 mm (35^1/$_2$ inch) aluminium expanded mesh sunscreen awning panel in 50 x 50 mm (2 x 2 inch) steel frame
13 100 x 100 mm (4 x 4 inch) square hollow section column
14 100 x 100 mm (4 x 4 inch) square hollow section diagonal strut
15 Aluminium-framed sliding glass windows
16 Aluminium sill flashing
17 Skimmed and painted plasterboard interior wall lining
18 Mineral wool insulation
19 Corrugated sheet metal external wall cladding over laminated foil condensation barrier
20 160 mm (6^1/$_4$ inch) thick concrete floor slab
21 50 mm (2 inch) rigid foam insulation
22 Metal decking permanent formwork
23 200 x 200 (8 x 8 inch) steel angle
24 12 mm (^{1}/$_2$ inch) steel cleats to anchor strut to facade
25 65 x 65 mm (2^1/$_2$ x 2^1/$_2$ inch) square hollow section cross bracing

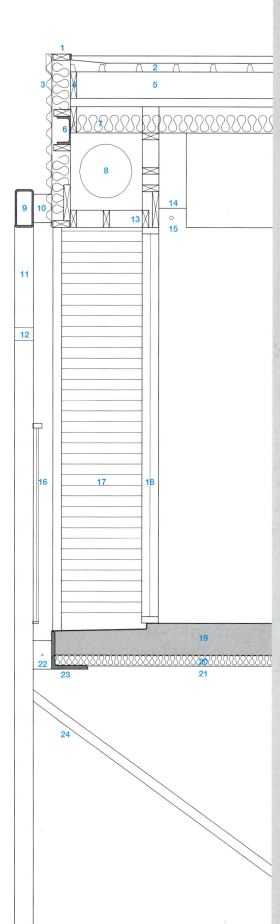

45.10
Section Detail
Through Living Room
East External Wall
1:20

1 Sheet metal parapet capping in colour to match cladding
2 Corrugated sheet metal roofing over laminated foil condensation barrier
3 Corrugated sheet metal external wall cladding over laminated foil condensation barrier
4 140 x 35 mm (5^1/$_2$ x 1^3/$_8$ inch) timber wall plate
5 140 x 45 mm (5^1/$_2$ x 1^3/$_4$ inch) timber rafters at 1200 mm (47^1/$_4$ inch) centres
6 150 mm (6 inch) pre-formed channel
7 Mineral wool insulation
8 Services void
9 200 x 100 mm (8 x 4 inch) rectangular hollow section
10 150 x 100 mm (6 x 4 inch) steel spacer
11 100 x 100 mm (4 x 4 inch) square hollow section column
12 100 x 100 mm (4 x 4 inch) square hollow section diagonal strut
13 Timber framed bulkhead
14 15 mm (^{5}/$_8$ inch) MDF pelmet
15 Light fixture
16 Terrace balustrade comprised of 50 x 25 mm (2 x 1 inch) steel flat baluster and 12 mm (^{1}/$_2$ inch) steel rod uprights at 125 mm (5 inch) centres
17 Timber cladding to terrace wall
18 Aluminium-framed sliding glass doors
19 160 mm (6^1/$_4$ inch) thick concrete floor slab
20 50 mm (2 inch) rigid foam insulation
21 Metal decking permanent formwork
22 12 mm (^{1}/$_2$ inch) steel cleats to anchor strut to facade
23 200 x 200 (8 x 8 inch) steel angle
24 65 x 65 mm (2^1/$_2$ x 2^1/$_2$ inch) square hollow section cross bracing

Maison Escalier
Paris, France

Client
Eric de Rugy

Project Team
Jacques Moussafir, Alexis Duquennoy,
Na An

Structural Engineer
CE Ingénierie, Malishev Wilson
Engineers

Contractors
Microsol, Lisandre, General Metal,
MGN, B2E, Tischlerei Bereuter

Built on the site of an old house set
between two buildings in the heart of
a well-preserved block in the centre of
Paris, Maison Escalier has been
designed as a tree-like structure rising
up in a confined space delimited on
three sides by the walls of the
neighbouring buildings. The house
relies entirely on the fully glazed south
facade and the roof to bring natural
light into the six half-levels that spiral
up around the central services core.

The plan is arranged as a series of
stairs connecting the gradually rising
floors. Starting at basement level with
a family room and home cinema, the
spaces rise up around the core, with
the living spaces on the entry level,
then upwards to the private spaces
including the bedroom and dressing
room, and culminating in a roof
terrace at the top of the house.
Interstitial spaces around the core are
utilized for secondary functions such
as an office, a sitting area and a
dressing room. Unusually, there was
no need to use partition walls to divide
the rooms as the constant change in
level introduces a sense of spatial
continuity from basement to roof
terrace, while maintaining privacy as
appropriate. The services core, around
which the spaces are arranged,
contains bathrooms in the basement
and top level and the kitchen on the
living floor.

The entirely steel structure consists
of cantilevered floors supported from
the central core and structurally
independent of the three outer walls,
which created the opportunity to glaze
the entire south wall. Here, electrically
operated filigree patterned steel
shutters are a sculptural feature of the
bedroom, the office, the living room
and the entrance hall. The laser cut
shutters can be slid open and stacked
against the steel frame, or closed for
shade and privacy.

1 A view of the south
facade with the
shutters stacked open
against the steel frame.
The entrance (right)
leads into the living
area (left), down into
the half basement
recreation spaces and
up to the bedroom, all
of which feature the
laser cut steel shutters.
2 The design of the
filigree patterned
shutters, set neatly into
a frame of steel
C-sections, echoes the
dappled light from the
trees.
3 At night, light from
the interior animates
the facade and
provides glimpses of
the building's
volumetric complexity.
4 A view of the living
room and the dining
area beyond. Moving
around the timber-clad
services core, the
rooms are linked by
short flights of steps.

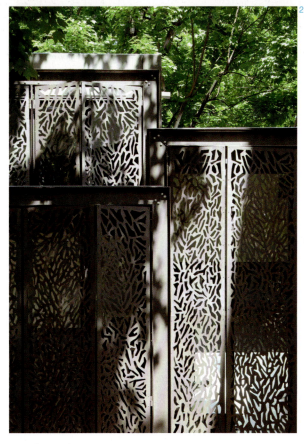

46.01
First Floor Plan
1:200
1 Void over dining
area below
2 Dressing room
3 Void over sitting
area below
4 WC
5 Bathroom
6 Bedroom
7 Stair to roof terrace
8 Void over stair
below

9 Terrace
10 Terrace to living
area below
11 Office

46.02
Ground Floor Plan
1:200
1 Dining area
2 Sitting area
3 Kitchen
4 Living area
5 Entrance hall

46.03
Basement Plan
1:200
1 Laundry
2 Home cinema
3 Bathroom
4 Family room

46.04
Section A–A
1:200
1 Bedroom
2 Roof terrace
3 Living area
4 Office
5 Family room
6 Entrance

46.05
Section B–B
1:200
1 Skylight
2 Door to bedroom
3 Roof terrace
4 Skylight
5 Bedroom
6 Office
7 Entrance
8 Dining area

46.06
Section C–C
1:200
1 Skylight
2 Bedroom
3 Bathroom
4 Roof terrace
5 Living area
6 Office
7 Kitchen
8 Entrance
9 Home cinema
10 Bathroom

46.07
Section D–D
1:200
1 Terrace
2 Bedroom
3 Bathroom
4 Dressing room
5 Living area
6 Kitchen
7 Dining area
8 Sitting area
9 Bathroom
10 Laundry

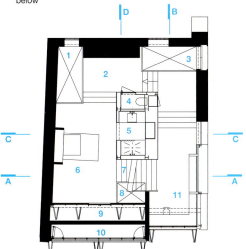

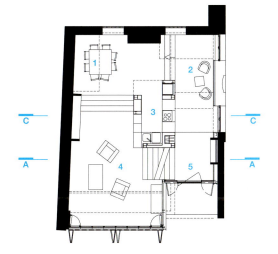

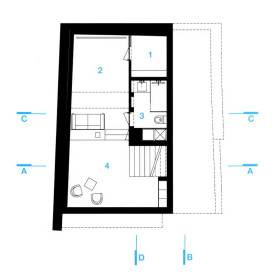

0   5m

0   15ft

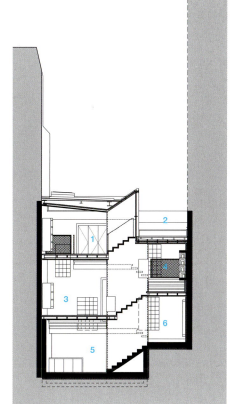

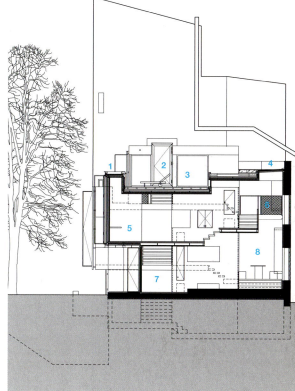

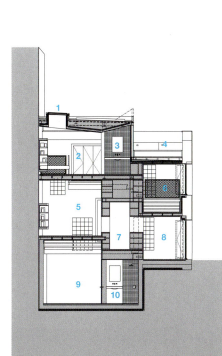

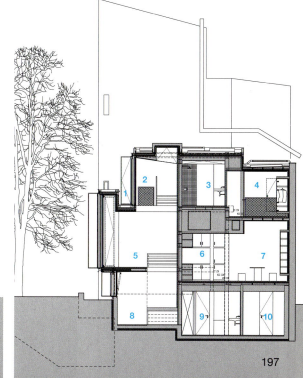

197

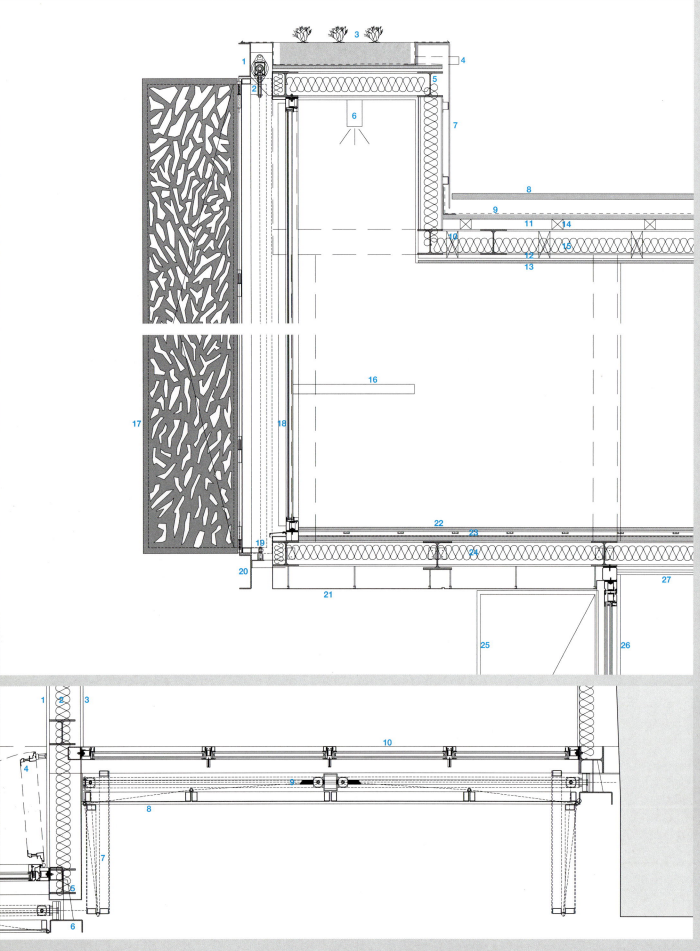

46.08
**Office Area Facade
and Shutters Section
Detail**
1:20
1 180 mm (7 inch)
steel C-section beam
2 Shutter guide and
motor
3 Planted roof
4 Drainage spigot
from planted roof
5 133 x 140 mm (5$\frac{1}{4}$
x 5$\frac{1}{2}$ inch) steel beam
6 Ceiling mounted
light fixture
7 Powder coated
aluminium sheet
external cladding
8 Ipe wood decking
to terrace
9 Waterproof
membrane
10 Timber framing
11 Plywood roofing
substrate
12 13 mm ($\frac{1}{2}$ inch) fire
rated plasterboard
ceiling substrate
13 Locust wood
boards to ceiling
14 Timber battens
15 Glasswool thermal
insulation
16 Timber desk to
office
17 Laser cut steel
shutter panel
18 Powder coated
steel framed fixed
double glazed window
19 Shutter guide
20 180 mm (7 inch)
steel C-section beam
21 Powder coated
aluminium sheet soffit
lining
22 Locust wood
floorboards over
underfloor heating
23 Acoustic separation
strips over structural
plywood flooring
substrate
24 Glasswool thermal
insulation
25 Shutter to entrance
facade
26 Glazed pivoting
entrance door
27 13 mm ($\frac{1}{2}$ inch)
painted plasterboard
ceiling

46.09
**Office Area Facade
and Shutters Plan
Detail**
1:20
1 13 mm ($\frac{1}{2}$ inch)
painted plasterboard
interior wall lining
2 Acoustic separation
strips over structural
plywood flooring
substrate
3 13 mm ($\frac{1}{2}$ inch)
painted plasterboard
interior wall lining
4 Clear glazed
casement window in
open position shown
dotted
5 133 x 140 mm (5$\frac{1}{4}$
x 5$\frac{1}{2}$ inch) steel
column
6 180 mm (7 inch)
steel C-section column
7 Laser cut steel
shutter panel in open
position shown dotted
8 Line of laser cut
steel shutter panel in
closed position
9 Shutter guide
10 Powder coated
steel framed fixed
double glazed window

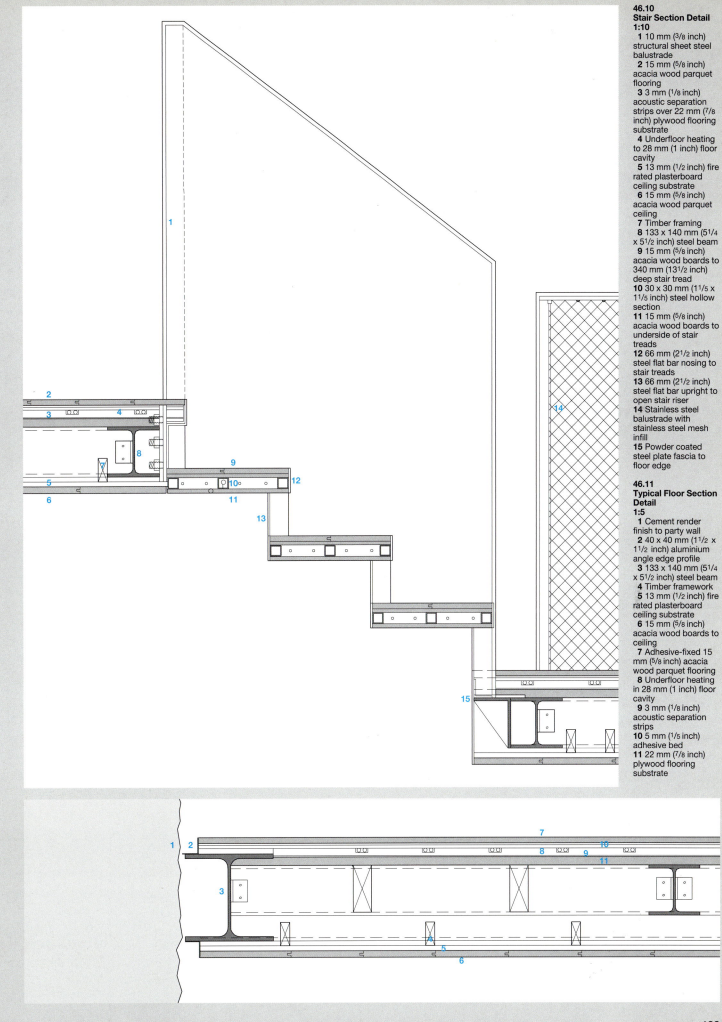

Stair Section Detail 1:10

1 10 mm (³/8 inch) structural sheet steel balustrade
2 15 mm (⁵/8 inch) acacia wood parquet flooring
3 3 mm (¹/8 inch) acoustic separation strips over 22 mm (⁷/8 inch) plywood flooring substrate
4 Underfloor heating to 28 mm (1 inch) floor cavity
5 13 mm (¹/2 inch) fire rated plasterboard ceiling substrate
6 15 mm (⁵/8 inch) acacia wood parquet ceiling
7 Timber framing
8 133 x 140 mm (5¹/4 x 5¹/2 inch) steel beam
9 15 mm (⁵/8 inch) acacia wood boards to 340 mm (13¹/2 inch) deep stair tread
10 30 x 30 mm (1¹/5 x 1¹/5 inch) steel hollow section
11 15 mm (⁵/8 inch) acacia wood boards to underside of stair treads
12 66 mm (2¹/2 inch) steel flat bar nosing to stair treads
13 66 mm (2¹/2 inch) steel flat bar upright to open stair riser
14 Stainless steel balustrade with stainless steel mesh infill
15 Powder coated steel plate fascia to floor edge

46.11
Typical Floor Section Detail 1:5

1 Cement render finish to party wall
2 40 x 40 mm (1¹/2 x 1¹/2 inch) aluminium angle edge profile
3 133 x 140 mm (5¹/4 x 5¹/2 inch) steel beam
4 Timber framework
5 13 mm (¹/2 inch) fire rated plasterboard ceiling substrate
6 15 mm (⁵/8 inch) acacia wood boards to ceiling
7 Adhesive-fixed 15 mm (⁵/8 inch) acacia wood parquet flooring
8 Underfloor heating in 28 mm (1 inch) floor cavity
9 3 mm (¹/8 inch) acoustic separation strips
10 5 mm (¹/5 inch) adhesive bed
11 22 mm (⁷/8 inch) plywood flooring substrate

Stereoscopic House
Sentosa Island, Singapore

Client
Private

Project Team
Erik G. L'Heureux

Structural Engineer
TEP Consultants

Mechanical Engineer
DMS Consulting Engineers

Architect of Record
Hk Hia & Associates

This luxury weekend house is located on the southern tip of Sentosa Island which lies just 500 metres (550 yards) off the southern coast of the main island of Singapore. A strategically important naval base until the late 20th century, the island has been transformed by government sponsored development over the last several decades into a popular resort with hotels, marinas, golf courses and luxury housing estates. Stereoscopic House is situated in one such estate, sandwiched between a golf course and the open waters of the Singapore Strait.

Arranged over four levels, this large house features staff accommodation, a wine cellar and a cinema in the basement. Living, dining and kitchen areas and a games room on the ground floor have direct access to the garden and pool. Bedrooms and bathrooms on the first floor take advantage of spectacular views across the strait, while on the top floor are a guest suite and roof terrace. Architecturally, the upper two levels are expressed as a timber-clad box with the pitched roof that is visible from the street cut away on the other side to create a cantilevered flat-roofed box. This timber-clad form sits on top of, and cantilevers over, the ground floor which is entirely clad in glass – translucent planks to the street facade to preserve privacy and clear sliding doors to the living spaces.

A number of passive environmental strategies mitigate the use of air-conditioning in the tropical climate, including low emissivity glazing, solar hot water heating, extensive cross ventilation, rain water harvesting and evaporative cooling. Striking sculptural perforated shade panels protect windows, skylights and terraces on the upper levels of the house from the tropical sun.

1 The most striking feature of the house is the timber clad upper volume. The timber is a sustainably sourced hard wood which is naturally resistant to rot and insects without the need for toxic treatments. The boards, laid in a striking herringbone pattern, is laid over a metal deck roof to create an additional barrier to the fierce tropical heat.
2 Laser cut aluminium shade panels are fully operable on the north-east street facade and fixed elsewhere, including here on the roof terrace to provide appropriate levels of light and shade.
3 A series of rooflights with perforated shade panels bring light into secondary spaces such as the bathrooms and dressing rooms.
4 The cool stone walls clad the walls and stair of the basement level which accommodates the wine cellar (left) and cinema.

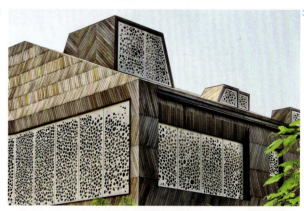

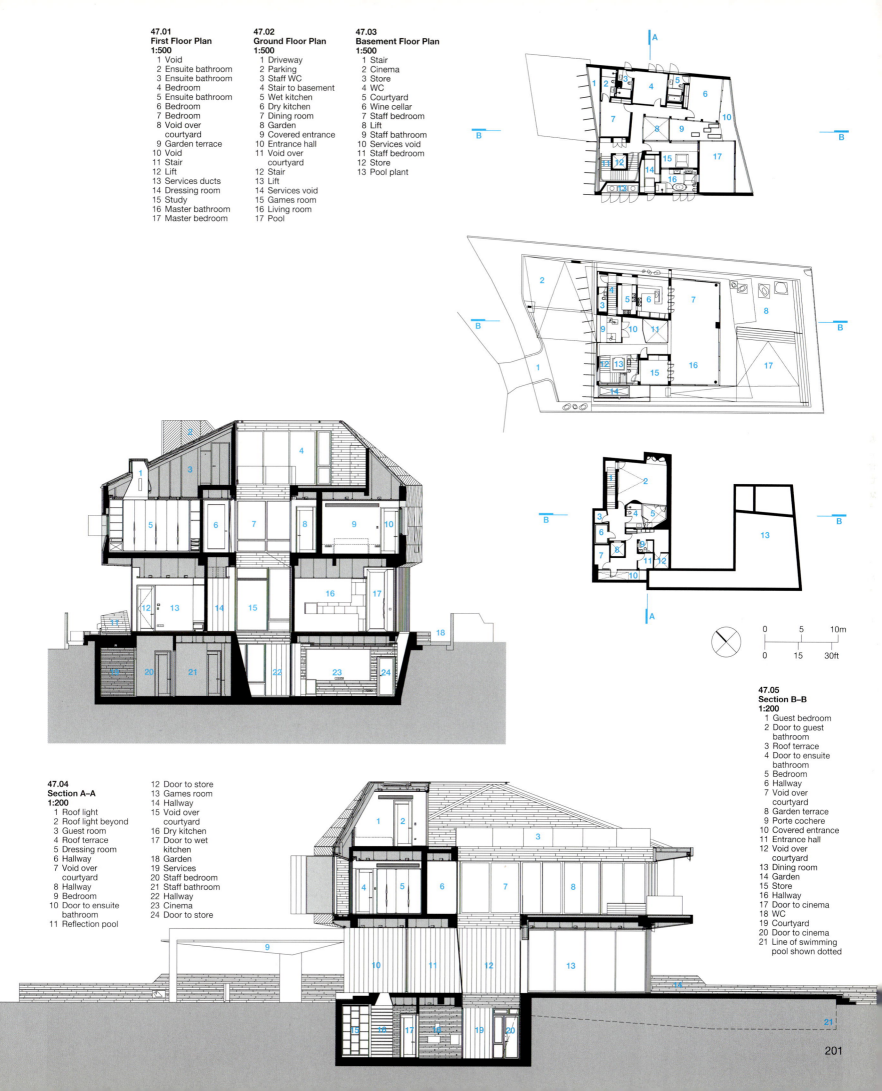

47.01
First Floor Plan
1:500
1 Void
2 Ensuite bathroom
3 Ensuite bathroom
4 Bedroom
5 Ensuite bathroom
6 Bedroom
7 Bedroom
8 Void over courtyard
9 Garden terrace
10 Void
11 Stair
12 Lift
13 Services ducts
14 Dressing room
15 Study
16 Master bathroom
17 Master bedroom

47.02
Ground Floor Plan
1:500
1 Driveway
2 Parking
3 Staff WC
4 Stair to basement
5 Wet kitchen
6 Dry kitchen
7 Dining room
8 Garden
9 Covered entrance
10 Entrance hall
11 Void over courtyard
12 Stair
13 Lift
14 Services void
15 Games room
16 Living room
17 Pool

47.03
Basement Floor Plan
1:500
1 Stair
2 Cinema
3 Store
4 WC
5 Courtyard
6 Wine cellar
7 Staff bedroom
8 Lift
9 Staff bathroom
10 Services void
11 Staff bedroom
12 Store
13 Pool plant

47.04
Section A–A
1:200
1 Roof light
2 Roof light beyond
3 Guest room
4 Roof terrace
5 Dressing room
6 Hallway
7 Void over courtyard
8 Hallway
9 Bedroom
10 Door to ensuite bathroom
11 Reflection pool
12 Door to store
13 Games room
14 Hallway
15 Void over courtyard
16 Dry kitchen
17 Door to wet kitchen
18 Garden
19 Services
20 Staff bedroom
21 Staff bathroom
22 Hallway
23 Cinema
24 Door to store

47.05
Section B–B
1:200
1 Guest bedroom
2 Door to guest bathroom
3 Roof terrace
4 Door to ensuite bathroom
5 Bedroom
6 Hallway
7 Void over courtyard
8 Garden terrace
9 Porte cochere
10 Covered entrance
11 Entrance hall
12 Void over courtyard
13 Dining room
14 Garden
15 Store
16 Hallway
17 Door to cinema
18 WC
19 Courtyard
20 Door to cinema
21 Line of swimming pool shown dotted

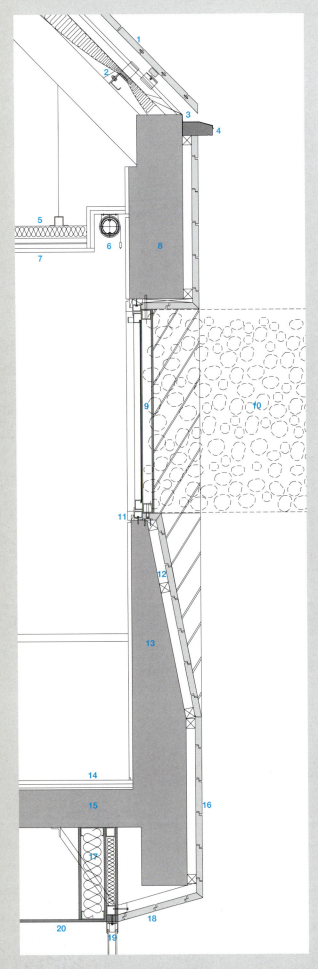

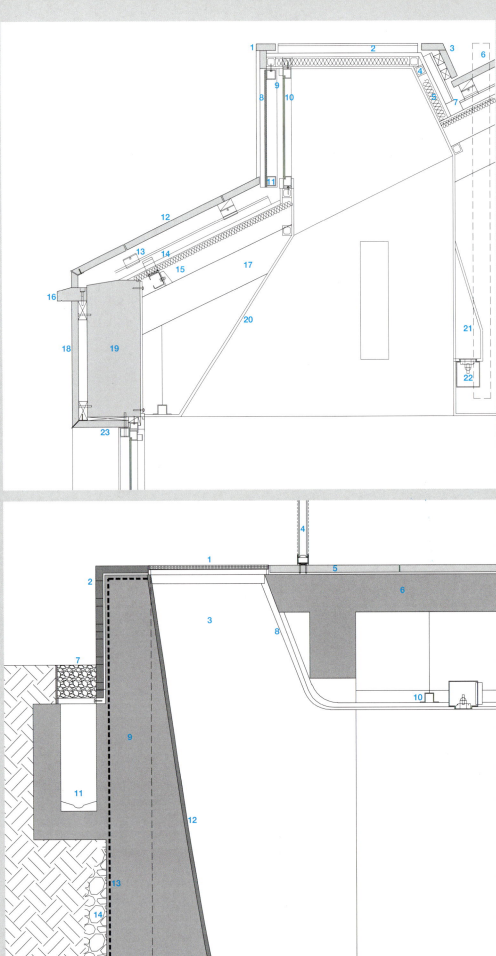

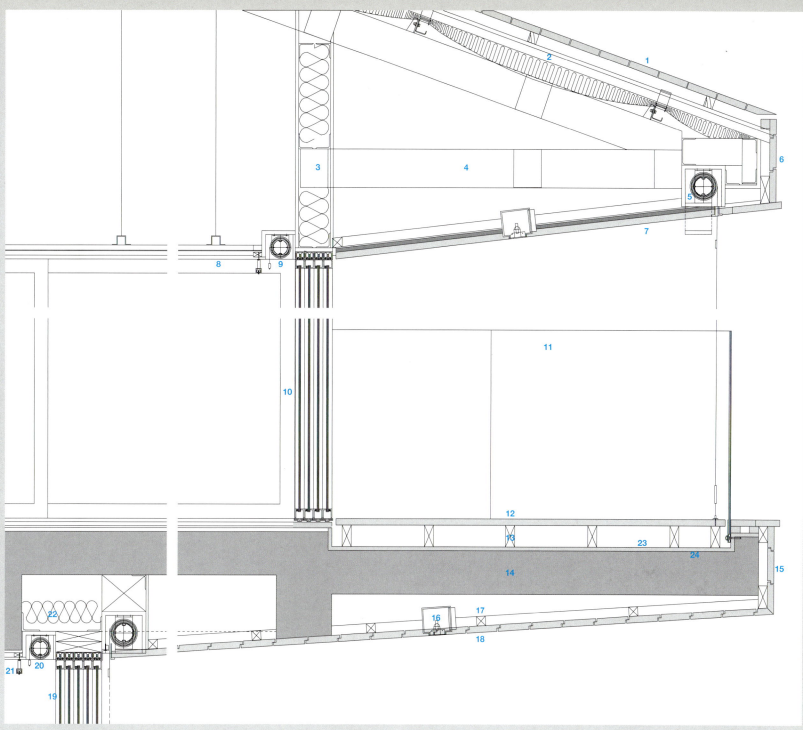

47.06
Roof and External Wall Overhang Section Detail
1:20
 1 25 mm (1 inch) thick ipe timber cladding to roof
 2 Metal roof sheeting on steel framing and insulation
 3 Metal flashing
 4 100 mm (4 inch) timber bullnose profile
 5 Insulated suspended ceiling
 6 Roller blind
 7 Painted plasterboard ceiling
 8 Reinforced concrete beam
 9 Aluminium-framed double glazed window
 10 Perforated aluminium shade panel
 11 Timber window reveal
 12 Timber battens and counter battens for

timber cladding
 13 Reinforced concrete wall
 14 18 mm (3/4 inch) thick timber floorboards
 15 Reinforced concrete floor slab and downstand beam
 16 25 mm (1 inch) thick ipe timber cladding to external wall
 17 Acoustic and thermally insulated wall head
 18 25 mm (1 inch) thick ipe timber cladding to external wall overhang
 19 Fixed double glazing
 20 Painted plasterboard ceiling

47.07
Skylight Detail
1:20
 1 100 mm (4 inch) timber corner piece to match external cladding
 2 Metal roof sheeting on steel framing and insulation
 3 25 mm (1 inch) thick ipe timber cladding to roof
 4 Metal hollow section structure
 5 Rockwool insulation
 6 25 mm (1 inch) thick ipe timber cladding beyond shown dotted
 7 Metal flashing
 8 Perforated aluminium shade panel
 9 Aluminium-framed window
 10 Aluminium reveal
 11 50 mm (2 inch) aluminium frame
 12 25 mm (1 inch)

thick ipe timber cladding to roof
 13 Clip support system for fixing timber
 14 Metal roof sheeting on steel framing and insulation
 15 Metal C-channel roof structure
 16 100 mm (4 inch) timber end piece
 17 Metal roof truss
 18 25 mm (1 inch) thick ipe timber wall cladding
 19 Reinforced concrete beam
 20 Painted plasterboard ceiling
 21 Frame and support for light fitting
 22 Concealed light fixture
 23 25 mm (1 inch) thick ipe timber window reveal

47.08
Basement Level Wall and Skylight Section Detail
1:20
 1 20 mm (3/4 inch) thick tempered glass to skylight
 2 8 mm (3/8 inch) external homogenous wall tiles
 3 Plastered wall to basement skylight
 4 Fixed glazing in aluminium channel
 5 Travertine floor tiles
 6 Reinforced concrete floor slab
 7 Gravel drain
 8 Painted plasterboard ceiling
 9 Reinforced concrete perimeter wall
 10 Suspended ceiling system
 11 External drain
 12 20 mm (3/4 inch) plaster finish

to concrete wall
 13 Waterproofing membrane
 14 Hardcore blinding

47.09
First Floor Terrace Detail
1:20
 1 25 mm (1 inch) thick ipe timber cladding to roof
 2 Metal roof sheeting on steel framing and insulation
 3 Steel framing to cantilevered roof
 4 Steel truss
 5 External roller blind
 6 25 mm (1 inch) thick ipe timber cladding to roof overhang edge
 7 25 mm (1 inch) thick ipe timber to soffit
 8 Painted plasterboard ceiling
 9 Internal roller blind
 10 Aluminium-framed sliding door to bedroom
 11 20 mm (3/4 inch) thick glass balustrade

 12 25 mm (1 inch) timber decking
 13 50 x 75 mm (2 x 3 inch) timber floor joists
 14 Cantilevered reinforced concrete floor slab
 15 25 mm (1 inch) thick ipe timber cladding
 16 Concealed light fixture
 17 50 x 50 mm (2 x 2 inch) timber battens and counter battens
 18 25 mm (1 inch) thick ipe timber cladding to soffit
 19 Aluminium-framed sliding door to living room
 20 Roller blind
 21 Curtain track
 22 Rockwool insulation
 23 Protective screed to terrace floor
 24 Waterproof membrane

**Streeter House
Deephaven, Minnesota, USA**

Client
Kevin Streeter

Project Team
David Salmela, Carly Coulson,
Souliyahn Keobounpheng, Scott
Muellner

Structural Engineer
Bruno Franck

Main Contractor
Streeter & Associates

Located on a small parcel of land in
Hennepin County near the shores of
Lake Minnetonka, Streeter House was
built on a site that many deemed
un-buildable due to the difficulties
posed by the presence of a pond to
the east and wetlands to the west.
However the client, a contractor of
high-end custom homes, felt that the
natural beauty of the site would be
perfect for his own home.

The house, designed for the client
and his son, is arranged over two
levels with the glass-walled ground
floor living spaces flowing through the
landscape. This low, attenuated, dark
grey masonry form supports two
cantilevered white boxes, each one
accessed via its own stair from the
ground floor. The east-west aligned
boxes each contain a bathroom and
dressing area on one side of the stair,
and a sleeping area on the other, with
a large terrace looking out over the
wooded landscape. A garage, an
expansive paved terrace with outdoor
fireplace, and a sauna pavilion
complete the accommodation and
extend the linear composition to the
north across the site.

The house is comprised of a kit of
standard parts, primarily glass,
concrete block, glu-lam beams, and
structural insulated panels (SIPs).
Locally manufactured black fly-ash
concrete blockwork is left exposed on
both the exterior and interior.
Prefabricated and predrilled glu-lam
beams sit on the concrete blockwork
and support the cantilevered bedroom
boxes. These two boxes, as well as all
of the non-masonry walls and roofs,
are constructed entirely of SIPs with a
factory-applied gypsum finish. The
increased insulation value of the SIPs
as well as the extensive use of glazing,
contribute to a highly energy efficient,
naturally lit home.

1 A view of the east
facade. The house
stretches across a
beautiful wooded site
in Minnesota, where
care has been taken to
have as little impact on
the natural
environment as
possible.
2 On the west side of
the building the sauna
pavilion (left) frames a
large outdoor terrace
and fireplace (centre
left). The large double
doors to the garage
(centre right) feature
porthole windows.
3 Contrasts in texture
and colour are an
important aspect of
the design. The dark
grey of the blockwork
to the ground floor is in
aesthetic opposition to
the white cantilevered
bedroom suites above.
4 The open plan
ground floor living
spaces feature large
expanses of clear
glazing both for
maximizing natural
light and to connect
with the landscape.
5 The interior is
characterized by a
regular grid of glu-lam
beams that support
the bedrooms. Two
separate staircases
rise up from the living
area giving access to
the self contained
suites.

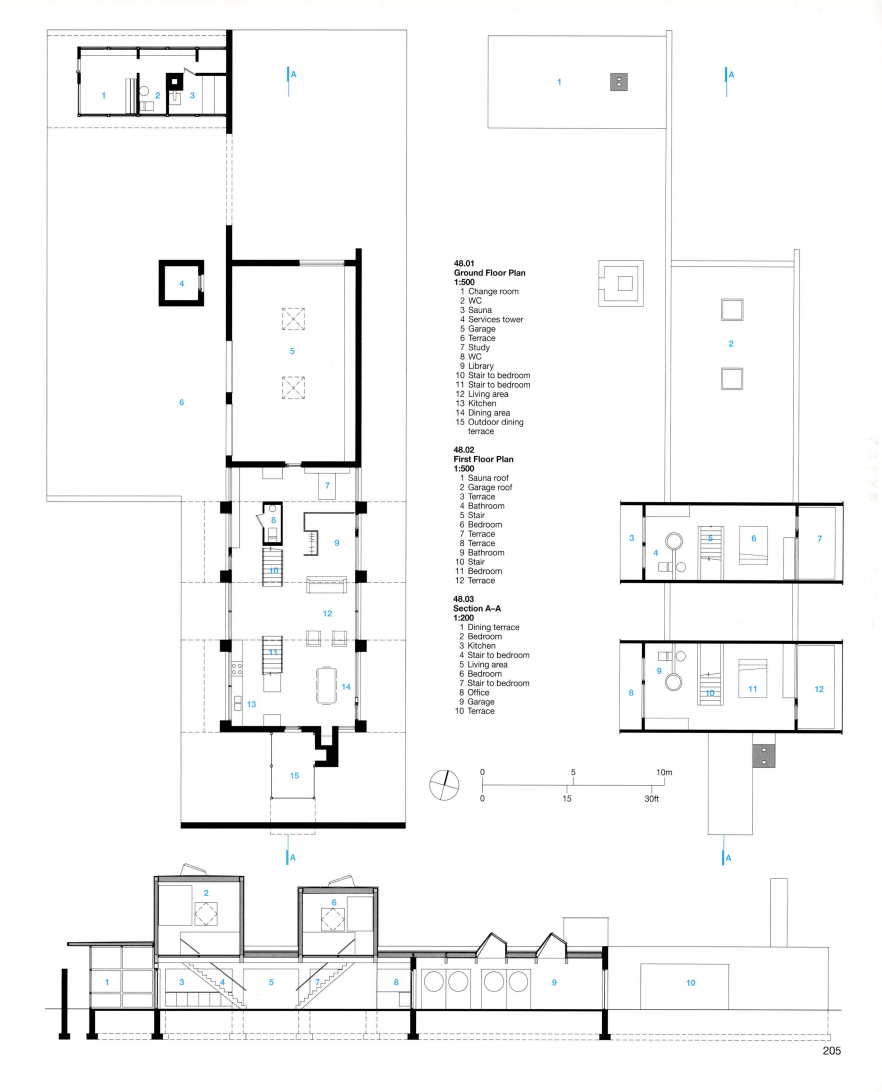

48.01
Ground Floor Plan
1:500
1 Change room
2 WC
3 Sauna
4 Services tower
5 Garage
6 Terrace
7 Study
8 WC
9 Library
10 Stair to bedroom
11 Stair to bedroom
12 Living area
13 Kitchen
14 Dining area
15 Outdoor dining
 terrace

48.02
First Floor Plan
1:500
1 Sauna roof
2 Garage roof
3 Terrace
4 Bathroom
5 Stair
6 Bedroom
7 Terrace
8 Terrace
9 Bathroom
10 Stair
11 Bedroom
12 Terrace

48.03
Section A–A
1:200
1 Dining terrace
2 Bedroom
3 Kitchen
4 Stair to bedroom
5 Living area
6 Bedroom
7 Stair to bedroom
8 Office
9 Garage
10 Terrace

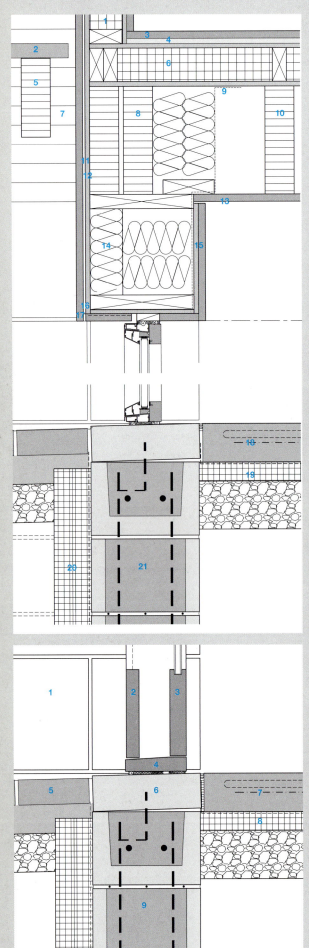

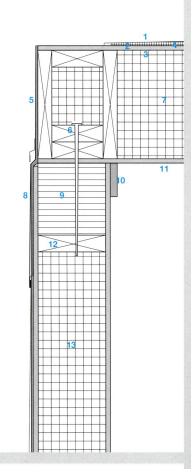

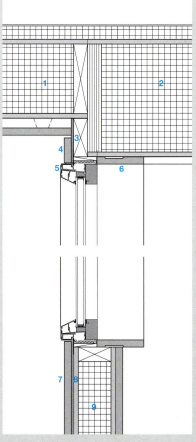

48.04
Ground Floor Window Head and Sill Section Detail
1:10
1 114 mm (4¹/₂ inch) thick structural insulated wall panel
2 Timber decking
3 18 mm (³/₄ inch) thick timber tongue-and-groove floorboards
4 12.5 mm (¹/₂ inch) acoustic isolation
5 84 x 210 mm (3¹/₄ x 8¹/₄ inch) glu-lam beam
6 165 mm (6¹/₂ inch) structural insulated floor panel
7 Timber tongue-and-groove cladding
8 84 x 286 mm (3¹/₄ x 11¹/₄ inch) thick glu-lam beam
9 Fire barrier
10 84 x 286 mm (3¹/₄ x 11¹/₄ inch) thick glu-lam beam
11 Waterproof membrane
12 12.5 mm (¹/₂ inch) thick oriented strand board
13 18 mm (³/₄ inch) timber tongue-and-groove boards to ceiling
14 Insulation
15 Vapour barrier
16 Insect mesh
17 Exposed edge to timber tongue-and-groove cladding
18 Polished concrete with underfloor heating
19 Rigid insulation
20 Rigid insulation
21 290 mm (11³/₈ inch) thick hollow black fly-ash concrete block foundation wall with internal core of reinforced concrete

48.05
Ground Floor Door Sill Section Detail
1:10
1 290 mm (11³/₈ inch) thick hollow black fly-ash concrete block wall
2 Custom timber framed sliding insect-screen door
3 Custom timber framed, double glazed door
4 Timber sill set on adhesive bed
5 Brick paving
6 Concrete block sill set on mortar and sloped to drain
7 Polished concrete with underfloor heating
8 Rigid insulation
9 290 mm (11³/₈ inch) thick hollow black fly-ash concrete block foundation wall with internal core of reinforced concrete

48.06
Typical Bedroom Roof Edge Section Detail
1:10
1 Black waterproof roofing
2 Vapour barrier
3 Double layer of oriented strand board roofing substrate
4 Tapered insulation
5 Folded zinc panel to roof edge
6 12.5 mm (¹/₂ inch) lag screws at 610 mm (24 inch) centres
7 311 mm (12¹/₄ inch) structural insulated roof panel
8 Zinc flatlock panels over waterproof membrane
9 184 x 190 mm (7¹/₄ x 7¹/₂ inch) glu-lam top plate
10 18 mm (³/₄ inch) timber batten to wall and ceiling junction
11 Fire rated gypsum board ceiling
12 50 x 200 mm (2 x 8 inch) timber framing between vertical reinforcing
13 210 mm (8¹/₄ inch) structural insulated wall panel

48.07
Skylight to Garage Roof Section Detail
1:10
1 Mounting bracket attached to curb
2 Roof membrane extending up over curb to side of skylight
3 Black aluminium cladding to skylight upstand
4 Structural waterproof plywood
5 Thermal insulation
6 Tapered rigid insulation
7 260 mm (10¹/₄ inch) structural insulated roof panel
8 Timber tongue-and-groove board lining to skylight interior
9 Fire rated gypsum ceiling
10 Timber junction batten

48.08
Bedroom Window Head and Sill Section Detail
1:10
1 210 mm (8¹/₄ inch) structural insulated roof panel to exterior
2 311 mm (12¹/₄ inch) structural insulated roof panel to interior
3 Insect barrier
4 18 mm (³/₄ inch) timber tongue-and-groove exterior wall cladding
5 Folded aluminium drip profile
6 Fir trim to window reveal
7 18 mm (³/₄ inch) timber tongue-and-groove exterior wall cladding
8 Waterproof membrane
9 114 mm (4¹/₂ inch) structural insulated wall panel

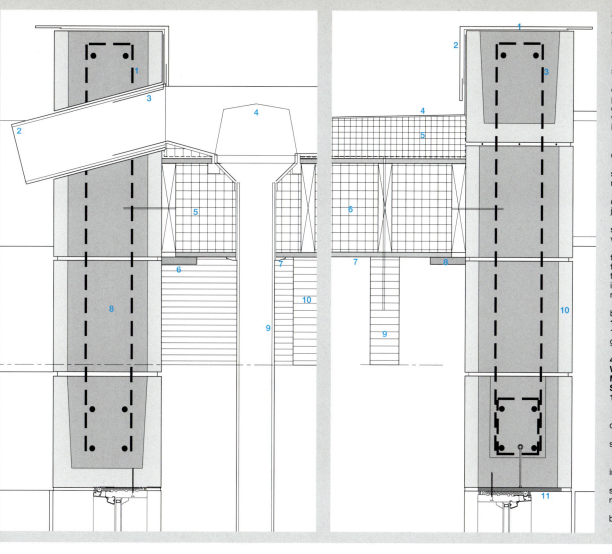

48.09
**Roof Drain Overflow
to Ground Floor Flat
Roof Section Detail
1:10**
1 Steel reinforcing
stirrups
2 150 mm (6 inch)
diameter steel pipe
painted black with
centre of pipe lined up
with blockwork joints
in both directions
3 Roof membrane
4 Black plastic roof
drain
5 311 mm (12¼ inch)
structural insulated
roof panel
6 Timber batten to
ceiling and wall
junction
7 Black metal ring
seal to pipe to maintain
vapour barrier
8 290 mm (11³/8 inch)
thick hollow black
fly-ash concrete block
foundation wall with
internal core of
reinforced concrete
9 100 mm (4 inch)
black steel pipe
10 84 x 286 mm (3¼ x
11¼ inch) exposed
glu-lam beam

48.10
**Window Head and
Masonry Wall Lintel
Section Detail
1:10**
1 Coping membrane
2 Black aluminium
coping
3 Steel reinforcing
stirrups
4 Roof membrane
5 Tapered rigid
insulation
6 311 mm (12¼ inch)
structural insulated
roof panel
7 Fire rated gypsum
board ceiling
8 Wood batten

9 84 x 286 mm (3¼ x
11¼ inch) exposed
glu-lam beam
10 290 mm (11³/8 inch)
thick hollow black
fly-ash concrete block
foundation wall with
internal core of
reinforced concrete
11 10 mm x 230 mm
(³/8 x 9 inch)
non-structural steel
plate running 50 mm (2
inch) beyond span on
either side of opening

48.11
**Window Head and
Soffit Section Detail
1:10**
1 18 mm (3/4 inch)
timber floor over
plywood subfloor
2 Void for plumbing
3 50 x 200 mm (2 x 8
inch) raised floor
framing at 610 mm (24
inch) centres
4 165 mm (6½ inch)
structural insulated
floor panel
5 84 x 286 mm (3¼ x
11¼ inch) glu-lam
beam
6 Vapour barrier
7 Thermal insulation
8 Composite timber
and aluminium double
glazed window
9 Insect mesh
10 Exposed edge to
timber tongue-and-
groove cladding

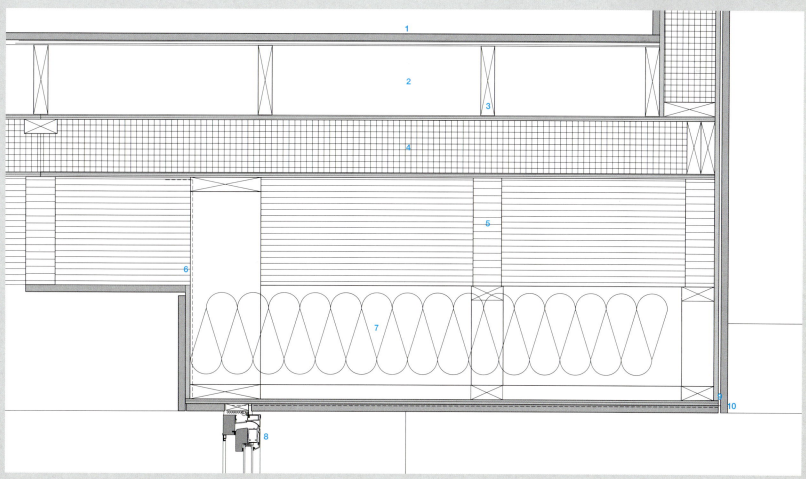

Tea Houses
Silicon Valley, California, USA

Client
Private

Project Team
Robert Swatt, Steven Stept, Ivan Olds,
Connie Wong, Jeanie Fan, Hiromi
Ogawa

Structural Engineer
Yu-Strandberg Engineering

Located in the grounds of the client's home on a large property near San Francisco in northern California, the three Tea Houses were designed to provide quiet, contemplative spaces away from the main house. The pavilions provide an opportunity to escape from the distractions of everyday life and as such have no television, internet, telephone or even music. The largest of the three pavilions, Visioning Tea House, provides a workspace that can also be used for hosting small parties, while the second, linked to the first via a skylit bathroom bridge, is called Sleeping Tea House and can be used as overnight accommodation. The third, Meditation Tea House, sits alone under the shelter of a large oak tree and was conceived as a meditative space for a single person.

Each tea house is designed as a transparent steel and glass pavilion, hovering like a lantern over the natural landscape. Cast in-situ concrete elements anchor the pavilions, supporting steel channel joists which cantilever beyond the concrete piers to support the floor and roof planes. The design treads lightly on the land, minimizing the need for cutting into the ground and preserving the delicate root systems of the native oaks. The interiors are executed with a simple palette of contrasting materials including crisply detailed steel and glass, unfinished board-formed, wire brushed concrete to expose the wood grain left by the formwork, and cedar boards, recycled from the remodeling of the main house.

The Tea Houses are passively cooled through louvred and sliding glazing to encourage cross ventilation, with additional cooling provided by shading from strategically located landscaping, including evergreen oaks, bamboo, deciduous maple and gingko trees. Heating is distributed through a quiet and efficient in-floor radiant system.

1 At night the structures glow like lanterns amongst the trees. Cantilevered out over the hillside, the floor to ceiling glazing looks out onto the native landscape.
2 View from the Sleeping Tea House looking out past the link bridge to the Visioning Tea House. The concrete box of the link accommodates a bath with a low level strip window that provides views of the landscape at eye level when in the bath.
3 Access to the pavilions is via a gravel terrace. A single timber step set into the concrete core negotiates the height between the ground and the pavilion floor.
4 In the Visioning Tea House, a large table is fashioned from a section of a large tree while cedar boards, recycled from the remodeling of the main house, line the ceiling and floor.

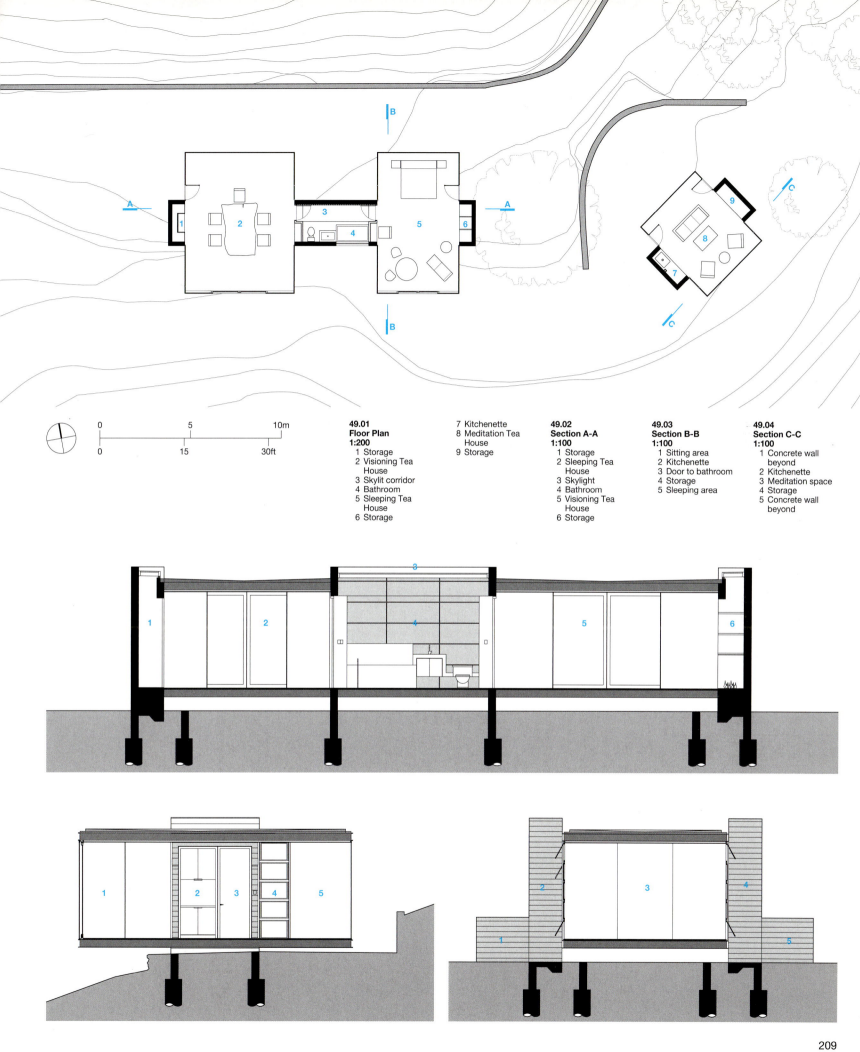

49.01
Floor Plan
1:200
1 Storage
2 Visioning Tea House
3 Skylit corridor
4 Bathroom
5 Sleeping Tea House
6 Storage
7 Kitchenette
8 Meditation Tea House
9 Storage

49.02
Section A-A
1:100
1 Storage
2 Sleeping Tea House
3 Skylight
4 Bathroom
5 Visioning Tea House
6 Storage

49.03
Section B-B
1:100
1 Sitting area
2 Kitchenette
3 Door to bathroom
4 Storage
5 Sleeping area

49.04
Section C-C
1:100
1 Concrete wall beyond
2 Kitchenette
3 Meditation space
4 Storage
5 Concrete wall beyond

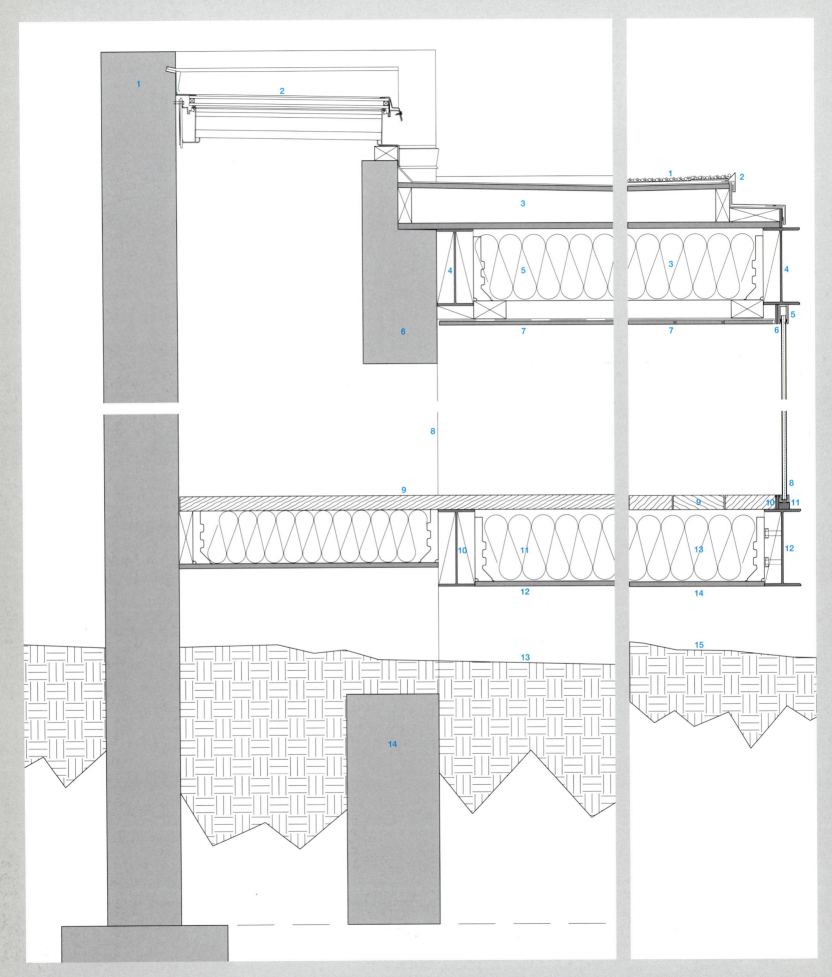

49.05
Wall, Roof and Skylight Section Detail
1:10
1 Cast in-situ board formed concrete wall
2 Skylight
3 Built up flat roof
4 Steel beam
5 Batt insulation between framing
6 Concrete beam
7 9.5 x 140 mm (3/8 x 51/2 inch) tongue-and-groove cedar cladding to ceiling on battens and counter battens
8 Line of concrete wall beyond
9 50 x 150 mm (2 x 6 inch) cedar floorboards
10 Steel beam
11 Batt insulation between framing
12 25 x 150 mm (1 x 6 inch) tongue-and-groove cedar boards to underfloor where visible and 12.5 mm (1/2 inch) cedar veneered plywood elsewhere
13 Natural ground line
14 Concrete beam and pier

49.06
Wall Section at Window Detail
1:10
1 Built up flat roof topped with gravel
2 Galvanized gravel stop and flashing on waterproof membrane
3 Batt insulation between framing
4 Steel beam
5 12.5 mm (1/2 inch) thick tempered glass set in 25 x 50 mm (1 x 2 inch) aluminium ceiling glazing channel painted to match steel beam
6 6.4 x 50 mm (1/4 x 2 inch) steel plate welded to steel beam and painted to match
7 9.5 x 140 mm (3/8 x 51/2 inch) tongue-and-groove cedar boards to ceiling on battens and counter battens, each board pre-drilled before installation
8 12.5 mm (1/2 inch) thick tempered glass set in 25 x 25 mm (1 x 1 inch) aluminium ceiling glazing channel painted to match steel beam
9 50 x 150 mm (2 x 6 inch) cedar floorboards
10 6 x 38 mm (1/4 x 11/2 inch) steel plate welded to steel beam and painted to match
11 19 mm (3/4 inch) steel plate welded to steel beam and painted to match
12 Steel beam
13 Batt insulation between framing
14 25 x 150 mm (1 x 6 inch) tongue-and-groove cedar boards to underfloor where visible and 12.5 mm (1/2 inch) cedar veneered plywood elsewhere
15 Natural ground line

49.07
Concrete Wall Parapet Detail
1:10
1 Galvanized steel sheet roofing
2 Concrete reglet with 75 mm (3 inch) lap joint and galvanized steel flashing
3 Pressure treated timber beam
4 63 mm (21/2 inch) diameter rainwater drain shown dotted
5 Pressure treated nailer
6 Cast in-situ board formed concrete wall

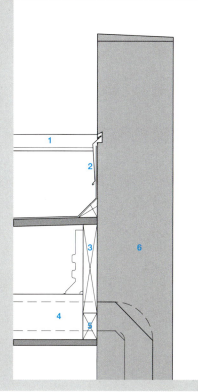

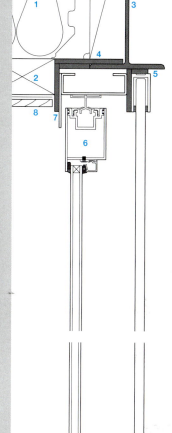

49.08
Window Jamb at Concrete Wall
1:5
1 Wall sconce light fixture centred on concrete wall
2 Concrete wall
3 50 x 64 mm (2 x 21/2 inch) steel angle closure plate
4 12.5 mm (1/2 inch) conduit for light fixture concealed within steel angle supports for window and doors
5 50 x 38 (2 x 11/2 inch) steel angle painted to match steel beam and secured to concrete wall with 9.5 mm (3/8 inch) diameter bolts at 400 mm (153/4 inch) centres
6 Sealant and backer rod
7 Steel window with equal jamb frames painted to match steel beams

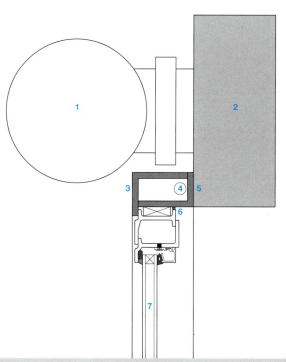

49.09
Aluminium Door Jamb Plan Detail
1:5
1 Aluminium-framed lift-and-slide double glazed door painted to match steel beams
2 6.4 x 25 mm (1/4 x 1 inch) steel flat bar window stop welded to steel support
3 Black silicone sealant
4 6.4 x 50 mm (1/4 x 2 inch) steel flat bar

vertical support welded to steel support and painted to match
5 Aluminium interlocker to lift-and-slide glazed door painted to match steel beams
6 12.5 mm (1/2 inch) fixed tempered glass with eased and polished edges in 25 x 25 mm (1 x 1 inch) aluminium glazing channel

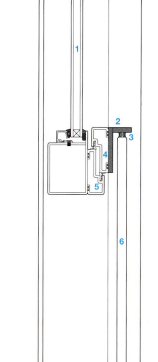

49.10
Aluminium Door Head and Sill Section Detail
1:5
1 Ceiling joists with batt insulation
2 Timber framing at 400 mm (153/4 inch) centres
3 Steel beam
4 Timber packing as required
5 Sealant and backer rod
6 Aluminium-framed lift-and-slide double glazed door head
7 6 x 50 mm (1/4 x 2 inch) steel plate welded to steel beam
8 9.5 x 140 mm (3/8 x 51/2 inch) tongue-and-groove cedar boards to ceiling on battens and counter battens
9 Aluminium-framed lift-and-slide double glazed door sill
10 50 x 150 mm (2 x 6 inch) cedar floorboards
11 12.5 mm (1/2 inch) fixed tempered glass in 25 x 25 mm (1 x 1 inch) aluminium glazing channel
12 Steel angle to support lift-and-slide sill welded to steel beam
13 Steel beam

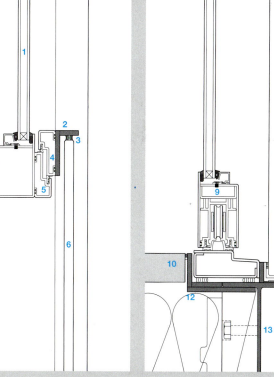

**House in Hieidaira
Shiga, Japan**

Client
Private

Project Team
Yo Shimada

Main Contractor
Takahashi Koumuten

Located in a rural part of Japan on the flank of Mount Hiei, north of Kyoto, this house was designed for an artist who required a studio and living space, as well as accommodation for his parents. The house has been designed as a collection of three independent but related structures that reference the local vernacular of predominantly small pitched-roof cottages.

It was thought that to try to accommodate all of the required programmatical functions in one structure would result in too large a building. Also there were concerns from the planning authority that activities in the studio may result in disturbance to neighbouring residents. The response was to design three independent forms, arranged in two separate buildings. At the front of the site, directly facing the street, the corrugated-sheet-metal clad studio stands sentinel, protecting the black clad residence behind. Due to the restricted budget, simple forms, materials and construction techniques were employed. The house is arranged over two levels with the ground floor accommodating a self contained apartment in a connected pavilion to the north. The link between the apartment and the main house is a circulation space and shared bathroom. The ground floor of the main house contains an open plan living, dining and kitchen space as well as a study.

Upstairs, two bedrooms have been carved out beneath the pitched roof. As ordinary vertical walls would have made the loft spaces too cramped, the partition walls lean to divide the space diagonally, creating a 'hill-like-floor' complete with skylights in both the ceiling and the floor to create interior and exterior views into and out of the loft bedrooms. The interior features a polished concrete floor, white painted walls and ceiling to the lower floor and exposed lauan-faced plywood to the upper floor.

1 The galvanized metal-clad studio (left) is contrasted with the black cladding of the residence behind (right). The simple square windows to the house have been scaled up to reduce the apparent size of the buildings and emphasize the cottage-like nature of the gabled forms.
2 In the main house, a steep ladder-like stair leads up to the bedrooms beneath the pitched roof.
3 In the upper storey, bedrooms have been carved out of the loft space using sloping plywood-clad planes that become both floor and wall. Cut outs in the sloping planes provide interior views over the living space below, while skylights in the roof bring in natural light.
4 The glazed north wall of the bathroom provides views over the mountain landscape.

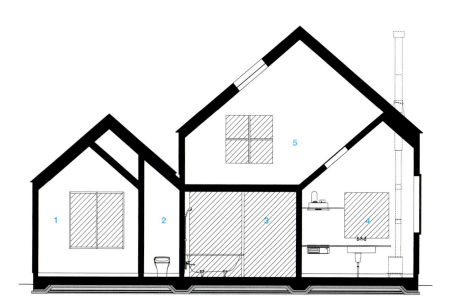

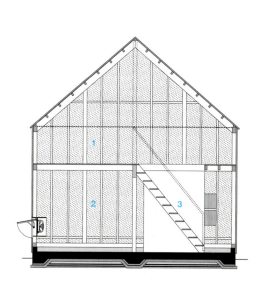

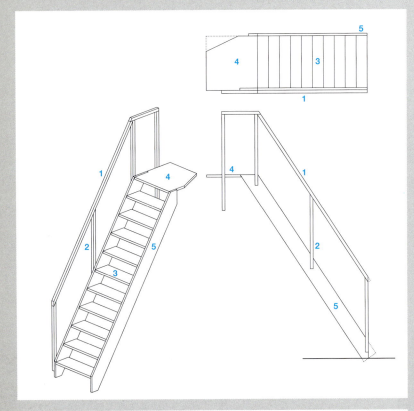

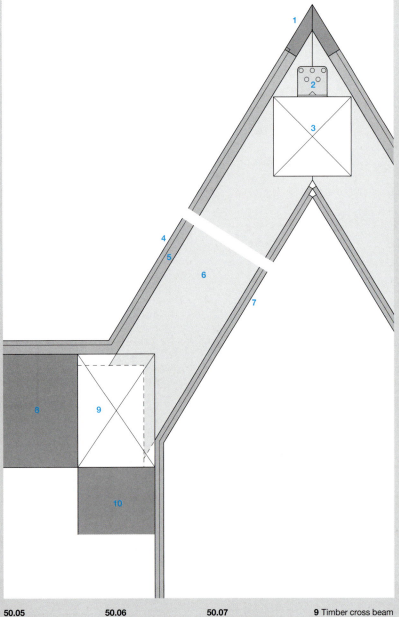

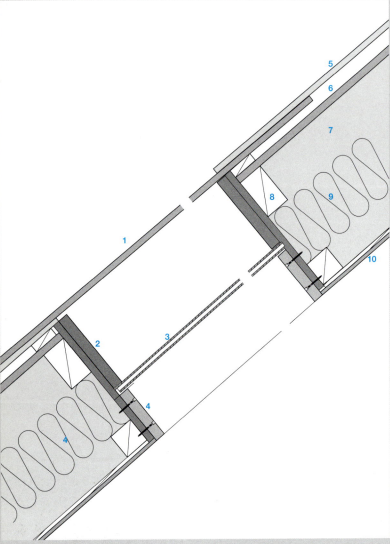

50.05
Stair Plan,
Axonometric and
Elevation Detail
1:50
1 40 x 40 mm (1^1/$_2$ x
1^1/$_2$ inch) timber
handrail
2 990 mm (39 inch)
high 40 x 40 mm (1^1/$_2$
x 1^1/$_2$ inch) timber
upright
3 690 mm (27^1/$_8$ inch)
wide, 221 mm (8^1/$_2$
inch) deep, 30 mm
(1^1/$_5$ inch) thick timber
stair treads
4 690 mm (27^1/$_8$ inch)
tapering to 518 mm
(20^3/$_8$ inch) timber stair
landing
5 30 mm (1^1/$_5$ inch)
thick, 200 mm (8 inch)
deep timber stringer

50.06
Skylight Section
Detail
1:5
1 1.5 mm (^{1}/$_{16}$ inch)
corrugated galvanized
sheet steel roofing
2 Two layers of
lauan-faced plywood,
one 12 mm (^{1}/$_2$ inch),
one 18 mm (^{3}/$_4$ inch) to
skylight reveal
3 Shatterproof fixed
glazing
4 Two layers of
lauan-faced plywood,
one 12 mm (^{1}/$_2$ inch),
one 18 mm (^{3}/$_4$ inch) to
skylight reveal
screw-fixed to timber
framing after glass
installation
5 1.5 mm (^{1}/$_{16}$ inch)
corrugated galvanized
sheet steel roofing
6 Ventilation cavity
7 Timber rafter
8 Timber framing
9 High performance
thermal insulation
10 Ceiling from two
layers of 6 mm (^{1}/$_4$
inch) thick lauan-faced
plywood

50.07
Interior Wall / Floor
Ridge Section Detail
Between Ground and
First Floor and
Between Loft
Bedrooms
1:5
1 18 mm (^{3}/$_4$ inch)
thick, 70 mm (2^3/$_4$
inch) long solid lauan
wood ridge cap, mitred
at apex
2 Steel plate beam
connector
3 105 x 105 mm (4^1/$_8$
x 4^1/$_8$ inch) timber
ridge beam
4 6 mm (^{1}/$_4$ inch)
thick lauan-faced
plywood floor
5 12 mm (^{1}/$_2$ inch)
thick structural
plywood flooring
substrate
6 45 x 105 mm (1^3/$_4$ x
4^1/$_8$ inch) timber joists
at 300 mm (12 inch)
centres
7 Ceiling from two
layers of 6 mm (^{1}/$_4$
inch) thick lauan-faced
plywood
8 Timber joist

9 Timber cross beam
10 Timber column

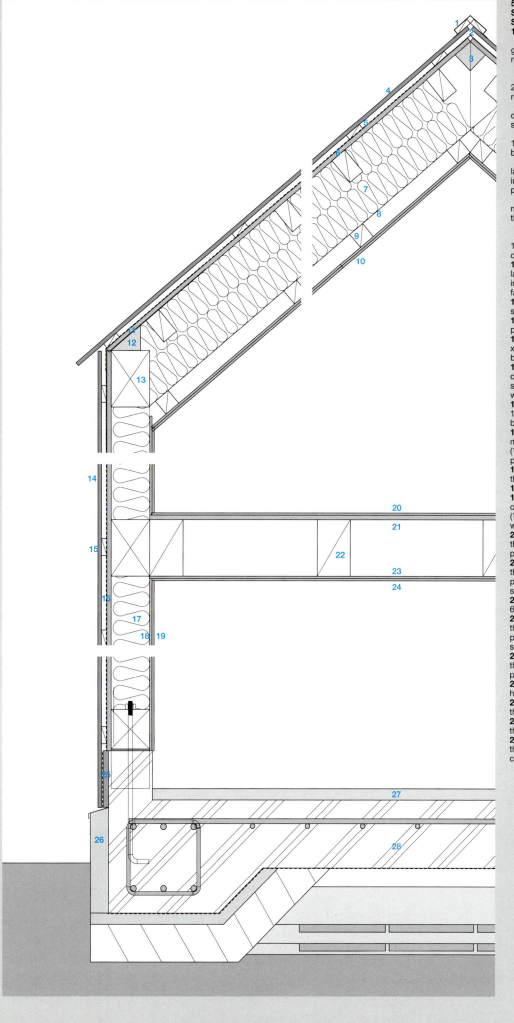

1 1.5 mm (1/16 inch) galvanized steel sheet ridge cap
2 Ridge vent
3 60 x 60 mm (2³/8 x 2³/8 inch) Douglas fir ridge beam
4 1.5 mm (1/16 inch) corrugated galvanized sheet steel roofing
5 14 x 45 mm (5/8 x 1³/4 inch) timber battens
6 Waterproof asphalt layer over 12 mm (1/2 inch) thick structural plywood
7 Two layers of 100 mm (4 inch) thick thermal insulation
8 Vapour barrier
9 45 x 45 mm (1³/4 x 1³/4 inch) timber ceiling joist
10 Ceiling of two layers of 6 mm (1/4 inch) thick lauan wood-faced plywood
11 Steel plate eaves stiffener
12 Douglas fir fillet packer
13 105 x 150 mm (4¹/8 x 6 inch) timber cross beam
14 1.5 mm (1/16 inch) corrugated galvanized sheet steel external wall cladding
15 14 x 45 mm (5/8 x 1³/4 inch) timber battens
16 Waterproof membrane over 12 mm (1/2 inch) structural plywood
17 100 mm (4 inch) thick thermal insulation
18 Vapour barrier
19 Internal wall lining of two layers of 6 mm (1/4 inch) thick lauan wood-faced plywood
20 6 mm (1/4 inch) thick lauan-faced plywood floor
21 12 mm (1/2 inch) thick structural plywood flooring substrate
22 90 x 150 mm (3¹/2 x 6 inch) floor joist
23 12 mm (1/2 inch) thick structural plywood ceiling substrate
24 6 mm (1/4 inch) thick lauan-faced plywood ceiling
25 150 mm (6 inch) high insulation board
26 50 mm (2 inch) thick insulation mortar
27 30 mm (1¹/5 inch) thick concrete screed
28 210 mm (8¹/4 inch) thick reinforced concrete floor slab

Directories,
Index and Credits

Directory of Details

Windows

Directory of Architects

Australia

Max Pritchard Architect
PO Box 808
Glenelg SA 5045
max@maxpritchardarchitect.com.au
T +61 (0) 8 8376 2314
www.maxpritchardarchitect.com.au
45 Bridge House

Austria

Judith Benzer Architektur
Hofmühlgasse 7a/16
1060 Wien
office@judithbenzer.com
T +43 (0) 699 1433 6448
www.judithbenzer.com
06 Summer House

Belgium

AST 77 Architecten
Goossensvest 45
3300 Tienen
info@ast77.be
T +32 (0) 1 681 10 77
www.ast77.be
01 Rostelaar House

Vincent Van Duysen Architects
Lombardenvest 34
2000 Antwerpen
vincent@vincentvanduysen.com
T +32 (0) 3 205 91 90
www.vincentvanduysen.com
29 VM Residence

Marie Jose Van Hee Architecten
Lieremanstraat 64
9000 Gent
info@mjvanhee.be
T +32 (0) 9 216 26 90
www.mjvanhee.be
24 House Van Aelten-Oosterlinck

Brazil

Studio MK27
Alamada Tietê, 505
Cerqueira César
01417-020 São Paulo
info@studiomk27.com.br
T + 55 11 30813522
www.studiomk27.com
09 Toblerone House

Chile

Marsino Arquitectos Asociados
Av. El Cerro 0179
Providencia , Santiago
informaciones@marsinoarquitectos.cl
T + 56 2 233 7812
www.marsinoarquitectos.cl
23 Diamante House

Croatia

DVA Arhitekta
Antuna Bauera 2
Hr-10000 Zagreb
dva-arhitekta@zg.t-com.hr
T +385 1 45 00 333
www.dva-arhitekta.hr
34 Jelenovac Residence

France

Moussafir Architectes
5/7 Rue d'Hauteville
75010 Paris
contact@moussafir.fr
T +33 (0) 1 48 24 38 30
www.moussafir.fr
46 Maison Escalier

**Bernard Quirot
architecte & associés**
16 Rue des Châteaux
70140 Pesmes
quirot.associes@orange.fr
T +33 (0) 3 84 31 27 99
www.quirotassocies.com
02 Sampans House

Germany

Käß Hauschildt
Könneritzstraße 30
04229 Leipzig
mail@kaesshauschildt.de
T +49 (0) 341 4637 8069
www.kaesshauschildt.de
36 KW House

Rost. Niderehe Architekten
Uferstraße 8e
22081 Hamburg
mail@rost-niderehe.de
T +49 (0) 40 22853 981 0
www.rost-niderehe.de
11 Eilbek Canal Houseboat

Uwe Schröder Architekt
Kaiserstraße 25
53113 Bonn
office@usarch.de
T +49 (0) 228 249946 0
www.usarch.de
28 Hundertacht House

Hungary

Budapesti Műhely
Erzsébet krt. 17
1073 Budapest
ez@budapestimuhely.hu
T +36 1 787 6105
www.budapestimuhely.hu
03 H House

India

SPASM Design Architects
310 Raheja Plaza
Shah Industrial Estate
New Andheri Link Road
Andheri West
Mumbai 400053
spasm@spasmindia.com
T +91 22 26735862
www.spasmindia.com
27 The Brick Kiln House

The Netherlands

Arjen Reas
Marlijnstraat 18
3192 BR Hoogvliet
Rotterdam
info@arjenreas.nl
T +31 (0)10 8400412
www.arjenreas.nl
40 Living on the Edge House

Bedaux de Brouwer Architecten
Dr. Keyzerlaan 2
5051 PB Goirle
post@bedauxdebrouwer.nl
T +31 (0)13 536 85 55
www.bedauxdebrouwer.nl
16 Villla Rotonda

70F Architecture
Stamerbos 34
1358 EP Almere
info@70f.com
T +31 (0)36 54 02 900
www.70f.com
15 Villa Frenay

Hoogte Twee Architecten
Prinsessestraat 13
6828 JT Arnhem
info@hoogtetwee.nl
T +31(0)26 351 77 22
www.hoogtetwee.nl
20 Dwelling-Workhouse HDT

Jack Hoogeboom
Walhallalaan 26
3072 EX Rotterdam
info@jackhoogeboom.nl
T +31(0) 6 16376222
www.jackhoogeboom.nl
05 Wellness Villa

Pasel Künzel Architects
Josephstraat 160-162
3014 TX Rotterdam
info@paselkuenzel.com
T +31 (0)10 462 42 02
www.paselkuenzel.com
25 V35K18

New Zealand

Strachan Group Architects
PO Box 26-038
Epsom, Auckland 1344
info@sgaltd.co.nz
T +64 (0)9 638 6302
www.sgaltd.co.nz
12 Owhanake Bay House

Japan

Harunatsu-arch
1-3-12 Nagamachi
Kanazawa-city
Ishikawa 920-0865
info@hn-arch.com
T +81(0) 76 216 5610
www.hn-arch.com
35 Villa 921

mA-style Architects
212-38 Hosoe
Makinohara-city
Sizuoka 421-0421
ma-style@yr.tnc.ne.jp
T +81(0) 548 23 0970
www.ma-style.jp
37 Riverbank House

Tato Architects
2-13-23 Kitano-cho
Chuo-ku, Kobe-city
Hyogo 650- 0002
daaas@e.email.ne.jp
T +81(0) 78 891 6382
www.tat-o.com
50 House in Hieidaira

Tezuka Architects
1-19-9 3F Todoroki
Setagaya-ku
Tokyo 158-0082
tez@sepia.ocn.ne.jp
T +81(0) 3 3703 7056
www.tezuka-arch.com
14 House to Catch the Mountain

Suga Atelier
1-3-20 Bandai
Abeno-ku Osaka-city
Osaka 545-0036
suga19@jasmine.ocn.ne.jp
+81(0) 6 6626 1920
www11.ocn.ne.jp/~suga
13 House of Cedar

Portugal

Pedro Reis Arquitecto
Rua da Emenda 30 CV 1
1200-170 Lisboa
info@pedroreis.pt
T +351 218 870 275
www.pedroreis.pt
38 House in Melides

Pedro Fonseca Jorge Arquitecto
Avenida da Igreja 32, 1°
2475-100 Benedita
egrojordep@gmail.com
T +351 918733099
www.pfj-arq.blogspot.com
26 House in Figueiral

Slovenia

Kombinat Arhitekti
Rimska cesta 22
1000 Ljubljana
info@kombinat-arhitekti.si
T +386 (0)590 19 080
www.kombinat-arhitekti.si
08 House MJ

South Korea

Byoung Soo Cho (BCHO)
55-7 Sil Building
Banpo 4-dong
Seocho-gu, Seoul 137-803
bc@bchoarchitects.com
T + 82 (0)2 537 8261
www.bchoarchitects.com
33 Earth House

Spain

Carlos Quintáns Eiras
Petunias 3 2° izquierda
15008 A Coruña
quintans@tectonica.es
T +34 881918005
www.carlosquintans.es
04 House in Paderne

A-cero
Parque Empresarial La Finca
Paseo Club Deportivo nº 1
Bloque 6 A, 28223 Madrid
a-cero@a-cero.com
T +34 917 997 984
www.a-cero.com
32 Concrete House

H Arquitectes
Montserrat 22, 2n 2a
08201 Sabadell
Barcelona
harquitectes@harquitectes.com
T +34 93 725 00 48
www.harquitectes.com
19 House 712

Sweden

Kjellgren Kaminsky Architecture
Ekmansgatan 3
411 32 Göteborg
sanna@kjellgrenkaminsky.se
T +46 (0) 31 761 20 01
www.kjellgrenkaminsky.se
07 Villa Nyberg

Switzerland

Wespi de Meuron Romeo
Via g. Branca Masa 9
6578 Caviano
info@wdmra.ch
T +41 (0) 91 794 17 73
www.wdmra.ch
31 Brione House

UK

Dow Jones Architects
39 Calbourne Road
London SW12 8LW
mail@dowjonesarchitects.com
T +44 (0) 20 8772 0507
www.dowjonesarchitects.com
43 Prospect House

Duggan Morris Architects
Unit 7, 16-24 Underwood Street
London N1 7JQ
info@dugganmorrisarchitects.com
T +44 (0) 20 7566 7440
www.dugganmorrisarchitects.com
17 Kings Grove House

Gort Scott
The Print House
18 Ashwin Street
London E8 3DL
info@gortscott.com
T +44 (0) 20 7254 6294
www.gortscott.com
18 Seafield House

Liddicoat & Goldhill
Studio 6
13 Ramsgate Street
London E8 2FD
info@liddicoatgoldhill.com
T +44 (0) 20 7923 2737
www.liddicoatgoldhill.com
22 The Shadow House

Jonathan Hendry Architects
10 Nickerson Way
Peacefields Business Park
Holton le Clay
Lincolnshire DN36 5HS
jh@jonathanhendryarchitects.com
T +44 (0) 1472 828320
www.jonathanhendryarchitects.com
44 Beach Chalet

Laura Dewe Mathews

Laura Dewe Mathews
104 Balcorne Street
London E9 7AU
studio@lauradewemathews.com
T +44 (0) 20 8986 8926
www.lauradewemathews.com
21 Gingerbread House

Carl Turner Architects
16 Clapham Park Terrace
Lyham Road
London SW2 5EA
info@ct-architects.co.uk
T +44 (0) 20 7274 1960
www.ct-architects.co.uk
42 Slip House

Nick Willson Architects
G2 Hoxton Works
128 Hoxton Street
London N1 6SH
info@nickwillsonarchitects.com
T +44 (0) 207 012 1674
www.nickwillsonarchitects.com
10 Flint House

**Witherford Watson Mann
Architects**
1 Coate Street
London E2 9AG
mail@wwmarchitects.co.uk
T +44 (0) 20 7613 3113
30 Astley Castle

USA

Bercy Chen Studio
1111 E.
11th Street Suite 200
Austin Texas 78702
info@bcarc.com
T +1 512 481 0092
www.bcarc.com
41 Edgeland House

Pencil Office
391 Schooner Ave
Jamestown RI 02835
info@penciloffice.com
www.penciloffice.com
47 Stereoscopic House

Swatt Miers Architects
5845 Doyle Street, Suite 104
Emeryville
California 94612
info@swattmiers.com
T +1 510 985 9779
www.swattmiers.com
49 Tea Houses

Salmela Architect
630 West 4th Street
Duluth MN 55806
david@salmelaarchitect.com
T +1 218 724 7517
www.salmelaarchitect.com
48 Streeter House

Vietnam

Vo Trong Nghia
85 Bis Phan Ke Binh,
DaKao, District 1
Ho Chi Minh City
hcmc@vtnaa.com
T +84 8 3 8297763
F +84 8 3 9110103
www.votrongnghia.com
39 Stacking Green House

Picture Credits

All architectural drawings are supplied courtesy of the respective architects and remain the © copyright of the architects, unless otherwise specified. These drawings are for private use and not for third party reproduction.

Photographic credits:
In all cases every effort has been made to credit the copyright holders, but should there be any omissions or errors, the publisher will insert the appropriate acknowledgement in any subsequent editions of the book.

10 © Steven Massart / Styling: Anneleen Claes
14 © Stephan Girard
18 © Tamás Bujnovszky
22 © Ángel Baltanás
26 John Lewis Marshall 1, 3
26 Jeroen Musch 2, 4
30 © Martin Weiss
34 © Kalle Sanner
38 © Klemen Ilovar & Matjaž Tančič
42 © Nelson Kon
46 © Gareth Gardner
50 © Hauke Dressler Fotograf 1, 2 3
50 © Jens Kroell / Hamburg 4
54 © Patrick Reynolds
58 Images courtesy Suga Shotaro Atelier 1, 4
58 Images courtesy Shintaro Amano 2, 3
62 Katsuhisa Kida / FOTOTECA
68 © Luuk Kramer
72 © Michel Kievits
76 © James Brittain / VIEW 1, 2, 4
76 © Edmund Sumner / VIEW 3
80 © David Grandorge
84 © Adrià Goula
88 © Thea van den Heuvel / DAPh
92 © Chloe Dewe Mathews
96 © Tom Gildon 1
96 © KeithCollie 2, 3

100 © Marsino Arquitectos Asociados
104 © David Grandorge
108 Marcel van der Burg
112 © Pedro Cavaco Leitão
116 © Sebastian Zachariah
120 Stefan Müller, Berlin
124 © Koen Van Damme
128 © Hélène Binet
132 © www.hanneshenz.ch
138 © Luis H. Segovia
142 © Courtesy BCHO Architects
146 © Robert Leš www.RobertLes.net
150 © Kai Nakamura
154 © Antje Quiram, Stuttgart
158 © Kai Nakamura
162 © Fernando Guerra / VIEW
166 © Oki Hiroyuki
172 © Kees Hageman
176 Paul Bardagjy
180 © Tim Crocker / VIEW
184 © David Grandorge
188 © David Grandorge
192 © Sam Noonan
196 © Hervé Abbadie
200 © Daniel Sheriff www.danielsheriff.com 1, 4
200 © Erik G.L'Heureux 2, 3
204 © Peter Bastianelli-Kerze
208 © Tim Griffith
212 © Satoshi Shigeta

About the CD

The attached CD can be read on both Windows and Macintosh computers. All the material on the CD is copyright protected and is for private use only. All drawings in the book and on the CD were specially created for this publication and are based on the architects' original designs.

The CD includes files for all of the drawings included in the book. The drawings for each building are contained in a numbered folder. They are supplied in two versions: the files with the suffix '.eps' are 'vector' Illustrator EPS files but can be opened using other graphics programs such as Photoshop; all the files with the suffix '.dwg' are generic CAD format files and can be opened in a variety of CAD programs.

Each file is numbered according to its original location in the book: project number, followed by the drawing number(s), followed by the scale. Hence, '01_01_200.eps' would be the eps version of the first drawing in the first project and has a scale of 1:200.

The generic '.dwg' file format does not support 'solid fill' utilized by many architectural CAD programs. All the information is embedded within the file and can be reinstated within supporting CAD programs. Select the polygon required and change the 'Attributes' to 'Solid', and the colour information should be automatically retrieved. To reinstate the 'Walls'; select all objects within the 'Walls' layer/class and amend their 'Attributes' to 'Solid'.